Getting straight "A"s doesn't have to be a mystery...

these practical, concise, and affordable study guides will tell you how!

The Harbrace Guides to
STUDENT SUCCESS
from Harcourt Brace Canada

Fit to Print: The Canadian Student's Guide to Essay Writing 3/e
Joanne Buckley

Learning for Success: Skills and Strategies for Canadian Students 2/e
Joan Fleet, Fiona Goodchild, Richard Zajchowski

Power over Time: Student Success with Time Management
Joan Fleet, Denise Reaume

Success in the Social Sciences: Writing and Research for Canadian Students
Richard Floyd

Getting into Law School: The Canadian Guide
Trevor Johnson

Speaking for Success: The Canadian Guide
Anthony Lieb

Transitions: Succeeding in College and University
Greta Hofmann Nemiroff

Graduate Student Success: The Canadian Guide
Manfred Szabo

Making your Mark: Learning to do Well on Exams
Catherine Taylor, Heather Avery, Lucille Strath

Career Success: The Canadian Guide
Shannon Whelan

Print Out: Using the Computer to Write
Wendy Wilson

*Look for copies of these best-selling books
in your college or university bookstore.*

The Dryden Accounting List

*Beechy	*Canadian Advanced Financial Accounting*
Bischoff	*Introduction to College Accounting*
Bloom and Elgers	*Issues in Accounting Policy: A Reader*
Bloom and Elgers	*Foundations of Accounting Theory: A Reader*
*Clowes	*EDP Auditing*
*Dauderis	*Financial Accounting: An Introduction to Decision Making*
Douglas	*Governmental and Nonprofit Accounting: Theory and Practice*
Everett, Raabe, and Fortin	*Income Tax Fundamentals 1995*
*Gaber, Davidson, Stickney, and Weil	*Financial Accounting*
*Gaber, Walgenbach, Hanson, and Hamre	*Introduction to Accounting*
*Lee, Gilbart, Hipwell, and Hales	*Accounting*
Miller	*GAAP Guide*
Miller	*GAAS Guide*
*Most	*Accounting Theory*
*Skinner	*Accounting Standards in Evolution*
*Williams, Deutsch, Stanga, and Holder	*Intermediate Accounting*

*denotes Canadian texts

Accounting

SECOND CANADIAN EDITION

NANCI LEE
American River College

ELAINE HALES
Georgian College

DRYDEN

Harcourt Brace & Company, Canada

Toronto Montreal Fort Worth New York Orlando
Philadelphia San Diego London Sydney Tokyo

Canadian Cataloguing in Publication Data

Lee, Nanci
    Accounting

2nd Canadian ed.
"Working papers included".
ISBN 0-03-922991-2

1. Accounting. 2. Accounting - Problems, exercises, etc. I. Hales, Elaine. II. Title.

HF5635.L44 1996   657'.042   C95-930060-0

Publisher: Heather McWhinney
Editor and Marketing Manager: Ken Nauss
Projects Manager: Liz Radojkovic
Projects Co-ordinator: May Ku
Director of Publishing Services: Jean Davies
Editorial Manager: Marcel Chiera
Supervising Editor: Semareh Al-Hillal
Production Editor: Laurel Parsons
Production Manager: Sue-Ann Becker
Production Co-ordinator: Carol Tong/Sheila Barry
Copy Editor: Jim Lyons, Wordsworth Communications
Cover Design: Jack Steiner Graphics
Cover Image: Andy Zito/The Image Bank of Canada
Typesetting and Assembly: Compeer Typographic Services Limited
Printing and Binding: Webcom Limited

This book was printed in Canada.

1 2 3 4 5   00 99 98 97 96

Preface

Accounting is written for students with little or no accounting background. It is designed to make learning as easy as possible and to give students a strong foundation in accounting fundamentals and a clear understanding of accounting terminology. After completing this first course in accounting, students will be prepared to enter the job market in entry-level accounting positions; will be able to understand the usefulness and importance of accounting procedures as business owners, managers, or office workers; and will be well prepared to continue their studies in advanced accounting courses.

Accounting has been consciously designed to help make students feel at ease with the text and with the subject matter. The new material presented in each chapter is kept to a minimum so that readers can absorb the content thoroughly before continuing. Difficult concepts are broken down into small segments where feasible so that readers can master the concepts a little at a time.

Concepts have been illustrated with true-to-life characters in everyday business situations. Extensive classroom testing of the material in this text has proved that student response is much greater to personal and realistic situations, and has made this book a concise, efficient, enjoyable learning tool.

While *Accounting* makes every attempt to communicate clearly with students, it is also designed with instructors in mind. The text is written to eliminate questions before they occur, thus making the job of teaching the class much easier. The friendly writing style encourages students to feel at ease with the material and stimulates class discussion.

While this text is an adaptation of the American text, *Accounting, An Introduction*, it has been completely fitted to the Canadian market. Chapters where tax laws or accounting procedures are different have been completely revamped to reflect Canadian law and procedures.

Chapter Organization

A number of special features reinforce students' learning. Each chapter contains the following features:

Learning objectives are listed at the beginning of each chapter. They clearly delineate for the reader what skills and concepts are to be gained from the chapter.

A list of the new accounting or accounting-related *vocabulary* appears at the beginning of each chapter. Each new word or term is defined before the student reads the material presented. When the words appear in the chapter, they are bold-faced and defined again in context. This enhances the students' comprehension of the material and reduces the number of questions about content. This approach also helps students augment their understanding of the English language while learning how to communicate effectively as accountants.

Discussion material is followed by numerous *illustrations*. T accounts, ledgers, journal entries, financial statements, and worksheets are used throughout the text to aid the reader in visually comprehending the written material.

Chapter summaries contain a concise review of the material presented in the chapter.

A *vocabulary review* follows each chapter. Two exercises are designed specifically to help the reader learn the definitions of the accounting and accounting-related words and terms.

Approximately ten *exercises* follow the vocabulary review at the end of each chapter. Exercises are relatively short and generally review one specific topic covered in the preceding material.

Problems follow the exercises; they are more comprehensive than the exercises and progress from easy to more difficult. The exercises and problems review all the major points discussed in the chapters.

There are three *comprehensive problems* in the text. The first one reviews the concepts presented in Chapters One–Six (the accounting cycle for a service business). The comprehensive problems are similar in nature to a practice set; all the working papers necessary for solving the problems are included in the student's packet of working papers. The second comprehensive problem appears after Chapter Eleven and covers the material presented in Chapters Seven–Eleven (special journals, bank reconciliation, and financial statements for a merchandising business). The third comprehensive problem appears at the end of the text and reviews the preparation of the payroll and the related tasks (completing individual employee earnings records, payments for union dues, registered pension plan contributions, workers' compensation insurance, employers' health tax, and the preparation of the T4 summary for Revenue Canada).

The *working papers* that accompany *Accounting* include answer spaces and forms for completing all the exercises, problems, and comprehensive problems in the text. Repetitive use of the forms provides a convenient and realistic link to real-world accounting and reinforces the students' confidence by means of practical application. For the benefit of both instructors and students, the working papers have been designed to correspond exactly with the solution pages in the instructor's manual.

The instructor's manual includes learning objectives, a summary of major concepts for each chapter, a "Message to the Instructor" with creative teaching suggestions, lecture notes, and a content analysis and the average time required for completion of each exercise and problem in the text. The instructor's manual also contains complete solutions for the exercises, problems, and the three comprehensive problems.

ACKNOWLEDGEMENTS

We would like to thank the reviewers whose valuable comments and suggestions helped to improve this text. They are

Michel K. Bauer	Sheridan College
Nancy Bury	Capilano College
Mike Cullimore	St. Lawrence College
Dave Eliason	S.A.I.T.
Sheila Simpson	Humber College
Ralph Sweet	Durham College.

Special thanks to Mel Sparks (Lambton College) for his significant input and for helping to error-check the final draft of this manuscript.

A Note from the Publisher

Thank you for selecting *Accounting*, Second Canadian Edition, by Nanci Lee and Elaine Hales. The authors and publisher have devoted considerable time to the careful development of this book. We appreciate your recognition of this effort and accomplishment.

We want to hear what you think about *Accounting*. Please take a few minutes to fill in the stamped reader reply card at the back of the book. Your comments and suggestions will be valuable to us as we prepare new editions and other books.

Contents

CHAPTER THREE

Understanding Debits and Credits and the Trial Balance

CHAPTER FOUR

The General Journal and the General Ledger

CHAPTER FIVE

Adjustments and the Ten-Column Worksheet

CHAPTER SIX Correcting and Closing Entries

CHAPTER SEVEN The Sales Journal and the Accounts Receivable Subsidiary Ledger

CHAPTER EIGHT ## The Purchases Journal and the Accounts Payable Subsidiary Ledger

CHAPTER NINE ## The Cash Receipts, Cash Payments, and Combined Cash Journals

CHAPTER TEN   # The Bank Account and Cash Funds

CHAPTER ELEVEN ## Worksheets, Financial Statements, and Closing Entries for a Merchandising Business

CHAPTER TWELVE ## Payroll—Employee Deductions

CHAPTER THIRTEEN **Payroll—Employer Taxes and Other Obligations**

Appendix: Check Figures for Problems

Index

CHAPTER ONE

Starting a Business and the Balance Sheet

Learning Objectives

When you have completed this chapter, you should
1. have an increased understanding of accounting terminology, particularly as it relates to the balance sheet.
2. know how management and accountants work together to make business decisions.
3. have a basic knowledge of the fundamental accounting equation.
4. after analyzing certain transactions that relate, be able to prepare a balance sheet.

Vocabulary

account   an individual record for each asset and liability and for the owner's capital

accounts payable   a liability of the business; a promise to pay a creditor for services or merchandise received

assets   items of value owned by a business; includes cash, equipment, land, buildings, furniture, etc.

capital account   a summary of the owner's investments, withdrawals, and the profits and losses of the business; sometimes called net worth or proprietorship

creditor   a person or a business to whom a debt is owed

current asset   an asset that is cash or that will be used up or converted to cash within a relatively short period of time (usually a year)

current liability   a liability (debt) due within a year's time

discrepancy   disagreement, as between facts or claims

fundamental accounting equation   Assets = Liabilities + Owner's Equity

liabilities   debts

long-term liabilities   debts that fall due more than one year beyond the balance sheet date

monetary   pertaining to money

owner's equity   that portion of the business assets to which the owner has direct claim

plant and equipment   assets that are held for an extended time and that are used to facilitate the production of goods and services for customers

Revenue Canada   the federal agency that is responsible for collecting income taxes

service business   a business that sells a service; examples are the businesses of doctors, dentists, veterinarians, lawyers, accountants, etc.

solvent   able to meet financial obligations; that is, able to pay bills when they are due

transaction   in this context, it refers to any business occurrence, such as a purchase, a sale, a receipt, or a payment of cash, that can be measured in dollars and cents and that must be recorded in the accounting records

Introduction

Many people have dreamed of opening their own business—maybe a restaurant, a riding school, an auto repair shop, or a consulting firm. While starting a business is relatively easy, keeping the business alive and healthy is much more difficult.

The accountant and the accounting records play a very important role in the life of any business. Accounting provides financial information about an economic entity (a business enterprise, a church, a club, a government organization, and so on.) The daily **transactions**, such as buying or selling goods and services, making a payment on a loan, or borrowing money—in short, anything that can be measured objectively in **monetary** terms—are recorded and classified. To make the information more usable, it is summarized in accounting reports, which are the basic tools for financial decision making.

Accounting is called the "language of business" because owners, managers, investors, creditors, bankers, and so on communicate with each other using terms such as *cost of goods sold*, *book value*, *net profit*, *operating expenses*, *return on net assets*, and *inventory turnover*. They read financial statements and other detailed accounting data to make intelligent decisions, such as: What price shall be charged? Shall we expand our hours? Hire new people? Take on new products? Offer new services? Borrow money? Cut back? Open another store? Take on a partner? Get out of the business altogether?

Without good records, a business would have difficulty remaining **solvent**, which means that a business has enough money on hand to pay its bills when they become due. Many new businesses close their doors in failure before the first year has passed, and poor management is frequently cited as the reason. Management must work hand in hand with accountants in analyzing the records in order to make the daily decisions that keep a business successful.

In addition, many persons outside the business are interested in the accounting records. The various government taxing agencies may want to see a firm's books on a regular basis to audit, for example, payroll tax and sales tax records. Good records can help keep a business out of trouble with various government agencies.

Accountants provide a valuable service both for businesses and for individuals. They are called upon to audit the records of companies to determine whether or not their figures are arrived at fairly. At the beginning of every year accountants are called upon to calculate the income taxes for millions of Canadians. They are hired regularly to prepare payroll and sales tax returns for businesses. Accountants may work for **Revenue Canada**. Their work there might include the auditing of income tax returns for businesses and for individuals. Accountants may be hired to tell you how best to invest your money, how to pay the least amount of income taxes, or how to plan for retirement. Accountants are a very important segment of our society; their services are constantly in demand.

The job of the accountant is normally one where she or he interprets the data in the accounting records, perhaps to help management make decisions or to project future business trends or to suggest several plans of action designed to give the best tax options. The job of a bookkeeper, on the other hand, is one of record keeping. Record keeping entails recording on a regular basis all the transactions of a business, classifying that information, and summarizing the data for presentation to the accountant, who will then interpret the results.

Starting a Business

Florence Hansen decides, after attending school and after working for two years to save the money, to start her own business. She plans to purchase a word processing system, hire an assistant, and then provide secretarial services to other businesses. She will call her business "The Instant Secretary." The business will not be selling a product as such (other than the talents and skills of Florence and her employee), and thus the business is a **service business**. Because Florence (or simply Flo) has studied accounting and knows she must carefully keep track of all business transactions, she is ahead of many people who start a new business.

The Fundamental Accounting Equation

The **fundamental accounting equation** governs how transactions are recorded. The equation is this:

$$\text{Assets} = \text{Liabilities} + \text{Owner's Equity.}$$

Assets are all things owned by the business (whether or not they are fully paid for). They may be tangible; that is, have a definite physical form such as office equipment, buildings, land, furniture, supplies, or cash—or they may be intangible, such as an investment in stocks or bonds, a copyright or patent, or amounts due from customers (accounts receivable).

Liabilities are debts owed by the business to various **creditors**.

Owner's equity is the difference between the assets and the liabilities. Therefore, the fundamental accounting equation may also be stated as:

$$\text{Assets} - \text{Liabilities} = \text{Owner's Equity}.$$

The assets of a business are supplied either by the owner or by some other person or company. That portion of the assets to which the owner has a claim is called the *owner's equity*. That portion to which creditors have a claim is called *liabilities*. If, for example, a business owner purchases new equipment that costs $10,000 by making a $6,000 down payment and agreeing to pay the other $4,000 over a year's time, the owner's equity in that asset at the time of purchase is $6,000. The rest of the price—the $4,000 still owed—is a liability. Thus, the equipment is owned by both the owner of the business and by a creditor. Each has an equity in the equipment until the debt is fully paid.

Transactions of a New Business

Now let's trace the transactions for The Instant Secretary to see how Flo went about getting ready to begin this business venture. We will see how every transaction affects the fundamental accounting equation. It is important to note here that Flo complies with the universally honoured practice of keeping all of her personal records separate from her business records. She owns her own home, a car, furniture, appliances, and cameras, and has personal debts. However, these personal assets and liabilities do not appear in the records of the business, where there is a separate record kept for each asset and liability and for the owner's equity. This separate record is called an **account**, and all increases and decreases are shown in the individual accounts.

TRANSACTION 1   **Establishing a Business Bank Account**   Flo withdraws $10,000 from her personal savings account, deposits the money in a business account, and orders personalized cheques for The Instant Secretary. The fundamental accounting equation looks like this after the deposit:

Assets	=	Liabilities	+	Owner's Equity
				Florence
				Hansen,
Cash	=			Capital
(1) $10,000	=			$10,000

The original investment, additional investments at a later date, and all profits and losses of the business are recorded in a separate account called the **Capital account**, or simply Capital, which is an owner's equity account. After this initial deposit, you will note that Assets = Owner's Equity. This is because at this point there are no debts.

TRANSACTION 2   **Purchasing Office Equipment and Paying Cash**   Flo purchases a desktop computer with word processing software from Business Equipment Company (BECO) at a total cost of $3,500. She writes a cheque for the equipment. The equation now looks like this:

	Assets			=	Liabilities	+	Owner's Equity
							Florence Hansen,
	Cash	+	Equipment	=			Capital
Previous							
Balances	$10,000						$10,000
(2)	−3,500		+3,500		_____		_____
New							
Balances	$6,500	+	$3,500	=			$10,000

Note that assets are still equal to owner's equity because there are no liabilities.

TRANSACTION 3

Purchasing Office Equipment on Account Flo purchases additional computer equipment, monitors, and printers from BECO at a total cost of $12,500. Flo does not pay for the equipment now, but agrees to pay the full amount within 12 months. Amounts owed to creditors are recorded in the liability account entitled **Accounts Payable**. The equation after this transaction looks like this:

	Assets			=	Liabilities	+	Owner's Equity
							Florence Hansen,
					Accounts		
	Cash	+	Equipment	=	Payable	+	Capital
Previous							
Balances	$6,500		$ 3,500	=			$10,000
(3)	_____		+12,500		+12,500		_____
New							
Balances	$6,500	+	$16,000	=	$12,500	+	$10,000

Notice that liabilities are now $12,500. This means that of the total assets of $22,500 ($6,500 + $16,000), the owner's share is $10,000.

At any time after a transaction has been recorded, total assets will equal total liabilities and owner's equity. You can always check the accuracy of your work by simply adding.

Assets		=	Liabilities + Owner's Equity	
Cash	$ 6,500		Accounts Payable	$12,500
Equipment	16,000		Florence Hansen, Capital	10,000
Total	$22,500		Total	$22,500

TRANSACTION 4

Purchasing Office Furniture, Making a Cash Down Payment Flo bought $4,500 worth of furniture from Andrews Office Furniture Company. She pays $2,500 down and agrees to pay the rest in six months' time. The equation now looks like this:

	Assets					=	Liabilities	+	Owner's Equity
	Cash	+	Equipment	+	Furniture	=	Accounts Payable	+	Florence Hansen, Capital
Previous Balances	$6,500		$16,000			=	$12,500		$10,000
(4)	−2,500				+4,500		+2,000		
New Balances	$4,000	+	$16,000	+	$4,500	=	$14,500	+	$10,000

Again, a quick check proves the accuracy of the work, because total assets must always equal total liabilities and owner's equity.

Assets		=	Liabilities + Owner's Equity	
Cash	$ 4,000		Accounts Payable	$14,500
Equipment	16,000		Florence Hansen, Capital	$10,000
Furniture	4,500			
Total	$24,500		Total	$24,500

TRANSACTION 5   **Purchasing of Office Supplies for Cash**   Flo writes a cheque for $800 for supplies. The equation after that transaction looks like this:

	Assets								=	Liabilities	+	Owner's Equity
	Cash	+	Equipment	+	Furniture	+	Supplies		=	Accounts Payable	+	Florence Hansen, Capital
Previous Balances	$4,000	+	$16,000	+	$4,500				=	$14,500	+	$10,000
(5)	−800						+800					
New Balances	$3,200	+	$16,000	+	$4,500	+	$800		=	$14,500	+	$10,000

TRANSACTION 6   **Contributing Personal Assets to the Business**   Flo has several dictionaries, office procedures manuals, and reference books that she contributes to the business. Since these books come from her personal library, their value increases the owner's capital account. Flo estimates the value of the books to be $200.

	Assets										=	Liabilities	+	Owner's Equity
	Cash	+	Equipment	+	Furniture	+	Supplies	+	Library		=	Accounts Payable	+	Florence Hansen, Capital
Previous Balances	$3,200	+	$16,000	+	$4,500	+	$800				=	$14,500	+	$10,000
(6)									+200					+200
New Balances	$3,200	+	$16,000	+	$4,500	+	$800	+	$200		=	$14,500	+	$10,200

At this point, do total assets equal the total of the liabilities and owner's equity? This question should be asked after each transaction.

TRANSACTION 7 **Paying Money to a Creditor** Flo pays $500 to BECO as partial payment of the $12,500 owed for the purchase of office equipment (see Transaction 3). Now the equation appears as follows:

		Assets				=	Liabilities +	Owner's Equity
	Cash +	Equipment +	Furniture +	Supplies +	Library =		Accounts Payable +	Florence Hansen, Capital
Previous Balances	$3,200 +	$16,000 +	$4,500 +	$800 +	$200 =		$14,500 +	$10,200
(7)	−500						−500	
New Balances	$2,700 +	$16,000 +	$4,500 +	$800 +	$200 =		$14,000 +	$10,200

Manipulating the Fundamental Accounting Equation

You can see from the transaction that total Assets equal $24,200, total Liabilities equal $14,000, and Owner's Equity is $10,200. The equation looks like this:

Assets	=	Liabilities	+	Owner's Equity
$24,200	=	$14,000	+	$10,200

Note that if any two parts of the equation are known, the missing part can easily be found.

ILLUSTRATION 1 **Assets = Liabilities + Owner's Equity (A = L + OE)** Liabilities are $14,000 and Owner's Equity is $10,200. What is the amount of the Assets?

Liabilities	+	Owner's Equity	=	Assets
$14,000	+	$10,200	=	$24,200

ILLUSTRATION 2 **Assets − Liabilities = Owner's Equity (A − L = OE)** Assets are $24,200 and Liabilities are $14,000. What is the amount of the Owner's Equity?

Assets	−	Liabilities	=	Owner's Equity
$24,200	−	$14,000	=	$10,200

ILLUSTRATION 3 **Assets − Owner's Equity = Liabilities (A − OE = L)** Assets are $24,200 and Owner's Equity is $10,200. What is the amount of the Liabilities?

Assets	−	Owner's Equity	=	Liabilities
$24,200	−	$10,200	=	$14,000

Total assets should always equal total liabilities plus owner's equity. If, for some reason, the equation is not in balance, a mistake in recording has occurred, and the error or **discrepancy** must be located before continuing.

If total assets increase, the total of liabilities and owner's equity must also increase by the same amount (see Transactions 1, 3, 4, and 6). If total assets decrease, the total of liabilities and owner's equity must decrease by the same amount (see Transaction 7). It is possible, too, for one asset to increase and another to decrease by the same amount, thus causing no change in total assets or in the fundamental accounting equation (see Transactions 2 and 5).

The Balance Sheet

Flo has purchased most of what she needs to begin her business and is ready to prepare her first financial statement, the balance sheet. The **balance sheet** contains a complete listing of all asset, liability, and owner's equity accounts. It is called a balance sheet because it proves that the total assets equal total liabilities and owner's equity, or, in other words, that the fundamental accounting equation is in balance.

Assets are recorded on the balance sheet at their original, or historic, cost. This is significant because many assets are worth an amount quite different from the one reflected on the balance sheet; such assets as land and buildings often appreciate, or become more valuable, over the years. Because assets are economic resources that are expected to benefit future operations, such assets as land, buildings, and equipment are for use and are not for sale. Most assets could not be sold without disrupting normal business activity.

Flo can see that by the use of her own $10,200 capital contribution plus credit of $14,000 extended to her (that is, liabilities), she now owns and controls a business that has assets costing $24,200. It is often said that the balance sheet is like a snapshot that shows the financial position or condition of the business at a moment in time. The balance sheet for The Instant Secretary on January 31 follows.

The Instant Secretary Balance Sheet January 31, 19XX		
Assets		
Cash	$ 2,700—	
Supplies	800—	
Equipment	16,000—	
Furniture	4,500—	
Library	200—	
Total Assets		$24,200—
Liabilities		
Accounts Payable	$14,000—	
Total Liabilities		$14,000—
Owner's Equity		
Florence Hansen, Capital, January 31, 19XX		10,200—
Total Liabilities and Owner's Equity		$24,200—

The Heading The balance sheet has a three-part heading that is centred and always includes, in this order: (1) the name of the business; (2) the name of the financial statement; and (3) the day for which the statement is prepared.

bond. 证券

copy copyright. 物版权著作权.

patent. 专利权

~~account~~ liability. => debt. 负债.

comply. ① 遵从.
② 同意答应.

(comply with?)

entitle ① 命名称. entitled...

Assets With this form of the balance sheet, called the *report form*, assets are listed first. The word *Assets* is centred over the actual listing of accounts. The listing of accounts begins with **current assets**, which are cash or assets that will be used up or converted to cash within a year's time. (Supplies is an example of an asset that will be used up.) The first asset listed is Cash, followed by Accounts Receivable and Notes Receivable. Receivables represent amounts owed to the business. The other current assets are listed following the receivables, in no particular order.

The **plant and equipment** titles are listed after the current assets. The plant and equipment assets are those that will be held for an extended time and that are used to facilitate the production of goods and services for customers. If there is an account for land, it will be shown last, following the other plant and equipment titles (furniture, fixtures, equipment, buildings, etc.) Account titles are written next to the vertical line, amounts to be added are entered in the left-hand column, and totals are entered in the right-hand column. A single line is drawn all the way across the column (from vertical line to vertical line) to indicate addition, then the total dollar amounts are entered, and *Total Assets* is written opposite that figure.

Liabilities Leave one blank line before centring the word *Liabilities* over the listing of account titles. There will be, in later chapters, more than one liability. Other account titles might be Taxes Payable, Notes Payable, Mortgage Payable, and so on. Those debts that are due within a year's time are listed first and are called **current liabilities**. In this category, the first listing is usually Accounts Payable, followed by Notes Payable. Notes Payable represent debt evidenced by the signing of a formal document in which the borrower promises to pay back a certain amount of money by a certain time and usually with interest. Other current liabilities are listed in any order after Accounts Payable. **Long-term liabilities** are listed next and are those debts that fall due more than one year beyond the balance sheet date.

Amounts to be added are written in the left-hand column and totals are entered in the right-hand column. In this case, where there is only one account, the amount could have been entered directly into the right-hand column because it is not necessary to find a column total.

Owner's Equity Again, leave one blank line before centring the words *Owner's Equity* over this last section. The capital account title is listed at the left-hand margin beneath the heading and the amount is listed in the right-hand column. A single line is drawn beneath the amount, which is added to the total liabilities figure. Write *Total Liabilities and Owner's Equity* opposite the sum obtained.

When a total for the assets and a total for the liabilities and owner's equity have been determined and the amounts are equal, a double horizontal line is drawn across the columns to indicate that the work is in balance and complete.

Dollar Signs and Lines A dollar sign appears at the beginning of each column and at totals. A line (ruling) must extend all the way across a column. A single line indicates addition or subtraction and a double line indicates that work is complete and in balance. Always use a ruler for drawing lines. Neatness is very important in accounting.

Cents When money amounts are in even dollars, write two zeros to represent cents. *Do not use XXs.* You may, however, choose to use a straight line or to omit the zeros to indicate even money amounts. For example, seven hundred forty-eight dollars may be written as $748.00, or $748—, or $748.

Summary

Accounting is the language of business and is used by owners, managers, investors, bankers—in short, nearly everyone concerned with business—to communicate vital information to one another. Daily transactions of economic units must be recorded, classified, and summarized into useful reports for management to make intelligent business decisions. Good accounting records help an organization to be profitable and remain solvent.

The fundamental accounting equation states that assets equal liabilities plus owner's equity; this relationship is shown on the balance sheet, which is prepared to show the financial picture of a business on a particular date. Assets are properties owned by a business; liabilities are the debts incurred by the business; and owner's equity is the owner's share in the assets, or that portion of the total asset value to which she or he has a direct claim. A business owner must always keep her or his personal assets and liabilities separate from those of the business.

On the balance sheet, current assets are listed first, followed by items of plant and equipment and land. In the liabilities section, current liabilities are listed first, followed by those due after a year's time.

Vocabulary Review

Following is a list of the words and terms for this chapter:

account   liabilities
accounts payable   long-term liabilities
assets   monetary
capital account   owner's equity
creditor   plant and equipment
current asset   Revenue Canada
current liability   service business
discrepancy   solvent
fundamental accounting equation   transaction

Fill in the blank with the correct word or term from the list.

1. The word _____ means pertaining to money.
2. _____ are things owned by the business.
3. Debts owed by the company are called _____.
4. A business that is able to pay its bills when they become due is said to be _____.
5. A purchase or a sale, receipt, or payment of cash or any business occurrence that can be measured in dollars and cents and that must be recorded on the books is called a/an _____.
6. A/An _____ exists when facts are not in agreement.
7. A/An _____ is a debt that is due within a year's time.
8. A person or business to whom money is owed is called a/an _____.
9. The owner's investments, profits, and losses are recorded in the _____.
10. A = L + OE is called the _____.
11. The federal agency responsible for the collecting of income taxes is _____.
12. An accounting firm is an example of a/an _____.
13. An asset that is cash or that will be used up or converted to cash within a year's time is a/an _____.

14. The owner's claim on the assets of the business is called _____.
15. The separate record for each asset and liability and the owner's equity is called a/an _____.
16. A/An _____ results when the business purchases a service or merchandise and agrees to pay later.
17. Assets that will be held for an extended time and are used to facilitate the production of goods and services for customers are called _____.
18. _____ are those debts that fall due more than one year beyond the balance sheet date.

Match the words and terms on the left with the definitions on the right.

19. solvent
20. monetary
21. current liability
22. discrepancy
23. transaction
24. creditor
25. assets
26. liabilities
27. plant and equipment
28. Revenue Canada
29. account
30. accounts payable
31. capital account
32. current asset
33. service business
34. owner's equity
35. fundamental accounting equation
36. long-term liabilities

a. things owned
b. one to whom money is owed
c. government income tax collecting agency
d. the owner's share of the assets
e. disagreement between facts
f. able to pay bills when they become due
g. debts
h. an individual record for assets, liabilities, and the owner's capital
i. an asset that is cash or that will be used up or converted to cash within a short period of time (usually a year)
j. a liability account
k. a business occurrence that can be measured in monetary terms and that is recorded on the books
l. an account that summarizes the owner's investments and the business profits and losses
m. pertaining to money
n. an accountant, a lawyer, a veterinarian, a dentist
o. A = L + OE
p. a debt due within a year's time
q. assets used to facilitate the production of goods and services and that will be held for an extended period of time
r. debts that fall due more than one year beyond the date of the balance sheet

Exercises

EXERCISE 1.1   Complete the following equations:
a. Assets = Liabilities + _____ _____
b. Liabilities + Owner's Equity = _____
c. A − L = _____
d. A − OE = _____
e. OE + L = _____
f. A − _____ = OE
g. A − _____ = L
h. A = L + _____
i. _____ − L = OE
j. _____ − OE = L

EXERCISE 1.2 Use the fundamental accounting equation to find the missing element in each of the following:

a. A = ?
    L   = $4,200
    OE = $7,100

b. A = $18,000
    L   = $6,600
    OE = ?

c. A = $21,000
    L   = $8,000
    OE = ?

d. A = $7,500
    L   = ?
    OE = $4,000

e. A = ?
    L   = $5,800
    OE = $9,470

f. A = $17,600
    L   = ?
    OE = $12,000

EXERCISE 1.3 Identify the following as an asset (A), a liability (L), or an owner's equity (OE) account:

_____ a. Cash

_____ b. Accounts Payable

_____ c. Jean Martin, Capital

_____ d. Supplies

_____ e. Furniture

_____ f. Building

_____ g. Equipment

_____ h. Wages Payable

_____ i. Library

_____ j. Payroll Taxes Payable

EXERCISE 1.4 Supply the missing figure in the following equations:

	Assets	=	Liabilities	+	Owner's Equity
a.	$_____	=	$2,500	+	$6,700
b.	14,700	=	7,400	+	_____
c.	12,600	=	_____	+	8,400
d.	_____	=	4,100	+	6,300
e.	4,800	=	0	+	_____

EXERCISE 1.5 Study the individual transactions within the equation and describe briefly what has occurred in each. Then determine the dollar value of the total assets and the dollar value of the total liabilities and owner's equity.

		Assets					=	Liabilities + Owner's Equity		
	Cash	+	Equipment	+	Furniture	=	Accounts Payable	+	Capital
a.	$15,000					=			$15,000
b.	−4,000		+4,000						
	11,000	+	4,000			=			15,000
c.					+500		+500		
	11,000	+	4,000	+	500	=	500	+	15,000
d.	−2,000		+6,000				+4,000		
	9,000	+	10,000	+	500	=	4,500	+	15,000
e.	−1,000						−1,000		
	$8,000	+	$10,000	+	$500	=	$3,500	+	$15,000

EXERCISE 1.6   Using the following account balances, determine the dollar amount of (a) total assets, (b) total liabilities, and (c) total owner's equity.

Cash	$3,500
Accounts Payable	2,400
Library	700
Equipment	2,850
Capital	7,800
Supplies	1,400
Taxes Payable	350
Furniture	2,100

EXERCISE 1.7   Following is a balance sheet for Jane Wade's Accounting Services. Calculate the dollar amount of the missing figures.

Jane Wade's Accounting Services
Balance Sheet
December 31, 19XX

Assets

Cash	$3,400	
Supplies	600	
Equipment	(a)	
Furniture	4,000	
Library	1,800	
Total Assets		$ (b)

Liabilities

Accounts Payable	$2,100	
Notes Payable	(c)	
Total Liabilities		$3,400

Owner's Equity

Jane Wade, Capital, December 31, 19XX		(d)
Total Liabilities and Owner's Equity		$10,200

EXERCISE 1.8   For each of the following indicate whether the transaction will cause total assets to increase (+), decrease (−), or not change (NC):
a. purchased office equipment for cash
b. purchased office equipment on account
c. owner invested cash into the business
d. purchased supplies for cash
e. purchased furniture on account
f. purchased a typewriter; made a cash down payment and agreed to pay the balance in six months
g. paid money on account
h. owner contributed personal assets to the business.

EXERCISE 1.9   Describe the effect of each transaction on the total assets, total liabilities, and owner's equity. Indicate an increase by (+), a decrease by (−), and no change by (NC). The first transaction has been completed for you.

Transaction	Total Assets	Total Liabilities	Owner's Equity
a. owner invested money from personal funds into the business	+	NC	+
b. purchased office equipment for cash	_____	_____	_____
c. purchased furniture for cash	_____	_____	_____
d. purchased equipment on account	_____	_____	_____
e. paid money on account	_____	_____	_____
f. owner donated personal library to the business	_____	_____	_____
g. purchased equipment; made a cash down payment and agreed to pay the balance in three months	_____	_____	_____

EXERCISE 1.10   Find answers for the following:
   a. The assets of the Lake Louise Riding School were $510,000 and the owner's equity was $275,000. What was the total amount of the liabilities?
   b. The liabilities of the Queen's Music School were $35,000. This amounted to one-fourth of the total assets. What was the amount of the owner's equity?
   c. On December 31 of Year 1, the assets of the Oxford Counselling Centre were $180,000. At the end of Year 2, they had increased by $32,000. The owner's equity at the end of Year 1 was one-third the value of the assets. The liabilities increased by $15,000 from Year 1 to Year 2. What is the value of the owner's equity at the end of Year 2?

Problems

PROBLEM 1.1   Darlene Shear began a pet-grooming business on May 1, 19XX. She completed the first transactions of the business as follows:
   a. withdrew $7,500 from her personal savings account and deposited it in a business bank account
   b. purchased grooming supplies for cash at a total cost of $1,400
   c. purchased office furniture at a total cost of $2,300, paying $1,000 down and agreeing to pay the balance within 90 days
   d. purchased office equipment at a total cost of $3,200, paying no money down but agreeing to pay the full amount within 90 days
   e. transferred her complete library of pet-grooming books and subscriptions worth $450 to the business
   f. purchased additional supplies for cash at a total cost of $800
   g. purchased additional equipment for cash at a total cost of $1,100.

INSTRUCTIONS   1. Record the transactions in equation form showing the increases, decreases, and the balance for each account after each transaction. The asset account titles used in this problem are Cash, Grooming Supplies, Office Furniture,

Office Equipment, and Library; the liability account is Accounts Payable; and the owner's equity account is Darlene Shear, Capital.

2. Prove the accuracy of your work by showing that total assets are equal to the total of liabilities and owner's equity.

PROBLEM 1.2   The following is a listing of the accounts and their balances for Sharon Christensen, public accountant:

Cash	$ 8,000
Supplies	500
Office Furniture	3,500
Office Machines	4,700
Accounts Payable	4,500
Sharon Christensen, Capital	12,200

INSTRUCTIONS

1. Prepare a balance sheet as of February 28, 19XX. Before you begin, review the form and rules for preparing the balance sheet that are explained in this chapter.
2. After completing the balance sheet, check the following:
   a. Is the heading centred?
   b. Does the heading contain three lines?
   c. Is the word *Assets* centred over the asset accounts?
   d. Does a dollar sign appear at the beginning of each column and at totals?
   e. Are the account titles for assets and for liabilities and owner's equity listed right next to the vertical lines?
   f. Is there a single rule that extends all the way across the column beneath the last asset listed and beneath the capital account amount?
   g. Is there a double rule beneath the total assets figure and beneath the total liabilities and owner's equity figure?
   h. Did you leave one blank line before you centred the words *Owner's Equity* over the capital account?

PROBLEM 1.3   Brian Jardin, a lawyer, opened a business on March 1, 19XX. Brian has done the following:
   a. deposited $18,000 into a business bank account
   b. bought $4,500 worth of books for the law library; paid cash
   c. bought office furniture for a total cost of $4,500; paid $2,500 cash down and agreed to pay the balance in six months
   d. purchased computer equipment costing $4,800; paid $2,500 cash down and agreed to pay the balance within six months
   e. contributed his personal library worth $3,500 to the business
   f. made a $1,000 cash payment on the computer equipment purchased in Transaction d
   g. made an $800 cash payment on the furniture purchased in Transaction c.

INSTRUCTIONS

1. Record the transactions in equation form, showing the increases, decreases, and the account balances after each transaction. Asset account titles used in this problem are: Cash, Library, Equipment, and Furniture; the liability account is Accounts Payable; and the owner's equity account is Brian Jardin, Capital.
2. Prove the accuracy of your work by showing that total assets is equal to the total of liabilities and owner's equity.
3. Prepare a balance sheet for Brian Jardin, Lawyer, as of March 31, 19XX.

PROBLEM 1.4   Nancy Samuels just opened an exercise salon called "No Weighting." The value of her exercise equipment is $9,500; the exercise mats cost $2,200; the stereo system cost $3,500; furniture cost $1,800; and the special lighting fixtures cost $875. Nancy owes $5,000 on the exercise equipment and $2,000 on the stereo system. Both of these amounts are due within one year. She has $2,700 cash in the bank.

INSTRUCTIONS
1. Calculate the amount of Nancy's capital account, following this procedure:
   a. List the asset amounts and their balances.
   b. Determine the dollar value of the total assets.
   c. Determine the total accounts payable.
   d. Subtract the total liabilities from the total assets.
2. Prepare a balance sheet for No Weighting as of March 31, 19XX.

PROBLEM 1.5   Pete Fredericks is getting ready to open a math-tutoring business called "Numbers Unlimited." During the month of April 19XX, Pete
   a. withdraws $2,500 from his personal chequing account and deposits the money in the business account
   b. buys a tape recorder and a typewriter (equipment) for $1,400 cash
   c. buys supplies for $200 cash
   d. purchases several desks, chairs, and tables for $2,000; pays $500 cash down and agrees to pay the balance in six months
   e. buys a couch and a chair for the waiting room for $870; pays no money down but agrees to pay the full amount due within one year
   f. invests another $1,000 cash from personal savings into the business.

INSTRUCTIONS
1. Record the transactions in equation form showing the increases, decreases, and the balance for each account after each transaction. The asset account titles used in this problem are Cash, Supplies, Equipment, and Furniture; the liability account is Accounts Payable; and the owner's equity account is Pete Fredericks, Capital.
2. Prove the accuracy of your work by showing that total assets is equal to total liabilities and owner's equity.
3. Prepare a balance sheet for Numbers Unlimited as of April 30, 19XX.

CHAPTER TWO

Profitability and the Income Statement

Learning Objectives

When you have completed this chapter, you should
1. have an increased understanding of accounting terminology, particularly as it relates to the income statement.
2. understand how owner's equity is increased or decreased.
3. understand how revenue and expenses affect owner's equity.
4. after analyzing certain transactions that relate, be able to prepare an income statement.
5. be able to prepare a statement of owner's equity detailing the changes that have occurred.

Vocabulary

accounting period   a designated time period (for example, a month, a quarter, or a year) for which a company's net income or net loss is calculated

accounts receivable   debts owed to the business, usually by customers who have received services or merchandise and who have agreed to pay at some future date

accrue   to increase or accumulate

drawing   amount withdrawn from the business for the personal use of the owner

entity   something that exists independently

entity concept   the accounting rule that maintains that a firm's transactions are kept separate from those of the owner

expenses   the costs incurred in obtaining revenue

17

incur   to become subject to

inflow   the act or process of flowing in

net income   profit, or the amount, if any, remaining when expenses are deducted from revenue

net loss   the amount by which expenses exceed revenue

proprietor   owner

revenue   the inflow of cash and other assets for goods sold and services performed

sole proprietorship   a business with one owner

Introduction

In Chapter One we learned that Florence Hansen was willing to invest $10,000 of her own money into a business venture called The Instant Secretary. Florence, and many others like her, is willing to take such financial risks for many reasons. Probably the most important reason, though, is that Flo thinks The Instant Secretary will earn a healthy profit. Another reason might be that she likes the idea of setting her own work hours. Maybe she believes that if she's going to work very hard, she wants the benefits to **accrue** to herself. Maybe she believes that she has a good idea for a business and that a lot of people will buy the service she will provide. Certainly Flo thinks that the business will be profitable or else she would not have been willing to risk the money that took her years to save.

In order for such a business to be profitable, the revenue must be greater than the expenses. When this is the case, the owner (or **proprietor**) profits by the gain. If, however, expenses become larger than revenues, the proprietor **incurs** a loss, and if the amount of cash on hand is reduced to a small amount, the business may not remain solvent—that is, it may not be able to pay its bills when they become due.

Revenue

Flo begins her business employing only herself and one full-time person. She has advertised The Instant Secretary in the newspapers and receives calls from local businesses right away. The Instant Secretary prepares letters, memos, and reports and performs other tasks for businesses. **Revenue** for The Instant Secretary results when services are performed and cash is received for those services, or when services are performed and an account receivable results.

An **account receivable** is a promise by a customer to pay at some future date. The company selling the service, in this case The Instant Secretary, stipulates when the account receivable must be paid. Flo requires that all accounts receivable be paid within 30 days.

A concise definition of revenue for a service business is this:

Revenue is the inflow of cash and other assets for services sold to customers.

It is important not to confuse cash and revenue, for not all cash coming into a business is revenue. Revenue results for Flo's business only when services are sold, but cash may come into the business from many other sources. For example, Flo may withdraw additional cash from her personal savings account and deposit that money into the business account. That would certainly not be considered revenue. The business may borrow money from a bank. Again, this is cash coming into the business, but it is not revenue. There are other examples, of course, and you will learn about them later.

Note that revenue is recorded on the books when it is earned, not necessarily when the cash is received. For example, Flo may perform services in the amount of $500 for a company on May 3, and may agree to accept payment for the services in June. Flo will record $500 as revenue for May, along with an account receivable for $500. When the cash is received in June, it will not be revenue at that time, but will be reducing the amount of the account receivable.

Revenue increases owner's equity, but it is recorded in a separate revenue account.

Expenses

Expenses are the necessary costs that relate to the earning of revenue. Examples are salaries for employees, payroll taxes, utilities, phone bills, advertising costs, and delivery charges. Expenses may be paid in cash as they are incurred, or the business may promise to pay at a later date. The latter, you will remember, results in an account payable.

Not all payments of cash are considered to be expenses. Paying back a loan, for example, is not an expense; rather, it is a reduction in a liability. Money paid for the purchase of equipment (as learned in Chapter One) is not an expense, but causes an increase in one asset and a decrease in another.

When an expense is incurred, it is recorded on the books, not necessarily when the cash is paid for it. For example, assume that Flo contracts for $1,000 of radio advertising to be done in May, but will not pay for it until July. She records $1,000 as an expense in May, along with a $1,000 increase in Accounts Payable. When Flo pays the bill in July, it is not recorded as an expense again; then it is a reduction of the amount owed (Accounts Payable).

Expenses decrease owner's equity and are recorded in separate accounts.

Net Income

When a business is making money, it is said to be operating profitably. Earning a profit is probably the most important reason people open their own businesses. The accounting term that we will use to describe profits is **net income**.

Net income may be defined simply as the excess of revenue over expenses, or, in other words, net income equals revenue minus expenses.

Net income must be measured for a specific period of time (say, one month or one year) in order for it to be meaningful. If, for example, one were to say, "I earned $5,000," it would not be particularly significant until we knew whether it took one year, one month, or one week (or some other period of time) to earn the $5,000.

Net Loss

Sometimes a business may have periods when the expenses incurred are greater than revenues; if this occurs, the business is said to have incurred a **net loss**, which is defined as the excess of expenses over revenue.

Owner's Withdrawals

With a small business that is not incorporated (for our purposes, a **sole proprietorship**), the owner is not considered to be a regular employee of the business. The salaries of employees are business expenses, and income taxes and payroll taxes are deducted from their paycheques. A proprietor of a small business, in contrast, personally pays income taxes based on the net income of the business for the year. That net income is considered to be the owner's salary for income tax purposes.

When the owner decides to withdraw money from the business (which he or she may do at any time), that withdrawal is not considered to be an expense. Rather, it is a reduction in the owner's equity and is recorded in a separate account called the Drawing account, or simply **Drawing**. Amounts withdrawn from the business by the owner decrease owner's equity, just as amounts invested into the business cause an increase in owner's equity. The drawing account will be used to record

1. all cash taken from the business by the owner for personal use,
2. any payments of personal bills by the owner with the business cheque book, and
3. the removal by the owner of a business asset for personal use (for example, a calculator taken from the business for home use).

Owner's Equity

The owner's equity account, Capital, may be affected by the following:

Increases in Owner's Equity
1. The owner invests cash or other assets in the business.
2. The business earns a net income.

Decreases in Owner's Equity
1. The owner withdraws cash or other assets from the business.
2. The business incurs a net loss.

An important accounting rule requires that business transactions be kept separate from the owner's personal transactions so that an accurate picture of the firm's earning power may be drawn. This principle is called the **entity concept**. For example, Flo maintains a personal chequing account under her name out of which she pays all of her personal bills. In addition, Flo maintains a business chequing account under the name of The Instant Secretary out of which all the business bills are paid. The Instant Secretary is an **entity** separate from Flo Hansen, and cash coming in and going out must be separately accounted for, as must all other assets and liabilities.

The Fundamental Accounting Equation with Revenue, Expense, and Drawing

It has already been noted that revenue increases owner's equity, that expenses and withdrawals decrease owner's equity, and that revenue, expenses, and withdrawals are recorded in separate accounts. Because revenue, expenses, and drawing directly affect the owner's equity, the fundamental accounting equation still looks like this:

$$\text{Assets} = \text{Liabilities} + \text{Owner's Equity}$$

but owner's equity must be regarded as being:

$$\frac{\text{Owner's}}{\text{Equity}} = \frac{\text{Owner's}}{\text{Investment}} + \text{Revenue} - \text{Expenses} - \text{Withdrawals}.$$

Let's look at some typical transactions for The Instant Secretary.

TRANSACTION 1 **Selling Services for Cash** Flo agrees to do some work for another local business. The work is completed in three days, and the charge for the service is $150. The customer pays cash. The fundamental accounting equation is shown with the previous balances taken from Chapter One. This particular transaction increases cash and increases revenue and affects the equation as follows:

	Assets					=	Liabilities + Owner's Equity				
	Cash +	Acc. Rec. +	Equip. +	Furn. +	Supp. +	Lib. =	Acc. Pay. +	Capital +	Rev. −	Exp. −	Draw.
Previous Balances	$2,700 +	0 +	$16,000 +	$4,500 +	$800 +	$200 =	$14,000 +	$10,200			
(1)	+150								+150		
New Balances	$2,850 +	0 +	$16,000 +	$4,500 +	$800 +	$200 =	$14,000 +	$10,200 +	$150		

TRANSACTION 2 **Selling Services on Account** The Instant Secretary agrees to do some work for Allen's Engineering Company over a two-week period. The total cost of The Instant Secretary's services for this job is $750. Allen's pays no money when the work is delivered but agrees to pay within 30 days, thus creating an account receivable for The Instant Secretary. The equation looks like this after both Revenue and the asset Accounts Receivable have been increased:

	Assets					=	Liabilities + Owner's Equity				
	Cash +	Acc. Rec. +	Equip. +	Furn. +	Supp. +	Lib. =	Acc. Pay. +	Capital +	Rev. −	Exp. −	Draw.
Previous Balances	$2,850 +	0 +	$16,000 +	$4,500 +	$800 +	$200 =	$14,000 +	$10,200 +	$150		
(2)		+750							+750		
New Balances	$2,850 +	$750 +	$16,000 +	$4,500 +	$800 +	$200 =	$14,000 +	$10,200 +	$900		

Note that the work performed is counted as revenue earned even though the money has not yet been collected for the service.

TRANSACTION 3   **Paying Cash for an Expense**   Flo pays a $60 phone bill for The Instant Secretary. The equation now looks like this:

	Assets					=	Liabilities + Owner's Equity				
	Cash +	Acc. Rec. +	Equip. +	Furn. +	Supp. +	Lib. =	Acc. Pay. +	Capital +	Rev. −	Exp. −	Draw.
Previous Balances	$2,850 +	$750 +	$16,000 +	$4,500 +	$800 +	$200 =	$14,000 +	$10,200 +	$900		
(3)	−60									−60	
New Balances	$2,790 +	$750 +	$16,000 +	$4,500 +	$800 +	$200 =	$14,000 +	$10,200 +	$900 −	$60	

TRANSACTION 4   **Paying Cash for an Expense**   Flo pays a $100 bill for equipment rental. The equation now looks like this:

	Assets					=	Liabilities + Owner's Equity				
	Cash +	Acc. Rec. +	Equip. +	Furn. +	Supp. +	Lib. =	Acc. Pay. +	Capital +	Rev. −	Exp. −	Draw.
Previous Balances	$2,790 +	$750 +	$16,000 +	$4,500 +	$800 +	$200 =	$14,000 +	$10,200 +	$900 −	$60	
(4)	−100									−100	
New Balances	$2,690 +	$750 +	$16,000 +	$4,500 +	$800 +	$200 =	$14,000 +	$10,200 +	$900 −	$160	

If you look carefully at the equation, you will see that Expenses are added together and the total is subtracted from Revenue to keep the equation in balance. Total Assets are now equal to Total Liabilities plus Capital plus Revenue minus Expenses. The equation now looks like this:

Assets	=	Liabilities	+	Capital	+	Revenue	−	Expenses
$24,940	=	$14,000	+	$10,200	+	$900	−	$160
	=			$24,940				

TRANSACTION 5   **Withdrawing Cash for Personal Use**   Flo withdraws $250 cash for her personal use. Remember that owner's withdrawals are not considered to be an expense of the business and are recorded in a separate account called *Drawing* or *Owner's Withdrawals*. The equation now looks like this:

	Assets					=	Liabilities + Owner's Equity				
	Cash +	Acc. Rec. +	Equip. +	Furn. +	Supp. +	Lib. =	Acc. Pay. +	Capital +	Rev. −	Exp. −	Draw.
Previous Balances	$2,690 +	$750 +	$16,000 +	$4,500 +	$800 +	$200 =	$14,000 +	$10,200 +	$900 −	$160	
(5)	−250										−250
New Balances	$2,440 +	$750 +	$16,000 +	$4,500 +	$800 +	$200 =	$14,000 +	$10,200 +	$900 −	$160 −	$250

TRANSACTION 6 **Paying Money to a Creditor** Flo pays $400 to a creditor, BECO, as partial payment for office equipment purchased earlier (see Chapter One, Transaction 3). The equation now looks like this:

	Assets					=	Liabilities + Owner's Equity				
	Cash +	Acc. Rec. +	Equip. +	Furn. +	Supp. +	Lib. =	Acc. Pay. +	Capital +	Rev. −	Exp. −	Draw.
Previous Balances (6)	$2,440 + −400	$750 +	$16,000 +	$4,500 +	$800 +	$200 =	$14,000 + −400	$10,200 +	$900 −	$160 −	$250
New Balances	$2,040 +	$750 +	$16,000 +	$4,500 +	$800 +	$200 =	$13,600 +	$10,200 +	$900 −	$160 −	$250

Remember, money paid on account is not an expense. Rather, it is a reduction in the liability, Accounts Payable.

TRANSACTION 7 **Incurring an Expense but Delaying Payment** Flo has some radio advertising done for The Instant Secretary in the amount of $375 and agrees to pay the bill within 60 days. Notice that this transaction does not affect assets at all. On the Liabilities and Owner's Equity side of the equation, the $375 is added as a Liability and will be subtracted as an Expense, thus causing no change in Total Liabilities and Owner's Equity. The equation now looks like this:

	Assets					=	Liabilities + Owner's Equity				
	Cash +	Acc. Rec. +	Equip. +	Furn. +	Supp. +	Lib. =	Acc. Pay. +	Capital +	Rev. −	Exp. −	Draw.
Previous Balances (7)	$2,040 +	$750 +	$16,000 +	$4,500 +	$800 +	$200 =	$13,600 + +375	$10,200 +	$900 −	$160 − −375	$250
New Balances	$2,040 +	$750 +	$16,000 +	$4,500 +	$800 +	$200 =	$13,975 +	$10,200 +	$900 −	$535 −	$250

Notice that expenses are recorded when they are actually incurred, not when they are paid.

TRANSACTION 8 **Receiving Money on Account** Allen's Engineering Service (see Transaction 2) pays $500 to The Instant Secretary as partial settlement of its account. The equation now looks like this:

	Assets					=	Liabilities + Owner's Equity				
	Cash +	Acc. Rec. +	Equip. +	Furn. +	Supp. +	Lib. =	Acc. Pay. +	Capital +	Rev. −	Exp. −	Draw.
Previous Balances (8)	$2,040 + +500	$750 + −500	$16,000 +	$4,500 +	$800 +	$200 =	$13,975 +	$10,200 +	$900 −	$535 −	$250
New Balances	$2,540 +	$250 +	$16,000 +	$4,500 +	$800 +	$200 =	$13,975 +	$10,200 +	$900 −	$535 −	$250

Note that one asset, Cash, has increased by $500 while another asset, Accounts Receivable, has decreased by $500, thus keeping the Total Assets the same. In addition, remember that when money is received on account, it is not considered to be revenue. It is, rather, a reduction in the asset, Accounts Receivable. For this particular transaction, the original entry (see Transaction 2) recorded the $750 revenue. When the customer actually pays the bill later, as is the case here, it would not be logical to count the money received as revenue again.

TRANSACTION 9 **Purchasing Equipment, Cash Down Payment** Flo purchases additional equipment at a total cost of $1,500. She makes a $300 cash down payment and agrees to make monthly payments of $100 for the next year. The equation is affected in the following way:

			Assets				=		Liabilities + Owner's Equity				
	Cash +	Acc. Rec. +	Equip. +	Furn. +	Supp. +	Lib. =		Acc. Pay. +	Capital +	Rev. −	Exp. −	Draw.	
Previous Balances	$2,540 +	$250 +	$16,000 +	$4,500 +	$800 +	$200 =		$13,975 +	$10,200 +	$900 −	$535 −	$250	
(9)	−300		+1,500					+1,200					
New Balances	$2,240 +	$250 +	$17,500 +	$4,500 +	$800 +	$200 =		$15,175 +	$10,200 +	$900 −	$535 −	$250	

Note that Total Assets have increased by $1,200 and that Total Liabilities have increased by $1,200, keeping the equation in balance.

TRANSACTION 10 **Investing Additional Cash** Flo decided to take an additional $3,000 from her personal savings account and deposit it in the business account.

			Assets				=		Liabilities + Owner's Equity				
	Cash +	Acc. Rec. +	Equip. +	Furn. +	Supp. +	Lib. =		Acc. Pay. +	Capital +	Rev. −	Exp. −	Draw.	
Previous Balances	$2,240 +	$250 +	$17,500 +	$4,500 +	$800 +	$200 =		$15,175 +	$10,200 +	$900 −	$535 −	$250	
(10)	+3,000								+3,000				
New Balances	$5,240 +	$250 +	$17,500 +	$4,500 +	$800 +	$200 =		$15,175 +	$13,200 +	$900 −	$535 −	$250	

Notice that this additional investment of $3,000 increases the Capital account but does not affect Revenue.

The preceding ten transactions are typical of the transactions that occurred during the entire month for The Instant Secretary. In addition to those already shown, The Instant Secretary performed additional services for cash in the amount of $2,400, thus increasing the Cash account from $5,240 to $7,640 and increasing the revenue earned from $900 to $3,300. Flo paid cash for wages expense, $800; utilities expense, $90; newspaper advertising, $72; and delivery expense, $18. These expenses, along with the others for the month, follow.

Phone Expense	$ 60
Equipment Rental Expense	100
Radio Advertising	375
Wages Expense	800
Utilities Expense	90
Newspaper Advertising	72
Delivery Expense	18
Total Expenses	$1,515

Note that the owner's withdrawals and the money paid on account are not listed as expenses. Total cash for The Instant Secretary, after earning the additional revenue and after paying the additional expenses, is $6,660.

The Income Statement

The income statement is the formal financial statement that is prepared to show total revenue, total expenses, and net income or net loss for a specific time period (a month, a quarter, a year), called an **accounting period**. Flo has decided to adopt a monthly accounting period for her business.

The income statement for The Instant Secretary, showing in detail all the revenue earned and the expenses incurred for the month of February, is as follows:

The Instant Secretary Income Statement For Month Ended February 28, 19XX		
Revenue		
Revenue from Services		$3,300—
Expenses		
Telephone Expense	$ 60—	
Equipment Rental Expense	100—	
Advertising Expense*	447—	
Wages Expense	800—	
Utilities Expense	90—	
Delivery Expense	18—	
Total Expenses		1,515—
Net Income		$1,785—

* Note that newspaper and radio advertising expenses are combined for the income statement under one account entitled *Advertising Expense.*

Rules for Preparing the Income Statement

The Heading   The income statement has a three-part heading that is centred and always includes, in this order: (1) the name of the business; (2) the name of the financial statement; and (3) the time period or the length of time for which the net income is measured.

Revenue   The word *Revenue* is written at the left next to the vertical line and, on the next line, the name of the revenue account is indented about half an inch. If there is more than one revenue account, the amounts are listed in the left-hand column. *Total Revenue* is written immediately below the last revenue account listed, and the total amount is written in the right-hand column as illustrated.

Revenue		
Revenue from Consulting	$1,450—	
Revenue from Teaching	2,700—	
Total Revenue		$4,150—

Expenses   Leave one blank line after the revenue accounts before writing the word *Expenses* at the left. Again, indent about half an inch and list the expense accounts. There is no particular order for listing expenses. The amounts are entered in the left-hand column and the total of the expenses is written in the right-hand column beneath the total revenue figure.

Net Income   The total of expenses is subtracted from the total revenue to obtain net income. If total expenses are larger than total revenue, a net loss has been incurred. Leave one blank line after total expenses before writing *Net Income* or *Net Loss*.

Dollar Signs and Lines   A dollar sign appears at the beginning of each column and by the net income figure. A single line appears under the amount for the last expense listed (Delivery Expense $18—) to indicate addition and a single line appears beneath the figure for total expenses to indicate subtraction. A double line appears beneath net income to show that work is completed. Remember, all lines are drawn with a ruler and extend all the way across the column.

Statement of Owner's Equity

Because revenue and expense accounts affect owner's equity, it is necessary to prepare the income statement before the balance sheet so that results of operations (net income or net loss) can be included in the owner's equity section of the balance sheet. Some people prefer, however, to prepare a statement of owner's equity separate from the balance sheet. This is the procedure that Flo chooses. The statement of owner's equity for The Instant Secretary detailing the changes in owner's equity for February is as follows:

The Instant Secretary Statement of Owner's Equity For Month Ended February 28, 19XX		
Florence Hansen, Capital, February 1, 19XX	$10,200—	
Add: Net Income for February	1,785—	
Additional Investment	3,000—	
Subtotal	14,985—	
Deduct: Florence Hansen, Drawing	250—	
Florence Hansen, Capital, February 28, 19XX		$14,735—

Note that net income and Flo's additional investment have increased owner's equity, while the withdrawals have caused a decrease. A net loss would also cause a decrease in owner's equity.

The following statement of owner's equity shows how a loss is handled for the A & M Consulting Service:

A & M Consulting Service Statement of Owner's Equity For Month Ended July 31, 19XX			
T.A. Adams, Capital, July 1, 19XX		$42,000—	
Add: Additional Investment		3,600—	
Subtotal		45,600—	
Deduct: Net Loss for July	$4,280—		
T.A. Adams, Drawing	2,700—		
Total Deductions		6,980—	
T.A. Adams, Capital, July 31, 19XX			$38,620—

The statement of owner's equity has a three-part heading similar to the heading of the balance sheet. It contains (1) the name of the company; (2) the name of the statement; and (3) the time period during which the changes occurred.

Calculations are completed in the left-hand column, and the total capital is entered directly into the right-hand column. Often, a third column is required for calculating, as is the case when the net loss must be added to the withdrawals.

The Balance Sheet—Not Detailing Changes in Owner's Equity

The balance sheet for The Instant Secretary looks similar to the one in Chapter One. When a separate statement of owner's equity is prepared, those changes are not reflected again on the balance sheet; only the ending capital figure appears in the owner's equity section.

The Instant Secretary Balance Sheet February 28, 19XX		
Assets		
Cash	$ 6,660—	
Accounts Receivable	250—	
Supplies	800—	
Equipment	17,500—	
Furniture	4,500—	
Library	200—	
Total Assets		$29,910—
Liabilities		
Accounts Payable	$15,175—	
Total Liabilities		$15,175—
Owner's Equity		
Florence Hansen, Capital, February 28, 19XX		14,735—
Total Liabilities and Owner's Equity		$29,910—

The Balance Sheet—Detailing Changes in Owner's Equity

If Flo were to choose not to prepare a separate statement of owner's equity, the balance sheet would reflect all the changes in the owner's capital account. The balance sheet for The Instant Secretary showing the changes in owner's equity for February is as follows:

The Instant Secretary Balance Sheet February 28, 19XX		
Assets		
Cash	$ 6,660—	
Accounts Receivable	250—	
Supplies	800—	
Equipment	17,500—	
Furniture	4,500—	
Library	200—	
Total Assets		$29,910—
Liabilities		
Accounts Payable	$15,175—	
Total Liabilities		$15,175—
Owner's Equity		
Florence Hansen, Capital, February 1, 19XX	$10,200—	
Add: Net Income for February	1,785—	
Additional Investment	3,000—	
Subtotal	14,985—	
Deduct: Florence Hansen, Drawing	250—	
Florence Hansen, Capital, February 28, 19XX		14,735—
Total Liabilities and Owner's Equity		$29,910—

The Accrual Method and the Cash Method of Measuring Net Income

The accrual method of accounting is a method whereby all revenue is recognized in the period in which the services are performed (or in the period in which the revenue is earned), whether or not cash is received for the performing of those services. Likewise, expenses are recognized (or counted) in the period in which they are incurred, whether or not cash payment for them is made right away. Revenue may be included in the total accounts receivable and expenses may show up in accounts payable.

For example, assume that a landscape contractor agrees to do some work for a client and sends the bill for the services after all the work is completed. The job was started on November 1 and completed on February 28 of the following year. The contractor would record a portion of the total revenue earned during each of the four months and would simply record an accounts receivable for amounts to be received after completion of the entire job. By the same token, the contractor would record all expenses related to this job when they were incurred, even if creditors agreed to accept payment at a later date. In short, the accrual method of accounting recognizes revenue when the services are performed and recognizes expenses as they are incurred.

The cash basis of accounting, in contrast, recognizes revenue when cash is actually received and recognizes expenses when cash is paid out. In the preceding example of the landscape contractor, revenue for the particular job would not be recognized until March when the cash was received, and expenses would be recorded when they were paid, not when they were incurred. Using the cash basis of accounting in this situation would distort the firm's financial position because the contractor was actually performing landscape services from November through February, yet all the revenue for this job by this method would be recognized in March, making that month's income as greatly overstated as the four preceding months' income was understated. An obvious advantage to the cash basis of accounting is its simplicity. However, since the cash basis distorts the amounts reported as revenues earned and expenses incurred for a particular time period, the accrual method of accounting will be used exclusively in this text.

Summary

Revenue is the **inflow** into the business of cash and other assets for services performed; expenses are the necessary costs relating to the earning of revenue. The fundamental accounting equation is now expanded to include revenue, expenses, and the owner's withdrawals. It is as follows:

$$\text{Assets} = \text{Liabilities} + \frac{\text{Owner's}}{\text{Capital}} + \text{Revenue} - \text{Expenses} - \text{Drawing}.$$

To earn a profit, revenue must be greater than related expenses. The proprietor is responsible for the business; he or she may take all profits but must also sustain all losses. The owner may be required to invest additional sums of money from time to time and may withdraw cash or other assets as needed.

The periodic income statement is the financial statement that shows whether or not the business is operating profitably. It lists the revenue accounts and total revenue, the expense accounts and total expenses, and the net income or net loss for the period.

The balance sheet reflects a firm's financial position on a certain date; it may detail the changes in the owner's capital account, or a separate statement of owner's equity may be prepared. The owner's capital account may be increased by a net income or by an additional investment by the owner. It may be decreased by a net loss or by the owner's withdrawals.

Vocabulary Review

Following is a list of the words and terms for this chapter:

accounting period	incur
accounts receivable	inflow
accrue	net income
drawing	net loss
entity	proprietor
entity concept	revenue
expenses	sole proprietorship

Fill in the blank with the correct word or term from the list.

1. The word meaning to increase or accumulate is _____.
2. An owner of a business is called a/an _____.
3. Money owed to the business by charge customers is called _____.
4. To _____ means to be subject to.
5. The amount by which expenses are greater than revenue is referred to as _____.
6. The word that means the process of flowing into is _____.
7. _____ is defined as the inflow of cash and receivables for services performed.
8. The rule that states that a firm's assets be kept separate on the books from the owner's assets is referred to as the _____.
9. The costs incurred in obtaining revenue are called _____.
10. A business owned by an individual is referred to as a/an _____.
11. The excess of revenue over expenses is _____.
12. Something that exists independently is called a/an _____.
13. A designated time period for which a company's net income or net loss is calculated is called a/an _____.
14. Money taken by the owner from the business is called _____.

Match the words and terms on the left with the definitions on the right.

15. inflow
16. accrue
17. proprietor
18. net income
19. entity concept
20. expenses
21. net loss
22. incur
23. sole proprietorship
24. accounts receivable
25. revenue
26. entity
27. accounting period
28. drawing

a. to increase or accumulate
b. the excess of expenses over revenue
c. money owed to the business by charge customers
d. a separate being
e. inflow of cash and receivables for services performed
f. costs incurred in obtaining revenue
g. the act or process of flowing into
h. to become subject to
i. the excess of revenue over expenses; profit
j. a time period of a month, a quarter, a year, etc., for which a company's net income or loss is determined
k. an owner
l. a business owned by one person
m. the accounting rule that a firm's assets be kept separate from the owner's assets
n. cash taken from the business by the owner for personal use

Exercises

EXERCISE 2.1   Identify the following as asset (A), liability (L), owner's equity (OE), revenue (R), or expense (E) accounts:

a. Accounts Receivable
b. Furniture
c. Don Jones, Capital
d. Accounts Payable
e. Equipment
f. Cash
g. Revenue from Services
h. Utilities Expense
i. Taxes Payable
j. Rent Expense
k. Don Jones, Drawing
l. Salaries Expense
m. Office Machines
n. Consulting Revenue

EXERCISE 2.2

	Cash +	Accounts Receivable +	Equipment =	Accounts Payable +	Capital +	Revenue −	Expenses −	Drawing
a.	$10,000				$10,000			
b.	−2,000		+2,000					
	8,000		2,000 =		10,000			
c.	+500					+500		
	8,500		+ 2,000 =		10,000 +	500		
d.		+800				+800		
	8,500 +	800 +	2,000 =		10,000 +	1,300		
e.	−400						−400	
	8,100 +	800 +	2,000 =		10,000 +	1,300 −	400	
f.	−600							−600
	7,500 +	800 +	2,000 =		10,000 +	1,300 −	400 −	600
g.			+900	+900				
	7,500 +	800 +	2,900 =	900 +	10,000 +	1,300 −	400 −	600
h.				+500			−500	
	7,500 +	800 +	2,900 =	1,400 +	10,000 +	1,300 −	900 −	600
i.	+100	−100						
	$7,600 +	$700 +	$2,900 =	$1,400 +	$10,000 +	$1,300 −	$900 −	$600

1. Does the left-hand side of the final line of the equation equal the right-hand side? (In other words, is the equation "in balance"? Do Total Assets equal Liabilities plus Capital plus Revenue minus Expenses minus Drawing?)
2. Tell what has occurred for each transaction.
3. What is the amount of net income?
4. What is the amount of the ending capital?

EXERCISE 2.3 Describe a transaction that could cause the following to occur:
a. increase one asset and decrease another asset by the same amount
b. increase an asset and increase revenue by the same amount
c. increase an asset and increase owner's equity by the same amount
d. decrease an asset and increase the drawing account by the same amount
e. decrease an asset and increase an expense by the same amount
f. decrease an asset and decrease a liability by the same amount
g. increase a liability and increase an expense.

EXERCISE 2.4

(a) Income Statement (b)		
(c)		
Revenue from Services	$12,200—	
Revenue from Consulting	(d)	
(e)		$16,200—
(f)		
Wages Expense	3,400—	
Advertising Expense	1,500—	
Telephone Expense	800—	
Utilities Expense	2,100—	
(g)		(h)
(i)		(j)

Shown on the previous page is a partially completed Income Statement for Eugene Evans, Veterinarian, for the month of June, 19XX. Prepare a corrected income statement and fill in the missing headings or figures.

EXERCISE 2.5 The following are some of the accounts and their balances for The Trend Styling Salon. Using only the revenue and expense accounts, prepare an income statement for the month ended June 30, 19XX.

Cash	$2,900
Accounts Receivable	640
Revenue from Haircutting	4,000
Advertising Expense	800
Furniture	3,000
Wages Expense	2,500
Rent Expense	1,750
Miscellaneous Expense	420
Accounts Payable	970
Revenue from Manicuring	620
Utilities Expense	280

EXERCISE 2.6 During May, Harry Brown, proprietor of Poodle Pruners, carried out the transactions listed below. In each case determine whether the transaction represents revenue for the month of May.

a. obtained a $5,000 business loan for the purchase of equipment and furniture

b. trimmed the fur of 14 poodles on May 10 and received $280 cash for the service

c. invested an additional $2,500 into the business

d. received $750 cash on account from customers whose dogs he had trimmed in April

e. trimmed and bathed eight poodles on May 31 at a total cost to customers of $450; five customers paid cash for the service amounting to $150, and the others agreed to pay within 30 days.

During July, Harry Brown carried out the following transactions. Determine which of the following represents expense for July.

f. on July 1, wrote a cheque for $1,500 in payment of the rent for July

g. on July 3, wrote a $500 cheque to himself to be deposited in his personal chequing account

h. on July 10, wrote a cheque for $725 in payment of an account payable resulting from radio advertising done in June

i. on July 15, wrote a cheque in payment for a desk for the computer and printer

j. on July 20, wrote a cheque for $1,000 to repay a non-interest-bearing loan obtained in February

k. on July 31, wrote a cheque for $120 for gasoline purchases for the business van for July.

EXERCISE 2.7

(a) (b) (c)		
(d)	$23,400—	
Add: Net Income	(e)	
Additional Investment	2,000—	
Subtotal	33,680—	
Deduct: Charles St. James, Drawing	(f)	
(g)		$32,880—

Charles St. James has an accounting practice called St. James Accounting. Shown on page 32 is a partially completed Statement of Owner's Equity for the three-month period ending March 31, 19XX. Calculate the amounts for the missing figures and prepare a complete statement of owner's equity.

EXERCISE 2.8   Heather Bullock runs an accounting service. Heather's capital account on May 1 had a balance of $7,800. During May, Heather invested an additional $2,000 into the business from her personal savings. Revenue for the month was $10,740 and expenses were $8,340. The balance in the drawing account on May 31 was $800. Prepare a statement of owner's equity for Heather's Accounting Service on May 31, 19XX.

EXERCISE 2.9   Roger Lemieux has a small business called "Equine Elegance." Roger grooms horses before their shows and gives advice on the proper care of horses. His capital account on November 1 showed a balance of $2,800. Revenue for November was $4,325 and expenses were $4,885. Roger's drawing account showed a balance on November 30 of $480. Prepare a statement of owner's equity for the month ended November 30, 19XX.

EXERCISE 2.10   Following you will find several different possibilities for the statement of owner's equity. Determine in each case the dollar value of the missing figure.

a. Capital, February 1	$ 8,000
Net loss for the month	1,500
Owner's withdrawals	800
Capital, February 28	?
b. Capital, May 1	$ 6,100
Net income for the month	1,800
Capital, May 31	7,000
Owner's withdrawals	?
c. Capital, October 31	$ 8,700
Net income for the month	1,650
Owner's withdrawals	1,000
Capital, October 1	?
d. Capital, March 1	$10,600
Owner's withdrawals	2,300
Net income for the month	1,700
Additional investment	1,000
Capital, March 31	?
e. Capital, September 1	$ 4,900
Owner's withdrawals	900
Capital, September 30	3,200
Net loss for the month	?

EXERCISE 2.11   The balance sheets for Huronia Legal Service at the beginning and the end of January showed the following balances:

	January 1	January 31
Total Assets	$27,600	$32,100
Total Liabilities	16,800	18,400

Determine the net income or loss of Huronia Legal Services for the month of January under the following unrelated assumptions:
   a. The owner, Ross Victor, invested an additional $3,000 into the business.
   b. The owner, Ross Victor, withdrew $1,750 from the business for personal use.
   c. The owner, Ross Victor, invested an additional $3,200 and withdrew $1,800 for personal use.

Problems

PROBLEM 2.1 Albert Mar, a decorator, began his own business on September 1 and completed the following transactions in the first month:

   a. deposited $5,500 in a bank account for Mar's Home Decorating
   b. bought furniture for the office at a total cost of $3,500; made a $1,000 cash down payment and agreed to pay the rest within six months
   c. purchased office equipment for $650 cash
   d. paid rent, $450
   e. received $800 for services rendered
   f. paid cash for supplies for the office, $280
   g. paid the salary of a part-time employee, $250
   h. received a bill for advertising, $380, and decided to pay it later (remember, expenses are recorded when they are incurred, not necessarily when they are paid)
   i. bought a typewriter, $1,000, and paid no money down; the full amount is due in 90 days
   j. performed services for a customer and sent a bill for $1,250; the customer agreed to pay within 90 days
   k. paid $100 on account (see Transaction h)
   l. Albert withdrew $500 from the business for personal use
   m. received a cheque (see Transaction j) for $475 from a customer in partial settlement of the account.

INSTRUCTIONS 1. Using the following headings, record each transaction and the new balances after each:

Accounts					Accounts				
Cash +	Receivable +	Supplies +	Furniture +	Equipment =	Payable +	Capital +	Revenue −	Expenses −	Drawing

   2. After recording all the transactions, check to make sure that the equation is in balance.
   3. Determine the amount of the net income or net loss for the month.
   4. Prepare a statement of owner's equity for the month ended September 30, 19XX.

PROBLEM 2.2 Krista Klein, owner of Krista's Katering, has just begun a catering business in which she caters for meetings, luncheons, and receptions. The accounts and their balances are listed below.

Catering Revenue	$9,500
Advertising Expense	1,400
Utilities Expense	2,200
Cash	2,400
Wages Expense	2,200
Krista Klein, Capital, July 1, 19XX	7,400
Food and Beverage Expense	3,550
Delivery Expense	650
Krista Klein, Drawing	1,000

INSTRUCTIONS

1. Prepare an income statement for the month ended July 31, 19XX.
2. Prepare a statement of owner's equity for the month ended July 31, 19XX.

PROBLEM 2.3

Paul Padilla established his own business called Paul's Parking. He completed the following transactions in the month of September:

a. deposited $6,000 into the business account
b. purchased office equipment from J.R.'s Office Supply Company for $1,800; paid $800 cash down and agreed to pay the balance within 90 days
c. paid rent, $1,000
d. paid $240 cash for supplies
e. paid wages, $300
f. received parking lot revenue, $2,000 cash
g. purchased office furniture from J.R.'s Office Supply Company for $2,000; paid $1,000 cash down and agreed to pay the balance within 60 days
h. paid $350 for advertising
i. paid utilities bill, $60
j. paid phone bill, $85
k. received $500 in cash revenue
l. sent bills totalling $650 to regular customers who have been using the parking lot but have not yet paid
m. paid wages, $300
n. wrote a cheque for $200 in partial settlement of the account owed to J.R.'s Office Supply Company (see Transactions b and g)
o. received a bill for advertising, $35; record it now, to be paid later
p. withdrew $400 for personal use.

INSTRUCTIONS

1. Using the following headings, record each transaction and the new balance:

Accounts						Accounts				
Cash +	Receivable +	Supplies +	Furniture +	Equipment =		Payable +	Capital +	Revenue −	Expenses −	Drawing

2. After recording all the transactions, check to make sure that the equation is in balance.
3. Determine the amount of net income or net loss for the month.
4. Prepare a balance sheet on September 30 that shows the changes that have occurred in owner's equity. Do not prepare a separate statement of owner's equity.

PROBLEM 2.4

Following is a list of the accounts and their balances on August 31, 19XX for Tim Hopwell, Child Psychologist.

Cash	$11,800	Accounts Receivable	$2,200
Counselling Revenue	8,600	Insurance Expense	600
Furniture	4,300	Equipment	1,560
Wages Expense	1,200	Utilities Expense	510
Accounts Payable	3,400	Tim Hopwell, Drawing	1,500
Rent Expense	650	Miscellaneous Expense	180
Tim Hopwell, Capital, August 1, 19XX	10,400	Teaching Revenue	2,100

INSTRUCTIONS
1. Prepare an income statement for the month ended August 31, 19XX.
2. Prepare a statement of owner's equity for the month ended August 31, 19XX.
3. Prepare a balance sheet as of August 31, 19XX.

PROBLEM 2.5
Using the figures given for Tim Hopwell, Child Psychologist, in Problem 2.4, prepare a balance sheet on August 31, 19XX that details the changes in the capital account in the owner's equity section.

PROBLEM 2.6
Rita Roth owns the Roth Real Estate Company. The income statement for the month of November shows a net income of $1,762. When the transactions were recorded for the month, however, several errors were made.
   a. Rita withdrew $1,200 during the month for personal use. The $1,200 was recorded as a deduction from cash and as an expense.
   b. The Roth Real Estate Company performed services amounting to $2,400 for Andy Blake during November, but since he would not be paying for the service until December, the bookkeeper decided to wait until then to record the transaction.
   c. A cheque for $700 in payment of an account payable to a local radio station for advertising done in October was recorded as an expense and as a deduction from cash.
   d. Rita performed services for E.Z. Agnos Company in November in the amount of $3,700. Agnos paid $2,000 cash and agreed to pay the balance in 60 days. The bookkeeper recorded the transaction by increasing cash by $2,000, increasing accounts payable by $1,700, and increasing revenue by $3,700.
   e. Rita made a $250 payment on a non-interest-bearing loan obtained in February. The bookkeeper recorded the payment as an expense and as a deduction from cash.
   f. A $375 bill was received for delivery services for the month of November. The bookkeeper decided to put off paying the debt until December, and thus did not record the liability.
   g. Rita donated office equipment valued at $5,000 to the Roth Real Estate Company. The transaction was recorded as an increase to assets and as an increase to revenue.

INSTRUCTIONS
1. Analyze each incorrect transaction and determine whether the error would cause net income to be overstated (O), understated (U), or not affected (NA).

Example   Rita's original $5,000 investment was recorded as an increase to cash and as an increase to revenue.

Solution   Overstated (revenue is higher than it should be).

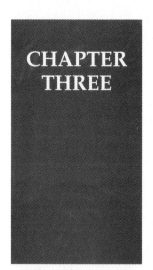

CHAPTER THREE

Understanding Debits and Credits and the Trial Balance

Learning Objectives

When you have completed this chapter, you should
1. have an increased understanding of accounting terminology.
2. be able to record transactions directly into T accounts, properly identifying the debit and credit amounts.
3. be able to determine account balances.
4. be able to prepare a trial balance from T accounts.
5. be able to prepare from the trial balance an income statement and a balance sheet that details the changes in owner's equity.

Vocabulary

account balance   the difference between the total debits and the total credits in an account; when the debit total exceeds the credit total, the account has a debit balance; when the credit total exceeds the debit total, the account has a credit balance

chart of accounts   the formal listing, in financial statement order, of a firm's accounts and their numbers

credit   an entry on the right-hand side of an account

debit   an entry on the left-hand side of an account

double-entry bookkeeping   a system of bookkeeping that requires for every debit entry there be a corresponding and equal credit entry or entries

normal balance   the debit or credit balance that an account is normally expected to have

notes payable   liabilities that are evidenced by a formal written promise to pay; often issued when money is borrowed and usually require a payment of interest

note receivable   assets that result when a customer signs a formal written promise to pay at some future date; may include an interest charge

T account   an informal ledger account drawn to look like a big T; used for illustrative purposes

trial balance   a two-column schedule that lists the accounts in financial statement order along with their balances; used to prove the equality of debits and credits

Introduction

In Chapters One and Two we followed Flo Hansen and her business, The Instant Secretary, through a full month's operations. You studied the fundamental accounting equation and the effects of various transactions on it. You recorded increases and decreases in the accounts by listing the account titles in equation form.

In actual practice, however, increases and decreases are not recorded that way. Transactions are first recorded in a book called a *journal* and then are transferred to individual accounts in a ledger. A *ledger* is a book with a separate page for each asset, liability, owner's equity, revenue, and expense account. The individual accounts summarize everything that has caused an increase or a decrease in them.

It is easier to understand the concepts of debits and credits if the ledger is presented first. You should remember, however, that transactions are recorded first in a journal, which will be presented in Chapter Four.

The T Account

The **T account** is called that because it is drawn to look like a big T. A T account has three basic parts: (1) the title, (2) a left-hand side, and (3) a right-hand side. The left-hand side of an account is called the **debit** side and the right-hand side is called the **credit** side.

Title of Account

Left-hand side	Right-hand side
Debit side	Credit side

Rules for Recording Debits and Credits in Balance Sheet Accounts

The debit and credit sides are used for recording increases and decreases in the accounts. When you make an entry on the left-hand side, you are debiting the account; when you make an entry on the right-hand side, you are crediting it. A debit entry sometimes causes an increase in the account and sometimes causes a decrease. The same is true for a credit entry. An easy way to remember the rules for debits and credits is to keep the fundamental accounting equation in mind:

$$\text{Assets} = \text{Liabilities} + \text{Owner's Equity.}$$

Assets appear on the left-hand side of the equation; assets increase by a left-hand, or debit, entry.

Asset Accounts

Debit side for recording **increases**	**Credit** side for recording **decreases**

When a debit increases an account, a credit decreases the same account. Again, let's look at the fundamental accounting equation:

$$\text{Assets} = \text{Liabilities} + \text{Owner's Equity.}$$

Notice that liabilities and owner's equity appear on the right-hand side of the equation. Note, too, that increases in liabilities and the owner's capital account are recorded on the right-hand, or credit, side.

Asset Accounts		=	**Liability Accounts**		+	**Owner's Capital**	
Debit side for recording **increases**	Credit side		Debit side	**Credit** side for recording **increases**		Debit side	**Credit** side for recording **increases**

Again, it is logical that when a credit records an increase in an account, a debit will record a decrease.

Assets		=	**Liabilities**		+	**Owner's Capital**	
Debit	Credit		Debit	Credit		Debit	Credit
+	−		−	+		−	+

The **account balance** is determined by subtracting the total of the smaller side from the total of the larger side. If the debit side is larger, the account is said to have a debit balance; if the credit side is larger, the account has a credit balance.

Let's look in detail at the asset account Cash. All the left-hand or debit entries in the account represent increases, or, in this case, deposits of cash into the bank. The ledger account does not show the source of the cash; the journal (discussed in detail in Chapter Four) must be consulted for that information. All the right-hand or credit entries represent cheques written or cash withdrawn. By a quick glance at the cash account, you can easily determine how much cash is on hand, or, in other words, the balance of the account.

The cash account looks like this at the end of October:

Cash

	10/1 Balance	25,000	10/5	4,000
Debit	10/7	3,000	10/10	2,200
Entries	10/14	3,500	10/14	500
	10/21	2,800	10/19	1,000
	10/28	3,900	10/26	1,400
			10/31	300
	Debit Balance	**28,800**		

(Credit Entries)

The account balance is determined as follows:
1. Total the debit entries.
2. Total the credit entries.
3. Subtract the smaller total from the larger.
4. Enter the balance on the side of the account with the larger total.

Bookkeepers use a pen and write very neatly when making entries in formal accounting records. They do make occasional errors but they do not erase or obliterate them; they simply draw a neat line through the incorrect figure and rewrite the figure above, below, or beside it, wherever it is most convenient.

The debit balance of $28,800 in the cash account represents cash in the bank. Asset accounts have a **normal balance** that is a debit. A credit balance in the cash account would indicate that more cash had been spent than deposited, a situation that could not continue for long. It would be difficult to imagine a situation, though, where an account for land would have a credit balance. Asset accounts have normal debit balances, and liabilities and the owner's capital account have normal credit balances.

The following reviews the relationship between the fundamental accounting equation and the rules for debit and credit in the accounts. Remember, assets appear on the left-hand side of the equation and increase on the left-hand, or debit, side of the account. Liabilities and owner's equity appear on the right-hand side of the equation and increase on the right-hand, or credit, side of the account. Carefully study the following T accounts:

Assets	=	Liabilities	+	Owner's Equity

Cash

Debit	Credit
+	−

Accounts Receivable

Debit	Credit
+	−

Office Supplies

Debit	Credit
+	−

Equipment

Debit	Credit
+	−

Land

Debit	Credit
+	−

Notes Payable

Debit	Credit
−	+

Accounts Payable

Debit	Credit
−	+

Taxes Payable

Debit	Credit
−	+

Mortgage Payable

Debit	Credit
−	+

Owner's Capital

Debit	Credit
−	+

Recording Transactions in the Accounts

Before the debit and credit amounts can be entered, the following questions must be answered:
1. Which accounts are affected?

2. What is the account classification for each account?
3. Which account(s) will be debited and which will be credited?
4. Do the debit entries equal the credit entries?

The **double-entry system of bookkeeping** requires that for every debit entry there be a corresponding credit entry or entries that will be equal in amount. Debits always equal credits (unless a mistake has been made).

Transactions Affecting the Balance Sheet

TRANSACTION 1

On November 1, 19XX, Ben Moore opens a janitorial service by depositing $15,000 from his personal funds into a business account entitled "A-1 Janitorial."

Analysis The entry increases Cash and increases Owner's Capital. An increase to Cash requires a debit to the account and an increase to Owner's Capital requires a credit.

Cash		110	Ben Moore, Capital		310
+	−		−	+	
11/1 15,000				11/1 15,000	
(Debit increase)				(Credit increase)	

TRANSACTION 2

On November 2, Ben purchases cleaning equipment for $5,000 cash.

Analysis This entry must increase the asset account Equipment; therefore, a debit to that account is required. To decrease the asset Cash, that account must be credited.

Equipment		150	Cash		110
+	−		+	−	
11/2 5,000			11/1 15,000	11/2 5,000	
(Debit increase)				(Credit decrease)	

Remember that double-entry bookkeeping requires that for every debit entry there be a corresponding and equal credit entry.

TRANSACTION 3

On November 5, Ben purchases $1,200 worth of cleaning supplies on account and agrees to pay within 60 days.

Analysis This entry will increase the asset account Supplies by a debit and will increase the liability Accounts Payable by a credit.

Supplies		130	Accounts Payable		210
+	−		−	+	
11/5 1,200				11/5 1,200	
(Debit increase)				(Credit increase)	

TRANSACTION 4   On November 6, Ben agrees to sell an unneeded vacuum cleaner to a friend for $650, the vacuum's original cost. The friend signs a non-interest-bearing, six-month **note receivable**.

Analysis   The Equipment account must be decreased, or credited, for $650. Notes Receivable must be increased, or debited, for $650.

Notes Receivable		125	Equipment			150
+	−			+	−	
11/6 650				11/2 5,000	11/6 650	
(Debits increase assets)					(Credits decrease assets)	

TRANSACTION 5   On November 6, Ben purchases a pickup truck costing $15,000. He pays $5,000 down and signs a **note payable** for the remainder.

Analysis   This entry increases the asset account Truck, decreases the asset account Cash, and increases the liability account Notes Payable. *Total* assets will increase by $10,000 and *total* liabilities will increase by $10,000, thus ensuring that the debits equal the credits.

Truck		140	Cash			110	Notes Payable		220
+	−		+	−			−	+	
11/6 15,000			11/1 15,000	11/2 5,000				11/6 10,000	
				11/6 5,000					

Assets
Net Increase $10,000   Liabilities
Net Increase $10,000

On any individual entry, there may be one or more debits and one or more credits as long as the total debits equal the total credits. A note payable is similar to an account payable except that a note is a formal instrument that is signed by the buyer; it usually includes an interest rate, when payments on the note and the interest must be made, and a due date.

TRANSACTION 6   On November 9, Ben makes a $300 payment on the cleaning supplies purchased in Transaction 3.

Analysis   The Cash account must be decreased (requiring a credit entry) and the Accounts Payable must be decreased (requiring a debit entry).

Accounts Payable		210	Cash			110
−	+		+	−		
11/9 300	11/5 1,200		11/1 15,000	11/2 5,000		
				11/6 5,000		
				11/9 300		
(Debit decrease)				(Credit decrease)		

TRANSACTION 7   On November 10, Ben withdraws $800 from the business for his personal use.

Analysis   Remember that in the fundamental accounting equation, drawing is subtracted from the liabilities and owner's equity side. In addition, in the statement of owner's equity, drawing is subtracted from the balance in the capital account. Since credit entries increase the capital account and debit entries decrease the capital account, it is logical that entries to the drawing account be debits, because drawing indirectly causes a decrease in capital.

Ben Moore, Drawing		320	Cash				110
+	−		+		−		
11/10 800			11/1 15,000		11/2	5,000	
					11/6	5,000	
					11/9	300	
					11/10	**800**	
(Debit increases drawing)					(Credit decreases cash)		

TRANSACTION 8   On November 10, Ben receives a cheque for $65 in partial payment of the note that resulted from selling the vacuum cleaner (see Transaction 4).

Analysis   The asset Cash must be increased by recording a debit entry and the asset Notes Receivable must be decreased by recording a credit.

Cash			110	Notes Receivable			125
+		−		+		−	
11/1 15,000		11/2	5,000	11/6 650		**11/10**	**65**
11/10 65		11/6	5,000				
		11/9	300				
		11/10	800				
(Debit increases cash)				(Credit decreases notes receivable)			

Rules for Recording Debits and Credits in Income Statement Accounts

A quick look at the Cash account for A-1 Janitorial will reveal that the only debits are the $15,000 original investment and the deposit that Ben made for the $65 received from the sale of an extra vacuum cleaner. Once the business has been established and the necessary items of equipment and supplies have been purchased, the source for additional cash will be the selling of the service or product. Let's review briefly the fundamental accounting equation to refresh our memories as to how revenue and expenses are handled.

$$\text{Assets} = \text{Liabilities} + \text{Owner's Equity} + \text{Revenue} - \text{Expenses} - \text{Drawing}$$

Revenue is added in the equation because it causes an increase in the owner's capital account, and expenses are subtracted because they cause a decrease. The rules for debiting and crediting these accounts directly relate to how they affect owner's equity.

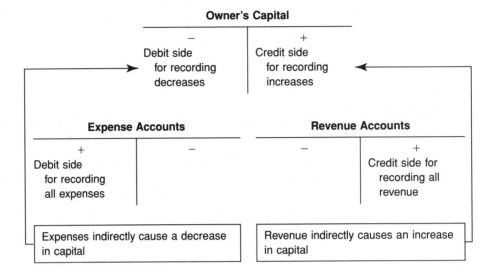

Think of revenue as indirectly causing an increase to the owner's capital account, thus requiring credit entries. In contrast, expenses indirectly cause a decrease in the capital account, thus requiring debit entries. While you are actually increasing the expenses by debits to the account, you will be indirectly decreasing the owner's capital. An actual change in the owner's capital account will take place at the end of the month when a net income or net loss is calculated. Transactions affecting the income statement follow.

TRANSACTION 9

On November 12, Ben advertises the services of his business in the local newspaper. He pays $95 cash for the advertising.

Analysis Expenses are recorded as debit entries because they indirectly cause a decrease in owner's capital. Cash is decreased by a credit entry.

Advertising Expense		610	Cash				110
+	−		+		−		
11/12	95		11/1	15,000	11/2	5,000	
			11/10	65	11/6	5,000	
					11/9	300	
					11/10	800	
					11/12	**95**	
(Expenses are recorded as debits)					(Credits decrease cash)		

TRANSACTION 10

On November 14, Ben receives a call from a local business and agrees to shampoo its carpets for $350 cash.

Analysis An increase of $350 must be recorded in the asset account Cash; therefore, cash must be debited. An increase in revenue is recorded by a credit.

Cash				110		Cleaning Revenue			410
+		–				–		+	
11/1	15,000	11/2	5,000					11/14	350
11/10	65	11/6	5,000						
11/14	**350**	11/9	300						
		11/10	800						
		11/12	95						

(Cash is increased by debits)   (Revenue is recorded as a credit)

TRANSACTION 11   On November 14, Ben purchases gas and oil for the delivery truck and pays $38 cash.

Analysis   Increases in expenses are recorded as debits and decreases in assets are recorded as credits.

Gas and Oil Expense			620		Cash				110
+		–			+		–		
11/14	**38**				11/1	15,000	11/2	5,000	
					11/10	65	11/6	5,000	
					11/14	350	11/9	300	
							11/10	800	
							11/12	95	
							11/14	**38**	

(Expenses are recorded as debits)   (Assets are decreased by credits)

TRANSACTION 12   On November 15, Ben agrees to clean the floors of a local clinic for $150. The clinic will pay on the fifteenth of the following month.

Analysis   Because we are using the accrual method of accounting, the revenue account will be increased by a credit entry even though the cash will be received at a later time. The accrual method recognizes revenue as earned when the services are performed. The corresponding debit entry will be to the asset Accounts Receivable.

Accounts Receivable			120		Cleaning Revenue			410
+		–			–		+	
11/15	**150**						11/14	350
							11/15	**150**

(Debits increase assets)   (Credits increase revenue)

TRANSACTION 13   On November 18, Ben decides to advertise the services of his business on a local radio station for a $425 fee, agreeing to pay in 30 days.

Analysis   Expenses have again increased, as have Accounts Payable. Increases in expenses are recorded as debits and increases in Accounts Payable are recorded as credits.

Advertising Expense			610	Accounts Payable			210
+		−		−		+	
11/12	95			11/9	300	11/5	1,200
11/18	**425**					**11/18**	**425**
(Expenses increase by debits)				(Liabilities increase by credits)			

TRANSACTION 14   On November 19, Ben makes a $492 payment on the note payable for the truck (see Transaction 5). Of the total payment, $295 applies toward the reduction of the amount borrowed and the rest, $197, is payment for interest. Interest is the charge to the borrower for the use of money. It will be discussed in more detail later.

Analysis   This transaction represents a compound entry because more than two accounts are involved. The increase in Interest Expense will be recorded as a debit; the reduction of the liability Notes Payable will be recorded as a debit; and the reduction in the asset Cash will be recorded as a credit.

Interest Expense			650	Notes Payable			220	Cash				110
+		−		−		+		+		−		
11/19	**197**			**11/19**	**295**	11/6	10,000	11/1	15,000	11/2	5,000	
								11/10	65	11/6	5,000	
								11/14	350	11/9	300	
										11/10	800	
										11/12	95	
										11/14	38	
										11/19	**492**	
(Expenses increase by debits)				(Liabilities decrease by debits)				(Assets decrease by credits)				

A Summary of the Rules for Debit and Credit

It is not customary for accountants to refer to accounts as either increasing or decreasing. They know automatically that a debit to cash is an increase, a credit to accounts payable is an increase, and so on. This information is second nature to them, as it will be to you shortly.

Study the chart that follows to help you memorize the debit–credit rules.

Accounts that Increase by Debits		Accounts that Increase by Credits	
Assets		**Liabilities**	
Debit side +	Credit side	Debit side	Credit side +
Owner's Withdrawals		**Owner's Capital**	
Debit side +	Credit side	Debit side	Credit side +

Expense Accounts		Revenue	
Debit side	Credit side	Debit side	Credit side
+			+

The Chart of Accounts

Each business has its own set of accounts. Each one is assigned an identification number and a specific name that is used when transactions are recorded. The accounts are arranged in financial statement order with the balance sheet accounts listed first, followed by the income statement accounts. Numbers are assigned to the accounts in family groups with, say, all the assets numbered in the 100s, all the liabilities in the 200s, the owner's equity accounts in the 300s, revenue in the 400s, and expenses in the 600s. Account numbers in the 500s will be assigned to a category of accounts entitled *cost of goods sold*, which will be discussed in a later chapter. Some numbers in each family group are left unassigned to allow for adding new accounts. Following is the **chart of accounts** for A-1 Janitorial. (Some accounts have been added to the ones mentioned earlier in this chapter.)

Chart of Accounts

Account Title	Account Number
Cash	110
Accounts Receivable	120
Notes Receivable	125
Supplies	130
Truck	140
Equipment	150
Accounts Payable	210
Notes Payable	220
Ben Moore, Capital	310
Ben Moore, Drawing	320
Cleaning Revenue	410
Advertising Expense	610
Gas and Oil Expense	620
Wages Expense	630
Utilities Expense	640
Interest Expense	650

The Trial Balance

The bookkeeper makes sure that for each transaction recorded during the accounting period the debits equal the credits. It logically follows that at the end of the accounting period, the total of all the debit entries will equal the total of all the credit entries. If they do not, a mistake has been made.

The **trial balance** is the device that accountants use to determine whether or not total debits are equal to total credits. The trial balance is prepared directly from the ledger on a two-column schedule. The steps in preparing the trial balance are:

1. Determine the balance of each ledger account.
2. Centre on the two-column schedule the three-part heading, which consists of the company name on the first line, the words *Trial Balance* on the

second line, and the day for which the trial balance is being prepared on the third line.
3. In chart of accounts order, list the account titles and their balances. Debit balances are entered in the left-hand column and credit balances in the right-hand column.
4. Total both columns and compare the totals to determine whether or not they are equal.
5. If the debit column equals the credit column, draw a double line across both columns to indicate that they are in balance.

The ledger accounts for A-1 Janitorial follow. Some transactions have been added to the original ones so that the entire month's transactions can be shown.

Cash   **110**

11/1	15,000	11/2	5,000
11/10	65	11/6	5,000
11/14	350	11/9	300
11/20	5,000	11/10	800
11/21	80	11/12	95
11/30	245	11/14	38
		11/19	492
		11/20	250
		11/21	46
		11/24	40
		11/28	315
		11/29	140
		11/30	45
	8,179		

Accounts Receivable   **120**

11/15	150		
11/27	70		
	220		

Notes Receivable   **125**

11/6	650	11/10	65
	585		

Supplies   **130**

11/5	1,200		

Truck   **140**

11/6	15,000		

Equipment   **150**

11/2	5,000	11/6	650
	4,350		

Accounts Payable   **210**

11/9	300	11/5	1,200
		11/18	425
			1,325

Notes Payable   **220**

11/19	295	11/6	10,000
			9,705

Ben Moore, Capital   **310**

		11/1	15,000
		11/20	5,000
			20,000

Ben Moore, Drawing   **320**

11/10	800		

Cleaning Revenue   **410**

		11/14	350
		11/15	150
		11/21	80
		11/27	70
		11/30	245
			895

Advertising Expense   **610**

11/12	95		
11/18	425		
	520		

Gas and Oil Expense		620		Wages Expense		630
11/14	38			11/20	250	
11/21	46			11/28	315	
11/24	40					
11/30	45				*565*	
	169					

Utilities Expense		640		Interest Expense		650
11/29	140			11/19	197	

The trial balance for A-1 Janitorial, taken directly from the T accounts, follows:

A-1 Janitorial **Trial Balance** **November 30, 19XX**	**Debit**	**Credit**
Cash	$ 8,179—	
Accounts Receivable	220—	
Notes Receivable	585—	
Supplies	1,200—	
Truck	15,000—	
Equipment	4,350—	
Accounts Payable		$ 1,325—
Notes Payable		9,705—
Ben Moore, Capital		20,000—
Ben Moore, Drawing	800—	
Cleaning Revenue		895—
Advertising Expense	520—	
Gas and Oil Expense	169—	
Wages Expense	565—	
Utilities Expense	140—	
Interest Expense	197—	
Totals	$31,925—	$31,925—

Trial Balance Limitations

The trial balance may prove that debit entries equal credit entries but may not show other errors that have been made. For example, if an entry is omitted from the ledger, the trial balance will not reveal that. Or the bookkeeper may debit office equipment rather than the furniture account. The trial balance won't show that either. Or the same wrong figure may be entered as a debit and a credit in the ledger. In short, the trial balance is very useful but only for proving that debits equal credits in the ledger.

Trial Balance Errors

If, when the trial balance is complete, the debits and credits are not equal, follow this procedure for locating your error. Working backward,
   1. Check to make sure that accounts with debit balances are correctly entered in the debit column of the trial balance and that accounts with credit balances are correctly entered in the credit column.
   2. Re-add the debit and credit columns.

3. Check to make sure that the balance of each account has been transferred correctly from the ledger account to the trial balance.
4. Recalculate the balances in the individual accounts.
5. Check to make sure that the correct debits and credits are entered in the accounts for each transaction.

The Income Statement and the Balance Sheet

Once the trial balance has been completed and is in balance, the income statement and the balance sheet may be prepared directly from it. The financial statements follow:

A-1 Janitorial Income Statement For Month Ending November 30, 19XX		
Revenue		
Cleaning Revenue		$ 895—
Expenses		
Advertising Expense	$520—	
Gas and Oil Expense	169—	
Wages Expense	565—	
Utilities Expense	140—	
Interest Expense	197—	
Total Expenses		1,591—
Net Loss		$ 696—

A-1 Janitorial Balance Sheet November 30, 19XX		
Assets		
Cash	$ 8,179—	
Accounts Receivable	220—	
Notes Receivable	585—	
Supplies	1,200—	
Truck	15,000—	
Equipment	4,350—	
Total Assets		$29,534—
Liabilities		
Accounts Payable	$ 1,325—	
Notes Payable	9,705—	
Total Liabilities		11,030—
Owner's Equity		
Ben Moore, Capital, November 1, 19XX	15,000—	
Add: Additional Investment	5,000—	
Subtotal	20,000—	
Deduct: Drawing	$800—	
Net Loss	696—	
Total Deductions	1,496—	
Ben Moore, Capital, November 30, 19XX		18,504—
Total Liabilities and Owner's Equity		$29,534—

Notice that all the changes in the owner's capital account are detailed in the owner's equity section of the balance sheet when a separate statement of owner's equity is not prepared.

Summary

A separate record is kept for each asset, liability, owner's equity, revenue, and expense account. The T account is the simplest form of an account; it has a title, a left-hand (debit) side, and a right-hand (credit) side. Debits and credits are used for recording increases and decreases in the accounts.

Transactions are entered first in a journal and then are transferred to the ledger. Double-entry bookkeeping requires that for every debit entry there be a credit entry that is equal in amount. The fundamental accounting equation may be used to help remember the rules for recording increases and decreases in the accounts.

1. Assets, which appear on the left-hand side of the equation, increase on the left-hand, or debit, side of the account.
2. Liabilities and owner's equity, which appear on the right-hand side of the equation, increase on the right-hand, or credit, side of the account.
3. Revenue, which indirectly increases capital, increases on the same side as the capital account, the credit side.
4. Expenses and owner's withdrawals, which indirectly decrease the owner's capital account, are recorded as debits, just as decreases to the capital account are recorded as debits.

The chart of accounts lists all the accounts in financial statement order and assigns a number to each. The trial balance lists all the accounts and their balances in financial statement order, and it proves the equality of debits and credits.

Vocabulary Review

Following is a list of the words and terms for this chapter:

account balance	normal balance
chart of accounts	notes payable
credit	notes receivable
debit	T account
double-entry bookkeeping	trial balance

Fill in the blank with the correct word or term from the list.

1. An entry on the right-hand side of an account is called a/an _____.

2. An account that is drawn to look like the letter T is called a/an _____.

3. The formal listing of a company's accounts and their numbers is called a/an _____.

4. A system of bookkeeping that requires a corresponding and equal credit entry for every debit entry is called _____.

5. An entry on the left-hand side of an account is a/an _____.

6. The debit or credit balance that an account is usually expected to have is referred to as its _____.

7. Liabilities that are evidenced by formal written promises to pay are referred to as _____.

8. The figure that is obtained when the smaller side of an account is subtracted from the larger side is called the _____.

9. A schedule that lists all the accounts in financial statement order and their balances and that proves the equality of debits and credits is called a/an _____.

10. Assets that result when customers sign formal written promises to pay at some future date are called _____.

Match the words and terms on the left with the definitions on the right.

11. debit
12. credit
13. double-entry bookkeeping
14. trial balance
15. T account
16. account balance
17. normal balance
18. chart of accounts
19. notes payable
20. notes receivable

a. a corresponding and equal credit entry is required for every debit entry
b. the formal listing of a company's accounts
c. an account that is drawn to look like a T
d. an entry on the right-hand side of an account
e. liabilities evidenced by formal written promises to pay
f. a listing of all the accounts in financial statement order and their balances
g. assets resulting when a customer signs a formal written promise to pay at a future date
h. an entry on the left-hand side of an account
i. the figure that is obtained when the smaller side of an account is subtracted from the larger side
j. the debit or credit balance that an account normally has

Exercises

EXERCISE 3.1 The debit and credit sides of the following T accounts are identified. Indicate the correct side for recording increases (+) and the correct side for recording decreases (−) for each T account. The solution to the first one is given as an example.

0. Example:

Cash	
Debit	Credit
+	−

1.

Owner, Capital	
Debit —	Credit +

2.

Accounts Receivable	
Debit +	Credit —

3.

Notes Payable	
Debit —	Credit +

4.

Rent Expense	
Debit +	Credit —

5.

Commission Revenue	
Debit —	Credit +

6.

Owner, Drawing	
Debit	Credit

7.

Supplies	
Debit	Credit

8.

Accounts Payable	
Debit	Credit

9.

Rental Revenue	
Debit	Credit

10.

Utilities Expense	
Debit	Credit

EXERCISE 3.2

(A) Tell whether the following would cause an increase (+) or a decrease (−) to the account mentioned:

1. a credit to Accounts Receivable
2. a debit to Drawing
3. a debit to Accounts Payable
4. a debit to Interest Expense
5. a credit to Capital
6. a credit to Cash
7. a debit to Notes Receivable
8. a credit to Accounts Payable
9. a debit to Accounts Receivable
10. a credit to Revenue
11. a debit to Cash
12. a debit to Advertising Expense
13. a credit to Notes Receivable
14. a debit to Capital
15. a debit to Mortgage Payable

(B) For each account listed, indicate whether the account has a normal debit balance or a normal credit balance:

16. Accounts Payable
17. Capital
18. Furniture
19. Drawing
20. Wages Expense
21. Cash
22. Revenue from Sales
23. Taxes Payable
24. Supplies
25. Equipment
26. Gas and Oil Expense
27. Commissions Revenue
28. Accounts Receivable
29. Automobile
30. Advertising Expense

EXERCISE 3.3

Determine the balance for each account listed, then prepare a trial balance for Sandra Samson, dentist, as of October 31, 19XX.

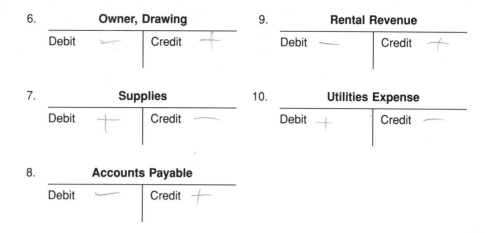

Cash				101
a)	15,000	b)		360
d)	1,100	c)		1,720
l)	250	e)		640
n)	780	h)		830
		i)		1,940
		j)		115
		k)		4,000
		m)		830
		q)		620
		r)		130

Accounts Payable				210
h)	830	c)		3,380
		f)		155

Notes Payable				215
		p)		28,000

Sandra Samson, Capital				301
		a)		15,000
		o)		2,200

Accounts Receivable				110
g)	950	n)		780

Sandra Samson, Drawing				305
m)	830			

Supplies			115
q)	† 620	—	

Dental Revenue				401
	—	d) †	1,100	
		g) †	950	
		l)	250	

Furniture			120
c)	⊤ 5,100	—	
k)	4,000		

Salary Expense			601
b)	† 360	—	
i)	1,940		

Library			125
o)	⊁ 2,200	—	

Rent Expense			605
e)	† 640	—	

Automobile			140
p)	⊣ 28,000	—	

Utilities Expense			610
j)	† 115	—	

Advertising Expense			615
f)	† 155	—	

Interest Expense			620
r)	⊤ 130	—	

EXERCISE 3.4 Using the T accounts for Exercise 3.3, briefly describe what has happened for each lettered transaction. The first one has been completed for you as an example.

Example Transaction a. This represents the owner's original investment in the business.

EXERCISE 3.5 Following is the trial balance for Susan St. Clair, Stylist, on April 30, 19XX. Susan has a new bookkeeper who is not entirely familiar with the process for preparing a trial balance. She has listed all the accounts in alphabetical order, and has made other errors. Find the errors and prepare a corrected trial balance for April 30, 19XX.

April 30, 19XX
Susan St. Clair, Stylist
Trial Balance

		Debit	Credit
120	Accounts Receivable	$ 3,200	
220	Accounts Payable		$ 7,000
640	Advertising Expense	350	
110	Cash	14,000	
130	Equipment	12,000	
620	Gas and Oil Expense		220 ✗
310	Susan St. Clair, Capital		33,000
320	Susan St. Clair, Drawing		600 ✗
135	Library	1,950	
225	Notes Payable	2,100 ✗	
610	Rent Expense	750	
410	Styling Revenue	3,370 ✗	
140	Truck	12,000	
630	Wages Expense	400	

EXERCISE 3.6 Following are the chart of accounts and T accounts for Jack Feder, consultant. Analyze each transaction separately, decide which accounts must be debited and credited, and then title the T accounts and enter the correct amounts. In each case, first enter the accounts to be debited. The first transaction has been completed for you.

Chart of Accounts

Assets	**Revenue**
100 Cash	410 Consulting Revenue
105 Accounts Receivable	
109 Supplies	
115 Office Equipment	
120 Land	

Liabilities	**Expenses**
205 Accounts Payable	610 Insurance Expense
210 Notes Payable	620 Utilities Expense
	625 Advertising Expense
Owner's Equity	630 Automobile Expense
301 Jack Feder, Capital	635 Rent Expense
310 Jack Feder, Drawing	645 Interest Expense

Transaction Number	Cash	Land	Jack Feder, Capital
Example Jack Feder invested $10,000 in cash and contributed a parcel of property worth $75,000 to establish his consulting business.	10,000	75,000	85,000
a. Jack purchased $20,000 in office equipment; he paid $5,000 cash down and signed a three-year interest-bearing note for $15,000.			
b. Jack paid $200 cash for an ad in a local magazine.			
c. Jack bought $1,200 in supplies; he paid $400 cash down and agreed to pay the balance in 30 days.			
d. Jack paid $800 for the first month's rent.			
e. Jack borrowed $10,000 from the bank; he signed a two-year interest-bearing note.			
f. Jack performed consulting services and received $1,400 cash.			
g. Jack wrote a cheque for $105 for the insurance premium for the month.			
h. Jack performed $800 in consulting services for a customer who agreed to pay in 30 days.			
i. Jack paid $500 on the supplies purchased in Transaction 3.			
j. Jack wrote a cheque for $175 for the electricity bill.			

k. Jack paid $625 on the note in Transaction 5; $415 is for repayment of principal and the rest is for payment of interest.

l. Jack performed $1,500 in consulting services for a customer who paid $900 in cash and agreed to pay the rest in 60 days.

m. Jack received $400 on account from a customer.

n. Jack wrote a cheque for $250 for gasoline and oil for the car for the month.

o. Jack withdrew $1,000 for personal use.

p. Jack wrote a cheque for $730 for the monthly payment on the note (see Transaction 1); $417 is for repayment of principal and the rest is for payment of interest.

EXERCISE 3.7 Determine for Lester Douglas, a lawyer, which of the following actions represent revenue (R), expense (E), or neither (N) for the month of July 19XX.

_____ a. received $500 in the mail from a client whose will he prepared in February

_____ b. invested an additional $3,000 into his law practice

_____ c. made a $450 payment on a note; $200 applies to the reduction of principal and $250 is for payment of interest

_____ d. bought a new couch for the office for $970 cash

_____ e. advised a client in July and received $200 cash

_____ f. withdrew $2,200 for personal use in July

_____ g. paid wages for July, $2,000

_____ h. donated a law library worth $3,500 to the business in July

_____ i. paid $300 for radio advertising done in May

_____ j. performed legal services for a client during the last two weeks in July and sent the client a bill for $600

EXERCISE 3.8 The following transactions were recorded in error by the bookkeeper for the Black Canyon Tour Guide Company in April. Determine how each affects revenue and expense. For each, indicate whether revenue and expense will be overstated (O), understated (U), or not affected (NA).

	Revenue	Expense
a. On April 5, the owner performed $630 in services on account. The bookkeeper debited Cash and credited Revenue.	✓	
b. The owner purchased office supplies on account for $320. The bookkeeper debited Office Supplies and credited Accounts Payable for $230.	✓	
c. The owner wrote a cheque for $196 for the April phone bill. The bookkeeper debited Rent Expense and credited Cash.		
d. On April 30, a bill was received for electricity for the month of April. The bookkeeper did not pay it or record it.	✓	
e. The owner invested $6,000 additional cash into the business. The bookkeeper debited Cash and credited Revenue.		

EXERCISE 3.9 Assume that a trial balance has been prepared and that the debit column does not equal the credit column. Considering each of the following errors separately, indicate whether the error would (1) cause the trial balance totals to be unequal and, if so, (2) which side, debit or credit, would be larger because of the error, and (3) by how much? The first item has been completed as an example.

Error	Will Trial Balance Totals Be Unequal?	If So, Which Column Will Be Larger?	How Much Larger Will It Be?
Example A $50 debit to cash was not recorded.	Yes	Credit	$50
a. A $25 debit to Accounts Receivable was recorded as a $25 debit to Cash.			
b. A $150 debit to Drawing was not recorded.			
c. A $75 credit to Accounts Payable was recorded twice.			
d. A $1,000 credit to Capital was recorded as a $100 credit to Capital.			
e. A $70 debit to Cash was recorded as a $700 debit to Cash.			
f. A $60 credit to Taxes Payable was not recorded.			
g. A $600 debit to Equipment was recorded as a $600 credit.			
h. A $90 credit to Notes Payable was recorded as a $90 debit.			
i. A $200 debit to Accounts Receivable was recorded as a $200 credit.			
j. A $10 debit to Accounts Payable was recorded as a $10 credit.			

Problems

PROBLEM 3.1 The T accounts and the transactions for November 19XX for the Tree Doctor follow:

Cash			110
a)	10,000	b)	6,000
f)	800	c)	2,000
j)	5,000	e)	600
k)	1,200	g)	400
s)	300	h)	150
t)	250	i)	900
		l)	250
		m)	140
		n)	200
		o)	900
		q)	300
		r)	500
		u)	175
		v)	200

Accounts Receivable			120
p)	600	t)	250
s)	400		

Supplies			130
d)	1,000		

Equipment			140
c)	5,000		

Truck			150
b)	12,000		

Accounts Payable			210
q)	300	d)	1,000
v)	200		

Notes Payable			220
o)	500	b)	6,000
		c)	3,000

Jack Pine, Capital			310
		a)	10,000
		j)	5,000

Jack Pine, Drawing			320
i)	900		
r)	500		

Revenue from Services			410
		f)	800
		k)	1,200
		p)	600
		s)	700

Truck Repairs Expense			610
l)	250		

Rent Expense			620
e)	600		

Utilities Expense			630
m)	140		

Advertising Expense			640
g)	400		
n)	200		

Interest Expense			650
o)	400		

Gas and Oil Expense			660
h)	150		
u)	175		

INSTRUCTIONS

1. Analyze each transaction and write a brief description telling what has occurred.
2. Determine the balance for each account.
3. Prepare a trial balance as of November 30, 19XX.
4. Prepare an income statement for the month ended November 30, 19XX.
5. Prepare a balance sheet on November 30, 19XX that details the changes in owner's equity. Do not prepare a separate statement of owner's equity.

PROBLEM 3.2   The chart of accounts and the transactions for the month of January 19XX for Shawn O'Brien, veterinarian, follow:

Chart of Accounts

100	Cash
110	Accounts Receivable
120	Medical Supplies
130	Office Supplies
140	Equipment
210	Accounts Payable
220	Notes Payable
310	Shawn O'Brien, Capital
320	Shawn O'Brien, Drawing
410	Revenue
610	Rent Expense
620	Salary Expense
630	Utilities Expense
650	Insurance Expense

TRANSACTIONS

a. Shawn wrote a personal cheque for $18,000 and deposited it in a business account entitled Shawn O'Brien, veterinarian
b. purchased medical supplies that cost $5,000 cash
c. purchased office supplies that cost $400, to be paid for within 30 days
d. purchased office equipment that cost $19,000; paid $3,000 cash down and signed a three-year non-interest-bearing note for the rest
e. cash revenue for the first week was $1,200
f. paid rent, $1,500
g. paid insurance premium, $800
h. paid office salaries of $375
i. made a $200 payment on office supplies purchased in Transaction c
j. performed $2,000 in services; $1,100 received in cash, the rest due in 30 days
k. bought examining room equipment that cost $99,000; paid $5,000 cash down and signed a two-year, non-interest-bearing note for the rest
l. received $450 on account from charge customers
m. performed $2,400 in services; received $1,700 in cash, the rest due in 30 days
n. bought office supplies, $620, on account
o. paid electricity bill, $210
p. paid office salaries, $375
q. received $500 from charge customers
r. paid $1,063 on the equipment purchased in Transaction k
s. paid $780 on the equipment purchased in Transaction d
t. performed $3,000 in services; received $1,700 cash, the rest due in 30 days
u. received $470 from charge customers
v. owner withdrew $1,500 for personal use

INSTRUCTIONS

1. Prepare and title the T accounts shown in the chart of accounts. Record a plus (+) or a minus (−) on the debit and credit side of each T account to indicate where the increases and decreases will be recorded.
2. Record the transactions in the T accounts, identifying each by letter.
3. Determine the balance for each account.
4. Prepare a trial balance as of January 31, 19XX.

PROBLEM 3.3

Pierre Trudeau has operated Pierre's Floral Shoppe for six months. The account balances and transactions for the month of August 19XX follow:

Chart of Accounts		
101	Cash	$10,500
110	Accounts Receivable	4,400
115	Office Supplies	970
120	Delivery Van	25,000
130	Computer Equipment	7,500
140	Office Equipment	11,600
210	Accounts Payable	7,500
215	Notes Payable	33,500
301	Pierre Trudeau, Capital	18,970
310	Pierre Trudeau, Drawing	
401	Floral Revenue	
601	Rent Expense	
605	Utilities Expense	
610	Advertising Expense	
615	Interest Expense	
620	Gas and Oil Expense	
625	Repairs Expense	
630	Insurance Expense	
640	Salaries Expense	

TRANSACTIONS
   a. purchased computer equipment at a cost of $5,400; paid $2,000 cash down and agreed to pay the balance in 90 days
   b. paid rent, $1,200
   c. paid utilities bill, $430
   d. received $720 from a customer paying on account
   e. made a $1,400 payment on the note payable; $530 of this amount is for interest
   f. delivered $1,720 of flowers to a customer; received $1,000 cash and the balance is to be received in 30 days
   g. received bill for advertising in the amount of $530 to be paid in 60 days
   h. paid $1,620 on accounts payable
   i. paid $27 from the business bank account to Cotty Cleaners for the owner's dry cleaning
   j. paid salaries, $640
   k. received $2,190 cash for flowers sold
   l. received $630 from a customer paying on account
   m. paid $220 for a tune-up on the delivery van
   n. withdrew $1,500 for personal use
   o. paid $530 on accounts payable
   p. delivered $3,400 worth of flowers to a customer who has agreed to pay in 30 days
   q. paid $615 for gas and oil for the delivery van
   r. paid radio advertising in the amount of $780
   s. received bill for auto repairs for $1,650 to be paid in 30 days
   t. made $1,200 payment on notes payable; $425 of this amount is for interest
   u. paid $420 for insurance
   v. withdrew $2,000 for personal use

INSTRUCTIONS
   1. Prepare and title the T accounts as named in the chart of accounts. Record a plus (+) or a minus (−) on the debit and credit side of each T account to indicate where increases and decreases will be recorded.
   2. Enter the beginning balances from the chart of accounts into the T accounts.
   3. Record the transactions in the T accounts, identifying each by letter.
   4. Determine the new balance of each account.
   5. Prepare a trial balance as of August 31, 19XX.
   6. Prepare an income statement for the month of August 19XX.
   7. Prepare a balance sheet as of August 31, 19XX that details the changes in owner's equity. Do not prepare a separate statement of owner's equity.

PROBLEM 3.4
Frances Schultz operates a dog-grooming business called "Pet's Pride." The chart of accounts, account balances, and transactions for September 19XX for Pet's Pride follow:

Chart of Accounts

100	Cash	$ 2,000
105	Accounts Receivable	1,800
110	Grooming Supplies	600
115	Grooming Equipment	5,700
120	Office Furniture	4,900
125	Van	18,000
201	Accounts Payable	3,000
210	Notes Payable	12,000
305	Frances Schultz, Capital	18,000
310	Frances Schultz, Drawing	
401	Grooming Revenue	
605	Rent Expense	
610	Utilities Expense	
612	Insurance Expense	
615	Advertising Expense	
620	Repairs Expense	
625	Gas and Oil Expense	
630	Interest Expense	

TRANSACTIONS

a. borrowed $5,000 from a local bank; signed an interest-bearing note, agreeing to repay the money within 24 months

b. paid $550 rent

c. received $200 cash from customers for services performed

d. bought a new couch for the waiting room, paid $400 cash down, and signed a 12-month, non-interest-bearing note for $600 for the rest

e. wrote a cheque for $800 to reduce amount owed on account to creditors

f. performed grooming services totalling $350 and received $120 in cash; the rest is due in 30 days

g. paid $95 for electricity for the office

h. bought gasoline for the van, $36

i. received a bill for $480 for radio advertising for September; record it now, to be paid at a later time

j. paid monthly insurance premium of $90

k. performed grooming services totalling $275 and received $175 in cash; the rest is due in 30 days

l. received $400 in the mail from charge customers

m. Frances wrote a cheque for $500 for personal use

n. paid $40 for a newspaper ad

o. paid $300 for repairs to equipment

p. performed grooming services and received $110 cash

q. made a loan payment of $800; $450 is interest, the rest applies to reduce the balance in Notes Payable (see Transaction a)

r. Frances withdrew $600 for personal use

s. paid $120 for phone bill

t. performed grooming services totalling $530 and received $300 in cash; the rest is due in 30 days

u. wrote a cheque for $700 to reduce amount owed on account

v. paid $200 for a tune-up for the van

w. received cheques in the mail totalling $470 from charge customers

x. Frances withdrew $300 for personal use

INSTRUCTIONS

1. Set up and title the necessary T accounts and enter the beginning balances in them.

2. Record September's transactions in the T accounts.

3. Determine the balance of each account.
4. Prepare a trial balance as of September 30, 19XX.
5. Prepare an income statement for the month ended September 30, 19XX.
6. Prepare a statement of owner's equity for the month ended September 30, 19XX.
7. Prepare a balance sheet as of September 30, 19XX.

PROBLEM 3.5   The T accounts and the trial balance for Maria's Appliance Repair follow. The trial balance, however, indicates that one or more mistakes have been made.

Cash			110
a)	25,000	b)	4,000
i)	450	d)	5,000
m)	1,050	e)	3,200
q)	520	f)	800
v)	1,500	g)	1,200
		k)	150
		l)	370
		o)	2,500
		r)	1,000
		s)	290
		t)	370
		u)	900

Accounts Receivable			120
j)	520	q)	520
p)	750		

Supplies		130
c)	4,500	
e)	3,200	

Equipment		140
b)	10,000	
d)	8,000	

Accounts Payable			210
o)	2,500	c)	4,500
s)	290	h)	600
		n)	290

Notes Payable			220
r)	1,000	b)	6,000
		d)	3,000

Maria Fore, Capital			310
		a)	25,000

Maria Fore, Drawing		320
u)	900	

Repair Revenue			410
		i)	450
		j)	520
		m)	1,050
		p)	750
		v)	1,500

Rent Expense		610
f)	800	

Utilities Expense		620
k)	150	

Salary Expense		630
l)	370	
t)	370	

Repair Parts Expense		640
n)	290	

Advertising Expense		650
g)	1,200	
h)	600	

Maria's Appliance Repair
Trial Balance
November 30, 19XX

	Debit	Credit
Cash	$ 8,470 6740	
Accounts Receivable	850 750	
Supplies	7,700	
Equipment	18000	$18,000
Accounts Payable		2,600
Notes Payable		8,000
Maria Fore, Capital		25,000
Maria Fore, Drawing	900	900
Repair Revenue		4,720 4270
Rent Expense	800	
Utilities Expense	150	
Salary Expense	640 740	
Repair Parts Expense	290	
Advertising Expense	1,800	
Totals	$56,700	$59,220 29870

INSTRUCTIONS

1. Locate the errors in the trial balance by using the following procedure:
   a. Re-add the debit and credit columns of the trial balance.
   b. If the trial balance does not balance at this point, check to make sure that the balance of each account has been properly transferred to the trial balance and that the balance is entered in the correct debit or credit column.
   c. If the trial balance does not balance at this point, recalculate the balances in the individual accounts.
   d. If the trial balance still does not balance, check the individual entries to make sure that there is a corresponding and equal credit entry for each debit entry.
2. Prepare a corrected trial balance.

PROBLEM 3.6

An income statement showing a net income of $7,200 was prepared for Seymour Enterprises for the month of April 19XX. When the bookkeeper was recording the transactions, however, some errors were made. The errors are as follows:

   a. The owner, Carl Seymour, withdrew $1,000 for his personal use, but the $1,000 was debited to Wages Expense and credited to Cash.
   b. Customers sent cheques totalling $2,500 through the mail to apply to their accounts from previous months. The bookkeeper debited Cash for $2,500 and credited Revenue for $2,500.
   c. Carl wrote a $300 cheque to pay for utilities for April. The bookkeeper debited Advertising Expense for $300 and credited Cash for $300.
   d. Carl wrote a cheque for $900 to a creditor to reduce the amount owed on account. The bookkeeper debited Supplies Expense for $900 and credited Cash for $900.
   e. Carl performed services on account in April totalling $3,000. The bookkeeper recorded this transaction by debiting Cash for $3,000 and crediting Accounts Payable for $3,000.
   f. A $900 bill for repairs to equipment was recorded as a debit to Repairs Expense for $90 and a credit to Cash for $90.
   g. A cheque for $75 was received from a customer who was paying on account. The bookkeeper debited Accounts Receivable for $75 and credited Cash for $75.

INSTRUCTIONS   (Consider each error separately.)
1. If the error made will affect net income, determine whether it causes net income to be overstated or understated.
2. Add or subtract the amounts of errors that affect net income to determine the correct net income figure for April.

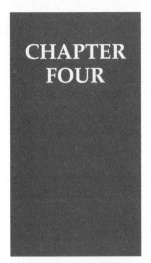

CHAPTER FOUR

The General Journal and the General Ledger

Learning Objectives

When you have completed this chapter, you should
1. have an increased understanding of accounting and accounting-related terminology.
2. be able to analyze and record transactions in a general journal.
3. be able to post general journal entries.
4. be able to prepare a trial balance directly from the general ledger and make an organized search for errors if the columns do not at first balance.

Vocabulary

accumulate   to gather, pile up, collect

book of original entry   the first place where transactions are recorded; a journal

chronological   arranged in order of time occurrence; in date order

compound journal entry   a journal entry with more than one debit and/or credit entry

corresponding   similar or equivalent (equal)

general journal   a journal that is used to record many different types of transactions

general ledger   a ledger that contains a separate record for each asset, liability, owner's equity, revenue, and expense account

journal   a book of original entry in a double-entry system in which transactions are recorded and the accounts to be debited and credited and their amounts are recorded

journalizing   the process of recording entries into the journal

posting   the process of transferring information from the journal to the ledger

posting reference   a cross-reference from the journal entry to its corresponding record in the ledger

slide   when the position of the decimal point is changed as the number is written down (for example, $62.45 is written as $624.50)

transposition   when the order of the numbers is changed (transposed) as they are written down (for example, 758 is written as 578)

verify   to determine or test the truth or accuracy of, as by comparison, investigation, or reference

Introduction

In Chapter Three you learned how to record transactions into T accounts and how to check the accuracy of your work by preparing a trial balance. You will remember, however, that transactions are not recorded directly into the accounts but are first recorded in a book called a **journal**. The journal is called the **book of original entry** because this is where transactions first appear. The **general journal**, which will be introduced in this chapter, may be used to record all different types of transactions, but there are many other kinds of special journals.

The process of recording transactions in a journal is called **journalizing**. Transactions are recorded **chronologically** (in the order of their time occurrence). We will use the transactions of Eppie Kondos to illustrate journalizing; he started a business for cleaning automobile interiors.

In the first transaction, Eppie deposited $15,000 from his personal account into a business account entitled Klean Kar. A debit to Cash and a credit to Capital were required. The general journal entry follows:

GENERAL JOURNAL				PAGE 1	
Date	**Description**	**Post. Ref.**	**Debit**		**Credit**
19XX Nov. 1	Cash		15000—		
	Eppie Kondos, Capital				15000—
	To Record Original Investment				

Analysis of a General Journal Entry

a. The year is written at the top of the date column.
b. The month and day on which the transaction occurred follow. The name of the month may be abbreviated and need be written only once at the top of the page. Transactions are recorded chronologically.
c. The debit entry (or entries) is always entered first and appears all the way to the left of the description column. The account name is written exactly as it appears in the chart of accounts.
d. The dollar amount of the debit entry is entered in the debit column.

e. Dollar signs are not used in the journal.
f. The credit entry (or entries) follows the debit entry on the next line. The names of the account(s) to be credited are indented about half an inch. Again, the account titles are written exactly as they appear in the chart of accounts.
g. The dollar amount of the credit entry is entered in the credit column.
h. A brief explanation of the transaction is written beneath the credit entry. The explanation is not indented.
i. One blank line is left between entries to make reading easier.
j. An entry with more than one debit and/or credit is called a **compound journal entry**. The debits are entered first (in no particular order) and all appear at the extreme left-hand side of the description column. The credit(s) appear next (again in no particular order) and are all indented about half an inch.
k. The **posting reference** column (which is blank with this entry) is used to record the account number *only* after the dollar amount is transferred to the **corresponding** account in the ledger.

Look over the general journal entries for November 1–6 for Klean Kar.

	GENERAL JOURNAL			PAGE 1
Date	Description	Post. Ref.	Debit	Credit
Nov. 1	Cash		15000 —	
	Eppie Kondos, Capital			15000 —
	To Record Original Investment			
2	Equipment		5000 —	
	Cash			5000 —
	Purchased Cleaning Equipment			
5	Supplies		1200 —	
	Accounts Payable			1200 —
	Purchased Cleaning Supplies; Total Due in 60 Days			
6	Notes Receivable		650 —	
	Equipment			650 —
	Sold Extra Vacuum Cleaner; Customer Signed a 6-month			
	Non-interest-bearing Note			
6	Truck		15000 —	
	Cash			5000 —
	Notes Payable			10000 —
	Paid 5,000 Cash Down on a Truck; $10,000 Balance			
	Due in 24 Months			

Compound Entry

Posting

The ledger, remember, is a book with a separate page for each account title in the chart of accounts. The journal has all the information about a particular transaction in one place, and the ledger has all the information about a particular account in one place. We **accumulate** all transactions affecting an account in the **general ledger**; for example, everything that happens to cash is shown in the Cash account. The process of transferring information from the journal to the ledger is called **posting**. In the journal, the column headed *Post. Ref.* or *PR* shows the number of the ledger account to which the posting is made; in the ledger, the *Post. Ref.* column shows the journal page number from which the posting came. Sometimes *F* replaces *PR*. *F* stands for folio and is often used as another word for posting reference.

The first transaction for Klean Kar is repeated now; the general journal entry is followed by the ledger accounts that are affected.

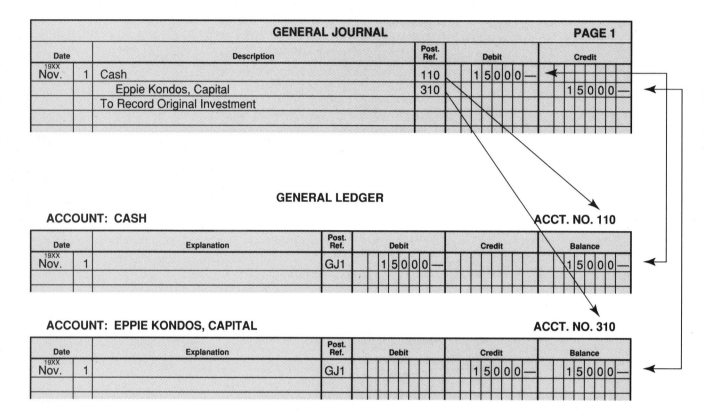

Analysis of Posting

a. Find the page in the general ledger for the first amount to be posted (in this case, Cash). Enter the year at the top of the date column, and enter the month and day as they appear in the journal. The month may be abbreviated.

b. Enter the dollar amount from the debit column of the journal to the debit column for the cash account. Do not use dollar signs in the ledger.

c. Enter the balance of the account into the balance column. Usually the balance must be calculated; in this case, however, there is only one figure.

d. In the posting reference column (PR) of the cash account, enter the initials *GJ* (which stand for general journal), and enter the journal page number from which the transaction was taken.

e. Enter the account number for cash in the posting reference column of the journal. This is not done until posting has been completed.

f. Repeat Steps a–e now as the credit entry to Eppie Kondos, Capital is posted.

g. Be especially careful when posting—it may save time later by avoiding errors at this point. It is a good idea to visually check each entry when it has been completed.

The General Ledger after Posting Is Completed

Following is the general ledger for Klean Kar showing all the transactions for November.

ACCOUNT: CASH ACCT. NO. 110

Date		Explanation	Post. Ref.	Debit	Credit	Balance
19XX Nov.	1		GJ1	1 5 0 0 0 —		1 5 0 0 0 —
	2		GJ1		5 0 0 0 —	1 0 0 0 0 —
	6		GJ1		5 0 0 0 —	5 0 0 0 —
	9		GJ1		3 0 0 —	4 7 0 0 —
	10		GJ1		8 0 0 —	3 9 0 0 —
	10		GJ1		9 5 —	3 8 0 5 —
	10		GJ1	6 5 —		3 8 7 0 —
	14		GJ2		3 8 —	3 8 3 2 —
	14		GJ2	3 5 0 —		4 1 8 2 —
	20		GJ2		2 5 0 —	3 9 3 2 —
	20		GJ2	5 0 0 0 —		8 9 3 2 —
	21		GJ2		4 6 —	8 8 8 6 —
	21		GJ2	8 0 —		8 9 6 6 —
	24		GJ2		4 0 —	8 9 2 6 —
	28		GJ3		3 1 5 —	8 6 1 1 —
	29		GJ3		1 4 0 —	8 4 7 1 —
	30		GJ3		4 5 —	8 4 2 6 —
	30		GJ3	2 4 5 —		8 6 7 1 —

ACCOUNT: ACCOUNTS RECEIVABLE ACCT. NO. 120

Date		Explanation	Post. Ref.	Debit	Credit	Balance
19XX Nov.	15		GJ2	1 5 0 —		1 5 0 —
	27		GJ2	7 0 —		2 2 0 —

ACCOUNT: NOTES RECEIVABLE ACCT. NO. 125

Date		Explanation	Post. Ref.	Debit	Credit	Balance
19XX Nov.	6		GJ1	6 5 0 —		6 5 0 —
	10		GJ2		6 5 —	5 8 5 —

ACCOUNT: SUPPLIES ACCT. NO. 130

Date		Explanation	Post. Ref.	Debit	Credit	Balance
19XX Nov.	5		GJ1	1 2 0 0 —		1 2 0 0 —

ACCOUNT: TRUCK ACCT. NO. 140

Date		Explanation	Post. Ref.	Debit	Credit	Balance
19XX Nov.	6		GJ1	1 5 0 0 0 —		1 5 0 0 0 —

ACCOUNT: EQUIPMENT   ACCT. NO. 150

Date		Explanation	Post. Ref.	Debit	Credit	Balance
19XX Nov.	2		GJ1	5 0 0 0 —		5 0 0 0 —
	6		GJ1		6 5 0 —	4 3 5 0 —

ACCOUNT: ACCOUNTS PAYABLE   ACCT. NO. 210

Date		Explanation	Post. Ref.	Debit	Credit	Balance
19XX Nov.	5		GJ1		1 2 0 0 —	1 2 0 0 —
	9		GJ1	3 0 0 —		9 0 0 —
	18		GJ2		4 2 5 —	1 3 2 5 —

ACCOUNT: NOTES PAYABLE   ACCT. NO. 220

Date		Explanation	Post. Ref.	Debit	Credit	Balance
19XX Nov.	6		GJ2		1 0 0 0 0 —	1 0 0 0 0 —

ACCOUNT: EPPIE KONDOS, CAPITAL   ACCT. NO. 310

Date		Explanation	Post. Ref.	Debit	Credit	Balance
19XX Nov.	1		GJ1		1 5 0 0 0 —	1 5 0 0 0 —
	20		GJ2		5 0 0 0 —	2 0 0 0 0 —

ACCOUNT: EPPIE KONDOS, DRAWING   ACCT. NO. 320

Date		Explanation	Post. Ref.	Debit	Credit	Balance
19XX Nov.	10		GJ1	8 0 0 —		8 0 0 —

ACCOUNT: CLEANING REVENUE   ACCT. NO. 410

Date		Explanation	Post. Ref.	Debit	Credit	Balance
19XX Nov.	14		GJ1		3 5 0 —	3 5 0 —
	15		GJ2		1 5 0 —	5 0 0 —
	21		GJ2		8 0 —	5 8 0 —
	27		GJ2		7 0 —	6 5 0 —
	30		GJ3		2 4 5 —	8 9 5 —

ACCOUNT: ADVERTISING EXPENSE   ACCT. NO. 610

Date		Explanation	Post. Ref.	Debit	Credit	Balance
19XX Nov.	12		GJ1	9 5 —		9 5 —
	18		GJ2	4 2 5 —		5 2 0 —

ACCOUNT: GAS & OIL EXPENSE   ACCT. NO. 620

Date		Explanation	Post. Ref.	Debit	Credit	Balance
19XX Nov.	14		GJ2	3 8 —		3 8 —
	21		GJ2	4 6 —		8 4 —
	24		GJ2	4 0 —		1 2 4 —
	30		GJ3	4 5 —		1 6 9 —

ACCOUNT: WAGES EXPENSE   ACCT. NO. 630

Date		Explanation	Post. Ref.	Debit	Credit	Balance
19XX Nov.	20		GJ2	2 5 0 —		2 5 0 —
	28		GJ3	3 1 5 —		5 6 5 —

ACCOUNT: UTILITIES EXPENSE   ACCT. NO. 640

Date		Explanation	Post. Ref.	Debit	Credit	Balance
19XX Nov.	29		GJ3	1 4 0 —		1 4 0 —

The Trial Balance

Once the journalizing and posting are completed, you are ready to prepare a trial balance that will **verify** that debit entries equal credit entries. The dollar amounts appearing on the trial balance are taken directly from the ledger.

Klean Kar Trial Balance November 30, 19XX	Debit	Credit
Cash	$ 8,671—	
Accounts Receivable	220—	
Notes Receivable	585—	
Supplies	1,200—	
Truck	15,000—	
Equipment	4,350—	
Accounts Payable		$ 1,325—
Notes Payable		10,000—
Eppie Kondos, Capital		20,000—
Eppie Kondos, Drawing	800—	
Cleaning Revenue		895—
Advertising Expense	520—	
Gas and Oil Expense	169—	
Wages Expense	565—	
Utilities Expense	140—	
Totals	$32,220—	$32,220—

If the columns of the trial balance do not equal each other, subtract the smaller side from the larger side to determine the amount of the difference. If, for example, the debit side totals $8,275 and the credit side totals $8,250, the difference is $25. Look for a $25 figure in the journal to see whether you may have posted only half of the entry to the ledger. Or, you might look for a $12.50 posting (half the amount of the difference), which could occur by posting, say, $12.50 as a credit to accounts receivable when you should have posted a $12.50 debit.

Transpositions and Slides

A **transposition** occurs when you transpose (change the order of) numbers as you write them down. For example, if the number you are supposed to record is 357 and the number you do record is 537, you have transposed the 3 and the 5. When a transposition occurs, the difference between the number as it should be and the transposed number will always be evenly divisible by 9.

	Number as It Should Be	Number Transposed	Difference	Divide Difference by 9
a.	357	537	537 − 357 = 180	180 ÷ 9 = 20
b.	978	789	978 − 789 = 189	189 ÷ 9 = 21
c.	1,042	1,024	1,042 − 1,024 = 18	18 ÷ 9 = 2
d.	14	41	41 − 14 = 27	27 ÷ 9 = 3

Table 1
Transpositions

Always subtract the smaller number from the larger number to avoid negative numbers.

A **slide** occurs when the decimal point is incorrectly placed. Let's assume that the correct figure is $7,125 and $71.25 is the figure recorded. This is a slide. As with a transposition, the difference between the number as it should be and the number as it is recorded will be evenly divisible by 9. Subtract $71.25 from $7,125 and the difference is $7,053.75. That number is evenly divisible by 9 ($7,053.75/9 = $783.75). Other examples:

	Number as It Should Be	Number as It Is Recorded	Difference	Divide Difference by 9
a.	7.85	78.50	78.50 − 7.85 = 70.65	70.65 ÷ 9 = 7.85
b.	204	2.04	204 − 2.04 = 201.96	201.96 ÷ 9 = 22.44
c.	60,469	604.69	60,469 − 604.69 = 59,864.31	59,864.31 ÷ 9 = 6,651.59
d.	10,250	1,025	10,250 − 1,025 = 9,225	9,225 ÷ 9 = 1,025

Table 2
Slides

Always subtract the smaller number from the larger to avoid negative numbers.

This information may be helpful when you have totalled the trial balance columns and find that they are not the same. Assume, for example, that the debit total is $10,072 and that the credit total is $10,108. The difference between those two numbers ($10,108 − $10,072), $36, is evenly divisible by 9 ($36/9 = 4). It may be suspected that the reason for the columns not being equal is a transposed number or a slide.

Summary

The journal is called the book of original entry because transactions are first recorded there. After a transaction has occurred, journalizing is the first step in the accounting process. The account(s) to be debited are always entered first and the account(s) to be credited are entered below and indented half an inch. A short explanation is written below the credit entry and one blank line is left between entries.

Posting is the second step in the accounting cycle and is the process of transferring the information from the journal to the ledger. Preparing a trial balance is the third step, and it involves listing the account titles and their amounts in the appropriate debit or credit column. If the trial balance columns are not equal, the bookkeeper must check to determine by how much the column totals differ. She or he will look for an entry that equals the amount by which the column totals differ or the figure that is half that amount. If the difference between the debit and credit columns of the trial balance is evenly divisible by 9, the error is very likely to be a transposition or a slide.

Vocabulary Review

Following is a list of the words and terms for this chapter:

accumulate	journal
book of original entry	journalizing
chronological	posting
compound journal entry	posting reference
corresponding	slide
general journal	transposition
general ledger	verify

Fill in the blank with the correct word or term from the list.

1. To determine or test the truth of, by comparison or investigation, is to _____.
2. A cross-reference from the journal to the ledger and vice versa is referred to as a/an _____.
3. A book of original entry is referred to as a/an _____.
4. Another word for to gather or pile up is _____.
5. A word that means arranged in date order is _____.
6. A/An _____ contains a separate record for each asset, liability, owner's equity, revenue, and expense account.
7. The process of transferring information from the journal to the ledger is called _____.
8. When the position of the decimal point is changed as the number is written down, a/an _____ has occurred.
9. The first place where transactions are recorded is referred to as the _____.
10. The number 652 copied as 625 is an example of a/an _____.
11. A journal entry with more than one debit and/or credit entry is referred to as a/an _____.
12. A word that means similar or equivalent is _____.
13. A journal that is used to record many different types of transactions is a/an _____.
14. The process of recording entries into the journal is called _____.

Match the words and terms on the left with the definitions on the right.

15. accumulate
16. book of original entry
17. chronological
18. compound journal entry
19. corresponding
20. general journal
21. general ledger
22. journal
23. journalizing
24. posting
25. posting reference
26. slide
27. transposition
28. verify

a. when the position of the entry decimal point is changed as the number is written down
b. in date order
c. similar or equivalent
d. a book of original entry
e. to gather
f. when the order of numbers is changed as they are written down
g. to test the accuracy of
h. the process of transferring information from the journal to the ledger
i. the process of recording transactions into a journal
j. the first place where transactions are recorded
k. a journal used to record many different kinds of transactions
l. a journal entry with more than one debit and/or credit
m. a ledger with separate accounts for asset, liability, owner's equity, revenue, and expense accounts
n. a cross-reference between the journal and the ledger

Exercises

EXERCISE 4.1

Transfer chronologically the transactions entered in the following T accounts into three-column balance ledger accounts in the following manner:
1. Write the account title and number at the top of the account.
2. Write the current year at the top of the date column.
3. Enter the month and day in the date column.
4. Write the amount in the appropriate debit or credit column.
5. Calculate the account balance after each entry.

Cash   **101**

12/1 GJ1	10,000	12/2 GJ1	5,000
12/10 GJ2	800	12/3 GJ1	1,000
12/26 GJ4	700	12/12 GJ2	1,500
12/27 GJ4	500	12/18 GJ3	85
		12/20 GJ3	250
		12/28 GJ4	420
		12/30 GJ5	1,000

Accounts Receivable   **110**

12/5 GJ1	500	12/27 GJ4	500
12/10 GJ2	300		
12/26 GJ4	900		

Supplies   **120**

| 12/3 GJ1 | 3,000 | | |

Equipment   **130**

| 12/2 GJ1 | 5,000 | | |

Accounts Payable   **210**

| 12/30 GJ5 | 1,000 | 12/3 GJ1 | 2,000 |

Y. Goldstein, Capital   **310**

| | | 12/1 GJ1 | 10,000 |

Y. Goldstein, Drawing		320
12/12 GJ2 1,500		

Revenue		405
	12/5 GJ1	500
	12/10 GJ2	1,100
	12/26 GJ4	1,600

Insurance Expense		610
12/28 GJ4 420		

Utilities Expense		620
12/18 GJ3 85		

Advertising Expense		630
12/20 GJ3 250		

EXERCISE 4.2 Post the following journal entries into three-column balance ledger accounts, calculating a new balance after each posting. Then enter the page number of the journal into the posting reference column of the ledger. The account titles and numbers are: Cash, 101; Accounts Receivable, 110; Supplies, 120; Equipment, 130; Accounts Payable, 210; Pat O'Henry, Capital, 310; Pat O'Henry, Drawing, 320; Revenue from Services, 410; and Utilities Expense, 610.

GENERAL JOURNAL				PAGE 28
Date	Description	Post. Ref.	Debit	Credit
19XX Nov. 1	Cash	101	8000—	
	Pat O'Henry, Capital	310		8000—
	To Record Original Investment			
3	Equipment	130	3000—	
	Cash	101		1000—
	Accounts Payable	210		2000—
	Purchased Equipment: Balance Due in 90 Days			
5	Supplies	120	400—	
	Accounts Payable	210		400—
	Purchased Supplies on Account			
9	Cash	101	270—	
	Revenue from Services	410		270—
	Performed Services for Cash			
10	Pat O'Henry, Drawing	101	650—	
	Cash	320		650—
	To Record Owner's Withdrawal			
12	Accounts Receivable	110	400—	
	Cash	101	250—	
	Revenue from Services	410		650—
	Performed Services for Cash and on Account			
14	Utilities Expense	610	90—	
	Cash	101		90—
	Paid Bill for Electricity			
18	Accounts Payable	210	400—	
	Cash	101		400—
	Paid Money to Creditor			
20	Cash	101	100—	
	Accounts Receivable	110		100—
	Received Money on Account			

EXERCISE 4.3   Determine the balance for each of the following accounts for Buck Jensen, trail guide. Then prepare a trial balance as of June 30, 19XX. (A check mark in the posting reference column of the ledger accounts indicates that the figure that appears in that column has not been posted from a journal, but, in this case, is a balance.)

ACCOUNT: CASH   ACCT. NO. 101

Date		Explanation	Post. Ref.	Debit	Credit	Balance
19XX May	31	Balance Forward	✓			2000—
June	1		GJ20	50—		
	7		GJ20	375—		
	8		GJ20		130—	
	10		GJ20		400—	
	14		GJ20	400—		
	15		GJ21		500—	
	15		GJ21		300—	
	16		GJ21		140—	
	18		GJ21		400—	
	25		GJ22		300—	
	28		GJ22	520—		
	29		GJ22		85—	
	30		GJ22	100—		

ACCOUNT: ACCOUNTS RECEIVABLE   ACCT. NO. 105

Date		Explanation	Post. Ref.	Debit	Credit	Balance
19XX May	31	Balance Forward	✓			500—
June	1		GJ20		50—	
	21		GJ21	250—		
	30		GJ22		100—	

ACCOUNT: SUPPLIES   ACCT. NO. 108

Date		Explanation	Post. Ref.	Debit	Credit	Balance
19XX May	31	Balance Forward	✓			400—
June	8		GJ20	130—		

ACCOUNT: EQUIPMENT   ACCT. NO. 110

Date		Explanation	Post. Ref.	Debit	Credit	Balance
19XX May	31	Balance Forward	✓			5000—

ACCOUNT: ACCOUNTS PAYABLE   ACCT. NO. 205

Date		Explanation	Post. Ref.	Debit	Credit	Balance
19XX May	31	Balance Forward	✓			2000—
June	10		GJ20	400—		
	18		GJ21	400—		

ACCOUNT: BUCK JENSEN, CAPITAL　　　　　　　　**ACCT. NO. 310**

Date		Explanation	Post. Ref.	Debit	Credit	Balance
19XX May	31	Balance Forward	✓			5900—

ACCOUNT: BUCK JENSEN, DRAWING　　　　　　　　**ACCT. NO. 311**

Date		Explanation	Post. Ref.	Debit	Credit	Balance
19XX June	15		GJ21	500—		
	25		GJ22	300—		

ACCOUNT: GUIDE REVENUE　　　　　　　　**ACCT. NO. 401**

Date		Explanation	Post. Ref.	Debit	Credit	Balance
19XX June	7		GJ20		375—	
	14		GJ20		400—	
	21		GJ21		250—	
	28		GJ22		520—	

ACCOUNT: STABLE EXPENSE　　　　　　　　**ACCT. NO. 610**

Date		Explanation	Post. Ref.	Debit	Credit	Balance
19XX June	16		GJ21	140—		
	29		GJ22	85—		

ACCOUNT: RENT EXPENSE　　　　　　　　**ACCT. NO. 620**

Date		Explanation	Post. Ref.	Debit	Credit	Balance
19XX June	15		GJ21	300—		

EXERCISE 4.4　　The chart of accounts for Sylvia Song, photographer, follows. Journalize the transactions for the month of April, 19XX, beginning on journal page 18. Indicate to which accounts the entries would be posted by writing the account numbers in the posting reference column, if the general ledger were available.

Chart of Accounts

101　Cash
105　Accounts Receivable
110　Supplies
120　Photographic Equipment
215　Accounts Payable
220　Notes Payable
305　Sylvia Song, Capital
310　Sylvia Song, Drawing
410　Photographic Revenue
620　Rent Expense
625　Utilities Expense
630　Insurance Expense
640　Advertising Expense

TRANSACTIONS

April 1   Sylvia photographed a wedding; $500 fee to be received within 10 days

April 2   paid $650 rent

April 3   received $420 in the mail from charge customer

April 4   took portraits and received $200 in cash; $300 is due in 30 days

April 5   made a loan payment of $150; the note is non-interest-bearing

April 8   paid $80 to reduce Accounts Payable

April 9   Sylvia withdrew $700 for personal use

April 10   paid a monthly insurance premium of $95

April 12   portrait revenue for the week is $1,200; $500 was received in cash, the rest is due in 30 days

April 14   paid telephone bill, $120

April 18   paid for advertising in high school newspaper, $50

April 20   bought a new lens for $825; paid $200 cash down and agreed to pay the rest in 60 days

April 25   portrait revenue is $1,400; $800 was received in cash, the rest is due in 30 days

April 26   received $500 in the mail from charge customers

April 28   paid bill for electricity, $75

April 29   paid cash for photographic supplies, $250

April 30   Sylvia withdrew $500 for personal use

EXERCISE 4.5

Tell whether the following numbers are evenly divisible by 9 following this procedure:

a. Find the sum of the digits of each number in Lines 1–10.

b. Determine whether or not the sum obtained in Step a is evenly divisible by 9. Answer yes or no in the space provided. If the sum of the digits is evenly divisible by 9, the number itself is evenly divisible by 9.

	Number	Sum of the Digits	Evenly Divisible by 9?
1.	306.42	_____	_____
2.	7,234.12	_____	_____
3.	46,728	_____	_____
4.	416,732.85	_____	_____
5.	8,334.00	_____	_____
6.	3,939.93	_____	_____
7.	423	_____	_____
8.	5.721	_____	_____
9.	46,901.30	_____	_____
10.	74,615.91	_____	_____

EXERCISE 4.6 For each of the following, find the difference between the number as it should be recorded and the number as it is actually recorded. In each case, divide the difference by 9 to prove that the difference between a transposed number or a slide as it should be recorded and as it is recorded will be evenly divisible by 9. The first one is completed for you.

	Number as It Should Be Recorded	Number as It Is Actually Recorded	Difference	Divide Difference by 9
0.	873	837	36	36 ÷ 9 = 4
1.	749	794		
2.	105.20	1,052.00		
3.	37,654	37,645		
4.	10.97	1.097		
5.	52	25		
6.	1.28	2.18		
7.	204	2,040		
8.	7.39	7.93		
9.	40,639	46,039		
10.	10,828	10,288		

EXERCISE 4.7 The following are trial balance totals where an error has been made and is as yet undiscovered. In each case, determine the difference between the debit and credit columns, find the sum of the digits of the difference, then determine whether or not the error is likely to be a slide or a transposition. (It is likely to be a slide or transposition if the difference is evenly divisible by 9.) The first one is completed for you.

	Debit Column	Credit Column	Difference	Sum of the Digits	Is Error Likely to Be a Slide or Transposition?
0.	17,604.21	18,522.48	918.27	27	yes
1.	70,732	70,822			
2.	10,450	10,498			
3.	21,732	22,722			
4.	106,549	105,326			
5.	185,410	176,320			

EXERCISE 4.8 The following transactions were journalized correctly, but errors were made when posting. For each, tell whether the errors would cause the trial balance totals to be unequal and, if so, by how much the columns will differ. Also indicate which column of the trial balance, debit or credit, will be larger.

	Will Trial Balance Totals Be Unequal?	If So, by How Much?	Which Column Will Be Larger?
a. A journal entry debiting Cash and crediting Accounts Receivable for $670 was posted as a debit to Cash of $760 and a credit to Accounts Receivable of $760.			
b. A journal entry debiting Cash and crediting Revenue for $200 was posted as a debit to Cash for $200 and a credit to Revenue for $2,000.			

c. A journal entry debiting Rent Expense and crediting Cash for $1,600 was posted as a debit to Advertising Expense for $1,600 and a credit to Cash for $1,600.   _____ _____ _____

d. A journal entry debiting Accounts Payable and crediting Cash for $350 was posted as a debit to Accounts Payable of $350 and a credit to Cash of $530.   _____ _____ _____

e. A journal entry debiting Accounts Receivable and crediting Revenue for $340 was posted as a debit to Accounts Receivable of $430 and a credit to Revenue of $430.   _____ _____ _____

f. A journal entry debiting Drawing and crediting Cash for $600 was posted as a debit to Drawing of $600 and a debit to Cash for $600.   _____ _____ _____

g. A journal entry debiting Equipment and crediting Accounts Payable for $2,400 was posted as a debit to Equipment of $2,400 and as a credit to Accounts Payable of $3,400.   _____ _____ _____

h. A journal entry debiting Cash and crediting Furniture for $460 was posted as a debit to Cash of $640 and a credit to Furniture of $460.   _____ _____ _____

EXERCISE 4.9   The following transactions were journalized and posted in error. Considering each separately, determine whether the error will cause total revenue, total expenses, and net income to be overstated (O), understated (U), or not affected (NA). (If revenue is *overstated*, net income will also be *overstated*; likewise, if revenue is *understated*, net income will be *understated*. If expenses are *overstated*, net income will be *understated*; and if expenses are *understated*, net income will be *overstated*.) The first one has been completed for you.

	Total Revenue	Total Expenses	Total Net Income
Example The owner withdrew $750 for personal use. The bookkeeper debited Wages Expense and credited Cash for $750.	NA	O	U
a. The owner invested an additional $5,000 into the business. The bookkeeper debited Cash and credited Revenue for $5,000.	_____	_____	_____
b. A cheque for $950 was written in payment of rent. The bookkeeper debited Repairs Expense and credited Cash for $950.	_____	_____	_____
c. A cheque for $375 was written in payment of an account. The bookkeeper debited Insurance Expense and credited Cash for $375.	_____	_____	_____
d. $620 was received from charge customers. The bookkeeper debited Accounts Receivable and credited Revenue for $620.	_____	_____	_____
e. $840 in services were performed on account. The bookkeeper debited Accounts Receivable and credited Capital for $840.	_____	_____	_____
f. A cheque was written for $775 in payment of the rent. The bookkeeper debited Building and credited Cash for $775.	_____	_____	_____
g. Salaries amounting to $415 were paid with cash. The bookkeeper debited Drawing and credited Cash for $415.	_____	_____	_____
h. A cheque was written for $62 in payment of the current month's phone bill. The bookkeeper debited Utilities Expense and credited Cash for $42.	_____	_____	_____

Problems

PROBLEM 4.1 The chart of accounts and the transactions for June 19XX for Dizzy's Flying School follow:

Chart of Accounts
101 Cash
105 Accounts Receivable
110 Supplies
115 Equipment
120 Airplane
220 Accounts Payable
230 Notes Payable
301 Dizzy Dawson, Capital
310 Dizzy Dawson, Drawing
401 Flying Revenue
610 Repairs Expense
615 Insurance Expense
620 Advertising Expense
630 Fuel Expense
640 Rent Expense
650 Interest Expense

TRANSACTIONS

June 1 Dizzy deposited $150,000 into a business account entitled Dizzy's Flying School

June 2 purchased an airplane for instruction purposes; paid $75,000 cash down and signed a five-year, 17 percent note for $200,000 for the balance

June 3 bought office supplies on account for $350

June 3 paid $3,780 cash for month's fuel for the plane

June 6 bought office equipment on account for $5,000; paid $2,500 cash down and agreed to pay the balance in 30 days

June 9 paid office rent, $750

June 10 paid monthly insurance premium, $900

June 12 Dizzy withdrew $3,500 for personal use

June 15 flying revenue for the first half of the month is $7,000; $4,300 was received in cash, the rest is due within 30 days

June 19 received in the mail a $265 bill for fuel; record it now, to be paid later

June 20 paid $500 due on Accounts Payable

June 24 paid $775 for repairs to the plane

June 26   paid $800 for advertising on the radio

June 30   paid $1,000 on account for office equipment purchased on June 6

June 30   made a $6,170 payment on the note for the amount due on the airplane; of that amount, $2,834 is for interest

June 30   flying revenue for the second half of the month is $4,700; $3,500 was received in cash, the rest is due within 30 days

June 30 $2,800 representing amounts due from charge customers received in the mail

INSTRUCTIONS

1. Journalize the transactions in a general journal. Number the journal beginning with page 28.
2. Post the transactions to the general ledger.
3. Prepare a trial balance as of June 30, 19XX.
4. Prepare an income statement for the month of June 19XX.
5. Prepare a balance sheet on June 30, 19XX detailing the changes in owner's equity.

PROBLEM 4.2

The chart of accounts and the account balances as of August 1, 19XX for Kwick Kleaners follows:

Chart of Accounts		
101	Cash	$ 6,500
110	Accounts Receivable	2,100
114	Cleaning Supplies	1,950
115	Cleaning Equipment	95,000
120	Office Equipment	8,000
210	Accounts Payable	4,500
220	Notes Payable	50,000
310	Nathaniel Emerson, Capital	59,050
320	Nathaniel Emerson, Drawing	
410	Cleaning Revenue	
601	Rent Expense	
605	Insurance Expense	
610	Advertising Expense	
620	Salary Expense	
630	Utilities Expense	
635	Interest Expense	

TRANSACTIONS

August 1   paid rent for August, $1,500

August 1   bought an electronic typewriter for the office; paid $500 cash down and agreed to pay the balance of $700 within 30 days

August 4   placed an ad in the newspaper for $100; the amount is due in 30 days

August 8   paid $125 for August insurance premium

August 10   bought $400 in cleaning supplies; will pay within 30 days

August 15   paid semimonthly salaries, $1,080

August 15   cleaning revenue for the first two weeks is $3,300, of which $1,600 is received in cash

August 17   received $2,225 in the mail from charge customers

August 18   paid $700 of the amount owed on the typewriter purchased August 1

August 22   paid $1,000 to reduce the amount owed on a note; $425 of the amount is for interest expense

August 25   paid the telephone bill, $305

August 28   cleaning revenue for the second two weeks is $3,800, of which $2,300 is received in cash

August 29   paid bill for electricity, $120

August 31   paid semimonthly salaries, $1,090

August 31   Nathaniel withdrew $1,800 for personal use

INSTRUCTIONS

1. Enter the balance from the chart of accounts into the ledger. Write *Balance* in the account explanation column and place a check mark (✓) in the posting reference column of each account for which a balance is entered.
2. Journalize the August transactions in a general journal. Number the journal beginning with page 39.
3. Post the transactions.
4. Prepare a trial balance.
5. Prepare an income statement for the month of August 19XX.
6. Prepare a statement of owner's equity for the month of August 19XX.
7. Prepare a balance sheet as of August 31, 19XX.

PROBLEM 4.3   The bookkeeper for David's Dance Studio was new and made several errors when recording the transactions for the first month of business. The chart of accounts and the general journal for the month of December follow:

Chart of Accounts

110	Cash
120	Accounts Receivable
130	Supplies
140	Equipment
150	Furniture
210	Accounts Payable
220	Notes Payable
310	David Starsky, Capital
320	David Starsky, Drawing
410	Dance Revenue
610	Utilities Expense
620	Wages Expense
630	Advertising Expense

GENERAL JOURNAL				PAGE 1	
Date	**Description**	**Post. Ref.**	**Debit**	**Credit**	
19XX Dec. 1	Cash		1 2 0 0 0 —		
	David Starsky, Capital			1 2 0 0 0 —	
	To Record Owner's Investment				
2	Equipment		4 0 0 0 —		
	Cash			1 0 0 0 —	
	Accounts Receivable			3 0 0 0 —	
	Bought Equipment; Paid $1,000 Down; Balance Due in				
	90 Days				
4	Furniture		2 0 0 0 —		
	Notes Payable			2 0 0 0 —	
	Bought Furniture: Signed a 6-month, 19% Note for $2,000				
5	Cash		5 0 0 —		
	Supplies			5 0 0 —	
	Paid Cash for Supplies				
6	Cash		4 0 0 —		
	Dance Revenue			4 0 0 —	
	To Record Week's Revenue; $400 Received in Cash;				
	$300 Balance Due within 30 Days				
9	Utilities Expense		1 0 5 —		
	Cash			1 0 5 —	
	Paid Bill for Electricity				
10	Cash		3 7 0 —		
	David Starsky, Drawing			3 7 0 —	
	To Record Owner's Withdrawal				
12	Utilities Expense		7 5 —		
	Accounts Payable			7 5 —	
	Received Phone Bill; Record Now to Be Paid Later				
15	Wages Expense		1 2 0 0 —		
	Cash			1 2 0 0 —	
	To Record Wages of $800 and Owner's				
	Withdrawal of $400				

GENERAL JOURNAL			PAGE 2	
Date	**Description**	**Post. Ref.**	**Debit**	**Credit**
19XX Dec. 18	Utilities Expense		75 —	
	Cash			75 —
	To Record Payment of Phone Bill Received and			
	Recorded on December 12			
20	Cash		300 —	
	David Starsky, Capital			300 —
	To Record Cash Received from Charge Customers			
23	Advertising Expense		175 —	
	Accounts Receivable			175 —
	To Record Bill Received for Newspaper Ad in December			
24	Equipment		1000 —	
	David Starsky, Capital			1000 —
	Owner Donated a Typewriter to the Business			
26	Wages Expense		700 —	
	Cash			700 —
	To Record Wages of $700			
28	Cash		500 —	
	Accounts Payable		600 —	
	Dance Revenue			1100 —
	To Record Revenue of $1,100; $500 Received in Cash			
30	Accounts Receivable		500 —	
	Cash			500 —
	To Record Payment Made on Equipment Purchased on			
	December 2			

INSTRUCTIONS

1. Look over each transaction carefully, including the description of the entry. If the entry is correct, recopy it onto a new journal page. If the entry is not correct, enter it as it should be on the new journal page. As in the illustration, use journal pages 1 and 2.
2. After entering the account names and numbers in the general ledger, post the correct transactions.
3. Prepare a trial balance as of December 31, 19XX.
4. Determine the amount of the net income or the net loss for December. Do not prepare a formal income statement.
5. Prepare a statement of owner's equity for the month of December 19XX.

PROBLEM 4.4

An income statement prepared for the Bowmer Company for the month of February 19XX showed a net income of $2,100. The following errors were made by the bookkeeper in recording the transactions for the month:

1. A $700 withdrawal by Barbara Bowmer was recorded by debiting Salary Expense and crediting Cash.
2. Received a bill for February advertising for $500, but did not pay it or record it on the books.
3. Received $950 in the mail from clients who received services in January and recorded the transaction as a debit to Cash and a credit to Revenue.
4. Recorded rent of $1,200 as a debit to Rent Expense of $120 and a credit to Cash of $120.
5. $1,500 cash received for services performed in February was recorded as a debit to Cash and a credit to Barbara Bowmer, Capital.
6. Services performed on account in February amounting to $1,100 were recorded as a debit to Revenue and a credit to Accounts Receivable.

INSTRUCTIONS

1. In each case, on general journal page 47 record the correct journal entry; write "correct entry" as the explanation. Number the entries 1–6.
2. Determine for each entry whether the error will (a) cause revenue to be overstated; (b) cause revenue to be understated; (c) cause expenses to be overstated; or (d) cause expenses to be understated.
3. If either revenue or expense is affected by the error, determine by how much each is overstated or understated.
4. Determine whether each incorrect entry will cause net income to be overstated or understated.
5. Determine the correct net income for the month. Use the headings listed to record your answers. The first error has been analyzed for you as an example.

Error	Will Revenue Be Overstated? By How Much?	Will Revenue Be Understated? By How Much?	Will Expenses Be Overstated? By How Much?	Will Expenses Be Understated? By How Much?	Will Net Income Be Overstated? By How Much?	Will Net Income Be Understated? By How Much?
1.	_____	_____	yes, $700	_____	_____	yes, $700

CHAPTER FIVE

Adjustments and the Ten-Column Worksheet

Learning Objectives

When you have completed this chapter, you should
1. have a better understanding of accounting terminology.
2. be able to calculate and record adjustments for supplies used, prepaid rent, insurance expense, depreciation, wages payable, and unearned revenue.
3. be able to prepare a ten-column worksheet.
4. be able to prepare financial statements directly from the worksheet.
5. be able to journalize adjusting entries directly from the worksheet.

Vocabulary

accounting cycle   the step-by-step procedure that begins with a transaction and ends with the closing of the books

acquisition   the act of acquiring possession

adjusting entry   an entry made at the end of the accounting period for which no transaction occurs and which brings certain accounts up to date

book value   the cost of an asset minus its accumulated depreciation

contra asset   an account with a credit balance that subtracts from its related asset account balance on the balance sheet

depreciation   the transferring of the cost of an asset to expense over the asset's useful life

prepaid expenses   expenses paid in advance and recorded initially as assets

salvage value   the estimated worth of an asset at the end of its useful life

useful life   the number of years over which an asset is depreciated

worksheet a ten-column form on which the trial balance is entered, adjustments are prepared, and the necessary information for preparing the income statement and balance sheet is accumulated

Introduction

The **accounting cycle** is a series of steps that are repeated for every accounting period. The accounting cycle begins when the first transaction occurs and ends when the bookkeeper closes the books for the period; the cycle is repeated for each accounting period.

The first steps in the accounting cycle are journalizing, posting, and preparing a trial balance. In this chapter, the trial balance will be placed directly onto a **worksheet**, which is a ten-column form used by the bookkeeper to organize the data necessary for preparing the adjusting and closing entries and the financial statements. After the trial balance has been completed and is in balance, the next steps in the accounting cycle are calculating adjustments and completing a worksheet.

An *accounting period*, which is the time span covered by the income statement, determines when (for example, a month, a quarter, a year) financial statements are prepared. Accounting periods must be equal in length so that comparisons can be made from one period to another. The measurement of net income should be as precise as possible, and the matching principle requires that all expenses incurred during an accounting period be subtracted from the revenue earned for that same period. Past or future revenue or expenses must not be recorded on current financial statements.

To help ensure accuracy in reporting net income, certain adjustments to the accounts are made before the financial statements are prepared. These adjusting entries are recorded first on the worksheet, next in the general journal, and finally are posted to the general ledger.

Prepaid Expenses

Businesses often make expenditures that will benefit more than one accounting period. For example, when supplies are purchased, they are expected to last for several accounting periods; insurance policies are frequently purchased for one-, two-, or three-year periods; and rent is often prepaid for several months. Such expenditures in advance are called **prepaid expenses** and are debited to an asset account at the time of payment; at the end of the accounting period, a portion of the cost will be recognized as an expense for the current period. The *unused* portion will remain on the books as an asset, but will eventually be converted to expense.

Adjusting Entries

Until now, when a transaction has been recorded, something has happened to prompt a journal entry. For example, a customer makes a payment on account, services are sold for cash, the owner withdraws money, or the rent is paid. With an **adjusting entry**, however, nothing external happens. Adjusting entries are made simply to bring certain accounts up to date or to make certain accounts accurately reflect their value. For example, the Office Supplies account is debited whenever supplies are purchased, but *no credit to the account* *is made when supplies are used up* until an adjusting entry is recorded. At the time a one-, two-, or three-year insurance policy is purchased, the total cost is debited to an asset account called Prepaid Insurance, but *no credits are recorded* to the account until an adjusting entry is made. Adjustments to the accounts are made at the end of the accounting period, which may be one month, three months, a year, or some other time.

Adjustment for Supplies Expense

Assume that on January 1, the Supplies account for Mary Tyus, M.D., has a balance of $255. Assume also that two purchases of supplies are made in January: one on January 14 for $60 and one on January 26 for $35. The general journal entries to record the purchases of supplies are as follows:

	GENERAL JOURNAL			PAGE 5	
Date	Description	Post. Ref.	Debit	Credit	
19XX Jan. 14	Supplies		60—		
	Cash			60—	
	To Record Purchase of Supplies				
26	Supplies		35—		
	Cash			35—	
	To Record Purchase of Supplies				

At the end of January, the Supplies account looks like this.

Supplies   **130**

1/1	Balance	255
1/14	GJ5	60
1/26	GJ8	35
		350

On January 31, a physical count of the supplies on hand shows their dollar balance to be $260, yet it appears from the account that $350 worth of supplies is on hand; this is not the case, because some of the supplies have been used. To reflect the accurate value ($260) of the account on January 31, an adjusting entry is made, transferring the used-up portion to the Supplies Expense account. The entry is as follows:

	GENERAL JOURNAL			PAGE 14	
Date	Description	Post. Ref.	Debit	Credit	
19XX	Adjusting Entries				
Jan. 31	Supplies Expense		90—		
	Supplies			90—	
	To Record Supplies Used for the Month				

The $90 figure used in the adjusting entry was determined by subtracting the ending value of supplies from the balance in the account ($350 − $260 = $90). The Supplies account should reflect the value of the ending inventory after the adjusting entry has been journalized and posted.

Supplies   **130**

1/1 Balance	255	1/31 GJ14 Adjusting	90
1/14 GJ5	60		
1/26 GJ8	35		
	260		

Supplies Expense   **605**

| 1/31 GJ14 Adjusting | 90 | | |

The Supplies account is an asset and will appear on the balance sheet; Supplies Expense is an expense and will appear on the income statement. Every adjusting entry will involve both a balance sheet account and an income statement account.

Adjustment for Prepaid Insurance

Assume that on January 2, 19XX Mary Tyus, M.D., purchases a 12-month fire insurance policy for $360. The entry in the general journal is as follows:

		GENERAL JOURNAL				PAGE 1	
Date		Description	Post. Ref.		Debit		Credit
19XX Jan.	2	Prepaid Insurance			3 6 0 —		
		Cash					3 6 0 —
		To Record Purchase of 12-Month Fire Insurance Policy					

The Prepaid Insurance account is an asset and will appear on the balance sheet. Insurance expense should not be debited at the time the policy is purchased, because the expense should logically be spread out over the 12-month period for which the policy is in force.

At the end of the month (or the accounting period), the adjusting entry for insurance is calculated as follows:

$$\$360 \div 12 \text{ Months} = \$30 \text{ Cost per Month.}$$

The general journal entry to transfer a portion of the asset Prepaid Insurance to Insurance Expense is as follows:

		GENERAL JOURNAL				PAGE 14	
Date		Description	Post. Ref.		Debit		Credit
19XX		Adjusting Entries					
Jan.	31	Insurance Expense			3 0 —		
		Prepaid Insurance					3 0 —
		To Record Insurance Expense for Month					

After the entry has been posted, the T accounts look like this:

Prepaid Insurance   **120**

| 1/2 GJ1 | 360 | 1/31 GJ14 Adjusting | 30 |

Insurance Expense   **660**

| 1/31 GJ14 Adjusting | 30 | |

Twelve $30 credits will be journalized and posted, one each month, until the entire $360 has been transferred to Insurance Expense.

Adjustment for Depreciation

The balance sheet is divided into two main categories of assets called *current assets* and *plant and equipment*. Plant and equipment items include assets such as buildings, furniture, office or store equipment, autos, and trucks. Plant and equipment assets are used in the production of other assets (for example, cash or accounts receivable) and generally are not for sale.

When an asset is purchased for use in the business, an asset account is debited. By recording **depreciation**, the cost of these assets is converted to expense over time. Assume, for example, that Mary Tyus purchases office equipment costing $10,600 on January 2. It is expected to have a **useful life** of four years and then have a **salvage value** of $1,000. In the general journal, the entry to record the **acquisition** of the asset is as follows:

GENERAL JOURNAL					PAGE 1
Date		Description	Post. Ref.	Debit	Credit
19XX Jan.	2	Office Equipment		1 0 6 0 0 —	
		Cash			3 0 0 0 —
		Notes Payable			7 6 0 0 —
		To Record Purchase of Office Equipment;			
		Signed a 12-Month, 10% Note			

Accountants may use several methods to determine how much depreciation expense may be recognized for an accounting period. The straight-line depreciation method recognizes the same amount of expense each accounting period. The bookkeeper must know three things to calculate the straight-line depreciation expense: (1) the cost of the asset, (2) the useful life of the asset, and (3) the estimated salvage value. Depreciation is calculated as follows:

1. Subtract the salvage value from the cost to determine the depreciable amount:

$$\$10,600 - \$1,000 = \$9,600.$$

2. Divide the depreciable amount by the number of years in the useful life to determine the annual depreciation:

$$\$9,600 \div 4 = \$2,400.$$

3. If the accounting period is one month, divide yearly depreciation by 12 to determine monthly depreciation:

$$\$2,400 \div 12 = \$200.$$

The adjusting entry to record the depreciation is as follows:

			GENERAL JOURNAL				PAGE 14	
Date			Description	Post. Ref.		Debit		Credit
19XX			Adjusting Entries					
Jan.	31		Depreciation Expense			2 0 0 —		
			Accumulated Depreciation: Office Equipment					2 0 0 —
			To Record Depreciation on Office Equipment					

When depreciation is recorded, credits are not entered directly into the asset account because accounts for depreciable assets show the historical cost. Depreciation amounts are recorded in an account called Accumulated Depreciation; it is a **contra asset** because it subtracts from its related asset on the balance sheet.

After the adjusting entry for depreciation has been posted, the T accounts look like this:

Office Equipment   **150**

1/2 GJ1	10,600	

Accumulated Depreciation: Office Equipment   **151**

	1/31 Adjusting GJ14	200

Depreciation Expense   **670**

1/31 Adjusting GJ14	200	

The Accumulated Depreciation account accumulates the depreciation for its related asset. The Office Equipment account and the contra asset account, Accumulated Depreciation, look like this six months after the purchase of the equipment:

Office Equipment   **150**

1/2 GJ1	10,600	

Accumulated Depreciation: Office Equipment   **151**

	1/31 Adjusting GJ14	200
	2/28 Adjusting GJ18	200
	3/31 Adjusting GJ22	200
	4/30 Adjusting GJ27	200
	5/31 Adjusting GJ32	200
	6/30 Adjusting GJ37	200

The cost of an asset minus its accumulated depreciation is called the asset's **book value**. The balance sheet will show cost, accumulated depreciation, and book value for every depreciable asset. A portion of the balance sheet on June 30 for the preceding purchase and six months' depreciation appears as follows:

Mary Tyus, M.D.
Balance Sheet
June 30, 19XX

Assets		
Cash		$8,100—

Office Equipment	$10,600—	
Less Accumulated Depreciation: Office Equipment	1,200—	$9,400—

Adjustment for Wages Payable

Assume that Mary Tyus incurs $150 in wages every day, Monday through Friday, and that paydays fall on Friday of each week. The end of the accounting period, however, falls on Tuesday, which is January 31, the end of the month. For January expenses to be properly recorded, two days of wages expense (Monday and Tuesday, January 30 and 31) must be recorded for January.

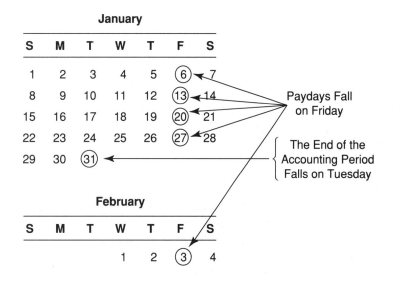

The adjusting entry to record this is as follows:

GENERAL JOURNAL						PAGE 14	
Date		Description	Post. Ref.	Debit		Credit	
19XX		Adjusting Entries					
Jan.	31	Wages Expense		3 0 0 —			
		Wages Payable				3 0 0 —	
		To Record Wages Expense for January 30 and 31					

Wages Payable is credited because the wages will not actually be paid until Friday, thus creating a short-term liability. After the adjusting entry is posted, the T accounts look like this:

Wages Expense   **640**

1/6	GJ2	750
1/13	GJ5	750
1/20	GJ7	750
1/27	GJ9	750
1/31	Adjusting GJ14	300

Wages Payable   **230**

1/31	Adjusting GJ14	300

On Friday, when the wages are actually paid, the balance from the Wages Payable account must be removed and three days' wages expense must be recognized for February. The entry to record payment of the wages is as follows:

GENERAL JOURNAL				PAGE 15	
Date	**Description**	**Post. Ref.**	**Debit**	**Credit**	
19XX Feb. 3	Wages Expense		450 —		
	Wages Payable		300 —		
	Cash			750 —	
	To Record Payment of Wages for Period				
	January 30–February 3				

After the entry for payment of the wages is posted, the T accounts for Wages Payable and Wages Expense look like this:

Wages Payable   **230**

2/3	GJ15	300	1/31	Adjusting GJ14	300

Wages Expense   **640**

1/6	GJ2	750
1/13	GJ5	750
1/20	GJ7	750
1/27	GJ9	750
1/31	Adjusting GJ14	300
2/3	GJ15	450

The Wages Expense account now accurately reflects $450 for the first week in February, and $300 of that week's total wages of $750 has been allocated to January.

Adjustment for Unearned Revenue

Often, a business receives money in advance for services it plans to deliver later. For example, magazine subscriptions are paid in advance, theatres sell season tickets, and dormitories collect room and board at the beginning of the quarter or semester. Cash received in advance of performing the services should not be recognized as revenue.

Assume that Mary Tyus receives $1,000 from Jorge Sanders on January 3 for consulting services that she will perform in the future. The entry to record the $1,000 received is as follows:

GENERAL JOURNAL				PAGE 2	
Date	Description	Post. Ref.	Debit	Credit	
19XX Jan. 3	Cash		1000—		
	Unearned Consulting Revenue			1000—	
	Cash Received for Services to Be Performed in the Future				

The Unearned Revenue account is a liability, because Mary owes the services to the customer and the $1,000 will not be recognized as revenue until the services are performed.

Assume that by the end of January Mary performs $600 of consulting services for Jorge Sanders. Through an adjusting entry, the $600 will be transferred from an Unearned Revenue account to Earned Revenue.

GENERAL JOURNAL				PAGE 14	
Date	Description	Post. Ref.	Debit	Credit	
	Adjusting Entries				
19XX Jan. 31	Unearned Consulting Revenue		600—		
	Consulting Revenue			600—	
	To Transfer $600 into Consulting Revenue				

After the adjusting entry has been posted, the T accounts appear as follows:

Unearned Consulting Revenue   **220**

1/31 Adjusting GJ14   600 | 1/3 GJ2   1,000

Consulting Revenue   **405**

                                    | 1/15 GJ11   900
                                    | 1/31 Adjusting GJ14   600

The balance in the Unearned Consulting Revenue account on January 31 is $400. When Mary performs the remainder of the consulting services, that balance, too, will be transferred to Consulting Revenue.

Adjustment for the Accrual of Revenue

In the previous example, Mary Tyus was paid for consulting before the services were performed. A more common occurrence would be one in which Mary performs services but does not receive payment by the end of the accounting period in which the financial statements are prepared. Assume that in January Mary performs medical services for a customer amounting to $2,000. At the end of the month, a bill is sent to the customer and the following adjusting entry to recognize the revenue earned is prepared.

GENERAL JOURNAL					PAGE 14	
Date	Description	Post. Ref.	Debit		Credit	
19XX Jan. 31	Accounts Receivable		2000—			
	Medical Revenue				2000—	
	To Record Services Performed and Bills					
	Sent to Customers					

The T accounts look as follows after the adjusting entry is prepared:

Accounts Receivable   **110**

1/1	Balance	400
1/15	GJ7	700
1/31	Adjusting GJ14	2,000

Medical Revenue   **401**

1/8	GJ5	2,700
1/15	GJ6	3,100
1/22	GJ8	3,300
1/29	GJ10	2,500
1/31	Adjusting GJ14	2,000

Effects of the Failure to Record Adjusting Entries

Every adjusting entry involves both an income statement account and a balance sheet account. Failure to record an adjustment causes an overstatement or an understatement of either expenses or revenue and an overstatement or an understatement of net income.

For example, failure to record an adjustment for an expense (such as the entry that debits Insurance Expense and credits Prepaid Insurance) would cause an understatement of expenses and a resulting overstatement of net income, while failure to record an adjustment for accrued revenue (such as the entry debiting Accounts Receivable and crediting Revenue) would cause an understatement of revenue and an understatement of net income.

Whenever there is a failure to record an adjustment, net income will be affected. Owner's equity will also be affected, because net income is added to the owner's capital account at the end of the accounting period. If net income is overstated, owner's capital will also be overstated; and if net income is understated, owner's capital will be understated.

Other accounts, too, will be affected. For example, the failure to record the adjustment for supplies used (a debit to Supplies Expense and a credit to Supplies) would cause an overstatement of total assets (Supplies), an understatement of total expenses (Supplies Expense), and an overstatement of net income.

The Ten-Column Worksheet

The worksheet is a ten-column form on which the trial balance, the adjustments, an adjusted trial balance, the income statement, and the balance sheet are first prepared. It is prepared in pencil because it is not a formal statement;

rather, it is the bookkeeper's tool and proves that the general ledger is in balance, and it accumulates the information for the adjustments and for the income statement and balance sheet *before* the adjustments are journalized and the formal statements are prepared in ink.

Trial Balance Columns of the Worksheet

The ten-column worksheet that follows is for Mary Tyus, M.D. The first two columns of the worksheet are for preparing the trial balance. The figures are taken directly from the ledger after all the posting for the period has been completed. The trial balance must be complete and in balance before continuing on to the adjustments columns of the worksheet. A single line to indicate addition is drawn across the debit and credit columns beneath the last item listed, and a double line extends across the debit and credit columns beneath the trial balance totals.

Mary Tyus, M.D.
Worksheet
For Month Ending January 31, 19XX

Acct. No.	Account Titles	Trial Balance Debit	Trial Balance Credit
101	Cash	12500—	
105	Accounts Receivable	1100—	
110	Notes Receivable	4700—	
120	Prepaid Insurance	360—	
130	Supplies	350—	
150	Office Equipment	10600—	
151	Accumulated Depreciation: OE		
201	Accounts Payable		2950—
210	Notes Payable		7600—
215	Payroll Taxes Payable		210—
220	Unearned Consulting Revenue		1000—
301	Mary Tyus, Capital		21692—
310	Mary Tyus, Drawing	4800—	
401	Medical Revenue		11600—
405	Consulting Revenue		900—
601	Rent Expense	3900—	
610	Interest Expense	76—	
615	Utilities Expense	1420—	
620	Repairs Expense	2416—	
630	Uniforms Expense	500—	
640	Wages Expense	3000—	
650	Payroll Tax Expense	230—	
	Totals	45952—	45952—

Adjustments Columns of the Worksheet

Once the trial balance is complete and in balance, the data for the adjustments are entered directly in the adjustments columns opposite their account titles. If the account title does not appear on the original trial balance, it may be added at the bottom of the worksheet.

The letter *a* is written next to the debit and credit amounts for the first adjustment, the letter *b* beside the next adjustment, and so on. The letters identify the adjustments and make them easier to journalize after the worksheet is complete.

The adjustment data for Mary Tyus, M.D., are as follows:

a. The Supplies Expense account is debited and Supplies is credited for $90 to recognize supplies used in January.
b. The Insurance Expense account is debited and Prepaid Insurance is credited for $30 to recognize insurance expense for January.
c. Depreciation Expense is debited and Accumulated Depreciation is credited for $200 to record depreciation expense for January.
d. Wages Expense is debited and Wages Payable is credited for $300 to record accrued wages expense.
e. The liability account Unearned Consulting Revenue is debited and Consulting Revenue is credited for $600 to recognize that portion of the consulting revenue that has been earned in January.
f. Accounts Receivable has been debited and Medical Revenue has been credited for $2,000 to recognize services performed but for which payment has not been received.

The worksheet on page 99 shows the trial balance and the adjustments columns.

Mary Tyus, M.D.
Worksheet
For Month Ended January 31, 19XX

Acct. No.	Account Titles	Trial Balance Debit	Trial Balance Credit	Adjustments Debit	Adjustments Credit
101	Cash	12500—			
105	Accounts Receivable	1100—		f. 2000—	
110	Notes Receivable	4700—			
120	Prepaid Insurance	360—			b. 30—
130	Supplies	350—			a. 90—
150	Office Equipment	10600—			
151	Accumulated Depreciation: OE				c. 200—
201	Accounts Payable		2950—		
210	Notes Payable		7600—		
215	Payroll Taxes Payable		210—		
220	Unearned Consulting Revenue		1000—	e. 600—	
301	Mary Tyus, Capital		21692—		
310	Mary Tyus, Drawing	4800—			
401	Medical Revenue		11600—		f. 2000—
405	Consulting Revenue		900—		e. 600—
601	Rent Expense	3900—			
610	Interest Expense	76—			
615	Utilities Expense	1420—			
620	Repairs Expense	2416—			
630	Uniforms Expense	500—			
640	Wages Expense	3000—		d. 300—	
650	Payroll Tax Expense	230—			
	Totals	45952—	45952—		
605	Supplies Used			a. 90—	
660	Insurance Expense			b. 30—	
670	Depreciation Expense			c. 200—	
230	Wages Payable				d. 300—
				3220—	3220—

Adjusted Trial Balance Columns of the Worksheet

The figures in the adjusted trial balance columns, not the ones on the original trial balance, are the ones that will be used by the accountant for preparing the financial statements. The correct procedure for completing the adjusted trial balance is to start with the first account, Cash, and if there is no adjustment, simply extend the balance to its correct debit or credit column of the adjusted trial balance. All accounts without adjustments are treated in the same fashion.

Accounts with adjustments are handled in one of four ways:

1. If the original account has a debit balance and the adjustment is also a debit, add the amounts together and extend the total to the adjusted trial balance as a debit. The adjustment to the Accounts Receivable account (f) is an example.
2. If the original account has a credit balance and the adjustment is also a credit, add the figures and extend the total to the adjusted trial balance as a credit. The adjustment to Medical Revenue (f) is an example.
3. If the account on the original trial balance has a debit balance and the adjustment is a credit, subtract and enter the new but smaller debit balance onto the adjusted trial balance. The adjustment to Supplies (a) is an example.
4. If the account on the original trial balance has a credit balance and the adjustment is a debit, subtract and extend the smaller credit balance to the credit side of the adjusted trial balance. The adjustment to Unearned Consulting Revenue (e) is an example.

The adjusted trial balance appears in the worksheet on page 101.

Mary Tyus, M.D.
Worksheet
For Month Ended January 31, 19XX

Acct. No.	Account Titles	Trial Balance Debit	Trial Balance Credit	Adj.	Adjustments Debit	Adj.	Adjustments Credit	Adjusted Trial Balance Debit	Adjusted Trial Balance Credit
101	Cash	12500						12500	
105	Accounts Receivable	1100		f.	2000			3100	
110	Notes Receivable	4700						4700	
120	Prepaid Insurance	360				b.	30	330	
130	Supplies	350				a.	90	260	
150	Office Equipment	10600						10600	
151	Accumulated Depreciation: OE					c.	200		200
201	Accounts Payable		2950						2950
210	Notes Payable		7600						7600
215	Payroll Taxes Payable		210						210
220	Unearned Consulting Revenue		1000	e.	600				400
301	Mary Tyus, Capital		21692						21692
310	Mary Tyus, Drawing	4800						4800	
401	Medical Revenue		11600			f.	2000		13600
405	Consulting Revenue		900			e.	600		1500
601	Rent Expense	3900						3900	
610	Interest Expense	76						76	
615	Utilities Expense	1420						1420	
620	Repairs Expense	2416						2416	
630	Uniforms Expense	500						500	
640	Wages Expense	3000		d.	300			3300	
650	Payroll Tax Expense	230						230	
	Totals	45952	45952						
605	Supplies Expense			a.	90			90	
660	Insurance Expense			b.	30			30	
670	Depreciation Expense			c.	200			200	
230	Wages Payable					d.	300		300
					3220		3220	48452	48452

Income Statement and Balance Sheet Columns of the Worksheet

Once the adjusted trial balance is complete and in balance, each figure is extended to the columns for either the balance sheet or the income statement. The procedure for extending the figures is as follows:

1. Starting at the top with Cash, extend the figures to their correct debit or credit column of the balance sheet. Repeat this procedure for each asset, liability, and owner's equity account that appears on the adjusted trial balance.
2. Beginning with the first revenue account, extend that balance into the credit column of the income statement, and extend all expense account balances into the debit column of the income statement.

Mary Tyus, M.D.
Worksheet
For Month Ended January 31, 19XX

Acct. No.	Account Titles	Trial Balance Debit	Trial Balance Credit	Adjustments Debit	Adjustments Credit
101	Cash	12500—			
105	Accounts Receivable	1100—		f. 2000—	
110	Notes Receivable	4700—			
120	Prepaid Insurance	360—			b. 30—
130	Supplies	350—			a. 90—
150	Office Equipment	10600—			
151	Accumulated Depreciation: OE				c. 200—
201	Accounts Payable		2950—		
210	Notes Payable		7600—		
215	Payroll Taxes Payable		210—		
220	Unearned Consulting Revenue		1000—	e. 600—	
301	Mary Tyus, Capital		21692—		
310	Mary Tyus, Drawing	4800—			
401	Medical Revenue		11600—		f. 2000—
405	Consulting Revenue		900—		e. 600—
601	Rent Expense	3900—			
610	Interest Expense	76—			
615	Utilities Expense	1420—			
620	Repairs Expense	2416—			
630	Uniforms Expense	500—			
640	Wages Expense	3000—		d. 300—	
650	Payroll Tax Expense	230—			
	Totals	45952—	45952—		
605	Supplies Expense			a. 90—	
660	Insurance Expense			b. 30—	
670	Depreciation Expense			c. 200—	
230	Wages Payable				d. 300—
				3220—	3220—
	Net Income				

3. Do not omit any of the accounts with adjustments that appear at the bottom of the original trial balance. Some are income statement accounts and others are balance sheet accounts. Supplies Expense, Insurance Expense, and Depreciation Expense are extended to the debit column of the income statement, while Wages Payable is a liability and must be extended to the credit column of the balance sheet.

4. Total the four columns of the income statement and the balance sheet and enter totals on the worksheet beneath a single ruled line.

Carefully study the worksheet as it appears after all figures have been extended from the adjusted trial balance columns to the balance sheet and income statement columns.

Adjusted Trial Balance		Income Statement		Balance Sheet	
Debit	Credit	Debit	Credit	Debit	Credit
12500 —				12500 —	
3100 —				3100 —	
4700 —				4700 —	
330 —				330 —	
260 —				260 —	
10600 —				10600 —	
	200 —				200 —
	2950 —				2950 —
	7600 —				7600 —
	210 —				210 —
	400 —				400 —
	21692 —				21692 —
4800 —				4800 —	
	13600 —		13600 —		
	1500 —		1500 —		
3900 —		3900 —			
76 —		76 —			
1420 —		1420 —			
2416 —		2416 —			
500 —		500 —			
3300 —		3300 —			
230 —		230 —			
	90 —	90 —			
	30 —	30 —			
200 —		200 —			
	300 —				300 —
48452 —	48452 —	12162 —	15100 —	36290 —	33352 —

Net Income on the Worksheet

The next steps will verify the accuracy of the bookkeeper's work and will complete the worksheet:

5. Determine the difference between the income statement debit and credit columns. If the credit total (revenue) is larger than the debit total (expenses), a net income has been earned. Enter the net income figure beneath the total on the debit side of the income statement and write the words *Net Income* in the Account Titles column of the worksheet on the same line.

6. Enter the net income figure obtained in Step 5 beneath the credit column total on the balance sheet. This is required because the net income is added to the owner's capital account (which has a credit balance) in the owner's equity section of the balance sheet.

7. Draw a single ruled line beneath the four columns of the income statement and the balance sheet beneath the net income figure.

8. Total the balance sheet columns. At this point, they must equal each other. If they do not, a mistake has been made and the bookkeeper must find it before continuing.

Mary Tyus, M.D.
Worksheet
For Month Ended January 31, 19XX

Acct. No.	Account Titles	Trial Balance Debit	Trial Balance Credit	Adjustments Debit	Adjustments Credit
101	Cash	12500—			
105	Accounts Receivable	1100—		f. 2000—	
110	Notes Receivable	4700—			
120	Prepaid Insurance	360—			b. 30—
130	Supplies	350—			a. 90—
150	Office Equipment	10600—			
151	Accumulated Depreciation: OE				c. 200—
201	Accounts Payable		2950—		
210	Notes Payable		7600—		
215	Payroll Taxes Payable		210—		
220	Unearned Consulting Revenue		1000—	e. 600—	
301	Mary Tyus, Capital		21692—		
310	Mary Tyus, Drawing	4800—			
401	Medical Revenue		11600—		f. 2000—
405	Consulting Revenue		900—		e. 600—
601	Rent Expense	3900—			
610	Interest Expense	76—			
615	Utilities Expense	1420—			
620	Repairs Expense	2416—			
630	Uniforms Expense	500—			
640	Wages Expense	3000—		d. 300—	
650	Payroll Tax Expense	230—			
	Totals	45952—	45952—		
605	Supplies Expense			a. 90—	
660	Insurance Expense			b. 30—	
670	Depreciation Expense			c. 200—	
230	Wages Payable				d. 300—
				3220—	3220—
	Net Income				

9. Total the income statement columns and draw a double ruled line across the income statement and balance sheet columns.

The debit column equals the credit column on the income statement, and the debit column equals the credit column on the balance sheet, but *the columns of the income statement do not equal the columns of the balance sheet*.

Net Loss on the Worksheet

A net *income* figure is added to the credit column of the balance sheet because net income is added to capital when the statement of owner's equity is prepared (credits increase the capital account). If, however, after totalling the income statement columns of the worksheet, the debit column (expenses) is larger than the credit column (revenue), a net loss has occurred; the amount of the net loss is entered beneath the debit column total on the balance sheet to complete the worksheet. A net loss will be subtracted from the owner's capital account when the statement of owner's equity is prepared. Study the partial worksheet for Paul's Preschool for March 19XX on page 106.

Adjusted Trial Balance		Income Statement		Balance Sheet	
Debit	Credit	Debit	Credit	Debit	Credit
12500				12500	
3100				3100	
4700				4700	
330				330	
260				260	
10600				10600	
	200				200
	2950				2950
	7600				7600
	210				210
	400				400
	21692				21692
4800				4800	
	13600		13600		
	1500		1500		
3900		3900			
76		76			
1420		1420			
2416		2416			
500		500			
3300		3300			
230		230			
90		90			
30		30			
200		200			
	300				300
48452	48452	12162	15100	36290	33352
		2938			2938
		15100	15100	36290	36290

Paul's Preschool
Worksheet
For Month Ended March 31, 19XX

Acct. No.	Account Titles	Adjusted Trial Balance Debit	Adjusted Trial Balance Credit	Income Statement Debit	Income Statement Credit	Balance Sheet Debit	Balance Sheet Credit
110	Cash	6720 —				6720 —	
115	Accounts Receivable	1200 —				1200 —	
120	Notes Receivable	905 —				905 —	
130	Prepaid Insurance	600 —				600 —	
140	Supplies	400 —				400 —	
145	Playground Equipment	16190 —				16190 —	
146	Accumulated Depreciation: PE		900 —				900 —
200	Accounts Payable		860 —				860 —
201	Notes Payable		9600 —				9600 —
210	Unearned Revenue		2500 —				2500 —
220	Wages Payable		220 —				220 —
301	Paul Pinchen, Capital		14334 —				14334 —
310	Paul Pinchen, Drawing	1560 —				1560 —	
410	Revenue		2780 —		2780 —		
601	Advertising Expense	105 —		105 —			
610	Rent Expense	800 —		800 —			
615	Utilities Expense	150 —		150 —			
620	Repairs Expense	235 —		235 —			
630	Depreciation Expense	300 —		300 —			
640	Wages Expense	1700 —		1700 —			
660	Payroll Tax Expense	102 —		102 —			
670	Interest Expense	127 —		127 —			
680	Supplies Used	60 —		60 —			
690	Insurance Expense	40 —		40 —			
	Totals	31194 —	31194 —	3619 —	2780 —	27575 —	28414 —
	Net Loss				839 —	839 —	
				3619 —	3619 —	28414 —	28414 —

Preparing the Financial Statements from the Worksheet

Once the worksheet is complete, the accountant can prepare the income statement and the balance sheet directly from the information already there. All the necessary figures, including the totals and the net income or loss, have already been calculated on the worksheet. The necessary figures for the preparation of the statement of owner's equity appear in the balance sheet columns as well as the figures required for the preparation of the balance sheet. There is only one exception: if the owner has made an additional investment during the period, the amount of that investment will be included in the balance of the capital account that appears on the trial balance. The bookkeeper must refer to the capital account in the ledger to determine whether such an additional investment has occurred during the period.

The Income Statement

Because the necessary figures for preparing the income statement are contained in the income statement columns of the worksheet, the bookkeeper simply copies the account names and balances onto the proper income statement form, and then determines the section totals and the net income. The income statement for Mary Tyus, M.D., follows. To check the accuracy of the statement, the net income figure should be checked to be sure that it is the same figure that appears on the worksheet.

Mary Tyus, M.D. Income Statement For Month Ended January 31, 19XX		
Revenue		
Medical Revenue	$13,600—	
Consulting Revenue	1,500—	
Total Revenue		$15,100—
Expenses		
Rent Expense	$ 3,900—	
Supplies Expense	90—	
Interest Expense	76—	
Utilities Expense	1,420—	
Repairs Expense	2,416—	
Uniforms Expense	500—	
Wages Expense	3,300—	
Payroll Tax Expense	230—	
Insurance Expense	30—	
Depreciation Expense	200—	
Total Expenses		12,162—
Net Income		$2,938—

Statement of Owner's Equity

Again, all the necessary figures for the preparation of the statement of owner's equity are contained within the balance sheet columns of the worksheet. The capital at the beginning of the period is that figure which appears on the adjusted trial balance and is extended to the balance sheet credit column. The statement of owner's equity for Mary Tyus, M.D., follows:

Mary Tyus, M.D. Statement of Owner's Equity For Month Ended January 31, 19XX		
Mary Tyus, Capital, January 1, 19XX	$21,692—	
Add: Net Income for January	2,938—	
Subtotal	24,630—	
Deduct: Mary Tyus, Drawing	4,800—	
Mary Tyus, Capital, January 31, 19XX		$19,830—

The Balance Sheet

The balance of all the asset and liability accounts appears in the worksheet columns for the balance sheet, and the ending balance for the capital account has been calculated in the statement of owner's equity. If there is no separate statement of owner's equity, of course, those calculations will be made in the owner's equity section of the balance sheet. The balance sheet for Mary Tyus, M.D., follows:

Mary Tyus, M.D. Balance Sheet January 31, 19XX			
Assets			
Cash		$12,500—	
Accounts Receivable		3,100—	
Notes Receivable		4,700—	
Prepaid Insurance		330—	
Supplies		260—	
Office Equipment	$10,600—		
Less: Accumulated Depreciation	200—	10,400—	
Total Assets			$31,290—
Liabilities			
Accounts Payable		$ 2,950—	
Notes Payable		7,600—	
Payroll Taxes Payable		210—	
Unearned Consulting Revenue		400—	
Wages Payable		300—	
Total Liabilities			$11,460—
Owner's Equity			
Mary Tyus, Capital, January 31, 19XX			19,830—
Total Liabilities and Owner's Equity			$31,290—

Finding Errors in the Income Statement and Balance Sheet Columns

Totalling the columns of the income statement and determining the net income or net loss will not show whether an error has been made. Only after the balance sheet columns are totalled and the net income or loss is added to the appropriate column will a mistake become apparent. If, for example, the credit column of the balance sheet does not equal the debit column after the net income is added to the credit column of the balance sheet, a mistake has been made. The error probably is *not* on the adjusted trial balance, because it was in balance before any figures were extended to the balance sheet and income statement. (The trial balance, and thus the adjusted trial balance, does not reveal all errors, however. It only proves the equality of debits and credits.) The following procedure can be used to locate errors on the worksheet:

1. Quickly look at each account on the adjusted trial balance to make sure that each has been extended to the correct financial statement column and in the appropriate debit or credit column. For example, the balance of the Drawing account may have been extended to the credit column of the balance sheet rather than to the debit column.
2. Check also to make sure that the amounts as extended are correct. A number can easily be transposed or a decimal point misplaced when numbers are transferred from one column to another.
3. Check the accounts at the bottom of the original trial balance to make sure that their balances have been extended to the correct income statement or balance sheet column.
4. Re-add the income statement columns.
5. Recalculate the net income or net loss figure.
6. Re-add the balance sheet columns.
7. Make sure that a net income figure appears in the credit column of the balance sheet and that a net loss figure appears in the debit column.
8. Finally, re-add the net income or loss figure to its correct balance sheet column total.

Journalizing the Adjusting Entries

Once the worksheet is complete, the bookkeeper must journalize and post the adjusting entries, because the adjustments will not appear in the ledger until these steps have been completed. The worksheet is used simply to accumulate the information needed to journalize the adjusting entries and to prepare the financial statements.

To begin, centre the words *Adjusting Entries* in the description column of the general journal. To journalize the adjustments, refer to the adjustments columns of the worksheet and, starting with the first adjustment (a), copy the debit account title and amount and the credit account title and amount into the general journal. After entering a concise explanation, continue with adjustments b, c, and so on. The general journal entries for the adjustments of Mary Tyus, M.D. follow. The general ledger after the adjustments have been posted appears in the next chapter.

GENERAL JOURNAL				PAGE 14
Date	Description	Post. Ref.	Debit	Credit
19XX	Adjusting Entries			
Jan. 31	Supplies Expense		90 —	
	Supplies			90 —
	To Record Supplies Used for the Month			
31	Insurance Expense		30 —	
	Prepaid Insurance			30 —
	To Record Insurance Expense for the Month			
31	Depreciation Expense		200 —	
	Accumulated Depreciation: Office Equipment			200 —
	To Record Depreciation on Office Equipment			
31	Wages Expense		300 —	
	Wages Payable			300 —
	To Record Wages Expense for January 30 and 31			
31	Unearned Consulting Revenue		600 —	
	Consulting Revenue			600 —
	To Transfer $600 into Consulting Revenue			
31	Accounts Receivable		2000 —	
	Medical Revenue			2000 —
	To Record Services Performed and Bill Sent to Customer			

Summary

The accounting cycle is a series of steps that are completed each accounting period. The steps covered so far include journalizing, posting, preparing the worksheet with adjustments, preparing the financial statements, and journalizing and posting the adjustments.

The worksheet is the ten-column form used by accountants to accumulate data for the adjusting entries and the financial statements. The following are examples of adjustments:

1. When supplies are purchased, the amount is debited to the asset account Supplies. As supplies are used up, however, no credit entries are made to the account to indicate this. An adjusting entry is required to record the supplies expense; it is recorded as a debit to the Supplies Expense account and a credit to the asset account Supplies.

2. When an insurance policy is purchased, the amount is debited to the asset account Prepaid Insurance. A portion of the cost of the policy is transferred to expense at the end of each accounting period by an adjustment that debits Insurance Expense and credits Prepaid Insurance.

3. When an asset such as equipment, furniture, a building, an automobile, or a truck is purchased, its historical cost is recorded in the asset account. At the end of each accounting period, a portion of the cost of each depreciable asset is transferred to expense by a debit to Depreciation Expense and a credit to the contra-asset account Accumulated Depreciation. Accumulated Depreciation subtracts from the balance of its related asset account on the balance sheet; the balance sheet shows the cost of each asset, its accumulated depreciation, and the difference between the two, the book value.

4. When a customer pays in advance for services, the recognition of the revenue must be deferred until the services are actually performed. To achieve this, the original entry debits Cash and credits a liability account (the *services* are owed to the customer) called Unearned Revenue. When the services are actually performed, the cash value of the work done is removed from the Unearned Revenue account by a debit and is entered into an Earned Revenue account by a credit.

5. At the end of the accounting period, services performed for which no payment has been received must be recorded. This is accomplished by an adjusting entry that debits the asset Accounts Receivable and credits Revenue.

6. Any liabilities that have accrued during the period but do not show on the books must be recorded as adjustments. The entry to record accrued wages is typical; Wages Expense is debited and Wages Payable is credited.

The adjusting entries are first entered in the adjustments columns of the worksheet. The amounts are combined with the figures on the original trial balance to produce an adjusted trial balance from which the figures used to prepare the income statement, statement of owner's equity, and balance sheet are obtained.

Vocabulary Review

Following is a list of the words and terms for this chapter:

accounting cycle	depreciation
acquisition	prepaid expenses
adjusting entry	salvage value
book value	useful life
contra asset	worksheet

Fill in the blank with the correct word or term from the list.

1. The number of years over which an asset is depreciated is the asset's _____.

2. An account that subtracts from its related asset account on the balance sheet is a/an _____.

3. A/an _____ is the act of acquiring possession.

4. The cost of an asset minus its accumulated depreciation is the asset's _____.

5. The periodic transferring of plant and equipment asset cost to expense is called _____.

6. The step-by-step procedure that begins with recording transactions and is repeated for each accounting period is the _____.

7. The ten-column form used to organize the data necessary for journalizing the adjustments and preparing the financial statements is the _____.

8. An accrual or deferral recorded at the end of the accounting period to bring the ledger up to date is a/an _____.

9. Expense items that are paid for prior to their use are called _____.

10. The expected worth of an asset at the end of its useful life is its _____.

Match the words and terms on the left with the definitions on the right.

11. accounting cycle
12. acquisition
13. adjusting entry
14. book value
15. contra asset
16. depreciation
17. prepaid expenses
18. salvage value
19. useful life
20. worksheet

a. the act of acquiring
b. the number of years over which an asset is depreciated
c. an account that subtracts from its related asset on the balance sheet
d. the accounting procedure that is repeated for each accounting period
e. the form on which the data for adjustments and the financial statements are first accumulated
f. the transferring of plant and equipment cost to expense
g. the value of an asset at the end of its useful life
h. a journal entry made at the end of the accounting period to record accruals and deferrals and for which no transaction occurs
i. the cost minus the accumulated depreciation of an asset
j. expense items that are paid for before they are incurred

Exercises

EXERCISE 5.1

On January 2, Phil's Automotive Engineering Company purchased a 12-month insurance policy for $540 cash.

1. Prepare the general journal entry required on January 2 to record the purchase of the policy.
2. Prepare the adjusting entry required on January 31 to record January's insurance expense.

EXERCISE 5.2

Every Friday, Acme Personnel pays its employees weekly salaries amounting to $25,000 ($5,000 per day, Monday through Friday).

1. Prepare the necessary entry on Wednesday, September 30 to record the wages expense for the last three days of September.
2. Prepare the general journal entry required on Friday, October 2 to record payment of the week's wages.

EXERCISE 5.3

On July 1, Andy's Delivery Service received a cheque for $1,500 from Pete's Laundry for delivery services to be performed in July, August, and September.

1. Record the journal entry required on July 1 to record the liability for the services and the receipt of the cash.
2. Prepare the required adjusting entry on July 31, assuming that Andy performs $400 of delivery services for Pete in July.

EXERCISE 5.4

The balance in the Supplies account for The Queen's Limos on September 1 was $235. Purchases of supplies for cash were recorded on September 5 for $110 and on September 19 for $185. The supplies inventory on September 30 as determined by a physical count was $215.

1. Prepare the two journal entries to record purchasing supplies on September 5 and 19.
2. Prepare the adjusting entry required on September 30 to record the supplies used during September.

EXERCISE 5.5

Sandra Smythe, public accountant, purchased a computer costing $12,000 for her office on January 3. It has a useful life of four years and no salvage value. Sandra paid $5,000 cash down for the computer and signed a 24-month, non-interest-bearing note for the remainder.

1. Prepare the general journal entry necessary to record the acquisition of the asset.
2. Prepare the adjusting entry on January 31 to record the depreciation on the computer.
3. Assuming that Sandra's accounting period is one year instead of one month, prepare the adjusting entry required on December 31 to record the depreciation.

EXERCISE 5.6

Mac's Repair Service performed $2,500 in services for T.A. Luong during the month of December for which no cash was received. On December 31, Mac sent a bill to Luong for $2,500 for the services performed; the bill stipulated that payment should be made within 30 days. Prepare the adjusting entry necessary on December 31 to record earning the revenue.

EXERCISE 5.7   Page 115 shows a portion of a worksheet for Ron Lee, Educational Consultant, on August 31, 19XX. The worksheet has been completed except for calculating the net income or net loss for the month and the final ruling.
1. Calculate the net income or net loss, label it in the account titles column, and enter the amount in the appropriate income statement and balance sheet columns.
2. Total and rule the worksheet.

EXERCISE 5.8   Page 115 shows a portion of a worksheet for Juanita Barbosa, Accountant, on November 30, 19XX. The worksheet has been completed except for calculating the net income or net loss for the month and the final ruling.
1. Calculate the net income or net loss, label it in the account titles column, and enter the amount in the appropriate income statement and balance sheet columns.
2. Total and rule the worksheet.

EXERCISE 5.9   Identify the following accounts as asset (A), contra asset (CA), liability (L), owner's equity (OE), revenue (R), or expense (E). Indicate whether the account has a normal debit or credit balance, and tell on which financial statement, the balance sheet (BS) or income statement (IS), each account will appear.

	Account Classification	Normal Debit or Credit Balance	Which Financial Statement?
Example Accounts Receivable	A	debit	BS
a. Notes Payable			
b. Rent Expense			
c. Revenue from Consulting			
d. Office Equipment			
e. Supplies			
f. Supplies Expense			
g. Accumulated Depreciation			
h. Prepaid Advertising			
i. Owner's Drawing			
j. Delivery Revenue			
k. Unearned Delivery Revenue			
l. Prepaid Rent			
m. Automobile			
n. Wages Payable			
o. Unearned Consulting Revenue			

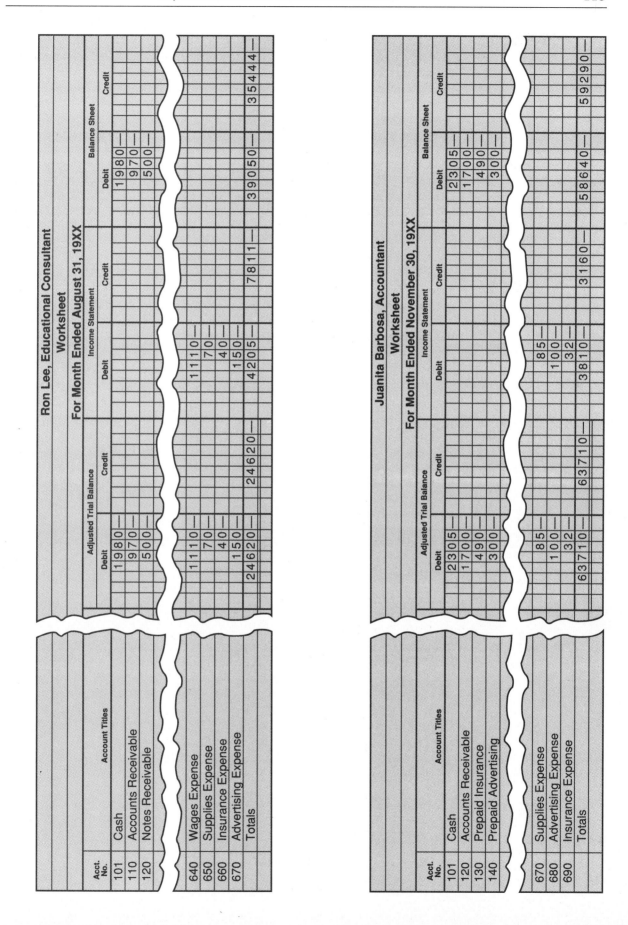

Ron Lee, Educational Consultant
Worksheet
For Month Ended August 31, 19XX

Acct. No.	Account Titles	Adjusted Trial Balance Debit	Adjusted Trial Balance Credit	Income Statement Debit	Income Statement Credit	Balance Sheet Debit	Balance Sheet Credit
101	Cash	1980 —				1980 —	
110	Accounts Receivable	970 —				970 —	
120	Notes Receivable	500 —				500 —	
640	Wages Expense	1110 —		1110 —			
650	Supplies Expense	70 —		70 —			
660	Insurance Expense	40 —		40 —			
670	Advertising Expense	150 —		150 —			
	Totals	24620 —	24620 —	4205 —	7811 —	39050 —	35444 —

Juanita Barbosa, Accountant
Worksheet
For Month Ended November 30, 19XX

Acct. No.	Account Titles	Adjusted Trial Balance Debit	Adjusted Trial Balance Credit	Income Statement Debit	Income Statement Credit	Balance Sheet Debit	Balance Sheet Credit
101	Cash	2305 —				2305 —	
120	Accounts Receivable	1700 —				1700 —	
130	Prepaid Insurance	490 —				490 —	
140	Prepaid Advertising	300 —				300 —	
670	Supplies Expense	85 —		85 —			
680	Advertising Expense	100 —		100 —			
690	Insurance Expense	32 —		32 —			
	Totals	63710 —	63710 —	3810 —	3160 —	58640 —	59290 —

EXERCISE 5.10   Following are the trial balance and adjustments columns of the worksheet for George Atkinson, Consultant, for the month of September 19XX. Recopy the information onto a ten-column worksheet and complete it.

George Atkinson, Consultant
Worksheet
For Month Ending September 30, 19XX

Acct. No.	Account Titles	Trial Balance Debit	Trial Balance Credit	Adjustments Debit	Adjustments Credit
101	Cash	12000—			
105	Accounts Receivable	8500—		e. 1250—	
110	Notes Receivable	14000—			
115	Office Supplies	1500—			a. 400—
120	Prepaid Insurance	1290—			b. 100—
128	Office Equipment	22000—			
129	Accumulated Depreciation: OE		5520—		d. 460—
201	Accounts Payable		1750—		
205	Notes Payable		9800—		
206	Payroll Taxes Payable		520—		
210	Unearned Consulting Revenue		1500—	f. 900—	
301	George Atkinson, Capital		42260—		
310	George Atkinson, Drawing	5000—			
401	Revenue from Teaching		8500—		e. 1250—
405	Revenue from Consulting		1500—		f. 900—
601	Rent Expense	2200—			
603	Utilities Expense	470—			
620	Advertising Expense	500—			
630	Wages Expense	3800—		c. 350—	
640	Interest Expense	90—			
	Totals	71350—	71350—		
650	Office Supplies Expense			a. 400—	
615	Insurance Expense			b. 100—	
220	Wages Payable				c. 350—
660	Depreciation Expense			d. 460—	
				3460—	3460—

EXERCISE 5.11   Following are several circumstances in which the accountant failed to correctly record adjusting entries. For each, tell whether the error in the adjustment would cause an overstatement of expenses and by how much; an understatement of expenses and by how much; an overstatement of revenue and by how much; an understatement of revenue and by how much; an overstatement of net income and by how much; or an understatement of net income and by how much. The first one has been completed as an example.

	Overstatement of Expenses	Understatement of Expenses	Overstatement of Revenue	Understatement of Revenue	Overstatement of Net Income	Understatement of Net Income
Example Accountant did not record adjusting entry for depreciation of $1,000.		$1,000			$1,000	
a. Accountant did not record supplies used for the period for $500.		500			500	
b. Accountant transferred $1,000 from Prepaid Advertising to Advertising Expense when the amount transferred should have been $100.	900					900
c. Accountant did not record accrued wages of $700.		700			700	
d. Accountant did not record revenue performed for which cash had not yet been received, and for which bills had not been sent for $5,000.			5000	5000		5000
e. Accountant did not record depreciation of $850 on the equipment.		850				
f. Accountant did not transfer $150 from Prepaid Insurance to Insurance Expense.		500				
g. Accountant debited Accounts Receivable and credited Revenue for $650 at the end of the month when a cheque for $650 was received from a customer who was paying on account.						

Problems

PROBLEM 5.1   Following on page 119 are the trial balance and adjustments columns of the worksheet prepared on May 31, 19XX for the Linowitz Trucking Company, owned by Paula Linowitz. The accounting period covers one month.

INSTRUCTIONS   1. Copy the trial balance and adjustments columns onto a ten-column worksheet.
2. Extend the figures to the adjusted trial balance and add the debit and credit columns. If they are equal, place the correct totals on the worksheet and rule the adjusted trial balance. In adjustments e, the three amounts for Accumulated Depreciation are combined into one amount for Depreciation Expense. The two credits to Trucking Revenue (g and h) are written on one line in the adjustments credit column. When extending, add both credit amounts to Trucking Revenue.
3. Starting with Cash, extend the asset, liability, and owner's equity account balances to the balance sheet columns of the worksheet.
4. Starting with Trucking Revenue, extend the revenue and expense account balances to the income statement columns of the worksheet.
5. Total the income statement columns of the worksheet, determine the net income, and total the balance sheet columns.
6. Enter the net income beneath the debit column total of the income statement and beneath the credit column total of the balance sheet. Add the column totals to the net income. The balance sheet debit and credit totals should be the same, as should the income statement debit and credit totals. If they are not, look for the error.
7. When the worksheet is complete and in balance, draw the correct rulings across the income statement and balance sheet columns.
8. Journalize the adjusting entries on page 30 in the general journal.

Linowitz Trucking Company
Worksheet
For Month Ended May 31, 19XX

Acct. No.	Account Titles	Trial Balance Debit	Trial Balance Credit	Adjustments Debit	Adjustments Credit
110	Cash	28000—			
115	Accounts Receivable	4320—		g. 4900—	
120	Notes Receivable	7600—			
125	Office Supplies	1490—			a. 560—
130	Trucking Supplies	7130—			b. 1840—
140	Prepaid Insurance	4700—			c. 300—
150	Prepaid Advertising	6900—			d. 2300—
160	Equipment	14200—			
161	Accumulated Deprec.: Equipment		37760—		e. 2360—
170	Trucks	73200—			
171	Accumulated Depreciation: Trucks		19520 0—		e. 12200—
180	Office Furniture	3970—			
181	Accumulated Depreciation: OF		1120—		e. 70—
200	Accounts Payable		6900—		
210	Notes Payable		41650 0—		
220	Payroll Taxes Payable		800—		
230	Unearned Revenue		4250—	h. 2000—	
300	Paula Linowitz, Capital		264101—		
310	Paula Linowitz, Drawing	3250—			
400	Trucking Revenue		37650—		g. 4900—
					h. 2000—
610	Interest Expense	6247—			
620	Rent Expense	1800—			
630	Repairs Expense	2404—			
640	Gas and Oil Expense	3170—			
650	Utilities Expense	1200—			
660	Wages Expense	8100—		f. 950—	
	Totals	964281—	964281—		
605	Office Supplies Expense			a. 560—	
615	Trucking Supplies Expense			b. 1840—	
625	Insurance Expense			c. 300—	
635	Advertising Expense			d. 2300—	
645	Depreciation Expense			e. 14630—	
240	Wages Payable				f. 950—
				27480—	27480—

PROBLEM 5.2   Following is the trial balance for Carol's Exercise Clinic on June 30, 19XX. The business is owned by Carol Goren, and the accounting period covers one month.

Carol's Exercise Clinic
Trial Balance
June 30, 19XX

Acct. No.	Account Titles	Debit	Credit
101	Cash	$ 4,250	
105	Accounts Receivable	1,535	
110	Notes Receivable	1,690	
120	Supplies	615	
130	Prepaid Insurance	500	
140	Van	23,600	
141	Accumulated Depreciation: Van		$10,200
150	Equipment	48,000	
151	Accumulated Depreciation: Equipment		2,000
201	Accounts Payable		400
205	Notes Payable		10,000
210	Unearned Revenue		1,000
220	Mortgage Payable		43,000
305	Carol Goren, Capital		14,590
310	Carol Goren, Drawing	2,600	
401	Revenue from Teaching		750
410	Revenue from Exercise Clinic		6,200
602	Utilities Expense	195	
604	Advertising Expense	250	
610	Interest Expense	760	
620	Wages Expense	2,800	
630	Payroll Tax Expense	170	
635	Gas and Oil Expense	130	
650	Repairs Expense	225	
660	Insurance Expense	820	
	Totals	$88,140	$88,140

INSTRUCTIONS

1. Copy the trial balance onto a ten-column worksheet.
2. Calculate the adjustments from the following data and enter them in the adjustments columns of the worksheet. Label the adjustments a, b, c, and so on. Additional account titles and numbers that will be required in this problem are: Supplies Expense, 670; Depreciation Expense, 685; and Wages Payable, 230.
   a. The beginning inventory of supplies was $475. A purchase of supplies was made on June 21 for $140, and the ending inventory of supplies was $270.
   b. The insurance policy was purchased for $600 on April 1 of this year. It prepaid the insurance for one year.
   c. The van was purchased on January 2 of last year. It has a useful life of five years and a salvage value of $2,000. The equipment was purchased on February 5 of this year. It is expected to last eight years and will have no salvage value.

d. June 30 falls on a Thursday. Wages of $100 a day are paid on each Friday. Record the wages expense for Monday through Thursday, June 27 through 30.

e. On June 1, Carol received a cheque for $1,000 from a local exercise firm to give ten aerobics lessons to its new instructors. Carol taught five of the lessons in June.

f. On June 30, services had been performed in the clinic totalling $1,200 for which no payment had been received and no bills had been sent.

3. Complete the worksheet.

4. Journalize the adjusting entries on page 42 of the general journal.

PROBLEM 5.3   Following is the trial balance for Dancing Dynamics on March 31, 19XX. The business is owned by Jon Phillips, and the accounting period covers three months.

Dancing Dynamics
Trial Balance
March 31, 19XX

Acct. No.	Account Titles	Debit	Credit
101	Cash	$ 1,950	
105	Accounts Receivable	2,700	
110	Supplies	560	
115	Prepaid Insurance	400	
120	Office Equipment	11,500	
121	Accumulated Depreciation: OE		
145	Van	18,000	
146	Accumulated Depreciation: Van		
201	Accounts Payable		$ 3,520
210	Notes Payable		15,500
215	Payroll Taxes Payable		145
220	Interest Payable		335
230	Unearned Lecturing Revenue		1,500
301	Jon Phillips, Capital		16,370
310	Jon Phillips, Drawing	4,000	
401	Revenue from Dancing		10,520
410	Revenue from Lecturing		840
601	Rent Expense	2,400	
610	Utilities Expense	600	
615	Advertising Expense	450	
620	Repairs Expense	420	
630	Gas and Oil Expense	550	
640	Interest Expense	1,000	
650	Wages Expense	4,200	
	Totals	$48,730	$48,730

INSTRUCTIONS   1. Copy the trial balance onto a ten-column worksheet.

2. Calculate the adjustments for a three-month period from the following data and enter them onto the adjustments columns of the worksheet. Label the adjustments a, b, c, and so on. Additional account titles and numbers required in this problem are: Supplies Expense, 660; Insurance Expense, 670; Depreciation Expense, 680; and Wages Payable, 240.

a. The beginning inventory of supplies on January 1 was $400. One pur-
   chase of supplies was made on February 27 for $160. The ending inven-
   tory of supplies on March 31, determined by a physical count, was $355.
b. The insurance policy was purchased on January 2 of this year. Its cost
   was $400, and it prepaid the insurance for six months.
c. Wages for Dancing Dynamics are $85 a day and are paid every Friday.
   March 31 falls on a Tuesday.
d. The office equipment was purchased on January 2 of this year. It has
   an expected useful life of four years and a salvage value of $1,500. The
   van was purchased on January 4 of this year and has an expected useful
   life of four years and a salvage value of $2,000.
e. Maybelle Johnson paid Jon $1,500 for five lectures he would be deliv-
   ering during February, March, and April. Jon has delivered three of the
   lectures by the end of March.
f. On March 31, $2,100 in dancing revenue services have been performed
   for which no cash has been received and no bills have been sent.

3. Complete the worksheet.
4. Prepare a statement of owner's equity for the three-month period January 1 through March 31.
5. Journalize the adjusting entries on general journal page 66.

PROBLEM 5.4 The trial balance columns of the worksheet for Marie's Bookkeeping Service
for the third quarter of 19XX follow.

Marie's Bookkeeping Service
Trial Balance
September 30, 19XX

Acct. No.	Account Titles	Debit	Credit
101	Cash	$ 4,120	
110	Accounts Receivable	1,780	
115	Office Supplies	920	
120	Prepaid Insurance	300	
125	Prepaid Advertising	600	
130	Office Equipment	18,050	
131	Accumulated Depreciation: OE		$ 3,000
150	Automobile	14,800	
151	Accumulated Depreciation: Automobile		4,500
201	Accounts Payable		1,100
210	Notes Payable		12,000
215	Payroll Taxes Payable		144
230	Unearned Consulting Revenue		900
301	Marie Himler, Capital		15,066
310	Marie Himler, Drawing	3,600	
401	Revenue from Bookkeeping		8,950
410	Revenue from Consulting		4,750
601	Rent Expense	1,800	
610	Repairs Expense	475	
620	Utilities Expense	450	
630	Advertising Expense	600	
640	Insurance Expense	305	
650	Gas and Oil Expense	210	
660	Wages Expense	2,400	
	Totals	$50,410	$50,410

INSTRUCTIONS

1. Copy the trial balance onto a ten-column worksheet.
2. Record the adjustments from the following data. Label the adjustments a, b, c, and so on. The accounting period covers three months. Additional account titles and numbers required in the problem are: Supplies Expense, 670; Depreciation Expense, 680; and Wages Payable, 250.
   a. The inventory of office supplies on September 30 is $520.
   b. The advertising was prepaid on July 1 for a six-month period. (Remember that the adjustment period is three months.)
   c. The $300 figure in Prepaid Insurance represents a six-month policy purchased on July 1.
   d. The auto was purchased on January 1 of the previous year. It has a useful life of four years and a salvage value of $2,800. The office equipment was purchased on July 1 of the previous year. It has a useful life of five years and a salvage value of $3,050.
   e. $700 of the unearned consulting revenue has been earned this period.
   f. Bookkeeping services for $2,200 have been performed but no cash has been received and no bills have been sent to customers.
   g. Wages totalling $75 per day are paid every Friday. September 30 falls on a Thursday.
3. Complete the worksheet for the three-month period.
4. Prepare an income statement for the third quarter.
5. Prepare a statement of owner's equity for the third quarter.
6. Prepare a balance sheet for the third quarter.
7. Journalize the adjusting entries on general journal page 39.

PROBLEM 5.5

The worksheet for Lori's Landscape Service for the month of April 19XX appears on pages 124–25. The trial balance and adjustments columns are without error, but the bookkeeper made several mistakes when extending the figures to the adjusted trial balance. The bookkeeper did not total the adjusted trial balance, but continued on, again making errors when extending figures to the income statement and balance sheet columns. As a result, when the net income was added to the credit column of the balance sheet, it did not balance.

INSTRUCTIONS

1. Look over the worksheet carefully. Check to make sure that the adjusted trial balance is correct. Look for transpositions as well as miscalculations and omissions. Write in all your corrections.
2. Re-add the adjusted trial balance. Do not continue until it is in balance.
3. Check extensions to the balance sheet and income statement columns. Carry forward all corrections made on the adjusted trial balance and check for other errors in these columns.
4. Re-add the balance sheet and income statement columns, write in correct figures, and rule the worksheet.

Lori's Landscape Service
Worksheet
For Month Ended April 30, 19XX

Acct. No.	Account Titles	Trial Balance Debit	Trial Balance Credit	Adjustments Debit	Adjustments Credit
101	Cash	3050—			
105	Accounts Receivable	1605—		g. 500—	
115	Office Supplies	495—			b. 205—
120	Garden Supplies	1840—			a. 720—
130	Prepaid Insurance	900—			c. 100—
140	Prepaid Advertising	800—			d. 200—
150	Office Equipment	8500—			
151	Accumulated Depreciation: OE		2300—		e. 150—
160	Garden Equipment	10000—			
161	Accumulated Depreciation: GE		4900—		e. 230—
170	Truck	25500—			
171	Accumulated Depreciation: Truck		10600—		e. 400—
201	Accounts Payable		1400—		
210	Notes Payable		15200—		
215	Payroll Taxes Payable		160—		
220	Unearned Landscape Revenue		1000—	h. 600—	
301	Lori Salzman, Capital		17970—		
310	Lori Salzman, Drawing	2000—			
401	Landscape Revenue		4750—		g. 500—
					h. 600—
601	Truck Expense	760—			
610	Repairs Expense	290—			
620	Rent Expense	550—			
630	Wages Expense	1600—		f. 340—	
640	Utilities Expense	390—			
	Totals	58280—	58280—		
650	Garden Supplies Expense			a. 720—	
660	Office Supplies Expense			b. 205—	
670	Insurance Expense			c. 100—	
680	Advertising Expense			d. 200—	
690	Depreciation Expense			e. 780—	
230	Wages Payable				f. 340—
				3445—	3445—

	Adjusted Trial Balance		Income Statement		Balance Sheet	
	Debit	Credit	Debit	Credit	Debit	Credit
	3050 —				3050 —	
	1105 —				1105 —	
	290 —				290 —	
	1130 —				1310 —	
	800 —				800 —	
	1000 —				1000 —	
	8500 —				8500 —	
		2450 —				2450 —
	10000 —				10000 —	
		5220 —				5220 —
	25500 —				25500 —	
		1100 —				1100 —
		1400 —				1400 —
		15200 —				15200 —
		160 —				160 —
		1600 —				1600 —
		19790 —				19970 —
	2000 —					
		4750 —		4750 —		
	670 —		670 —			
	290 —		290 —			
	550 —		550 —			
	1600 —		1600 —			
	390 —		390 —			
	720 —		720 —			
	250 —		250 —			
	100 —		100 —			
	200 —		200 —			
	780 —		780 —			
		340 —	340 —			

Handwritten margin notes:
- 2105 ←
- 1120 ←
- 600 ←
- 5130 ←
- 11000 ←
- 400 ←
- 17970 ←
- 5850 ←
- 760 ←
- 1440
- 205 ←

PROBLEM 5.6   Before preparing adjusting entries, Jon Smythe, Flight Trainer, calculated his net income for November to be $5,700. His accountant, however, calculated the following necessary adjustments to the accounts:

a. depreciation on the airplane, $3,500
b. services performed for which payment had not been received and for which no bills had yet been sent, $1,400
c. accrued wages expense, $425
d. supplies used in November, $190
e. insurance expense, $1,500
f. $500 of the balance of $1,300 in unearned revenue had been earned in November.

INSTRUCTIONS   1. Consider the effect each adjusting entry will have on net income. Determine whether the adjustment will cause net income to be reduced (and by how much) or whether the adjustment will cause net income to increase (and by how much). The first transaction has been recorded as an example.

Adjustment	Reduces Net Income by This Amount	Increases Net Income by This Amount
a.	$3,500	_____

2. Considering the effect the adjusting entries will have, determine the correct amount of net income or loss for the month.

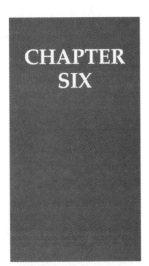

CHAPTER SIX

Correcting and Closing Entries

Learning Objectives

When you have completed this chapter, you should
1. have a better understanding of accounting terminology.
2. be able to analyze an incorrect journal entry and determine how to correct it.
3. be able to journalize and post the closing entries.
4. be able to prepare a post-closing trial balance.

Vocabulary

calendar year   January 1 through December 31

closing entries   journal entries that, when posted, bring the account balances of revenue and expense accounts and the drawing account to zero and update the capital account

counteract   to reverse the effects of a previous act

erroneous   wrong or inaccurate

fiscal year   any 12-month period used by a business for determining net income or loss; it may or may not be a calendar year

nominal accounts   all the temporary accounts that will be closed at the end of the accounting period; revenue, expense, and drawing accounts

post-closing   after closing

real accounts   assets, liabilities, and the owner's capital account

temporary proprietorship accounts   another term for nominal accounts

Introduction

If an error is made when journalizing and that incorrect journal entry is posted, the bookkeeper must prepare a new journal entry that will **counteract** the effects of the first entry. Once the correcting entry is posted, the general ledger will be correct.

Chapter Five showed how bookkeepers have developed the worksheet to help them sort out and organize the information required for the adjusting entries and financial statements. The worksheet is also used to help in one of the last steps in the accounting cycle—journalizing the closing entries. The **closing entries** bring all revenue and expense account balances and the owner's drawing account balance to zero and update the capital account.

Correcting Entries

When an error is made in a journal entry and it is discovered before it is posted, it may be corrected by drawing a line through the incorrect account title(s) and amount(s) and writing the correct title(s) and amount(s) in small letters and figures immediately above the incorrect entry. It is not acceptable in actual practice to erase in the journal or ledger.

GENERAL JOURNAL				PAGE 25		
Date	Description	Post. Ref.	Debit		Credit	
19XX Jan. 11	Cash		1 6 0 —			
	Accounts ~~Payable~~ Receivable				1 6 0 —	
	Received Cash on Account					

Often, however, the error is not discovered right away and the incorrect amounts are posted. When this happens, the easiest way to correct the entry is to make a new entry that will counteract the effects of the first entry. For example, assume that on January 4 a firm pays $250 cash for office supplies. The bookkeeper debits Medical Supplies and credits Cash for $250. The entry is posted to the ledger. Before the accounting cycle has been completed, the wrong entry is discovered and corrected by debiting Office Supplies and crediting Medical Supplies for $250 in the general journal. Once this entry has been posted, the general ledger will be correct. The entry looks like this:

GENERAL JOURNAL				PAGE 26		
Date	Description	Post. Ref.	Debit		Credit	
19XX	Correcting Entry					
Jan. 28	Office Supplies		2 5 0 —			
	Medical Supplies				2 5 0 —	
	To Correct Entry of January 4					

Debiting Office Supplies for $250 puts the correct amount in that account for the first time, and crediting Medical Supplies for $250 removes the incorrect amount from that account. Another example might be when a customer sends in a cheque for $500 on February 10 to apply to his or her account, and the bookkeeper debits Accounts Receivable and credits Cash for $500 and posts the figures. This error, when discovered on February 28, will be corrected in the following manner:

GENERAL JOURNAL				PAGE 34	
Date	Description	Post. Ref.	Debit	Credit	
19XX	Correcting Entry				
Feb. 28	Cash		1000—		
	Accounts Receivable			1000—	
	To Correct Entry of February 10				

By debiting Cash for $1,000, the effects of the incorrect entry will have been counteracted: a $500 debit is required to reverse the effects of the incorrect $500 credit to Cash and another $500 debit is required for the correct entry. The same logic holds true for the error in Accounts Receivable.

Incorrect amounts, as well as incorrect account titles, may be recorded in error. For example, on March 3, $1,100 is spent on a new typewriter for the office. The bookkeeper **erroneously** records a debit to Office Equipment of $1,000 and a credit to Cash of $1,000 and posts the incorrect amounts. When the error is discovered at the end of the month, it will be handled this way:

GENERAL JOURNAL				PAGE 43	
Date	Description	Post. Ref.	Debit	Credit	
19XX	Correcting Entry				
Mar. 31	Office Equipment		100—		
	Cash			100—	
	To Correct Entry of March 3				

Correcting entries may occur at any time, and they vary a great deal. Both what was done and what should have been done must be considered before journalizing. Each incorrect entry must be carefully analyzed to determine its effects on the accounts involved; using T accounts may be helpful in the analysis. In each case, the words *Correcting Entry* must be centred in the description column of the general journal before the actual entry is made.

Closing Entries

Closing an account means bringing it to a zero balance, and the journal entries that accomplish this are called closing entries. All the revenue and expense accounts are closed and the net income or net loss is transferred to the owner's capital account by closing entries; for this reason, revenue and expense accounts are called **temporary proprietorship accounts** or **nominal accounts**.

By bringing the revenue and expense account balances to zero at the end of each accounting period, a new net income or loss figure can more easily be calculated for the next accounting period. The revenue and expense figures of one accounting period should not be running into those of the next.

Closing entries also update the capital account by crediting it for the amount of the net income and debiting it for the amount of the drawing. This procedure is repeated in the statement of owner's equity. If the accounting period shows a net loss, the owner's capital account will be debited for that amount in the closing process.

The illustrations in this chapter show the closing process at month's end, but many businesses close their books quarterly or at the end of the **fiscal year**. A fiscal year is any 12-month period chosen by a business owner during which the yearly net income or loss is determined and federal and provincial income taxes are calculated. A **calendar year** is the period beginning January 1 and ending December 31. A fiscal year and a calendar year may or may not be the same.

The closing process involves recording the entries in the general journal and posting them to the general ledger. The four closing entries (1) close all revenue accounts; (2) close all expense accounts; (3) close the income summary account by transferring the net income or net loss to the owner's capital account; and (4) close the drawing account by transferring the balance of the drawing account to the owner's capital account.

The Income Summary Account

The Income Summary account is a special account used only in the closing process. Though it is given an account number in the owner's equity category, this account does not appear on the trial balance or on the balance sheet. It is both opened and closed in the closing process and is not used again until the end of the next accounting period.

The Worksheet and the Closing Process

Because the worksheet accumulates all the revenue and expense accounts and the net income in one place, it may be used when journalizing the closing entries. The bookkeeper uses the debit and credit columns of the income statement to determine the account titles and amounts to be used in the closing process. As the closing entries are journalized, check marks (✓) are placed by the amounts in the debit or credit columns. A check mark by each amount in the income statement columns of the worksheet ensures that no accounts have been omitted in the closing process.

Closing the Revenue Accounts

The bookkeeper will close all revenue accounts in the first closing entry. Because revenue accounts have credit balances, debits are required for closing them. The corresponding credit will be to the Income Summary account. Consult the income statement columns of the worksheet to determine the number of revenue accounts, their account titles, and their balances. A portion of the worksheet and the required entry to close the revenue accounts for Mary Tyus, M.D., follows.

Mary Tyus, M.D.
Worksheet
For Month Ending January 31, 19XX

Acct. No.	Account Titles	Adjusted Trial Balance Debit	Adjusted Trial Balance Credit	Income Statement Debit	Income Statement Credit
101	Cash	12500—			
105	Accounts Receivable	3100—			
110	Notes Receivable	4700—			
120	Prepaid Insurance	330—			
130	Supplies	260—			
150	Office Equipment	10600—			
151	Accumulated Depreciation: OE		200—		
201	Accounts Payable		2950—		
210	Notes Payable		7600—		
215	Payroll Taxes Payable		210—		
220	Unearned Consulting Revenue		400—		
301	Mary Tyus, Capital		21692—		
310	Mary Tyus, Drawing	4800—			
401	Medical Revenue		13600—		13600— ✓
405	Consulting Revenue		1500—		1500— ✓
601	Rent Expense	3900—		3900—	
610	Interest Expense	76—		76—	
615	Utilities Expense	1420—		1420—	
620	Repairs Expense	2416—		2416—	
630	Uniforms Expense	500—		500—	
640	Wages Expense	3300—		3300—	
650	Payroll Tax Expense	230—		230—	
	Totals				
605	Supplies Expense	90—		90—	
660	Insurance Expense	30—		30—	
670	Depreciation Expense	200—		200—	
230	Wages Payable		300—		
		48452—	48452—	12162—	15100— ✓
	Net Income			2938—	
				15100—	15100—

GENERAL JOURNAL					PAGE 15	
Date		Description	Post. Ref.	Debit	Credit	
19XX		Closing Entries				
Jan.	31	Medical Revenue		13600—		
		Consulting Revenue		1500—		
		Income Summary			15100—	
		To Close Revenue Accounts				

As the first closing entry is journalized, check marks (✓) are placed by the revenue amounts on the worksheet to indicate that those accounts have been closed. The following T accounts for Medical Revenue, Consulting Revenue, and Income Summary look like this after the first closing entry is posted:

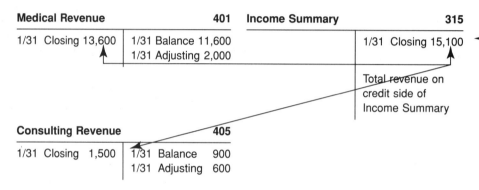

Medical Revenue   401

  1/31 Closing 13,600 | 1/31 Balance 11,600
                      | 1/31 Adjusting 2,000

Income Summary   315

                      | 1/31 Closing 15,100

Total revenue on credit side of Income Summary

Consulting Revenue   405

  1/31 Closing   1,500 | 1/31 Balance   900
                      | 1/31 Adjusting   600

The debit and credit sides of the revenue accounts are now equal, and the accounts have a zero balance. The Income Summary account contains on its credit side a total of all the revenue for the period.

Closing the Expense Accounts

The account titles and amounts necessary for preparing the second closing entry may be taken directly from the income statement debit column of the worksheet. The journal entry to close the expense accounts is as follows:

GENERAL JOURNAL					PAGE 15	
Date		Description	Post. Ref.	Debit	Credit	
19XX		Closing Entries				
Jan.	31	Income Summary		12162—		
		Rent Expense			3900—	
		Interest Expense			76—	
		Utilities Expense			1420—	
		Repairs Expense			2416—	
		Uniforms Expense			500—	
		Wages Expense			3300—	
		Payroll Tax Expense			230—	
		Supplies Expense			90—	
		Insurance Expense			30—	
		Depreciation Expense			200—	
		To Close Expense Accounts				

The adjusted trial balance and the income statement columns of the worksheet for Mary Tyus, M.D., follow. Look at it carefully; pay special attention to the check marks that have been entered on the worksheet opposite the revenue and expense amounts. The T accounts also follow to show how they appear after the closing entries have been posted.

Mary Tyus, M.D.
Worksheet
For Month Ending January 31, 19XX

Acct. No.	Account Titles	Adjusted Trial Balance Debit	Adjusted Trial Balance Credit	Income Statement Debit	Income Statement Credit
101	Cash	12500—			
105	Accounts Receivable	3100—			
110	Notes Receivable	4700—			
120	Prepaid Insurance	330—			
130	Supplies	260—			
150	Office Equipment	10600—			
151	Accumulated Depreciation: OE		200—		
201	Accounts Payable		2950—		
210	Notes Payable		7600—		
215	Payroll Taxes Payable		210—		
220	Unearned Consulting Revenue		400—		
301	Mary Tyus, Capital		21692—		
310	Mary Tyus, Drawing	4800—			
401	Medical Revenue		13600—		13600— ✓
405	Consulting Revenue		1500—		1500— ✓
601	Rent Expense	3900—		3900— ✓	
610	Interest Expense	76—		76— ✓	
615	Utilities Expense	1420—		1420— ✓	
620	Repairs Expense	2416—		2416— ✓	
630	Uniforms Expense	500—		500— ✓	
640	Wages Expense	3300—		3300— ✓	
650	Payroll Tax Expense	230—		230— ✓	
	Totals				
605	Supplies Expense	90—		90— ✓	
660	Insurance Expense	30—		30— ✓	
670	Depreciation Expense	200—		200— ✓	
230	Wages Payable		300—		
		48452—	48452—	12162— ✓	15100— ✓
	Net Income			2938—	
				15100—	15100—

Rent Expense 601

1/31 Balance 3,900	1/31 Closing 3,900

Supplies Expense 605

1/31 Adjusting 90	1/31 Closing 90

Interest Expense 610

1/31 Balance 76	1/31 Closing 76

Utilities Expense 615

1/31 Balance 1,420	1/31 Closing 1,420

Repairs Expense 620

1/31 Balance 2,416	1/31 Closing 2,416

Uniforms Expense 630

1/31 Balance 500	1/31 Closing 500

Wages Expense 640

1/31 Balance 3,000	1/31 Closing 3,300
1/31 Adjusting 300	

Payroll Tax Expense 650

1/31 Balance 230	1/31 Closing 230

Insurance Expense 660

1/31 Adjusting 30	1/31 Closing 30

Depreciation Expense 670

1/31 Adjusting 200	1/31 Closing 200

Income Summary 315

1/31 Closing 12,162	1/31 Closing 15,100
Total expenses on debit side	Total revenue on credit side

After the second closing entry has been posted, the Income Summary account has a credit balance of $2,938, the net income for the period. The balance is logical, because the total revenue appears on the credit side of the Income Summary account and total expenses appear on the debit side. After the first two closing entries have been posted, the balance in the Income Summary account will always represent the net income or net loss for the period.

Transferring the Net Income (or Loss) to Owner's Capital

The third closing entry transfers the net income or net loss to the owner's capital account. A net income must be added to capital, which requires a credit to the Capital account; a net loss, on the other hand, requires a debit to capital to reduce the Capital account by the amount of the loss. This third closing entry begins the process of updating the Capital account in the general ledger by adding to it the net income or subtracting from it the net loss.

The actual dollar amount of the net income or loss is obtained from the income statement columns of the worksheet, where it is first calculated. The third closing entry transferring the net income to capital for Mary Tyus, M.D., follows.

		GENERAL JOURNAL			**PAGE 15**
Date		**Description**	**Post. Ref.**	**Debit**	**Credit**
19XX		Closing Entries			
Jan.	31	Income Summary		2938—	
		Mary Tyus, Capital			2938—
		To Transfer Net Income to Capital			

After this third closing entry has been posted, the Income Summary account is closed and the Capital account is increased by the amount of the net income for the period, $2,938.

Income Summary				**315**	
All expenses and net income	1/31 Closing	12,162	1/31 Closing	15,100	All revenue
	1/31 Closing	2,938			
		15,100		*15,100*	

Mary Tyus, Capital				**301**	
			1/1 Balance	21,692	
			1/31 Closing	2,938	(Net income)

Transferring Drawing to Capital

The owner's Drawing account is the only balance sheet account that is closed. Drawing is subtracted from capital in the statement of owner's equity and in the ledger as one of the steps to determine the ending capital figure. The last closing entry closes the Drawing account and transfers its balance to the Capital account.

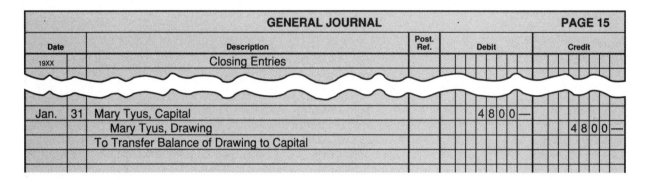

A check mark by the $4,800 Drawing account figure on the worksheet completes the journalizing of the closing entries. After the entry has been posted, the Drawing account and Capital account look like this:

Mary Tyus, Drawing			310
1/31 Balance	4,800	1/31 Closing	4,800

	Mary Tyus, Capital			301
(Drawing subtracted)	1/31 Closing 4,800	1/1 Balance	21,692	
		1/31 Closing	2,938	(Net income added)
		2/1 Balance	**19,830**	

The new balance of the capital account is $19,830, as revealed when the statement of owner's equity was prepared in Chapter Five.

The financial statements, including the statement of owner's equity, may be prepared before the closing entries are journalized and posted. Thus, the financial statements may be accurate and up to date (because their source of information is the worksheet) before the data are actually posted.

The Journal and Ledger Illustrated

The closing entries are recorded in the general journal immediately following the adjusting entries. Adjusting entries are always posted before closing entries. Either the word *Adjusting* or the word *Closing* is entered in the explanation column of the ledger account. The closing entries and the general ledger accounts for Mary Tyus, M.D., follow. Those accounts that have not been affected by the adjusting or closing entries are shown with only their January 31 balances.

	GENERAL JOURNAL			PAGE 15	

GENERAL JOURNAL — **PAGE 15**

Date		Description	Post. Ref.	Debit	Credit
19XX		Closing Entries			
Jan.	31	Medical Revenue	401	1 3 6 0 0 —	
		Consulting Revenue	405	1 5 0 0 —	
		Income Summary	315		1 5 1 0 0 —
		To Close Revenue Accounts			
	31	Income Summary	315	1 2 1 6 2 —	
		Rent Expense	601		3 9 0 0
		Interest Expense	610		7 6
		Utilities Expense	615		1 4 2 0
		Repairs Expense	620		2 4 1 6
		Uniforms Expense	630		5 0 0
		Wages Expense	640		3 3 0 0
		Payroll Tax Expense	650		2 3 0
		Supplies Expense	605		9 0
		Insurance Expense	660		3 0
		Depreciation Expense	670		2 0 0
		To Close Expense Accounts			
	31	Income Summary	315	2 9 3 8 —	
		Mary Tyus, Capital	301		2 9 3 8 —
		To Transfer Net Income to Capital			
	31	Mary Tyus, Capital	301	4 8 0 0 —	
		Mary Tyus, Drawing	310		4 8 0 0 —
		To Transfer Balance of Drawing to Capital			

ACCOUNT: CASH   ACCT. NO. 101

Date		Explanation	Post. Ref.	Debit	Credit	Balance
19XX Jan.	31	Balance	✓			1 2 5 0 0 —

ACCOUNT: ACCOUNTS RECEIVABLE   ACCT. NO. 105

Date		Explanation	Post. Ref.	Debit	Credit	Balance
19XX Jan.	31	Balance	✓			1 1 0 0 —
	31	Adjusting	GJ14	2 0 0 0 —		3 1 0 0 —

ACCOUNT: NOTES RECEIVABLE   ACCT. NO. 110

Date		Explanation	Post. Ref.	Debit	Credit	Balance
19XX Jan.	31	Balance	✓			4 7 0 0 —

ACCOUNT: PREPAID INSURANCE   ACCT. NO. 120

Date		Explanation	Post. Ref.	Debit	Credit	Balance
19XX Jan.	2		GJ5	360—		360—
	31	Adjusting	GJ14		30—	330—

ACCOUNT: SUPPLIES   ACCT. NO. 130

Date		Explanation	Post. Ref.	Debit	Credit	Balance
19XX Jan.	1	Balance	✓			255—
	14		GJ5	60—		315—
	26		GJ8	35—		350—
	31	Adjusting	GJ14		90—	260—

ACCOUNT: OFFICE EQUIPMENT   ACCT. NO. 150

Date		Explanation	Post. Ref.	Debit	Credit	Balance
19XX Jan.	2		GJ5	10600—		10600—

ACCOUNT: ACCUMULATED DEPRECIATION: OFFICE EQUIPMENT   ACCT. NO. 151

Date		Explanation	Post. Ref.	Debit	Credit	Balance
19XX Jan.	31	Adjusting	GJ14		200—	200—

ACCOUNT: ACCOUNTS PAYABLE   ACCT. NO. 201

Date		Explanation	Post. Ref.	Debit	Credit	Balance
19XX Jan.	31	Balance	✓			2950—

ACCOUNT: NOTES PAYABLE   ACCT. NO. 210

Date		Explanation	Post. Ref.	Debit	Credit	Balance
19XX Jan.	31	Balance	✓			7600—

ACCOUNT: PAYROLL TAXES PAYABLE   ACCT. NO. 215

Date		Explanation	Post. Ref.	Debit	Credit	Balance
19XX Jan.	31	Balance	✓			210—

ACCOUNT: UNEARNED CONSULTING REVENUE ACCT. NO. 220

Date		Explanation	Post. Ref.	Debit	Credit	Balance
19XX Jan.	3		GJ5		1000—	1000—
	31	Adjusting	GJ14	600—		400—

ACCOUNT: WAGES PAYABLE ACCT. NO. 230

Date		Explanation	Post. Ref.	Debit	Credit	Balance
19XX Jan.	31	Adjusting	GJ14		300—	300—

ACCOUNT: MARY TYUS, CAPITAL ACCT. NO. 301

Date		Explanation	Post. Ref.	Debit	Credit	Balance
19XX Jan.	31	Balance	✓			21692—
	31	Closing	GJ15		2938—	24630—
	31	Closing	GJ15	4800—		19830—

ACCOUNT: MARY TYUS, DRAWING ACCT. NO. 310

Date		Explanation	Post. Ref.	Debit	Credit	Balance
19XX Jan.	31	Balance	✓			4800—
	31	Closing	GJ15		4800—	0

ACCOUNT: INCOME SUMMARY ACCT. NO. 315

Date		Explanation	Post. Ref.	Debit	Credit	Balance
19XX Jan.	31	Closing	GJ15		15100—	15100—
	31	Closing	GJ15	12162—		2938—
	31	Closing	GJ15	2938—		0

ACCOUNT: MEDICAL REVENUE ACCT. NO. 401

Date		Explanation	Post. Ref.	Debit	Credit	Balance
19XX Jan.	31	Balance	✓			11600—
	31	Adjusting	GJ14		2000—	13600—
	31	Closing	GJ15	13600—		0

ACCOUNT: CONSULTING REVENUE ACCT. NO. 405

Date		Explanation	Post. Ref.	Debit	Credit	Balance
19XX Jan.	31	Balance	✓			900—
	31	Adjusting	GJ14		600—	1500—
	31	Closing	GJ15	1500—		0

ACCOUNT: RENT EXPENSE   ACCT. NO. 601

Date		Explanation	Post. Ref.	Debit	Credit	Balance
Jan. 19XX	31	Balance	✓			3900 —
	31	Closing	GJ15		3900 —	0

ACCOUNT: SUPPLIES EXPENSE   ACCT. NO. 605

Date		Explanation	Post. Ref.	Debit	Credit	Balance
Jan. 19XX	31	Adjusting	GJ14	90 —		90 —
	31	Closing	GJ15		90 —	0

ACCOUNT: INTEREST EXPENSE   ACCT. NO. 610

Date		Explanation	Post. Ref.	Debit	Credit	Balance
Jan. 19XX	31	Balance	✓			76 —
	31	Closing	GJ15		76 —	0

ACCOUNT: UTILITIES EXPENSE   ACCT. NO. 615

Date		Explanation	Post. Ref.	Debit	Credit	Balance
Jan. 19XX	31	Balance	✓			1420 —
	31	Closing	GJ15		1420 —	0

ACCOUNT: REPAIRS EXPENSE   ACCT. NO. 620

Date		Explanation	Post. Ref.	Debit	Credit	Balance
Jan. 19XX	31	Balance	✓			2416 —
	31	Closing	GJ15		2416 —	0

ACCOUNT: UNIFORMS EXPENSE   ACCT. NO. 630

Date		Explanation	Post. Ref.	Debit	Credit	Balance
Jan. 19XX	31	Balance	✓			500 —
	31	Closing	GJ15		500 —	0

ACCOUNT: WAGES EXPENSE   ACCT. NO. 640

Date		Explanation	Post. Ref.	Debit	Credit	Balance
Jan. 19XX	6		GJ2	750 —		750 —
	13		GJ6	750 —		1500 —
	20		GJ9	750 —		2250 —
	27		GJ12	750 —		3000 —
	31	Adjusting	GJ14	300 —		3300 —
	31	Closing	GJ15		3300 —	0

ACCOUNT: PAYROLL TAX EXPENSE

ACCT. NO. 650

Date		Explanation	Post. Ref.	Debit	Credit	Balance
19XX Jan.	31	Balance	✓			2 3 0 —
	31	Closing	GJ15		2 3 0 —	0

ACCOUNT: INSURANCE EXPENSE

ACCT. NO. 660

Date		Explanation	Post. Ref.	Debit	Credit	Balance
19XX Jan.	31	Adjusting	GJ14	3 0 —		3 0 —
	31	Closing	GJ15		3 0 —	0

ACCOUNT: DEPRECIATION EXPENSE

ACCT. NO. 670

Date		Explanation	Post. Ref.	Debit	Credit	Balance
19XX Jan.	31	Adjusting	GJ14	2 0 0 —		2 0 0 —
	31	Closing	GJ15		2 0 0 —	0

The Post-Closing Trial Balance

Once the closing entries have been posted, the remaining step in the accounting cycle is to prepare the **post-closing** trial balance. The accounts that appear on the post-closing trial balance are the **real accounts** and include assets, liabilities, and the owner's capital account. The post-closing trial balance is prepared as a last check to ensure that after the adjusting and closing entries have been posted, the ledger is in balance. The post-closing trial balance for Mary Tyus, M.D., follows.

Mary Tyus, M.D. Post-Closing Trial Balance January 31, 19XX	Debit	Credit
Cash	$12,500—	
Accounts Receivable	3,100—	
Notes Receivable	4,700—	
Prepaid Insurance	330—	
Supplies	260—	
Office Equipment	10,600—	
Accumulated Depreciation: Office Equipment		$ 200—
Accounts Payable		2,950—
Notes Payable		7,600—
Payroll Taxes Payable		210—
Unearned Consulting Revenue		400—
Wages Payable		300—
Mary Tyus, Capital		19,830—
Totals	$31,490—	$31,490—

Steps in the Accounting Cycle

The accounting cycle begins with transactions and the journalizing of them and ends with the closing of the books and the post-closing trial balance. The steps in the accounting cycle are:

1. Journalize the transactions.
2. Post the transactions.
3. Prepare a worksheet.
   a. Prepare a trial balance.
   b. Prepare the adjustments.
   c. Prepare an adjusted trial balance.
   d. Complete the worksheet by extending figures first to the balance sheet and then to the income statement columns.
4. Prepare the financial statements.
5. Journalize the adjusting entries.
6. Post the adjusting entries.
7. Journalize the closing entries.
8. Post the closing entries.
9. Prepare the post-closing trial balance.

Summary

If a general journal entry has not been posted, any errors that have been made when journalizing may be corrected simply by drawing a line through the incorrect account title(s) and/or amount(s) and entering the correct title(s) and/or amount(s) above. If the journal entry has been posted, however, a new entry must be made that will counteract the effects of the first entry. When the error is discovered, the bookkeeper simply centres the words *Correcting Entry* in the description column of the journal and journalizes the entry required to correct the one in error.

The closing entries are journalized following the adjusting entries. All the nominal accounts, or the temporary proprietorship accounts, are brought to a zero balance during the closing process, and the owner's capital account is updated. Temporary proprietorship accounts include drawing, revenue, and expense accounts. The closing process takes place at the end of the accounting period, which may be at the end of a month, a quarter, or a fiscal year. The four closing entries (1) close all revenue accounts, (2) close all expense accounts, (3) transfer net income or loss to capital, and (4) transfer the balance of drawing to capital.

The Income Summary account is used only in the closing process. All the revenue, expenses, and net income or loss are transferred to it during closing. The Income Summary account opens and closes when the first three closing entries have been journalized and posted.

The information for the closing entries is available in the income statement and balance sheet columns of the worksheet, the ledger accounts, or the financial statements themselves. Check marks should be placed next to all of the amounts in the income statement columns as they are journalized and next to the drawing account balance as it is closed.

Only the real accounts (assets, liabilities, and owner's capital) remain open after the closing entries have been posted. A post-closing trial balance verifies that they are in balance before the next accounting cycle is begun.

Vocabulary Review

Following is a list of the words and terms for this chapter:

calendar year   fiscal year
closing entries   nominal accounts
counteract   post-closing
erroneous   real accounts
                            temporary proprietorship accounts

Fill in the blank with the correct word or term from the list.

1. All the revenue and expense accounts are referred to as _____.
2. Journal entries that bring account balances to zero are called _____.
3. All the asset and liability accounts and the owner's capital account are called _____.
4. _____ means "after closing."
5. To perform an act that will reverse the effects of a previous act is to _____.
6. January 1 through December 31 is a/an _____.
7. Something that is wrong or inaccurate is _____.
8. Any 12-month period chosen by a business owner for determining net income is a/an _____.
9. Nominal accounts are also known as _____.

Match the words and terms on the left with the definitions on the right.

10. closing entries
11. counteract
12. erroneous
13. post-closing
14. nominal accounts
15. real accounts
16. fiscal year
17. calendar year
18. temporary proprietorship accounts

a. asset, liability, and the owner's capital account
b. to reverse the effects of a previous act
c. revenue and expense accounts
d. wrong or inaccurate
e. January 1 through December 31
f. after closing
g. journal entries that bring revenue and expense account balances to zero and update the capital account
h. April 1 through March 31
i. the asset, liability, and capital accounts

Exercises

EXERCISE 6.1   Ly Vo owns The Reading School. Following are examples of transactions that have been erroneously journalized and posted by the bookkeeper. Prepare the correcting entry for each. Write the letter of each entry in the date column on page 6 of the general journal. You may omit explanations.

   a. Ly Vo wrote a cheque for $220 for office supplies. The bookkeeper debited Office Supplies for $200 and credited Cash for $200.

b. A cheque for $89 was received from a customer of The Reading School who was paying on account. The bookkeeper debited Cash for $89 and credited Accounts Payable for $89.

c. A cheque for $440 was received from a customer of The Reading School who was paying on account. The bookkeeper debited Accounts Payable for $440 and credited Cash for $440.

d. Ly Vo wrote a cheque for $50 to pay an outstanding account. The bookkeeper debited Accounts Receivable for $50 and credited Cash for $50.

e. Ly Vo wrote a cheque for $250 for office furniture. The bookkeeper debited Office Equipment for $250 and credited Accounts Payable for $250.

EXERCISE 6.2   Following are the closing entries on July 31, 19XX for Reliable Answering Service. Post them to accounts with the following titles and account balances.

Chart of Accounts

301	Daniel Black, Capital	$8,750
310	Daniel Black, Drawing	2,400
315	Income Summary	0
401	Revenue	4,000
601	Utilities Expense	190
605	Rent Expense	575
610	Wages Expense	900
615	Advertising Expense	250
620	Payroll Tax Expense	55
630	Supplies Expense	70
640	Depreciation Expense	50

GENERAL JOURNAL   PAGE 24

Date		Description	Post. Ref.	Debit	Credit
19XX		Closing Entries			
July	31	Revenue		4000—	
		Income Summary			4000—
		To Close Revenue Account			
	31	Income Summary		2090—	
		Utilities Expense			190—
		Rent Expense			575—
		Wages Expense			900—
		Advertising Expense			250—
		Payroll Tax Expense			55—
		Supplies Expense			70—
		Depreciation Expense			50—
		To Close Expense Accounts			
	31	Income Summary		1910—	
		Daniel Black, Capital			1910—
		To Transfer Net Income to Capital			
	31	Daniel Black, Capital		2400—	
		Daniel Black, Drawing			2400—
		To Transfer Balance of Drawing to Capital			

EXERCISE 6.3 Following are the balances of the T accounts for Wayne's Windsurfers on June 30, 19XX. Journalize the closing entries on page 14. The four entries will (1) close all revenue accounts, (2) close all expense accounts, (3) close the income summary account and transfer the profit or loss to the capital account, and (4) close the Drawing account and transfer the balance to the capital account. Post the entries to the T accounts and determine the amount of the ending capital balance.

Wayne Werner, Capital	301
	6/1 Balance 5,250

Revenue	401
	6/30 Balance 2,100

Wayne Werner, Drawing	310
6/30 Balance 1,000	

Rent Expense	601
6/30 Balance 400	

Income Summary	315

Insurance Expense	605
6/30 Balance 75	

Advertising Expense	610
6/30 Balance 250	

Repairs Expense	615
6/30 Balance 320	

Depreciation Expense	650
6/30 Balance 450	

Supplies Expense	660
6/30 Balance 30	

EXERCISE 6.4 Tell whether each of the following will cause an increase (+), cause a decrease (−), or have no effect (NE) on net income for March. Assume that adjusting and closing entries are prepared monthly.

_____ a. withdrawals in March by the owner for personal use
_____ b. a purchase of equipment for cash on March 31
_____ c. a bill for electricity for March is received and recorded but not paid
_____ d. an additional investment by the owner on March 9
_____ e. cash paid on an account payable on March 29
_____ f. an adjusting entry to record wages payable
_____ g. an adjusting entry on March 31 to record depreciation on the automobile
_____ h. a receipt of $3,000 cash on March 1 from a customer who is paying in advance for services to be performed in April, May, and June
_____ i. a $10,000 non-interest-bearing business loan obtained on March 13
_____ j. an adjusting entry to record $500 of services performed for which no cash has been received

EXERCISE 6.5 For the following accounts, indicate on which financial statement each will appear (income statement or balance sheet) and whether the account has a normal debit or credit balance. The first one has been completed as an example.

	Which Financial Statement?	Normal Debit or Credit Balance?
Example Capital	balance sheet	credit
a. Equipment		
b. Wages Payable		
c. Supplies Expense		
d. Accumulated Depreciation		
e. Unearned Consulting Revenue		
f. Prepaid Advertising		
g. Wages Expense		
h. Supplies		
i. Revenue from Services		
j. Advertising Expense		
k. Prepaid Insurance		
l. Depreciation Expense		
m. Unearned Medical Revenue		
n. Insurance Expense		
o. Consulting Revenue		

EXERCISE 6.6 Following are selected ledger accounts for the Tri-More Company on January 31, 19XX. All of the revenue and expense accounts are listed. Journalize the four required closing entries on journal page 27.

230	Unearned Consulting Revenue	$1,000
601	Rent Expense	900
201	Accounts Payable	2,740
310	Sandra Nielsen, Drawing	2,770
401	Revenue	3,055
301	Sandra Nielsen, Capital, January 1, 19XX	6,120
605	Insurance Expense	275
171	Accumulated Depreciation: Office Equipment	1,000
610	Advertising Expense	350
615	Wages Expense	1,890
620	Payroll Tax Expense	114
315	Income Summary	0
640	Depreciation Expense	200
160	Supplies	190
660	Supplies Expense	75

EXERCISE 6.7 Using the information in Exercise 6.6, prepare a statement of owner's equity on January 31, 19XX for the Tri-More Company.

EXERCISE 6.8 Following is the Income Summary account for Kay Song, Consultant, on April 30, 19XX, after the first two closing entries have been posted.

Income Summary   **315**

4/30 Closing	15,820	4/30 Closing	12,485

1. What is the balance of the account before the third closing entry is posted to it?
2. Is the account balance a debit or a credit?
3. After the first two entries have been posted to the Income Summary account, does a debit balance represent a net income or a net loss for the period?
4. After the first two closing entries have been posted, does the credit side of the Income Summary account represent total revenue or total expenses for the period?
5. Will the third closing entry, which transfers net loss to capital, be recorded as a debit or as a credit to Capital? To Income Summary?
6. If there is a net income for the period, will the amount of the net income be recorded as a debit or as a credit to Capital? To Income Summary?

EXERCISE 6.9 Following are the closing entries for Gregory Bronski, Counsellor, on May 31, 19XX. The entries have not been posted. Assuming that the first two entries are correct, determine what is wrong, if anything, with the last two. If you find one or both of them to be incorrect, draw a line through the account title and/or amount and enter the correct account title and/or amount directly above the line. The balance of the Capital account on May 1 was $6,240, and the balance of Drawing on May 31 was $1,800.

Date		Description	Post. Ref.	Debit	Credit
		GENERAL JOURNAL			**PAGE 4**
19XX		Closing Entries			
May	31	Revenue from Counselling		1916—	
		Income Summary			1916—
		To Close Revenue Account			
	31	Income Summary		2334—	
		Rent Expense			890—
		Utilities Expense			225—
		Wages Expense			800—
		Payroll Tax Expense			79—
		Supplies Expense			45—
		Insurance Expense			75—
		Depreciation Expense			220—
		To Close Expense Accounts			
	31	Income Summary		318—	
		Gregory Bronski, Capital			318—
		To Transfer Net Income to Capital			
	31	Gregory Bronski, Drawing		1800—	
		Gregory Bronski, Capital			1800—
		To Transfer Balance of Drawing to Capital			

EXERCISE 6.10 Following are several examples of incorrect journal entries that have already been posted to the ledger. Tell whether the incorrect entry will affect net income for the month. If so, determine whether it will be overstated (O) or understated (U) and determine by how much the net income will be overstated or understated.

	Will Error Affect Net Income?	If So, Will Net Income Be Overstated or Understated?	By How Much?
a. Services were performed for $500 cash; recorded by a $500 debit to Accounts Receivable and a $500 credit to Revenue.	No		
b. $100 was received from a customer who was paying on account; recorded by a $110 debit to Cash and a $110 credit to Accounts Receivable.	No		
c. Owner's withdrawal of $900 was recorded as a $900 debit to Salary Expense and a $900 credit to Cash.	Yes	Understated	$900
d. A cheque was written for $175 for payment on account; recorded as a $175 debit to Utilities Expense and a $175 credit to Cash.	Yes	Understated	$175
e. $800 in services were performed on account; recorded as an $800 debit to Accounts Receivable and an $800 credit to owner's Capital.	Yes	Understated	$800
f. $1,200 in services were performed on account; recorded as a $1,200 debit to Cash and a $1,200 credit to Revenue.	No		
g. A $168 telephone bill was paid and recorded as a $186 debit to Utilities Expense and a $186 credit to Cash.	Yes	understated	$18
h. The owner invested an additional $1,000 in the business. It was recorded as a $1,000 debit to Cash and a $1,000 credit to Revenue.	Yes	overstated	$1000
i. A $250 cash payment was made for equipment repairs. It was recorded as a $250 debit to Equipment and a $250 credit to Cash.	Yes	overstated	$250
j. A $190 payment was made for gas and oil for a delivery van. Utilities Expense was debited for $190 and Cash was credited for $190.	No		

Problems

PROBLEM 6.1 Following are several examples of journalizing errors that have been posted.

  a. A firm wrote a cheque for $550 for shop supplies. The bookkeeper recorded a debit of $550 to Office Supplies and a Credit of $550 to Cash.

  b. A firm wrote a cheque for $550 for shop supplies. The bookkeeper recorded a debit of $505 to Shop Supplies and a credit of $505 to Cash.

  c. A firm wrote a cheque for $550 for shop supplies. The bookkeeper recorded a debit of $650 to Shop Supplies and a credit of $650 to Cash.

  d. A cheque for $420 was received from a customer paying on account. The bookkeeper recorded a debit to Cash of $402 and a credit to Accounts Receivable for $402.

  e. A cheque for $420 was received from a customer paying on account. The bookkeeper recorded a debit to Accounts Receivable for $420 and a credit to Cash for $420.

  f. A cheque for $420 was received from a customer paying on account. The bookkeeper recorded a debit to Accounts Receivable for $410 and a credit to Cash for $410.

  g. A firm wrote a cheque for $840 to pay an outstanding debt. The bookkeeper recorded a debit to Accounts Payable for $860 and a credit to Cash for $860.

  h. A firm wrote a cheque for $840 to pay an outstanding debt. The bookkeeper recorded a debit to Cash of $840 and a credit to Accounts Payable of $840.

  i. A firm wrote a cheque for $840 to pay an outstanding debt. The bookkeeper recorded a debit to Accounts Receivable of $840 and a credit to Cash for $840.

  j. A firm wrote a cheque for $840 to pay an outstanding debt. The bookkeeper recorded a debit to Accounts Receivable of $480 and a credit to Cash for $480.

INSTRUCTIONS Prepare correcting entries on page 49 of the general journal. Explanations may be omitted. Enter the letter of the transaction in the date column of the journal.

PROBLEM 6.2   The adjusted trial balance and income statement columns of the worksheet for Dandee Delivery Service for the month of September 19XX follow.

Dandee Delivery Service
Worksheet (Partial)
For Month Ended September 30, 19XX

Acct. No.	Account Titles	Adjusted Trial Balance Debit	Adjusted Trial Balance Credit	Income Statement Debit	Income Statement Credit
101	Cash	4020—			
105	Accounts Receivable	850—			
110	Supplies	490—			
115	Prepaid Insurance	300—			
120	Equipment	3465—			
121	Accumulated Depreciation: Equipment		1590—		
130	Truck	18500—			
131	Accumulated Depreciation: Truck		8200—		
201	Accounts Payable		300—		
210	Notes Payable		10550—		
220	Unearned Delivery Revenue		800—		
301	Dee Snyder, Capital		7870—		
310	Dee Snyder, Drawing	3200—			
401	Revenue from Delivery		4720—		4720—
601	Truck Expense	310—		310—	
610	Rent Expense	950—		950—	
615	Utilities Expense	255—		255—	
630	Advertising Expense	580—		580—	
640	Interest Expense	260—		260—	
650	Insurance Expense	100—		100—	
660	Supplies Expense	75—		75—	
670	Depreciation Expense	675—		675—	
	Totals	34030—	34030—	3205—	4720—
	Net Income			1515—	
				4720—	4720—

INSTRUCTIONS
1. Prepare the four closing entries required on September 30, 19XX on journal page 39. The account number for Income Summary is 315.
2. Post the entries to the general ledger.
3. Prepare a post-closing trial balance.

PROBLEM 6.3 The income statement and balance sheet columns of the worksheet for Softee Diaper Service for the year ended December 31, 19XX follow.

Softee Diaper Service
Worksheet (Partial)
For Year Ended December 31, 19XX

Acct. No.	Account Titles	Income Statement Debit	Income Statement Credit	Balance Sheet Debit	Balance Sheet Credit
101	Cash			7064—	—
110	Accounts Receivable			1500—	
115	Notes Receivable			3002—	
120	Supplies			775—	
125	Prepaid Insurance			400—	
135	Prepaid Advertising			1550—	
136	Equipment			24000—	
137	Accumulated Depreciation: Equipment				4500—
140	Furniture			4540—	
141	Accumulated Depreciation: Furniture				1600—
150	Truck			22000—	
151	Accumulated Depreciation: Truck				7000—
201	Accounts Payable				1765—
210	Notes Payable				30000—
220	Unearned Consulting Revenue				3500—
301	Alex Agnos, Capital				37041—
310	Alex Agnos, Drawing			12000—	
401	Revenue from Services		42625—		
601	Delivery Expense	5100—			
605	Repairs Expense	6204—			
610	Rent Expense	12000—			
615	Interest Expense	6396—			
620	Advertising Expense	1000—			
630	Utilities Expense	2400—			
640	Insurance Expense	100—			
650	Wages Expense	15000—			
660	Payroll Tax Expense	900—			
670	Supplies Expense	600—			
680	Depreciation Expense	1500—			
		51200—	42625—	76831—	85406—
	Net Loss		8575—	8575—	
		51200—	51200—	85406—	85406—

INSTRUCTIONS

1. Journalize the four closing entries required on December 31, 19XX on journal page 30. The account number for Income Summary is 315.
2. Prepare an income statement for the year ended December 31, 19XX.
3. Prepare a statement of owner's equity for the year ended December 31, 19XX.
4. Prepare a balance sheet as of December 31, 19XX.

PROBLEM 6.4   Following is the worksheet for Robert's Hair Styling for the month of December 19XX.

		Robert's Hair Styling				
		Worksheet				
		For Month Ended December 31, 19XX				
Acct. No.	Account Titles	Trial Balance			Adjustments	
		Debit	Credit	Debit		Credit
101	Cash	6400—				
110	Accounts Receivable	1250—		f. 300—		
120	Beauty Supplies	2800—			a.	1290—
125	Office Supplies	980—			b.	430—
130	Prepaid Insurance	1440—			c.	240—
135	Hair Styling Equipment	18000—				
136	Accumulated Depreciation: HSE		5500—		e.	250—
140	Office Equipment	10500—				
141	Accumulated Depreciation: OE		1837—		e.	167—
150	Furniture	6200—				
151	Accumulated Depreciation: Furn.		1100—		e.	100—
160	Automobile	18200—				
161	Accumulated Depreciation: Auto.		3663—		e.	333—
205	Accounts Payable		2940—			
220	Notes Payable		15600—			
230	Unearned Hair Styling Revenue		500—	g. 200—		
301	Robert Goodwin, Capital		36526—			
310	Robert Goodwin, Drawing	2500—				
401	Hair Styling Revenue		6150—		f.	300—
					g.	200—
601	Rent Expense	1800—				
610	Advertising Expense	500—				
620	Utilities Expense	470—				
630	Repairs Expense	220—				
640	Interest Expense	156—				
650	Wages Expense	2200—		d. 330—		
655	Payroll Tax Expense	200—				
	Totals	73816—	73816—			
615	Beauty Supplies Expense			a. 1290—		
625	Office Supplies Expense			b. 430—		
635	Insurance Expense			c. 240—		
240	Wages Payable				d.	330—
670	Depreciation Expense			e. 850—		
				3640—		3640—
	Net Loss					

INSTRUCTIONS

1. Journalize and post the adjusting entries. Write Adjusting in the explanation column of each ledger account as you post. Use general journal page 27.
2. Journalize and post the closing entries. Write Closing in the explanation column of each ledger account as you post. Use general journal page 28. The account number for Income Summary is 315.
3. Prepare an income statement for the month of December 19XX.
4. Prepare a balance sheet as of December 31. Include the statement of owner's equity on the balance sheet.
5. Prepare a post-closing trial balance.

Adjusted Trial Balance		Income Statement		Balance Sheet	
Debit	Credit	Debit	Credit	Debit	Credit
6400—				6400—	
1550—				1550—	
1510—				1510—	
550—				550—	
1200—				1200—	
18000—				18000—	
	5750—				5750—
10500—				10500—	
	2004—				2004—
6200—				6200—	
	1200—				1200—
18200—				18200—	
	3996—				3996—
	2940—				2940—
	15600—				15600—
	300—				300—
	36526—				36526—
2500—				2500—	
	6650—		6650—		
1800—		1800—			
500—		500—			
470—		470—			
220—		220—			
156—		156—			
2530—		2530—			
200—		200—			
1290—		1290—			
430—		430—			
240—		240—			
	330—				330—
850—		850—			
75296—	75296—	8686—	6650—	66610—	68646—
			2036—	2036—	
		8686—	8686—	68646—	68646—

PROBLEM 6.5   Following is the trial balance for Uncle Ray's Party Service for the third quarter of 19XX.

<table>
<tr><td colspan="4" align="center">**Uncle Ray's Party Service**
Trial Balance
September 30, 19XX</td></tr>
<tr><td>**Acct.
No.**</td><td>**Account Titles**</td><td>**Debit**</td><td>**Credit**</td></tr>
<tr><td>101</td><td>Cash</td><td>$ 5,214</td><td></td></tr>
<tr><td>110</td><td>Accounts Receivable</td><td>279</td><td></td></tr>
<tr><td>115</td><td>Party Supplies</td><td>895</td><td></td></tr>
<tr><td>116</td><td>Prepaid Insurance</td><td>300</td><td></td></tr>
<tr><td>120</td><td>Party Equipment</td><td>6,500</td><td></td></tr>
<tr><td>121</td><td>Accumulated Depreciation: Party Equipment</td><td></td><td>$ 750</td></tr>
<tr><td>130</td><td>Van</td><td>18,000</td><td></td></tr>
<tr><td>131</td><td>Accumulated Depreciation: Van</td><td></td><td>1,250</td></tr>
<tr><td>201</td><td>Accounts Payable</td><td></td><td>756</td></tr>
<tr><td>205</td><td>Notes Payable</td><td></td><td>11,404</td></tr>
<tr><td>210</td><td>Unearned Party Revenue</td><td></td><td>600</td></tr>
<tr><td>301</td><td>Ray Whittier, Capital</td><td></td><td>19,714</td></tr>
<tr><td>310</td><td>Ray Whittier, Drawing</td><td>4,500</td><td></td></tr>
<tr><td>401</td><td>Revenue from Party Services</td><td></td><td>8,742</td></tr>
<tr><td>601</td><td>Wages Expense</td><td>4,046</td><td></td></tr>
<tr><td>610</td><td>Repairs Expense</td><td>750</td><td></td></tr>
<tr><td>620</td><td>Rent Expense</td><td>1,500</td><td></td></tr>
<tr><td>630</td><td>Payroll Tax Expense</td><td>125</td><td></td></tr>
<tr><td>640</td><td>Utilities Expense</td><td>507</td><td></td></tr>
<tr><td>670</td><td>Advertising Expense</td><td>600</td><td></td></tr>
<tr><td></td><td>Totals</td><td>$43,216</td><td>$43,216</td></tr>
</table>

INSTRUCTIONS

1. Copy the trial balance onto the trial balance columns of a ten-column worksheet.
2. Record the adjustments from the following data for the three-month period ending September 30, 19XX. Account numbers that you will need to complete this problem include: Party Supplies Expense, 680; Insurance Expense, 690; Depreciation Expense, 675, Wages Payable, 220; and Income Summary, 320.
   a. The inventory of party supplies on September 30 is $585.
   b. The insurance policy was purchased on July 1 for $300 for a 12-month period.
   c. The party equipment was purchased on January 2 of this year. It has a useful life of four years and a salvage value of $500. The van was purchased on April 1 of this year. It has a useful life of three years and a salvage value of $3,000.
   d. One-half of the balance in the Unearned Party Revenue account has been earned this quarter.
   e. September 30 falls on a Wednesday. Record three days' wages expense at $100 a day for September 28 through 30.
   f. Ray performed services amounting to $900 for which no cash has been received or bills sent.
3. Complete the worksheet.
4. Journalize the adjusting entries. Assign page number 84 to the journal.
5. Journalize the closing entries. Use general journal page 85.

PROBLEM 6.6   Because of errors, the trial balance of the Banff Springs Delivery Service as of November 30, 19XX does not balance.

Banff Springs Delivery Service
Trial Balance
November 30, 19XX

Acct. No.	Account Titles	Debit	Credit
101	Cash	$ 9,280	
110	Accounts Receivable	2,130	
115	Supplies	780	
120	Office Equipment	3,215	
125	Furniture	1,450	
130	Delivery Van	2,500	
210	Accounts Payable		$ 4,990
215	Notes Payable		11,230
301	Dan McNaughton, Capital		14,200
310	Dan McNaughton, Drawing	2,180	
401	Delivery Revenue		6,250
605	Rent Expense	1,120	
610	Salary Expense	2,240	
615	Insurance Expense	1,435	
620	Advertising Expense	820	
630	Interest Expense	1,385	
	Totals	$28,535	$36,670

While looking over the accounting records, the accountant discovers the following errors:

a. On November 15, services were performed on account for $815. The entry was recorded as a credit to Delivery Revenue and a credit to Accounts Payable.

b. A $900 cash withdrawal on November 29 by the owner was recorded as a debit to Capital and a credit to Cash.

c. A $360 bill was received for advertising done in November; it was decided to pay the bill in 60 days. It was recorded as a debit to Advertising Expense and a credit to Accounts Receivable.

d. An additional $2,000 investment by the owner on November 30 was correctly recorded as a credit to Capital, but no corresponding debit entry was made.

e. A $1,000 withdrawal by the owner on November 20 was recorded as a debit to Salary Expense and a credit to Cash.

f. A receipt of $655 from a customer paying on account was recorded as a $650 debit to Cash and a $655 credit to Accounts Receivable.

g. A cheque in the amount of $2,750 in payment of a note payable was recorded as a $2,750 debit to Notes Payable and a $7,250 credit to Cash.

INSTRUCTIONS   1. Individually analyze each error and its effect on the accounts; then calculate new balances for the accounts affected. (It may be helpful to use T accounts for the analysis.)

2. Prepare a corrected trial balance as of November 30, 19XX.

Comprehensive Problem 1 for Review of Chapters One–Six

Following are the chart of accounts and account balances on October 1, Year 3, for the Rocky Mountain Reporter, a newspaper. Also following are the transactions for the month of October, Year 3.

Chart of Accounts			
110	Cash	$ 17,540.63	
120	Accounts Receivable	12,409.15	
130	Supplies	1,962.00	
135	Prepaid Insurance	600.00	
140	Equipment	75,000.00	
141	Accumulated Depreciation: Equipment		$ 19,800.00
150	Delivery Van	21,640.00	
151	Accumulated Depreciation: Delivery Van		10,800.00
160	Furniture	4,300.00	
161	Accumulated Depreciation: Furniture		2,145.00
170	Building	195,000.00	
171	Accumulated Depreciation: Building		24,750.00
180	Land	36,000.00	
210	Accounts Payable		4,203.32
220	Notes Payable		31,490.60
225	Unearned Consulting Revenue		
230	Mortgage Payable: Building		122,400.00
240	Wages Payable		
310	Emerson Browne, Capital		148,862.86
320	Emerson Browne, Drawing		
330	Income Summary		
410	Revenue from Subscriptions		
420	Consulting Revenue		
610	Utilities Expense		
620	Wages Expense		
630	Advertising Expense		
640	Gasoline and Oil Expense		
650	Building Repairs Expense		
655	Van Repairs Expense		
660	Interest Expense		
670	Supplies Expense		
680	Insurance Expense		
690	Depreciation Expense		

TRANSACTIONS

October 1   wrote cheque #2169 for $2,400 for the personal use of Emerson Browne

October 2   received $1,000 in cash from the Alberta Centre for Learning for ten hours of consulting services to be provided by Emerson Browne in the future (credit to Unearned Consulting Revenue)

October 3   wrote cheque #2170 for $375.62 for payment of telephone bill

October 5   wrote cheque #2171 for $147.70 for payment for gasoline for the van

October 6   bought $420 in supplies; agreed to pay within 30 days

October 7   wrote cheque #2172 for $570.61 to pay bill for electricity

October 7   recorded $5,200 in subscription revenue for the week; $4,010 was received in cash and the rest is due within 30 days

October 9   wrote cheque #2173 for $1,760.50 in payment of monthly mortgage on building; $1,240.10 is for payment of interest, and the rest applies toward reduction of the principal (the amount borrowed)

October 10   wrote cheque #2174 for $1,460.82 for repairs to the building

October 12   received cheques totalling $2,060.49 from charge customers

October 13   purchased office supplies costing $1,540.22; wrote cheque #2175 for $850.22 as a cash down payment and agreed to pay the balance in 60 days

October 14   wrote cheque #2176 for $2,100 for personal use of Emerson Browne

October 14   wrote cheque #2177 for $3,410.77 to pay wages from October 1 through 14

October 15   recorded $6,100 in subscription revenue for the week; $4,650.25 was received in cash, and the rest is due within 30 days

October 16   wrote cheque #2178 for $217.40 to pay for repairs to the van

October 17   wrote cheque #2179 for $168.40 for gasoline and oil for the van

October 19   received cheques from charge customers totalling $1,971.14

October 20   wrote cheque #2180 for $2,462.90 to pay for television advertising

October 21   recorded $4,742.80 in subscription revenue for the week; $3,960.20 was received in cash, and the rest is due within 30 days

October 23   received a bill for radio advertising for $950 (record it now to be paid within 30 days)

October 24   wrote cheque #2181 for $1,500 for personal use of Emerson Browne

October 25   wrote cheque #2182 for $542.68 for building repairs

October 26   wrote cheque #2183 for $650 to reduce the amount owed on account

October 28   recorded $5,001 in subscription revenue for the week; $4,019.50 was received in cash, and the rest is due within 30 days

October 28   wrote cheque #2184 for $3,410.77 to pay wages from October 15 through 28

October 29   wrote cheque #2185 for $822.86 for payment on note; $640.32 is payment for interest, and the rest applies to reduction of the principal

October 30   wrote cheque #2186 for $260.14 for gasoline and oil for the van

October 31   wrote cheque #2187 for $420 to reduce the amount owed to creditors

INSTRUCTIONS

1. Enter the account names, numbers, and balances into the general ledger.
2. Record October's transactions in a general journal. Begin numbering with page 20.
3. Post the transactions to the general ledger.
4. Prepare a trial balance on the first two columns of a ten-column worksheet.
5. Prepare the adjustments from the following data:
   a. The inventory of supplies on October 31, determined by a physical count, is $1,140.75.
   b. The $600 figure in the Prepaid Insurance account on October 1 represents the remaining balance of a 12-month insurance policy purchased on April 1 of this year for $1,200.
   c. The equipment was purchased in January of Year 1. It has a useful life of 10 years and a salvage value of $3,000.
   d. The delivery van was purchased in July of Year 1. It has a useful life of four years and a salvage value of $2,440.
   e. The furniture was purchased in January of Year 1. It has a useful life of five years and a salvage value of $400.
   f. The building was purchased in January of Year 1. It has a useful life of 20 years and a salvage value of $15,000.
   g. Three hours of consulting (at $100 per hour) were performed by Emerson Browne during October for the Alberta Centre for Learning. (Refer to October 2 transaction.)
   h. October 31 falls on a Monday. Record one day's wages expense at $341.07.
   i. Unrecorded Subscription Revenue during October (for which customers have not paid) is $2,017.15.
6. Complete the worksheet.
7. Prepare an income statement for the month of October 19XX.
8. Prepare a statement of owner's equity for the month of October 19XX.
9. Prepare a balance sheet as of October 31, 19XX. Include only the ending capital figure in the owner's equity section.

10. Journalize the adjusting entries in the general journal. Continue in the same journal. Centre the words "Adjusting Entries" in the description column of the journal before recording the entries.
11. Post the adjusting entries to the general ledger.
12. Journalize the closing entries in the general journal. Continue in the same journal as before. Centre the words "Closing Entries" in the description column of the journal before recording the entries.
13. Post the closing entries to the general ledger.
14. Prepare a post-closing trial balance.

CHAPTER SEVEN

The Sales Journal and the Accounts Receivable Subsidiary Ledger

Learning Objectives

When you have completed this chapter, you should
1. have an increased understanding of accounting terminology.
2. have an increased understanding of merchandising businesses.
3. be able to record entries directly into the special sales journal and perform summary posting.
4. be able to post to the accounts receivable subsidiary ledger and prepare a schedule of accounts receivable.
5. be able to calculate and account for sales tax.
6. be able to account for sales returns and allowances and sales discounts.

Vocabulary

contra   indicates against or opposing

control accounts   the accounts receivable or accounts payable accounts in the general ledger with balances representing the total of all customer or creditor balances in the accounts receivable or accounts payable ledgers

credit memorandum   a document issued by the seller that informs the buyer that her or his account receivable has been credited (reduced) because of a return or an allowance

merchandise   goods that may be bought or sold

merchandising business   a business that buys and sells merchandise

merchant   a person who operates a merchandising business

retailer   one who sells goods in small quantities to customers

subsidiary   secondary in importance; subordinate

summary posting   when journal totals are posted to the general ledger

wholesaler   one who sells goods in large quantities, as to a retailer

Introduction

So far in our study of accounting, we have discussed only service businesses. We are now ready to expand our learning to include merchandising businesses and the special kinds of accounting procedures used by such businesses.

A service business, you will remember, sells the services of its owner and/ or employees. A **merchandising business**, in contrast, sells a product, sometimes along with a service.

The product usually has to be bought by the **merchant** before it can be resold. Therefore, when determining at what price to sell, the owner must take into account not only all the related expenses, but also the cost price of the **merchandise** to be sold as well as the amount of profit desired.

In this and the chapters to come, you will become familiar with some new accounts and journals and with two new ledgers.

Special Journals

In addition to the general journal, many firms use special journals. An important advantage of using special journals is the amount of time saved by the bookkeeper when journalizing and posting. In addition, when more than one journal is being used, more than one person may be recording journal entries at one time.

There are four special journals about which you will learn. Their names and functions are listed as follows:

Journal	Function	Posting Reference
Sales Journal	Used to record all sales of merchandise on account	S
Purchases Journal	Used to record all purchases of merchandise for resale on account	P
Cash Receipts Journal	Used to record all incoming cash	CR
Cash Payments Journal	Used to record all outgoing cash	CP

The special journals may be designed to fit the needs of the individual business. Each one may be a little different from the other, but the principles for recording and posting remain the same. When the four special journals and the general journal are used simultaneously, it is called a "5" journal system.

The Sales Account

When merchandise is sold, the amount is credited to a revenue account called Sales. It is handled in the same way as Revenue from Consulting, Medical Revenue, or any of the other revenue accounts used to record services performed. The Sales account appears as the first item on the income statement under the Revenue from Sales heading. Assume that merchandise is sold on November 28 for $500 cash. After the sale is posted, the T accounts look like this:

Cash		105	Sales		400
11/28	500			11/28	500

Sales and Sales Invoices

Frank Phelps owns a **retail** sporting goods store called "Sports Haven." He purchases tennis rackets, racquetball shoes, running shorts, exercise bikes, and so on from **wholesalers**. He then calculates how much he wants to mark up each item and adds the amount of the markup to the cost price to determine the selling price. Frank must consider three things when determining the markup: (1) the cost of the merchandise; (2) the related expenses that will be incurred in selling the item; and (3) the average amount of profit desired on the merchandise sold.

In general journal form, a sale on account to P.R. Collins appears as follows:

GENERAL JOURNAL						PAGE 6	
Date	Description	Post. Ref.		Debit		Credit	
19XX June 1	Accounts Receivable—P.R. Collins			1 2 5 —			
	Sales					1 2 5 —	
	To Record Sale on Account; Invoice 507						

Frank does not, however, use a general journal for the recording of sales. His reasons are:

1. For each entry, the words *Accounts Receivable* (or *Cash*) and *Sales* must be laboriously written into the general journal.
2. For each entry, two amounts must be posted to the general ledger from the general journal.

Both of these tasks take up the bookkeeper's valuable time. When using a special sales journal, much of this time is saved.

Entries in the sales journal may be made directly from the sales invoices. Multiple copies of prenumbered sales invoices are prepared at the time a sale is made; one copy goes to the customer and another goes to the accounting department. The invoice shows the quantity of the item sold, a brief description of the item, the unit price, and the total price. The customer's name appears on the invoice and, for credit sales, the customer's address. A sample invoice for Sports Haven follows.

```
                    S P O R T S   H A V E N              No. 507

                          740 Main Street
                        Barrie, Ontario  L4M 3X9

                                                   I N V O I C E
                                                   Terms:  net 30
                                                   Date:   6/1/XX

       Sold to:  P.R. Collins
                 176 Oak Avenue
                 Midhurt, Ontario


       Quantity    Description              Unit      Total
                                            Price     Price

          2        Running Shorts           5.00      10.00
          1        Running Shoes           45.00      45.00
          1        Tennis Racket           70.00      70.00
                                                     125.00
```

The Sales Journal

A sales journal, remember, is used for the recording of sales of merchandise on account. Therefore, every entry in the sales journal is a debit to accounts receivable and a credit to sales. Because this is known automatically by the bookkeeper, it is not necessary to record a separate debit to accounts receivable and credit to sales each time a credit sale is made. What is necessary to record is: (1) the date; (2) the invoice number; (3) the customer's name; and (4) the amount, so that when billing is done, we will know exactly how much each customer owes.

Following is a single-column sales journal for the month of June 19XX for Sports Haven.

SALES JOURNAL

Date		Sales Invoice Number	Customer's Name	Post. Ref.	Amount					
19XX June	1	507	P.R. Collins				1	2	5	—
	3	508	A.O. Brickner				2	7	5	—
	7	509	Z.A. Mysine					4	5	—
	10	510	B.L. Laws					7	6	—
	13	511	J.R. Custer				1	9	5	—
	16	512	A.O. Brickner				1	0	9	—
	20	513	C.L. Lindsay					1	7	—
	25	514	J.R. Custer				4	7	5	—
	30	515	W.W. Ho				2	6	6	—
			Total	110/401		1	5	8	3	—

When totalling a single-column journal, special care must be taken. Because there is only one column, if a mistake is made, there is no double-check to tell you something is wrong. Be sure to check your column total by adding it twice. Then draw a single line across the amount ... der the last figure entered, write the word *Total*, and ent... total credit sales. A double line is then draw... customer's name column.

It should be noted that ... s now virtually obsolete in Canada. In 1991, tl... l the goods and services tax (GST), which requ... llect 7 percent GST and remit these amounts ... e appropriate intervals. This 7 percent GST is ... ansaction, right down to the consumer. The mo... column sales journal is presented later in this chapter.

Posting the Sales Journal

Once you have determined that the total is accurate, it must be posted to two different accounts in the general ledger; (1) a debit of $1,583 must be posted to accounts receivable, and (2) a credit of $1,583 must be posted to sales. The posting reference notation *S6* is entered in the ledger accounts to indicate that the transaction was taken from page 6 of the sales journal. In addition, after the posting has been completed, write the account numbers for accounts receivable (110) and sales (401) in the posting reference column of the journal opposite the word *Total* $\boxed{^{110}/_{401}}$.

When column totals are posted rather than each individual entry, it is called **summary posting**. The two general ledger accounts affected are shown after the sales journal has been posted. (Assume there were no previous balances in the accounts.)

ACCOUNT: ACCOUNTS RECEIVABLE   **ACCT. NO. 110**

Date	Explanation	Post. Ref.	Debit	Credit	Balance
19XX June 30		S6	1 5 8 3 —		1 5 8 3 —

ACCOUNT: SALES   **ACCT. NO. 401**

Date	Explanation	Post. Ref.	Debit	Credit	Balance
19XX June 30		S6		1 5 8 3 —	1 5 8 3 —

As you can readily see, if all the sales on account for June for Sports Haven had been recorded in a general journal, nine separate postings would have been required to accounts receivable and nine to sales.

The Accounts Receivable Subsidiary Ledger

The accounts receivable account in the general ledger shows the *total* amount owed by all customers. It does not show amounts owed by *individual* customers. A business owner must know how much individual customers have charged and paid on their accounts so that billing can be carried out. Amounts owed by individual customers could be kept in the general ledger, and it might then read: Accounts Receivable, Adams; Accounts Receivable, Brown; Accounts Receivable, Coulson, and so on. This would, of course, be very unwieldy, and the trial balance might have hundreds or thousands of account titles using this method. This would make the trial balance nearly impossible to prepare and to read, and the chances for making errors would be much greater. Accountants long ago decided to keep the accounts receivable account in the general ledger simple by showing only the totals owed by charge customers. It is therefore called a **control account** because its balance provides a check; the total of all the individual balances that are kept in the accounts receivable subsidiary ledger must equal the balance in the accounts receivable control account in the general ledger.

In the accounts receivable subsidiary ledger, each customer has a separate page for the recording of his or her charge purchases and any payments made on the account. The accounts receivable ledger is called a **subsidiary** ledger because it is under the control of the accounts receivable account in the general ledger.

The accounts receivable subsidiary ledger is not meant to replace the general ledger; rather, it is designed to give specific information that the general ledger does not give.

Posting to the Accounts Receivable Subsidiary Ledger

The postings to the accounts receivable subsidiary ledger come primarily from the sales journal, where the charge sales are first recorded, and from the cash receipts journal, where customers' payments on account are recorded.

The sales journal, the general ledger accounts affected, and the accounts receivable subsidiary ledger (arranged in alphabetical order) follow.

SALES JOURNAL   **PAGE 6**

Date	Sales Invoice Number	Customer's Name	Post. Ref.	Amount
19XX June 1	507	P.R. Collins	✓	1 2 5 —
3	508	A.O. Brickner	✓	2 7 5 —
7	509	Z.A. Mysine	✓	4 5 —
10	510	B.L. Laws	✓	7 6 —
13	511	J.R. Custer	✓	1 9 5 —
16	512	A.O. Brickner	✓	1 0 9 —
20	513	C.L. Lindsay	✓	1 7 —
25	514	J.R. Custer	✓	4 7 5 —
30	515	W.W. Ho	✓	2 6 6 —
		Total	110/401	1 5 8 3 —

General Ledger

Accounts Receivable   **110**

6/30 S6	1,583	

Sales   **401**

	6/30 S6	1,583

Accounts Receivable Subsidiary Ledger

A.O. Brickner

| 6/3 S6 | 275 | |
| 6/16 S6 | 109 | |

P.R. Collins

| 6/1 S6 | 125 | |

J.R. Custer

| 6/13 S6 | 195 | |
| 6/25 S6 | 475 | |

W.W. Ho

| 6/30 S6 | 266 | |

B.L. Laws

| 6/10 S6 | 76 | |

C.L. Lindsay

| 6/20 S6 | 17 | |

Z.A. Mysine

| 6/7 S6 | 45 | |

When the amount is posted to the accounts receivable ledger, a check mark (✓) is placed in the posting reference column of the sales journal. Account numbers are not used in subsidiary ledgers in this text because the ledgers will be arranged alphabetically.

The Schedule of Accounts Receivable

At the end of the accounting period, a schedule of accounts receivable is prepared directly from the accounts receivable subsidiary ledger. Each customer and the balance owed are listed on the schedule. The total owed by customers as shown on the schedule of accounts receivable must equal the balance in the accounts receivable control account in the general ledger, which also, you will remember, shows the total owed by all customers. If the totals do not agree, a mistake has been made.

The accounts receivable subsidiary ledger, the schedule of accounts receivable, and the accounts receivable control account from the general ledger follow:

ACCOUNTS RECEIVABLE SUBSIDIARY LEDGER

ACCOUNT: A.O. BRICKNER

Date		Explanation	Post. Ref.	Debit	Credit	Balance
19XX June	3		S6	2 75 —		2 75 —
	16		S6	1 09 —		3 84 —

ACCOUNT: P.R. COLLINS

Date		Explanation	Post. Ref.	Debit	Credit	Balance
19XX June	1		S6	1 25 —		1 25 —

ACCOUNT: J.R. CUSTER

Date		Explanation	Post. Ref.	Debit	Credit	Balance
19XX June	13		S6	1 95 —		1 95 —
	25		S6	4 75 —		6 70 —

ACCOUNT: W.W. HO

Date		Explanation	Post. Ref.	Debit	Credit	Balance
19XX June	30		S6	2 66 —		2 66 —

ACCOUNT: B.L. LAWS

Date		Explanation	Post. Ref.	Debit	Credit	Balance
19XX June	10		S6	76 —		76 —

ACCOUNT: C.L. LINDSAY

Date		Explanation	Post. Ref.	Debit	Credit	Balance
19XX June	20		S6	17—		17—

ACCOUNT: Z.A. MYSINE

Date		Explanation	Post. Ref.	Debit	Credit	Balance
19XX June	7		S6	45—		45—

Sports Haven
Schedule of Accounts Receivable
June 30, 19XX

A.O. Brickner	$384—	
P.R. Collins	125—	
J.R. Custer	670—	
W.W. Ho	266—	
B.L. Laws	76—	
C.L. Lindsay	17—	
Z.A. Mysine	45—	
Total		$1,583—

GENERAL LEDGER

ACCOUNT: ACCOUNTS RECEIVABLE   **ACCT. NO. 110**

Date		Explanation	Post. Ref.	Debit	Credit	Balance
19XX June	30		S6	1583—		1583—

Note that the illustration shows only debit entries to accounts receivable. Normally, the accounts receivable account would have credit entries in it also. For example, when a customer pays on account, the debit to cash and the credit to accounts receivable are recorded in the cash receipts journal. The credit to accounts receivable will be posted to both the control account and the subsidiary ledger.

Provincial Sales Tax and Federal GST Charged

Many retail merchants are required by law to collect provincial sales taxes and GST (Goods and Services Tax) from their customers. These taxes are then remitted to the appropriate government agency by the merchant.

Wholesalers are not usually required to collect provincial sales tax when they sell to retailers because it is normally the end user, the final customer, who pays it. However, GST must be collected from everyone. The requirements for tax collection vary from province to province, but regardless of varying exemptions and amounts, the accounting principles remain the same.

Assume that provincial tax is 8 percent and GST is 7 percent. On July 9, a retailer makes a $240 taxable sale on account to Spencer Chatterly. To calculate the taxes:

1. Provincial $240 \times .08 = \$19.20$
2. GST $240 \times .07 = \$16.80$

The customer will be charged for the amount of the sale ($240) and the amount of the provincial tax ($19.20) and GST ($16.80).

In general journal form, the sale on account looks like this:

GENERAL JOURNAL					PAGE 8	
Date	Description	Post. Ref.	Debit		Credit	
19XX July 9	Accounts Receivable—Spencer Chatterly		276 —			
	Sales				240 —	
	Provincial Sales Tax Payable				19 20	
	GST Charged				16 80	
	To Record Sale on Account, Plus Taxes					

The Provincial Sales Tax Payable and GST Charged accounts are current liabilities and will reflect on the balance sheet with the other liabilities. The taxes collected by the business are not a business expense because it is the customer who pays them. The business owner merely collects the taxes and then remits them to the provincial or federal government. At the appropriate time, the entry to pay the amount of taxes due will look like this:

GENERAL JOURNAL					PAGE 14	
Date	Description	Post. Ref.	Debit		Credit	
19XX Aug. 7	Provincial Sales Tax Payable		590 —			
	Cash				590 —	
	To Record Payment of Provincial Sales Taxes					
7	GST Charged		430 —			
	Cash				430 —	
	To Record Payment of Federal Taxes					

Posting Accounts Receivable from the General Journal

From now on, when any general journal entry is made that involves accounts receivable, double posting will be required. For example, assume that a charge sale was made to Barbara Sanders on September 11 in the amount of $530, plus 8 percent provincial sales tax and 7 percent GST. The entry is:

GENERAL JOURNAL				PAGE 9	
Date	Description	Post. Ref.	Debit	Credit	
19XX Sept. 11	Accounts Receivable—Barbara Sanders		609 50		
	Sales			530 —	
	Provincial Sales Tax Payable			42 40	
	GST Charged			37 10	
	To Record Sale on Account, Plus Taxes				

The amount charged to accounts receivable must be posted to the accounts receivable control account in the general ledger. In addition, the sales and taxes payable amounts must be posted to the general ledger. The T accounts after posting appear as follows:

General Ledger   **Accounts Receivable Subsidiary Ledger**

Accounts Receivable   **110**   **Barbara Sanders**

9/11 GJ9   609.50   9/11 GJ9   609.50

Provincial Sales Tax Payable   **225**

                          9/11 GJ9   42.40

GST Charged   **235**

                          9/11 GJ9   37.10

Sales   **401**

                          9/11 GJ9   530.00

The posting reference column of the general journal after posting has been completed for this transaction looks like this:

GENERAL JOURNAL				PAGE 9	
Date	Description	Post. Ref.	Debit	Credit	
19XX Sept. 11	Accounts Receivable—Barbara Sanders	110/✓	609 50		
	Sales	401		530 —	
	Provincial Sales Tax Payable	225		42 40	
	GST Charged	235		37 10	
	To Record Sale on Account, Plus Taxes				

Notice that a diagonal line is placed in the posting reference column of the general journal opposite the debit entry to accounts receivable. When the posting to the accounts receivable control account has been completed, the account number is placed before the diagonal line 110/ . When the amount is posted to Sanders's account in the accounts receivable subsidiary ledger, a check mark is placed after the diagonal line 110/✓ .

The Multicolumn Sales Journal

If both provincial sales tax and GST are collected regularly, it is desirable to design the sales journal to accommodate recording them because it is a lot less work to use a specially designed sales journal than to use a general journal. Such a journal might look like this:

SALES JOURNAL								PAGE 43
Date	Invoice Number	Customer's Name	Post. Ref.	Accounts Receivable Debit	PST Payable Credit	GST Charged Credit		Sales Credit
Oct. 1	7643	P.R. Jones	✓	460—	32—	28—		400—
4	7644	C.Y. Little	✓	172 50	12—	10 50		150—
9	7645	J.L. King	✓	862 50	60—	52 50		750—
	etc.	etc.	✓	5290—	368—	322—		4600—
		Totals		6785—	472—	413—		5900—
				(110)	(225)	(235)		(401)

After the multicolumn sales journal is totalled, a proof of balance must be constructed of the column totals. The debit total must equal the credit totals. Simply add the credit columns:

$$\begin{array}{r} \$\ 472— \\ 413— \\ \underline{5,900—} \\ \underline{\underline{\$6,785—}} \end{array}$$

Since the total of the credit columns ($6,785—) is equal to the total of the debit column ($6,785—), the bookkeeper may now post the totals. After an amount has been posted, place the account number under the column total. Once the summary posting has been completed, individual amounts should be posted to the customers' accounts in the accounts receivable subsidiary ledger; then a check mark is placed in the posting reference column of the journal opposite each customer's name.

Sales Returns and Allowances

The Sales Returns and Allowances account is used to record a return of merchandise by the customer or to record an allowance granted by the seller because of inferior or defective or damaged merchandise. When such returns or allowances occur, a **credit memorandum** is given to the customer. It is called a credit memorandum because it indicates that the customer's account receivable will be credited. The credit memorandum is, like the sales invoice, prepared with multiple copies; one copy goes to the customer and one to the accounting department. Although it might be feasible simply to debit the sales account for returns and allowances, it is not desirable because owners and managers prefer to keep track of how many returns there are, who is making the returns, and which merchandise is being returned. Too many returns may indicate customer dissatisfaction with the merchandise and may require considering of a new supplier.

A sales return reverses the effects on the books of the original sale. Therefore, the sales returns and allowances account has a debit balance; ultimately, it will be a subtraction from sales on the income statement. For this reason, the sales returns and allowances account is called a **contra** sales account. It is included in the revenue category on the chart of accounts even though its balance is opposite that of the sales account.

Assume that on October 3, 19XX, Sports Haven sold four tennis rackets on account to Schwartz Company for $110 each. The transaction was recorded in Sports Haven's sales journal. On October 10, 19XX, Schwartz Company returned one of the rackets because the strings were faulty. Sales returns, when they relate to credit sales, are recorded in the general journal. The entry to record the return follows:

		GENERAL JOURNAL				PAGE 47	
Date		Description	Post. Ref.	Debit		Credit	
19XX Oct.	10	Sales Returns and Allowances	450	1 1 0 —			
		Accounts Receivable—Schwartz Co.	110/✓			1 1 0 —	
		To Record Return of Faulty Tennis Racket					

Following are the general ledger accounts affected and Schwartz Company's account in the accounts receivable subsidiary ledger after the sale and return have been posted. Normally, the individual sale to Schwartz Company would not appear in the accounts receivable control account because only the total of the sales journal is posted there. It is included here only for the purpose of illustration.

General Ledger

Accounts Receivable Subsidiary Ledger

Accounts Receivable			110		Schwartz Company		
10/3	S29	440	10/10 GJ47	110	10/3 S29	440	10/10 GJ47	110

Sales			401
		10/3 S29	440

Sales Returns and Allowances		450
10/10 GJ47	110	

If a customer is charged tax when a sale is made and later returns the merchandise, credit must be given to the customer not only for the merchandise returned, but also for the tax.

For example, assume that on October 4, 19XX Sports Haven sold two warm-up suits on account to Arlene Davidson for $70 each plus 8 percent provincial sales tax and 7 percent GST. The entry, in general journal form, looks like this:

		GENERAL JOURNAL				PAGE 47	
Date		Description	Post. Ref.	Debit		Credit	
19XX Oct.	4	Accounts Receivable—Arlene Davidson		1 6 1 —			
		Sales				1 4 0 —	
		Provincial Sales Tax Payable				1 1 20	
		GST Charged				9 80	
		To Record Sale on Account, Plus Taxes					

Assume that on October 6, Arlene returned one of the warm-up suits for credit. The entry to record the return looks like this:

		GENERAL JOURNAL			PAGE 47	
Date		Description	Post. Ref.	Debit	Credit	
19XX Oct.	6	Sales Returns and Allowances		7 0 —		
		Provincial Sales Tax Payable		5 60		
		GST Charged		4 90		
		Accounts Receivable—Arlene Davidson			8 0 50	
		To Record Return of Merchandise				

Notice that the sales returns and allowances account is debited for the amount of the original selling price of the returned item. Taxes payable are debited for the amount of the taxes relating to the returned item. The tax payable accounts must be reduced because if the merchandise is returned, a sale has been reversed and no tax is required.

Sales Discounts

When a credit sale is made and no discount is offered for paying early, the terms may be expressed on the invoice as net 30, which means that the full amount of the invoice is due within 30 days. Often, however, a wholesaler will grant discount terms to credit buyers. The terms will indicate that a certain percent of the purchase price will be deducted if the buyer pays the invoice within a certain time period. Such terms might be 2/10, n/30 (read as two-ten, net-thirty), which means that a 2 percent discount will be allowed if the invoice is paid within 10 days of the invoice date. The discount is applied to the value of merchandise only. If the invoice is not paid within 10 days, the total invoice price must be paid within 30 days of the invoice date.

When the sale is made, the seller does not know whether the buyer will take advantage of credit terms. Therefore, sales are recorded in the sales journal at their full invoice price. It is only when the customer pays that it becomes evident whether a discount has been taken or not. If a discount has been taken, it is recorded in a special account called sales discounts. Sales discounts has a debit balance and, like sales returns and allowances, subtracts from sales on the income statement. The sales discount account is classified as a contra revenue account and is assigned a number in the revenue category.

Assume that on October 3 a credit sale is made by A-1 Plumbing Supplies (a wholesaler) to Joe's Hardware in the amount of $5,000 plus 7 percent GST. The terms are 1/10, n/30. (A 1 percent discount is allowed if the invoice is paid within 10 days of the invoice date, or the net amount is due within 30 days.) The entry is recorded on page 30 of the sales journal as illustrated:

			SALES JOURNAL					PAGE 30	
Date		Sales Invoice Number	Customer's Name	Post. Ref.	Accounts Receivable Debit	GST Charged Credit	Sales Credit		
19XX Oct.	3	1046	Joe's Hardware	✓	5 3 5 0 —	3 5 0 —	5 0 0 0 —	

You will notice that the sales journal in this example does not have a PST payable column. Since A-1 Plumbing Supplies is a wholesaler, they are not required to collect provincial sales tax.

Joe's Hardware has 10 days from the date of the invoice to pay and receive the 1 percent discount; it has, then, until October 13 (3 + 10). (When calculating a due date, do not count the first day.) Assume that on October 13 a cheque is received by A-1 Plumbing from Joe's Hardware. The cheque is for the amount of the sale of October 3 minus the 1 percent discount. The discount is calculated like this:

1. Change 1 percent to its decimal equivalent (1% = 01. = .01) by moving the decimal point two places to the left.
2. Multiply .01 by $5,000 to get $50, the amount of the discount. (Note that the discount relates only to the sale itself. No discount is allowed on the GST charged.)

The entry in general journal form looks like this:

GENERAL JOURNAL				PAGE 20	
Date	Description	Post. Ref.	Debit	Credit	
19XX Oct. 13	Cash	101	5 3 0 0 —		
	Sales Discount	430	5 0 —		
	Accounts Receivable—Joe's Hardware	110/✓		5 3 5 0 —	
	To Record Amount Due on Invoice 1046,				
	Less 1% Discount				

Notice that Accounts Receivable is credited for the full amount of the sale, $5,350, even though the customer remitted only $5,300. This is necessary so that no balance remains in Accounts Receivable. The customer has paid in full by taking advantage of the sales discount. After posting has been completed, the ledger accounts look like this:

General Ledger

Accounts Receivable Subsidiary Ledger

Cash   101   Joe's Hardware

10/13 GJ20   5,300   10/3 S30   5,350 | 10/13 GJ20   5,350

Accounts Receivable   110

10/3 S30   5,350 | 10/13 GJ20   5,350

GST Charged   215

            | 10/3 S30   350

Sales   401

            | 10/3 S30   5,000

Sales Discounts   430

10/13 GJ20   50 |

Sales Returns and Allowances and Sales Discounts on the Income Statement

Both sales discounts and sales returns and allowances are contra sales accounts and subtract from sales on the income statement. A portion of the income statement for A-1 Plumbing Supplies is reproduced here.

A-1 Plumbing Supplies Income Statement For Month Ended October 31, 19XX			
Revenue			
Sales		$12,570—	
Less: Sales Returns and Allowances	$75—		
Sales Discounts	60—	135—	
Net Sales			$12,435—

Note that net sales represents total (or gross) sales minus all returns, allowances, and discounts.

Summary

A merchandising business sells a product, perhaps along with a service; thus, accounting procedures for merchandising firms are different from those for service businesses. In addition to the general journal, four special journals may be used. They are: (1) the sales journal, for recording sales of merchandise on account; (2) the purchases journal, for recording purchases of merchandise for resale on account; (3) the cash receipts journal, for recording all cash coming into the business; and (4) the cash payments journal, for recording all outgoing cash. The special journals save the bookkeeper a great deal of time because they cut down on the amount of writing required in the journal and on the number of individual postings.

When a credit sale of merchandise is made, that sale is recorded in a special sales journal by entering the date, the invoice number, the customer's name, and the amount. The total of the sales journal is posted to accounts receivable as a debit and to sales as a credit. In addition, each entry in the sales journal must be posted as a debit to the customer's account in the accounts receivable subsidiary ledger. The total owed by each customer is listed on a schedule of accounts receivable at the end of the accounting period; that total must equal the balance in the accounts receivable control account in the general ledger.

Customer returns of merchandise (or allowances) are recorded as a debit in the contra sales account entitled sales returns and allowances. Another contra sales account, sales discounts, is used when customers pay within a certain specified time in order to receive a discount.

Businesses will often grant a sales discount to credit customers if those customers pay within a certain time. For example, credit terms of 2/10, n/30 indicate that a 2 percent discount will be granted if the invoice is paid within 10 days of the invoice date. If it is not, the customer has 30 days from the invoice date in which to pay.

Both sales returns and allowances and sales discounts are subtracted from sales on the income statement.

Many firms are required to collect provincial sales taxes and GST from their customers and remit those taxes to the government. Taxes collected are recorded in liability accounts entitled provincial sales tax payable and GST charged. Taxes collected from customers and later remitted to the government are not an expense; they are shown on the balance sheet as current liabilities.

Vocabulary Review

Following is a list of the words and terms for this chapter:

contra	merchant
control account	retailer
credit memorandum	subsidiary
merchandise	summary posting
merchandising business	wholesaler

Fill in the blank with the correct word or term from the list.

1. The word that indicates opposition is _____.
2. The accounts receivable account in the general ledger contains a summary of all the postings to accounts receivable and is called a/an _____.
3. Another word for a person who operates a merchandising business is _____.
4. One who sells in large quantities to other businesses is called a/an _____.
5. One who sells in small quantities to customers is called a/an _____.
6. When the totals of a journal are posted rather than the individual entries, it is referred to as _____.
7. A word that means secondary in importance is _____.
8. A service business sells a service; a/an _____ sells a product.
9. A document issued by the seller to the buyer to inform him or her that his or her account receivable is being credited because of a return or an allowance is called a/an _____.
10. Goods that may be bought or sold are referred to as _____.

Match the words and terms on the left with the definitions on the right.

11. contra
12. control account
13. credit memorandum
14. merchandise
15. merchandising business
16. merchant
17. retailer
18. subsidiary
19. summary posting
20. wholesaler

a. when journal totals are posted
b. goods that may be bought or sold
c. secondary in importance
d. a person who operates a merchandising business
e. a person who sells goods in small quantities to customers
f. indicates opposition
g. a person who sells in large quantities to a retailer
h. a business that buys and sells merchandise
i. the accounts receivable account in the general ledger
j. a document issued by the seller informing the buyer that his or her account receivable has been reduced on the seller's books

Exercises

EXERCISE 7.1   In each case, determine the amount of the sales discount and the last day on which the discount may be taken. The months of the year and the number of days in each are included for your reference.

Month	Number of Days	Month	Number of Days
January	31	July	31
February	28	August	31
March	31	September	30
April	30	October	31
May	31	November	30
June	30	December	31

February has 29 days in leap years. An easy way to tell whether or not any particular year is a leap year is to determine whether the year is evenly divisible by 4. For example, 2008 is a leap year because 2008 ÷ 4 = 502. The division comes out even.

	Invoice Amount	Invoice Date	Terms	Amount of Discount	Last Day to Pay and Receive Discount
a.	$ 1,200	January 26	1/15, n/60	_____	_____
b.	3,780	March 22	2/10, n/30	_____	_____
c.	10,460	June 20	2/15, n/30	_____	_____
d.	475	July 29	1/10, n/60	_____	_____
e.	520	August 30	2/15, n/60	_____	_____
f.	1,650	September 30	2/10, n/30	_____	_____
g.	5,720	November 16	1/15, n/60	_____	_____
h.	15,240	October 19	2/15, n/60	_____	_____

EXERCISE 7.2   Claudia Shayne owns a retail shop called "Pick-A-Wick"; she sells unusual candles. Record the following in general journal form and post to the general ledger and the accounts receivable subsidiary ledger. Use journal page 24 and the following account titles and numbers: Cash, 101; Accounts Receivable, 110; Provincial Sales Tax Payable, 210; GST Charged, 230; Sales, 405; and Sales Returns and Allowances, 410.

December 5   sold ten candles to Roger Merino on account; $215 plus 8 percent provincial sales tax and 7 percent GST; invoice 16432

December 6   issued credit memo 203 to Roger Merino, who returned two candles priced at $15 each plus 8 percent provincial sales tax and 7 percent GST

December 23   sold candles to Roger Merino for $48 cash plus 8 percent provincial sales tax and 7 percent GST

December 30   received payment in full from Roger Merino for the balance owed on invoice 16432 less the December 6 return

EXERCISE 7.3 Lee Kawasaki owns a wholesale waterbed store. He sells to retailers and offers credit terms of 2/10, n/30. No provincial sales tax is collected; however, 7 percent GST must be collected. Record the following entries in general journal form; use page 16. Post your entries to the general ledger and to the accounts receivable subsidiary ledger. Use the following account titles and numbers: Cash, 101; Accounts Receivable, 110; GST Charged, 235; Sales, 401; Sales Returns and Allowances, 405; and Sales Discounts, 410.

April 2   sold $4,000 worth of merchandise on account to Waterbeds Galore; terms 2/10, n/30; invoice 2111-40

April 4   Waterbeds Galore reported that three frames from the April 2 purchase were damaged in shipment; Lee issued credit memo 40-32 for $75, plus 7 percent GST

April 12   received a cheque from Waterbeds Galore for the total amount owed minus the April 4 return and the discount

EXERCISE 7.4 Following are T accounts for Carolyn's Candy & Confectionery with a series of transactions related to a sale on account to one customer. The posting reference CR indicates that a payment on account has been received by Carolyn's and has been recorded in the cash receipts journal. The posting reference CP indicates that a payment has been made by Carolyn's and has been recorded in the cash payments journal. Briefly describe what has occurred on (a) June 3, (b) June 6, (c) June 13, and (d) July 12.

Cash			**101**
6/13 CR9	115.00	7/12 CP12	15.00

Accounts Receivable			**110**
6/3 GJ8	172.50	6/6 GJ8	57.50
		6/13 CR9	115.00

Provincial Sales Tax Payable			**220**
6/6 GJ8	4.00	6/3 S6	12.00
7/12 CP12	8.00		

GST Charged			**225**
6/6 GJ8	3.50	6/3 S6	10.50
7/12 CP12	7.00		

Sales			**401**
		6/3 S6	150.00

Sales Returns and Allowances			**405**
6/6 GJ8	50.00		

EXERCISE 7.5   Following is the sales journal for Clay Pots for November 19XX and the general journal entries relating to sales returns and allowances. The terms are 2/10, n/30.

SALES JOURNAL					Accounts Receivable Debit	GST Charged Credit	Sales Credit	PAGE 14
Date	Sales Invoice Number	Customer's Name	Post. Ref.		Accounts Receivable Debit	GST Charged Credit	Sales Credit	
19XX Nov. 1	1762	Barbara Boone			2 2 4 70	1 4 70	2 1 0 —	
3	1763	Buster Jayne			3 6 3 80	2 3 80	3 4 0 —	
8	1764	Jana Trickle			1 9 2 60	1 2 60	1 8 0 —	
10	1765	Barbara Boone			9 6 30	6 30	9 0 —	
15	1766	Bud Marengo			4 8 1 50	3 1 50	4 5 0 —	
18	1767	John Stamas			2 3 5 40	1 5 40	2 2 0 —	
25	1768	Jana Trickle			8 0 25	5 25	7 5 —	
30	1769	Barbara Boone			1 7 1 20	1 1 20	1 6 0 —	
		Total			1 8 4 5 75	1 2 0 75	1 7 2 5 —	

GENERAL JOURNAL			Debit	Credit	PAGE 9
Date	Description	Post. Ref.	Debit	Credit	
19XX Nov. 5	Sales Returns and Allowances	405	4 0 —		
	GST Charged	235	2 80		
	Accounts Receivable—B. Boone	110/✓		4 2 80	
	To record return of merchandise				
10	Sales Returns and Allowances	405	3 0 —		
	GST Charged	235	2 10		
	Accounts Receivable—J. Trickle	110/✓		3 2 10	
	To record return of merchandise				

Answer the following:
   a. Where will the totals of the sales journal be posted?
   b. Including both the sales and general journals, how many separate postings must be made to the accounts receivable subsidiary ledger? To the accounts receivable control account?
   c. If Barbara Boone sends a cheque to Clay Pots on November 11 to cover her total purchases up until that date, how much should she remit?
   d. If Jana Trickle sends a cheque to Clay Pots on November 23, how much should she remit?
   e. What is the last day on which Bud Marengo may pay and still receive the discount? How much will be due on that date?
   f. What is the last day on which Barbara Boone may pay and still receive the discount for her November 30 purchase? How much will be due on that date?

EXERCISE 7.6   Pete Agnos owns a retail men's clothing store called "Man's Choice." Pete's total sales for October 19XX were $28,700. Sales returns and allowances were 1 percent of the gross sales, and sales discounts were 2 percent of the credit sales, which were $12,700. Prepare the revenue section of the income statement for Man's Choice for the month of October 19XX.

EXERCISE 7.7   Following is the accounts receivable subsidiary ledger for Marie's Auto Parts. Calculate the balance after each transaction and prepare a schedule of accounts receivable on March 31, 19XX. The balance in the accounts receivable control account on March 31 is $1,480. CR in the posting reference column indicates that a payment on account has been recorded in the cash receipts journal.

ACCOUNTS RECEIVABLE SUBSIDIARY LEDGER

ACCOUNT: BUG REPAIR SHOP

Date	Explanation	Post. Ref.	Debit	Credit	Balance
19XX Mar. 1		S3	870—		
11		CR4		400—	
15		S4	550—		
19		GJ5		150—	

ACCOUNT: FOREIGN AUTO REPAIR

Date	Explanation	Post. Ref.	Debit	Credit	Balance
19XX Mar. 12		S4	65—		
14		S4	170—		
15		GJ5		40—	

ACCOUNT: JOANNA GRIMM

Date	Explanation	Post. Ref.	Debit	Credit	Balance
19XX Mar. 15		S4	375—		
25		CR4		375—	
28		S4	425—		
31		GJ6		125—	

ACCOUNT: KURT ZANDER

Date	Explanation	Post. Ref.	Debit	Credit	Balance
19XX Mar. 20		S4	206—		
24		S4	115—		
25		S4	65—		
26		GJ6		65—	
30		CR4		206—	

EXERCISE 7.8   Sure Sound Stereos uses a multicolumn sales journal to record its sales on account to customers. It is required to collect 8 percent provincial sales tax and 7 percent GST on all sales. Following is a partial chart of accounts.

110	Accounts Receivable
230	Provincial Sales Tax Payable
235	GST Charged
405	Sales

Complete the multicolumn sales journal and indicate how it would look after all postings have been completed.

																		SALES JOURNAL												PAGE 7			
Date		Sales Invoice Number	Customer's Name	Post. Ref.	Accounts Receivable Debit								PST Payable Credit							GST Charged Credit							Sales Credit							
May	3	305	R. Joyce																												2	4	0	—
	7	306	L. Hemming																												7	8	0	—
	11	307	T. Ayotte																											1	2	1	5	—
	15	308	F. Brooks																													8	4	—
	23	309	L. Lyons																												5	3	0	—
	29	310	C. Little																											1	9	2	0	—
	31	311	N. Thomas																												2	3	0	—
			Total																															

Problems

PROBLEM 7.1   Roxanne Simas owns a feed store called "R & S Feed and Supplies." Roxanne sells to ranchers and is not required to collect provincial sales tax, but she must collect 7 percent GST. Following are the transactions relating to credit sales for March 19XX:

March 1   sold alfalfa to Bar-D Ranch; $800; invoice 1660

March 3   sold grain to Sleepy River Ranch; $180; invoice 1661

March 5   sold supplies to Oak Hill Ranch; $570; invoice 1662

March 7   sold supplies to Sleepy River Ranch; $270; invoice 1663

March 8   issued credit memorandum 420-D to Oak Hill Ranch for supplies returned; $150

March 11   sold supplies to Bar-D Ranch; $950; invoice 1664

March 15   issued credit memorandum 421-D to Bar-D Ranch for supplies returned; $200

March 20   sold hay to Angus Acres; $1,500; invoice 1665

March 24   sold salt blocks to Sleepy River Ranch; $120; invoice 1666

March 25   issued credit memorandum 422-D to Sleepy River Ranch for merchandise returned; $60

March 29   sold grain to Angus Acres; $550; invoice 1667

INSTRUCTIONS   1. Enter the following account titles, numbers, and March 1 balances into the general ledger and the accounts receivable subsidiary ledger.

	General Ledger		Accounts Receivable Subsidiary Ledger	
110	Accounts Receivable	$1,005	Angus Acres	$250
205	GST Charged		Bar-D Ranch	175
400	Sales		Oak Hill Ranch	460
410	Sales Returns and Allowances		Sleepy River Ranch	120

2. Use page 3 for the sales journal and page 7 for the general journal.
3. Assuming that the terms of sales are net 30, record sales on account in the sales journal (use the one in Exercise 7.5 as a model), and record sales returns and allowances in the general journal.
4. Post to the accounts receivable subsidiary ledger immediately after each transaction.
5. After carefully checking the addition, total and rule the sales journal.
6. Post to the general ledger first from the sales journal and then from the general journal.
7. Prepare a schedule of accounts receivable as of March 31. Compare its total with the balance in the accounts receivable control account.

PROBLEM 7.2   Henry Hicks sells small appliances to retailers. He is not required to collect provincial sales tax, but he must collect 7 percent GST. Following are the transactions relating to credit sales for June 19XX for Henry's store, H & H Appliances.

June 1   sold irons and hair dryers to Bestco; $850; invoice 1835

June 4   sold toasters and waffle irons to Buy 'N Save; $1,500; invoice 1836

June 6   issued credit memorandum 704-13 to Bestco for merchandise returned; $250

June 10   sold blenders and mixers to Buy 'N Save; $1,475; invoice 1837

June 15   sold crepe makers to Apco; $750; invoice 1838

June 18   issued credit memo 704-14 to Buy 'N Save for merchandise returned; $50

June 20   sold toaster ovens and car vacuums to Bestco; $1,720; invoice 1839

June 26   sold electric knives to Apco; $460; invoice 1840

June 28   issued credit memorandum 704-15 to Bestco for damaged merchandise; $100

June 30   sold electric fry pans to Apco; $625; invoice 1841

INSTRUCTIONS   1. Enter the following account titles, numbers, and June 1 balances into the general ledger and the accounts receivable subsidiary ledger.

	General Ledger		Accounts Receivable Subsidiary Ledger	
110	Accounts Receivable	$1,980	Apco	$650
205	GST Charged		Bestco	490
401	Sales		Buy 'N Save	840
410	Sales Returns and Allowances			

2. Use page 6 for the sales journal and page 18 for the general journal.
3. Assuming that the terms of sale are net 30, record sales on account in the sales journal and record sales returns and allowances in the general journal. Use the sales journal in Exercise 7.5 as a model.
4. Post to the accounts receivable subsidiary ledger immediately after each transaction.
5. After carefully checking the addition, total and rule the sales journal.

6. Post to the general ledger first from the sales journal and then from the general journal.

7. Prepare a schedule of accounts receivable as of June 30. Compare its total with the balance in the accounts receivable control account.

PROBLEM 7.3   The transactions relating to credit sales for August 19XX for Wanda's Beauty Supplies follow. Wanda is a retailer who sells directly to consumers and is required to collect 8 percent provincial sales tax and 7 percent GST on all sales.

August 1   sold supplies to Andy Johnson; $50; invoice 4302

August 4   sold supplies to Georgia Keene; $125; invoice 4303

August 6   sold supplies to Byron Metzinger; $75; invoice 4304

August 8   issued credit memorandum 16032-A to Georgia Keene for supplies returned; $30

August 10   sold supplies to Andy Johnson; $30; invoice 4305

August 14   sold supplies to Joe Nagasaki; $220; invoice 4306

August 18   issued credit memorandum 16033-A to Byron Metzinger for damaged merchandise; $10

August 22   sold supplies to Andy Johnson; $40; invoice 4307

August 24   issued credit memo 16034-A to Joe Nagasaki for merchandise returned; $20

August 26   sold supplies to Byron Metzinger; $75; invoice 4308

August 29   sold supplies to Georgia Keene; $165; invoice 4309

August 30   issued credit memorandum 16035-A to Georgia Keene for merchandise returned; $50

INSTRUCTIONS   1. Enter the following account titles, numbers, and August 1 balances into the general ledger and the accounts receivable subsidiary ledger.

General Ledger		Accounts Receivable Subsidiary Ledger	
110	Accounts Receivable	$500	Andy Johnson	$125
210	Provincial Sales Tax Payable	120	Georgia Keene	80
230	GST Charged	105	Byron Metzinger	240
410	Sales		Joe Nagasaki	55
420	Sales Returns and Allowances			

2. Use page 8 for the sales journal and page 14 for the general journal.

3. Assuming that the terms of sale are net 30, record sales plus 8 percent provincial sales tax and 7 percent GST in the multicolumn sales journal and record sales returns in the general journal.

4. Post to the accounts receivable subsidiary ledger immediately after each transaction.

5. After carefully checking the addition, total and rule the sales journal.

6. Post to the general ledger first from the sales journal and then from the general journal.

7. Prepare a schedule of accounts receivable as of August 31. Compare its total with the balance in the Accounts Receivable control account.

PROBLEM 7.4 Wiley Manual owns a wholesale furniture warehouse called "The House of Wiley." No provincial sales tax is charged to his customers, but 7 percent GST is collected on all sales. The following transactions relating to credit sales took place during the month of May 19XX. Be sure to read through all the instructions before beginning the problem.

May 1   sold merchandise on account to Mack's Bar Stools; $3,000, terms 2/10, n/30; invoice 2000

May 4   sold merchandise on account to Kitchen Korner; $4,500, terms 2/10, n/30; invoice 2001

May 6   issued credit memorandum 14-280 to grant a $200 allowance to Mack's Bar Stools on the May 1 purchase because of damage to several stools

May 10   received a cheque from Mack's Bar Stools for the balance owed on May 1 purchase less the return on May 6

May 15   sold merchandise on account to House of Maple; $970, terms 2/10, n/30; invoice 2002

May 16   received a cheque from Kitchen Korner for the balance owed on May 4 purchase

May 19   sold merchandise on account to Mack's Bar Stools; $1,500, terms 2/10, n/30; invoice 2003

May 22   issued credit memorandum 14-281 to House of Maple; it returned $200 of May 15 purchase

May 24   sold merchandise on account to Chairs, Inc.; $1,050, terms 2/10, n/30; invoice 2004

May 25   received a cheque from House of Maple for payment of the balance owed on May 15 invoice less the return on May 22

May 27   sold merchandise on account to Chairs, Inc.; $500, terms 2/10, n/30; invoice 2005

May 30   sold merchandise on account to House of Maple; $700, terms 2/10, n/30; invoice 2006

INSTRUCTIONS 1. Enter the following account titles and numbers into the general ledger and the accounts receivable subsidiary ledger. The accounts receivable control account on May 1 has a zero balance because all customers had paid in full as of that date.

	General Ledger		Accounts Receivable Subsidiary Ledger	
101	Cash	$4,620	Chairs, Inc.	0
110	Accounts Receivable	0	House of Maple	0
235	GST Charged		Kitchen Korner	0
401	Sales		Mack's Bar Stools	0
406	Sales Discounts			
411	Sales Returns and Allowances			

2. Use page 5 for the sales journal and page 11 for the general journal.
3. Record sales on account in a sales journal and record sales returns and allowances in the general journal. Record receipt of cash and sales discounts in the general journal. (Later on, you will record all incoming cash in the cash receipts journal.)
4. Post to the accounts receivable subsidiary ledger immediately after each transaction.
5. After carefully checking the addition, total and rule the sales journal.
6. Post to the general ledger first from the sales journal and then from the general journal.
7. Prepare a schedule of accounts receivable as of May 31. Compare its total with the balance in the accounts receivable control account.

PROBLEM 7.5   Following are the transactions for Super Shirts, a retail shirt and sweater store, relating to credit sales for the month of November 19XX. Eight percent provincial sales tax and 7 percent GST must be collected on all sales. Credit terms for all customers are 3/10, n/30.

November 1   sold merchandise to Gabrielle Ladouceur; $250; invoice 3301

November 3   sold merchandise to Jana Harris; $560; invoice 3302

November 5   sold merchandise to Lynda Bruining; $650; invoice 3303

November 9   issued credit memorandum 4062-A to Jana Harris for damaged merchandise; $30

November 10   received a cheque from Gabrielle Ladouceur for payment of November 1 invoice

November 13   received a cheque from Jana Harris in payment of November 3 invoice less the November 9 return

November 15   sold merchandise to Denise Vernon; $95; invoice 3304

November 18   sold merchandise to Gabrielle Ladouceur; $80; invoice 3305

November 20   sold merchandise to Lynda Bruining; $150; invoice 3306

November 22   received a cheque from Lynda Bruining in payment of November 5 invoice

November 24   issued credit memorandum 4063-A to Denise Vernon for merchandise returned; $20

November 25 received a cheque from Denise Vernon in payment of November 15 invoice less the return of November 24

November 27 issued credit memorandum 4064-A to Lynda Bruining for damaged merchandise, $50

November 29 sold merchandise to Jana Harris; $240; invoice 3307

November 30 received a cheque from Lynda Bruining in payment of November 20 invoice less the return of November 27

INSTRUCTIONS

1. Enter the following account titles and numbers into the general ledger and the accounts receivable subsidiary ledger. The accounts receivable control account on November 1 has a zero balance because all customers had paid in full as of that date.

	General Ledger		Accounts Receivable Subsidiary Ledger
101	Cash	$3,740	Lynda Bruining
110	Accounts Receivable		Jana Harris
210	Provincial Sales Tax Payable		Gabrielle Ladouceur
215	GST Charged		Denise Vernon
401	Sales		
405	Sales Discounts		
410	Sales Returns and Allowances		

2. Use page 11 for the sales journal and page 26 for the general journal.
3. Record sales on account in a sales journal and record sales returns and allowances in the general journal. Record receipts of cash and sales discounts in the general journal. (Later on, you will record all incoming cash in the cash receipts journal.)
4. Post to the accounts receivable ledger immediately after each transaction.
5. After carefully checking the addition, total and rule the sales journal.
6. Post to the general ledger first from the sales journal and then from the general journal.
7. Prepare a schedule of accounts receivable and compare its total with the balance in the accounts receivable control account.

The Purchases Journal and the Accounts Payable Subsidiary Ledger

Learning Objectives

When you have completed this chapter, you should
1. have an increased understanding of accounting terminology.
2. be able to record entries directly into the purchases journal and perform summary posting.
3. be able to post to the accounts payable subsidiary ledger and prepare a schedule of accounts payable.
4. be able to account for freight charges.
5. be able to account for purchases returns and allowances.
6. be able to calculate and account for purchases discounts.
7. be able to calculate single trade discounts.
8. recognize several different forms of credit terms.

Vocabulary

debit memorandum   a document issued by the buyer that informs the seller that his or her account payable has been debited because of a return or an allowance

FOB destination   free on board to destination; the seller will pay the freight charges to the destination of the goods, where title to the goods passes to the buyer

FOB shipping point   free on board to shipping point; the seller will pay for the cost of loading the goods at the shipping point, where the title of the goods passes to the buyer; the buyer will pay freight charges

in transit   in the process of being moved from one place to another

list price   the price listed in the seller's catalogue

net price   the list price minus the trade discount

purchase invoice   the invoice that is received by the buyer when the ordered goods are shipped; from the point of view of the seller, it is a sales invoice and is prepared by the seller

purchase order   a form prepared, usually by the purchasing department, giving written authorization to buy the merchandise

purchase requisition   a form made out by a department requesting the purchasing department to prepare a formal purchase order

trade discount   a discount given to the buyer at the time of purchase; may be given as an incentive to the buyer

vendor   a seller of merchandise

Introduction

In Chapter Seven, we learned how Frank Phelps, owner of Sports Haven, dealt with some of the special accounting needs of merchandising businesses. Specifically, the unit dealt with credit sales of merchandise. In this unit, we will see how Frank handles the purchase of merchandise for resale.

Purchases and the Purchase Invoice

In a small firm, a purchase order may be made directly and simply. Often, the sales representative will obtain an order from the owner or manager when he or she makes a regular call on the particular business. Or, a purchase order may be placed by phone. When the merchandise is delivered, it is important for the buyer to receive a copy of the seller's invoice and to check carefully the goods received against that invoice.

In larger firms, a more formal approach to purchasing is used. A **purchase requisition** is made by any department and is forwarded to the purchasing department. Purchase requisitions are made with multiple copies; one of the copies is sent to the purchasing department and one is kept by the department that issues the request. No accounting entry is made at this time.

When the proper authority in the purchasing department approves the requisition, a formal **purchase order** is prepared. Purchase orders are numbered consecutively and are carefully accounted for. Multiple copies are usually prepared: the original will be sent to the supplier from whom the merchandise is being purchased; one copy is retained by the purchasing department; one copy goes to the department that placed the order; and one copy goes to the receiving clerk. When the merchandise is received, the receiving clerk will check the actual sales invoice from the **vendor** against the purchase order to make sure that everything ordered was actually delivered and will verify that the terms on the sales invoice are the same terms originally agreed upon. It is good practice to send copies of purchase orders to the accounting department, too, so that invoice calculations may be verified and prices checked against the sales invoice.

When the sales invoice arrives, either with the merchandise ordered or before it, a copy of the invoice is sent to the accounting department to be recorded. The sales invoice received from the vendor is, from the point of view of the buyer, a **purchase invoice**. Therefore, at this point in time, the accountant will be recording the purchase of merchandise.

Following is the purchase invoice that arrived with the shipment when Frank Phelps ordered skis and bindings from Cold Weather Sports, Inc.

Cold Weather Sports, Inc.			**Invoice No. 5307**
204 Superior St.			
Sault Ste. Marie, Ontario		**Invoice Date**	**Your Order No. & Date**
P6B 4K9		June 4 — 608 — June 1	

Terms	**FOB**	**Shipped Via**	**Shipped from**
2/15, n/30	Shipping Point	Provincial Transport	Sault Ste. Marie

Sold to:	**Ship to:**
Sports Haven	Same
740 Main St.	
Barrie, Ontario	
L4M 3X9	

Quantity Shipped	**Description**	**Unit Price**	**Extension**
6	Tuf-Lite, 170 mm, Skis, #S46130	85.00	510.00
10	Tuf-Lite, 190 mm, Skis, #S46132	85.00	850.00
8	Ski-Rite, 150 mm, Skis, #Q04329	50.00	400.00
20	Eazy-On Bindings, #J46523	40.00	800.00
			2,560.00
	7% GST		179.20
	Total		$2,739.20

When this shipment arrives from Cold Weather Sports, Inc., the person who receives the goods should check the incoming order to make sure that everything that appears on the invoice is included with the shipment. The receiving person will be asked to sign the invoice indicating that all the goods are there and are in satisfactory condition. If a careful check is not made at this point, it may be discovered later that a portion of the shipment is missing or that some items have been damaged **in transit**.

GST Accounts

In Chapter Seven, the GST Charged account was introduced; it was used each time a sale or a sales return and allowance was made. Remember that the GST Charged account is a *liability* because the tax is collected on behalf of the federal government and the money must be remitted to Revenue Canada, Customs and Excise, at appropriate intervals.

The goods and services tax (GST) is a multistage tax that applies to most transactions throughout the production and marketing process. The majority of goods and services sold or provided in Canada are taxable under the GST at the rate of 7 percent. Some examples of goods and services taxed at 7 percent include:

- automobiles
- gasoline and car repairs
- soft drinks, candies, and confections
- restaurant meals
- clothing and footwear
- advertising services
- taxi and limousine fares
- legal and accounting fees
- hotel accommodations
- barbers' and hairstylists' services.

A limited number of goods and services, such as sales of basic groceries and prescription drugs, are also taxable, *but at a rate of 0 percent*. Some examples include:

- basic groceries (milk, bread, vegetables)
- agricultural and most fishery products (wheat, grain, raw wool, unprocessed tobacco, fish for human consumption, and farm livestock, with some exceptions such as horses)
- prescription drugs and drug dispensing fees
- medical devices (hearing aids, wheelchairs, eyeglasses, etc.)
- exports.

Not only are the customers of a business charged 7 percent GST when a *sale* is made to them, but also the business is charged 7 percent GST when a *purchase* is made. The account used to show the amount of GST that must be paid on a purchase is called GST Paid and it, too, is classified as a liability. Each time a purchase is made, GST Paid is debited because, even though it is classified as a liability, it really represents an *expense* to the business. The total of GST paid (on purchases) is deducted from the total of GST charged (on sales), with the difference either remitted to or claimed from the federal government.

The Purchases Account

All merchandise that is purchased for resale is debited to a special account called Purchases; it is assigned a number in the new category, cost of goods sold. Accounts that appear in the cost of goods sold category will be used in calculating the actual cost price of the merchandise that is sold. Cost of goods sold will be discussed in detail in Chapter Eleven.

Assume that Sports Haven recorded the credit purchase of ski equipment from Cold Weather Sports, Inc. in a general journal. The entry would look like this:

GENERAL JOURNAL					PAGE 11	
Date		Description	Post. Ref.	Debit	Credit	
19XX June	4	Purchases		2560 —		
		GST Paid		179 20		
		Accounts Payable—Cold Weather Sports, Inc.			2739 20	
		To Record Purchase; Terms 2/15, n/30				

Remember that the purchases account is debited only for the purchase of merchandise for resale. When merchandise is purchased that is not for resale, it is debited to its appropriate asset account. For example, assume that Frank purchased a small computer on account for use by his bookkeeper. The entry would be a debit to Office Equipment and a credit to Accounts Payable and would be recorded in the general journal rather than the purchases journal.

The Purchases Journal

Sports Haven uses special journals to record sales, purchases, cash receipts, and cash payments. The general journal is not used for recording purchases on account because: (1) for each entry, the words *Purchases, GST Paid,* and *Accounts Payable* would have to be written into the journal; and (2) for each entry, three amounts would have to be posted to the general ledger.

As is true with the sales journal, use of the purchases journal saves the bookkeeper's valuable time. The purchases journal is used only for the recording of credit purchases of merchandise for resale. Because this is the case, every entry in the purchases journal will result in a debit to purchases, a debit to GST Paid, and a credit to accounts payable. As with the sales journal, it is not necessary to write the words *Purchases, GST Paid,* and *Accounts Payable* with each entry. It is necessary only to enter the date, the creditor's name, the invoice number and date, and the correct amounts in the appropriate columns.

Following is the purchases journal for Sports Haven for the month of June 19XX:

PURCHASES JOURNAL						PAGE 6
Date	Supplier's Name	Invoice Number	Post. Ref.	Purchases Debit	GST Paid Debit	Accounts Payable Credit
June 4	Cold Weather Sports, Inc.	5307		2560 —	179 20	2739 20
8	Running World	1042		574 —	40 18	614 18
10	Racquet Warehouse	879		740 —	51 80	791 80
14	Running World	1078		760 —	53 20	813 20
19	Sports Supplies	7061		1409 —	98 63	1507 63
21	Cold Weather Sports, Inc.	5390		962 —	67 34	1029 34
28	Running World	1091		416 —	29 12	445 12
	Total			7421 —	519 47	7940 47

After the purchases journal has been totalled, add the columns to ensure that the total of the debit columns is equal to the total of the credit column.

$$\begin{array}{r} \$7,421.00 \\ \underline{519.47} \\ \$7,940.47 \end{array}$$

Once the proof has been constructed, draw a single line across the amount columns and a double line beneath the totals across all columns of the journal except the supplier's name column.

Posting the Purchases Journal

The total of the purchases journal must be posted to the general ledger. Following are the general ledger accounts affected.

ACCOUNT: ACCOUNTS PAYABLE   **ACCT. NO. 205**

Date	Explanation	Post. Ref.	Debit	Credit	Balance
19XX June 30		P6		7 9 4 0 47	7 9 4 0 47

ACCOUNT: GST PAID   **ACCT. NO. 215**

Date	Explanation	Post. Ref.	Debit	Credit	Balance
19XX June 30		P6	5 1 9 47		5 1 9 47

ACCOUNT: PURCHASES   **ACCT. NO. 511**

Date	Explanation	Post. Ref.	Debit	Credit	Balance
19XX June 30		P6	7 4 2 1 —		7 4 2 1 —

If all of Sports Haven's credit purchases had been recorded in the general journal, not only would the journalizing have been much more time-consuming, but seven separate postings to the purchases account and seven separate postings to the GST Paid and accounts payable accounts would have been required. Summary posting (when journal totals are posted) saves a great deal of time.

The Accounts Payable Subsidiary Ledger

The accounts payable subsidiary ledger shows the amounts owed to individual creditors. All charge purchases, purchases returns and allowances, and payments made to creditors appear in this ledger. The accounts payable account in the general ledger is, like accounts receivable, a control account. The balance in the accounts payable account represents the total amount owed to all creditors. The accounts payable subsidiary ledger shows the individual amounts owed. Of course, the total of the individual creditors' balances must equal the balance in the control account.

You will be working with three different ledgers from now on. They are:
1. the general ledger, which contains separate records for all assets, liabilities, owner's equity, revenue, cost of goods sold, and expense accounts;
2. the accounts receivable subsidiary ledger, which contains individual accounts for all charge customers showing all credit sales made to them, their sales returns and allowances, and all payments received; and,
3. the accounts payable subsidiary ledger, which contains individual accounts for all creditors showing all credit purchases, purchases returns and allowances, and all payments made.

The accounts receivable and accounts payable subsidiary ledgers are frequently referred to as simply the accounts receivable ledger and the accounts payable ledger.

Posting to the Accounts Payable Subsidiary Ledger

Credit postings to the accounts payable subsidiary ledger come primarily from the purchases journal. Debit entries come mainly from the cash payments journal (when money is paid on account). Debit or credit entries may also come from the general journal; for example, a correcting entry may be made or a purchases return or allowance may be granted.

The purchases journal, the general ledger accounts affected when the total is posted, and the accounts payable ledger (arranged in alphabetical order) follow.

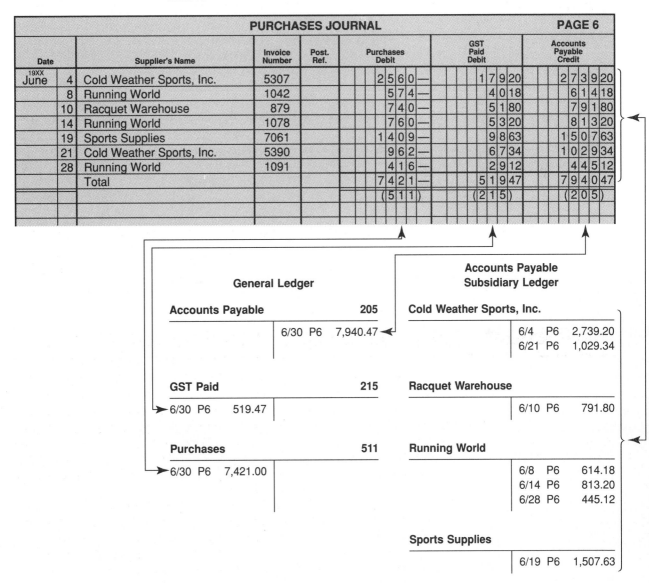

PURCHASES JOURNAL   **PAGE 6**

Date	Supplier's Name	Invoice Number	Post. Ref.	Purchases Debit	GST Paid Debit	Accounts Payable Credit
June 4	Cold Weather Sports, Inc.	5307		2560 —	179 20	2739 20
8	Running World	1042		574 —	40 18	614 18
10	Racquet Warehouse	879		740 —	51 80	791 80
14	Running World	1078		760 —	53 20	813 20
19	Sports Supplies	7061		1409 —	98 63	1507 63
21	Cold Weather Sports, Inc.	5390		962 —	67 34	1029 34
28	Running World	1091		416 —	29 12	445 12
	Total			7421 —	519 47	7940 47
				(511)	(215)	(205)

General Ledger

Accounts Payable   **205**

	6/30 P6	7,940.47

GST Paid   **215**

6/30 P6	519.47

Purchases   **511**

6/30 P6	7,421.00

Accounts Payable Subsidiary Ledger

Cold Weather Sports, Inc.

6/4	P6	2,739.20
6/21	P6	1,029.34

Racquet Warehouse

6/10	P6	791.80

Running World

6/8	P6	614.18
6/14	P6	813.20
6/28	P6	445.12

Sports Supplies

6/19	P6	1,507.63

When an amount is posted to the accounts payable ledger, place a check mark (✓) opposite the creditor's name in the posting reference column of the purchases journal and write P and the page number in the creditor's account in the ledger. When the total of the purchases journal is posted, indicate that by writing the account numbers for purchases, GST paid, and accounts payable under the column totals.

The Schedule of Accounts Payable

A schedule of accounts payable is prepared at the end of the accounting period and alphabetically lists each creditor and the amount owed. The total of the schedule of accounts payable must be compared with the balance in the accounts payable control account. The two figures must be the same; if they are not, the bookkeeper must search for the error.

    The accounts payable subsidiary ledger, the schedule of accounts payable, and the accounts payable control account follow.

ACCOUNTS PAYABLE SUBSIDIARY LEDGER

ACCOUNT: COLD WEATHER SPORTS, INC.

Date	Explanation	Post. Ref.	Debit	Credit	Balance
19XX June 4		P6		2 7 3 9 20	2 7 3 9 20
21		P6		1 0 2 9 34	3 7 6 8 54

ACCOUNT: RACQUET WAREHOUSE

Date	Explanation	Post. Ref.	Debit	Credit	Balance
19XX June 10		P6		7 9 1 80	7 9 1 80

ACCOUNT: RUNNING WORLD

Date	Explanation	Post. Ref.	Debit	Credit	Balance
19XX June 8		P6		6 1 4 18	6 1 4 18
14		P6		8 1 3 20	1 4 2 7 38
28		P6		4 4 5 12	1 8 7 2 50

ACCOUNT: SPORTS SUPPLIES

Date	Explanation	Post. Ref.	Debit	Credit	Balance
19XX June 19		P6		1 5 0 7 63	1 5 0 7 63

Sports Haven **Schedule of Accounts Payable** **June 30, 19XX**		
Cold Weather Sports, Inc.	$3,768.54	
Racquet Warehouse	791.80	
Running World	1,872.50	
Sports Supplies	1,507.63	
Total		$7,940.47

ACCOUNT: ACCOUNTS PAYABLE   **ACCT. NO. 205**

Date		Explanation	Post. Ref.	Debit	Credit	Balance
19XX June	30		P6		7 9 4 0 47	7 9 4 0 47

The accounts payable account would normally have more than one entry in it. For example, payments made on account would be posted to it from the cash payments journal (which will be introduced in the next chapter), and purchases returns and allowances would be posted to it from the general journal.

The Freight In Account

Often, freight charges are incurred when merchandise is purchased. Such charges are logically considered to be an added cost of the merchandise purchased, because it is usually the buyer who pays the freight charges, either directly or indirectly through higher prices for the merchandise purchased. For this reason, the cost of freight could be debited directly to the purchases account. Most businesses, however, prefer to keep freight costs separate from the cost of purchases. Knowing exactly how much is spent for various methods of transporting goods is valuable to management in controlling costs. Decisions have to be made concerning which type of transportation (air, truck, rail) to use; keeping careful accounting records of freight costs provides valuable information in making those decisions.

An account called Freight In is debited for freight costs. Sports Haven's journal entry to record the transportation charge on the shipment of skis and bindings from Sault Ste. Marie is as follows:

		GENERAL JOURNAL				PAGE 6	
Date		Description	Post. Ref.	Debit		Credit	
19XX June	8	Freight In		1 75 —			
		GST Paid		1 2 25			
		Accounts Payable—Provincial Transport				1 8 7 25	
		To Record Freight Charges on Cold Weather Sports,					
		Inc., Invoice 5307					

Of course, if the freight charges were paid by cash, the entry would appear in the cash payments journal.

The freight in account is, like purchases, a cost of goods sold account, and its balance will be added to net purchases on the income statement as shown:

Net Purchases	$7,421
Add Freight In	175
Cost of Purchases	$7,596

FOB Shipping Point and FOB Destination

Before goods are shipped, there must be an agreement between buyer and seller as to which party will pay the freight charges. The purchase order and the seller's invoice will stipulate either FOB shipping point or FOB destination. **FOB shipping point** means free on board to the shipping point, or the seller will pay to have the goods loaded at the point of shipment, but will not pay the transportation costs from the shipping point to the destination. Title to the goods passes to the buyer at the shipping point, and the buyer will pay the freight charges upon arrival of the merchandise.

If the terms are **FOB destination**, that means free on board to the destination agreed upon, and the seller will pay the freight charges. Title to the goods passes to the buyer when the goods arrive.

Whether the freight terms are FOB shipping point or FOB destination, it may be assumed that the buyer will pay the transportation charges, either directly or indirectly.

Debit and Credit Memoranda

When damaged or unsatisfactory merchandise is returned, or when the buyer is given an allowance for such, the buyer issues a **debit memorandum** to the seller indicating that the buyer's account payable has been debited or reduced. When the bookkeeper receives a debit memorandum, she or he records it by crediting an account called purchases returns and allowances and debiting accounts payable in the general journal. This same transaction on the books of the seller would be recorded as a debit to sales returns and allowances and as a credit to accounts receivable. If the seller (instead of the buyer) had issued the memo, it would have been called a credit memorandum, because on the books of the seller, a credit to accounts receivable is being recorded. Thus, a credit memorandum can reduce accounts receivable or increase accounts payable, and a debit memorandum can increase accounts receivable or reduce accounts payable, depending on whom (buyer or seller) is issuing it.

Purchases Returns and Allowances

Although it would be possible simply to credit the purchases account for returns and allowances, it is good accounting practice to keep a separate record for them. It may help management to make future decisions about which merchandise to buy or which vendor to contact for a particular product. An excessive number of returns of any product or to any vendor may indicate that the purchasing policy needs revision.

Assume that on June 9 Frank Phelps, owner of Sports Haven, contacted Cold Weather Sports by telephone to report that the Eazy-On bindings that it had sent were factory-damaged and had to be adjusted before they could be used. The manager of Cold Weather Sports suggested that if Frank would keep the bindings and make the necessary adjustments, he would give Sports Haven a $10 allowance on each binding ordered. Frank agreed and a $200 debit memorandum was issued by Sports Haven on June 9. The general journal entry and the related T accounts for Sports Haven's recording of the allowance follow. Note that the original purchase from Cold Weather Sports is shown in the accounts payable control account even though such individual entries are not usually shown in the control account. (Credit purchases, remember, are individually recorded in the purchases journal, but only the totals of the columns are posted to the general ledger.)

GENERAL JOURNAL					PAGE 6
Date	Description	Post. Ref.	Debit		Credit
June 9	Accounts Payable—Cold Weather Sports, Inc.	205/✓	2 1 4 —		
	GST Paid	215			1 4 —
	Purchases Returns and Allowances	512			2 0 0 —
	To Record Debit Memorandum, Invoice 5307				

General Ledger

Accounts Payable   205

6/9 GJ6 214.00	6/4 P6 2,739.20

GST Paid   215

6/4 P6 179.20	6/9 GJ6 14.00

Purchases Returns and Allowances   512

	6/9 GJ6 200.00

Accounts Payable Subsidiary Ledger

Cold Weather Sports, Inc.

6/9 GJ6 214.00	6/4 P6 2,739.20

The Purchases Returns and Allowances account appears in the cost of goods sold category on the chart of accounts along with purchases. Purchases returns and allowances is a contra purchases account because its balance is subtracted from the balance of purchases on the income statement.

Purchases Discounts

Many times the buyer will be allowed a discount if the invoice is paid within a certain number of days. The terms indicated on invoice 5307 from Cold Weather Sports, Inc. are 2/15, n/30. If Sports Haven pays within 15 days of the invoice date, a 2 percent discount may be deducted from the total invoice price of the merchandise. Remember, too, that Sports Haven received a $200 allowance for damaged merchandise on invoice 5307. The procedure for calculating the amount due if it is paid within the discount period is as follows:

Step 1.   Calculate the last day for payment within the discount period. Terms are 2/15, n/30 and the invoice date is June 4.

June 4
+   15 (2/15, n/30)
June 19 last day for payment within the discount period.

Step 2.   Calculate the balance owed on the merchandise by referring to the T account for Cold Weather Sports.

Cold Weather Sports, Inc.

6/9 GJ6	214.00	6/4 P6	2,739.20
			2,525.20

Step 3.   Calculate the cash discount. Remember, it must be figured on the *actual price of the merchandise* minus the return *without GST*.

a. $2,560 - $200 = $2,360
b. $2,360 × .02 = $47.20

Step 4.   Calculate the amount owed on the invoice.
Subtract the amount of the discount from the balance in Cold Weather Sports, Inc.'s Account.

$2,525.20 - $47.20 = $2,478.00

The invoice must be paid by June 19 in order to receive the 2 percent discount. On or before that date, a cheque for $2,478 may be remitted to Cold Weather Sports, Inc. The discount is recorded as a credit to an account called Purchases Discounts. It, like Purchases Returns and Allowances, is shown in the cost of goods sold category on the chart of accounts. Purchases Discounts is a contra purchases account and will be subtracted from the balance of purchases on the income statement. The general journal entry on Sports Haven's books to record the payment of Cold Weather Sports' invoice 5307 looks like this:

GENERAL JOURNAL				PAGE 6	
Date	**Description**	**Post. Ref.**	**Debit**	**Credit**	
19XX June 19	Accounts Payable—Cold Weather Sports, Inc.	205/✓	2 5 2 5 20		
	Cash	101		2 4 7 8 —	
	Purchases Discounts	513		4 7 20	
	To Record Payment in Full of Invoice 5307				

Note that accounts payable has been debited for $2,525.20, the balance owed on the invoice, even though only $2,478 was actually paid. This is necessary to show that Sports Haven has, in effect, saved $47.20 by taking advantage of the discount and does not owe any more on this particular invoice.

The following T accounts outline Sports Haven's original purchase from Cold Weather Sports, the purchase allowance, and the payment of the invoice within the discount period.

The entries are outlined as follows:

a. a debit to Purchases, a debit to GST Paid, and credits to Accounts Payable and Cold Weather Sports to record the original purchase.

b. a debit to Accounts Payable and Cold Weather Sports, a credit to GST Paid, and a credit to Purchases Returns and Allowances to record the $200 debit memorandum issued by Sports Haven.

c. a debit to Accounts Payable and Cold Weather Sports and credits to Purchases Discounts and Cash to record payment of the invoice within the discount period.

General Ledger

Accounts Payable Subsidiary Ledger

Cash				101
6/1 Balance 10,000.00		6/19 GJ6	2,478.00 (c)	

Cold Weather Sports, Inc.				
(b) 6/9 GJ6	214.00	6/4 P6	2,739.20 (a)	
(c) 6/19 GJ6	2,525.20			

Accounts Payable				205
(b) 6/9 GJ6	214.00	6/4 P6	2,739.20 (a)	
(c) 6/19 GJ6	2,525.20			

GST Paid				215
(a) 6/4 P6	179.20	6/9 GJ6	14.00 (b)	

Purchases		511
(a) 6/4 P6	2,560.00	

Purchases Returns and Allowances			512
	6/9 GJ6	200.00 (b)	

Purchases Discounts			513
	6/19 GJ6	47.20 (c)	

Purchases discounts and purchases returns and allowances are subtracted from purchases on the income statement. This is logical because a return or an allowance is like a purchase not made, and the purchases discount reduces the cost of the merchandise. The portion of the income statement that shows Purchases and its related accounts looks like this:

Partial Income Statement			
Cost of Goods Sold			
Purchases		$45,000	
Less: Purchases Returns and Allowances	$2,700		
Purchases Discounts	$2,900	5,600	
Net Purchases		39,400	
Add Freight In		1,200	
Cost of Purchases			$40,600

Single Trade Discounts

Most sellers print catalogues from which buyers may choose their merchandise. The catalogues list the seller's prices, and the catalogue price is thus called the **list price**. Sellers may grant a discount at the time of the sale to the buyer, and that discount is called a **trade discount**. The list price minus the trade discount is known as the **net price**. By changing the trade discount offered, the seller may easily change the price charged. It is easier and more economical for the seller to change the discount offered than to change the entire catalogue. In addition, larger trade discounts may be offered to customers who place larger orders.

Trade discounts are not recorded on the books of the seller or the buyer. Only the actual price charged for the merchandise is recorded. It is necessary, though, for the bookkeeper to be able to calculate trade discounts so that invoices may be checked for accuracy.

Assume that on June 21 a sales representative from Running World calls on Frank Phelps of Sports Haven. Frank orders 30 pairs of running shoes with a list price of $25 per pair minus a 10 percent trade discount. The total price paid for the shoes is calculated as follows:

Step 1.   Calculate the total list price.
           30 pairs × $25 = $750

Step 2.   Calculate the trade discount (10 percent).

           a. Move the decimal point two places to the left in 10 percent.
              10% = 10. = .10
           b. Multiply the list price by the trade discount.
              $750 × .10 = $75

Step 3.   Calculate the net price of the invoice.

           Calculate the total purchase price by subtracting the trade discount from the list price.
           $750 − $75 = $675

Step 4.   Calculate the total invoice price.

           a. Multiply the net price of the invoice by 7 percent GST.
              $675 × .07 = $47.25
           b. Add the net price of the invoice to the 7 percent GST.
              $675 + $47.25 = $722.25

The net price of the invoice is $675; the total invoice price is $722.25. On the books of Sports Haven, the entry will be recorded as a debit to Purchases for the net price of $675, a debit to GST Paid for $47.25, and a credit to Accounts Payable for the full amount owing of $722.25. On the books of Running World, the entry will be recorded as a debit of $722.25 to Accounts Receivable, a credit to GST Payable of $47.25, and a credit to Sales of $675.

Remember, the amount of the trade discount is not recorded on the books of the buyer or the seller.

Trade Discounts and Credit Terms on the Same Invoice

Frequently, a trade discount will be offered to the buyer along with credit terms to encourage early payment of the invoice.

For example, assume that on July 11 Sports Haven purchased merchandise from Racquet Warehouse with a list price of $1,500 minus a trade discount of 5 percent. In addition, credit terms of 2/10, n/30 were offered. The net price for the purchase is:
  a. $1,500 × .05 = $75
  b. $1,500 − $75 = $1,425 (net invoice price).

The total invoice price is:

c. $1,425 \times .07 = \$99.75$

d. $\$1,425 + \$99.75 = \$1,524.75$ (total invoice price).

The entry will be recorded in the purchases journal as follows:

PURCHASES JOURNAL						PAGE 7	
Date	Supplier's Name	Invoice Number	Post Ref.	Purchases Debit	GST Paid Debit	Accounts Payable Credit	
19XX July 11	Racquet Warehouse	956		1425—	99 75	1524 75	

The last day for payment of the invoice within the discount period is July 21 (July 11 + 10 days). The discount is 2 percent of $1,425, or $28.50.

The entry in general journal form to record the payment of the invoice is as follows:

GENERAL JOURNAL				PAGE 8	
Date	Description	Post. Ref.	Debit	Credit	
19XX July 21	Accounts Payable—Racquet Warehouse		1524 75		
	Cash			1496 25	
	Purchases Discounts			28 50	
	To Record Payment of Invoice 956				

Note that the trade discount was not recorded on the books. Rather, it was calculated and subtracted from the list price ($1,500 − $75 = $1,425). The purchases discount was calculated on the actual purchase price, $1,425.

Credit Terms

There are many different credit terms offered to buyers. Some of the more common ones are listed here.

Terms	
2/10, n/30	A 2 percent discount is offered if the invoice is paid within 10 days of the invoice date; or, the net amount of the invoice is due within 30 days of the invoice date.
2/10, EOM	A 2 percent discount is allowed if the invoice is paid within 10 days after the end of the current month.
n/10, EOM	No discount is allowed. The net amount is due within 10 days after the end of the current month.
30 days	No discount is allowed. The net amount is due within 30 days after the date of the invoice.
COD	Cash on delivery or collect on delivery. The amount of the invoice must be paid at the time the goods are delivered.

Accounting for GST

In Chapter Seven, it was pointed out that each time a sale was made, 7 percent GST was credited to the GST Charged account. If there was a sales return or allowance granted to a customer, the GST relating to the sales return or allowance was debited to GST Charged; this reduced the amount owing to the federal government.

In this chapter, for every purchase made, GST Paid is debited. The GST that must be paid on all purchases is in effect an expense and that is why it must be *debited* to the GST Paid account. Each time there is a purchase return or allowance, GST Paid is credited because the expense has decreased.

There is a third GST account that is also classified as a liability — GST Owing (Refund). In Chapter Seven, the GST Charged account was used as a liability to record the amount collected on sales on behalf of the federal government. In this chapter, GST Paid is used to record the tax expense on purchases.

At the appropriate intervals, both the GST Charged account and the GST Paid account must be closed out to GST Owing (Refund) account. If the GST Owing (Refund) account has a credit balance, that amount must be remitted to the federal government. If the GST Owing (Refund) account has a debit balance, that amount is owing to the business as a refund *from* the federal government. In most instances, the GST Owing (Refund) account will have a credit balance, because successful businesses sell merchandise at a higher price than the price for which it was purchased.

Summary

In many large firms, the purchasing process requires that a purchase requisition be filled out by the department making the request, and a purchase order be filled out by the purchasing department. The accounting entry is recorded upon receipt of the goods ordered and purchase invoice. All goods bought for resale will be debited to an account called purchases. A new category of accounts called cost of goods sold will include the purchases account, freight in, purchases returns and allowances, and purchases discounts.

A special journal, the purchases journal, is used to record all credit purchases of merchandise for resale. Summary posting, or the posting of column totals, is used in the purchases journal. In addition, each entry in the purchases journal is posted as a credit to the individual creditors' accounts in the accounts payable subsidiary ledger. At the end of the accounting period, a schedule of accounts payable is prepared, and the total is compared with the balance of the accounts payable account in the general ledger. The figures must be the same. If they are not the same, an error has been made that must be located and corrected.

Freight charges are considered to be part of the cost of the merchandise purchased and are debited to an account called freight in. The balance of the freight in account is added to the balance of net purchases on the income statement to arrive at the cost of purchases. On the seller's invoice, either FOB shipping point or FOB destination will be indicated. FOB shipping point means free on board to the point of shipment and the buyer will reimburse the carrier; FOB destination means free on board to the destination and the seller will pay the carrier.

When purchased merchandise is returned or is damaged, the buyer will issue a debit memorandum to the seller that indicates that the buyer's accounts payable account is being reduced by a debit. When the seller receives the debit memo, the accounts receivable account on the books of the seller must also be reduced by the same amount if the buyer has a valid claim. The return of merchandise is recorded on the buyer's books as a credit to purchases returns and allowances, a credit to GST Paid, and a debit to accounts payable (or cash, in case a refund is being made); the same return on the seller's books will be recorded as a debit to sales returns and allowances, a debit to GST Charged, and a credit to accounts receivable (or cash).

A trade discount may be granted to the buyer. If that is the case, the buyer subtracts the amount of the trade discount from the list price of the merchandise and records only the actual purchase price. Trade discounts are not recorded on the books of the buyer or the seller.

In addition to the trade discount, credit terms may be offered on the same invoice by the seller to encourage prompt payment.

Vocabulary Review

Following is a list of the words and terms for this chapter:

debit memorandum   purchase invoice
FOB destination   purchase order
FOB shipping point   purchase requisition
in transit   trade discount
list price   vendor
net price

Fill in the blank with the correct word or term from the list.

1. _____ means in the process of being moved from one place to another.
2. The invoice that is received by the buyer when goods ordered have been shipped is referred to, from the viewpoint of the buyer, as a/an _____.
3. Another term for a seller of merchandise is _____.
4. When the purchasing department prepares a form ordering merchandise, the form is referred to as a/an _____.
5. A form made out by a department that requests the purchasing department to order merchandise is referred to as a/an _____.
6. A discount granted to the buyer at the time of purchase, often for volume buying, is referred to as a/an _____.
7. The price of merchandise that is shown in the seller's catalogue is referred to as the _____.
8. The catalogue price minus the trade discount is referred to as the _____.
9. When the seller pays the freight charges all the way to the buyer's destination, the freight terms are _____.
10. When the seller pays only for loading the merchandise at the point of shipment, the freight terms are _____.
11. A document issued by the buyer to the seller, indicating that the accounts payable account is being reduced on the books of the buyer, is referred to as a/an _____.

Match the words and terms on the left with the definitions on the right.

12. debit memorandum
13. FOB destination
14. FOB shipping point
15. in transit
16. list price
17. net price
18. purchase invoice
19. purchase order
20. purchase requisition
21. trade discount
22. vendor

a. freight charges paid by the seller to the buyer's destination
b. the invoice that is received with the ordered merchandise
c. a request to the purchasing department that merchandise be ordered
d. catalogue price minus trade discount
e. one who sells merchandise
f. a formal order for merchandise made by the purchasing department
g. the catalogue price
h. the cost of loading merchandise at the point of shipment is paid by the seller; the buyer pays to the destination
i. a document issued by the buyer indicating that the buyer's accounts payable account is being reduced
j. a discount granted to the buyer at the time of purchase
k. in the process of being moved

Exercises

EXERCISE 8.1   In each case, determine (1) the last day on which the invoice may be paid to receive the discount; (2) the last day on which the invoice may be paid after the discount period; and (3) the amount of the discount. For a list of the months and the number of days in each, refer to Chapter Seven, Exercise 7.1.

	Invoice Amount	Invoice Date	Terms	Last Day for Discount	Last Day for Payment after Discount	Amount of Discount
a.	$1,000	January 18	1/15, n/60	_____	_____	_____
b.	4,750	February 20	2/10, EOM	_____	_____	_____
c.	500	April 25	2/10, n/30	_____	_____	_____
d.	8,040	June 27	1/15, n/30	_____	_____	_____
e.	3,000	July 29	60 days	_____	_____	_____
f.	5,500	September 11	2/10, n/60	_____	_____	_____
g.	7,420	November 21	1/15, n/60	_____	_____	_____
h.	9,000	December 14	1/10, EOM	_____	_____	_____

EXERCISE 8.2   Sylvia McMurtry owns Sylvia's Sandwich Shop. Record the following in general journal form. Use journal page 8.

April 10   Sylvia purchased 40 kg of prime rib for $160 plus 7 percent GST from Restaurant Supplies, Inc.; terms, 2/10, EOM.

April 11   Sylvia called the manager of Restaurant Supplies, Inc. to complain about the quality of the prime rib delivered on April 10. She suggested that Restaurant Supplies, Inc. grant a 20 percent allowance. It agreed, and she issued a debit memo for $32 plus 7 percent GST to Restaurant Supplies, Inc.

April 30   Sylvia issued a cheque to Restaurant Supplies, Inc. to pay the balance owed on the April 10 purchase.

EXERCISE 8.3   In Exercise 8.2, you recorded three transactions for Sylvia's Sandwich Shop. They related to a purchase, a return, and a payment. Now record the same transactions for Restaurant Supplies, Inc. as they will relate to the same sale, return, and receipt of payment on April 10, 11, and 30. Use journal page 17.

EXERCISE 8.4   Record the following in general journal form for Dino's Deli. Use journal page 14.

July 1   Dino purchased 200 kg of whole wheat flour and 75 kg of cracked wheat flour from Nature's Lifestyle Products, an out-of-town vendor. The list price for the whole wheat flour is $50 and the list price for the cracked wheat flour is $26. Nature's Lifestyle allowed a 10 percent trade discount. Seven percent GST is paid on all purchases and the credit terms are 2/15, n/30.

July 2   Dino wrote a cheque to United Delivery Service for $15 plus GST for delivering the goods ordered from Nature's Lifestyle Products.

July 2   Dino issued a $50 debit memorandum to Nature's Lifestyle Products because of damaged merchandise.

July 16   Dino sent a cheque to Nature's Lifestyle Products for the amount owed on the July 1 purchase.

EXERCISE 8.5   In Exercise 8.4, you recorded for Dino's Deli four transactions that related to a purchase, a payment for freight, a return, and a payment for the purchase. Now record in general journal form the same transactions for Nature's Lifestyle Products as they relate to the sale, the return, and the receipt of payment. Use journal page 18.

EXERCISE 8.6   Following are T accounts for Plant City that relate to one purchase and the subsequent returns and payment of the invoice. Briefly describe what has occurred on August 10 (two transactions), August 12, and August 20. The posting reference notation *CP* refers to an entry in the cash payments journal.

Cash   101

	Aug. 10 CP12 53.50
	Aug. 20 CP12 945.00

Purchases   501

Aug. 10 P8 1,000.00	

Accounts Payable   210

Aug. 12 GJ9 107.00	Aug. 10 P8 1,070.00
Aug. 20 CP12 963.00	

Purchases Returns and Allowances   520

	Aug. 12 GJ9 100.00

GST Paid   220

Aug. 10 P8 70.00	Aug. 12 GJ9 7.00
Aug. 10 CP12 3.50	

Purchases Discounts   530

	Aug. 20 CP12 18.00

Freight In   540

Aug. 10 CP12 50.00	

EXERCISE 8.7   Following is the purchases journal for Plant City for the month of September 19XX and the general journal entries that relate to purchases returns and allowances:

PURCHASES JOURNAL   **PAGE 9**

Date	Supplier's Name	Invoice Number	Post. Ref.	Purchases Debit	GST Paid Debit	Accounts Payable Credit
Sept. 1	Planters Unlimited	9721		270—	18 90	288 90
6	Green Growers	10649		500—	35—	535—
16	Plant Food, Inc.	4298		190—	13 30	203 30
21	Planters Unlimited	9846		940—	65 80	1005 80
26	ABC Nursery	17408		1620—	113 40	1733 40
30	Green Growers	10841		650—	45 50	695 50
	Total			4170—	291 90	4461 90

GENERAL JOURNAL   **PAGE 14**

Date	Description	Post. Ref.	Debit	Credit
Sept. 2	Accounts Payable—Planters Unlimited		107—	
	GST Paid			7—
	Purchases Returns and Allowances			100—
	To Record Debit Memo 604-C; Invoice 9721			
27	Accounts Payable—ABC Nursery		214—	
	GST Paid			14—
	Purchases Returns and Allowances			200—
	To Record Debit Memo 605-C; Invoice 17408			

Answer the following:
a. Where will the totals of the purchases journal be posted?
b. Including both the purchases journal and the general journal, how many separate postings must be made to the accounts payable subsidiary ledger?

c. How much money must be sent on September 11 to Planters Unlimited in full payment of invoice 9721? (Terms: 1/10, n/30.)

d. What is the last day for payment within the discount period on the September 16 purchase from Plant Food, Inc., invoice 4298? What amount must be remitted to Plant Food, Inc. on that date? (Terms: 1/10, EOM.)

EXERCISE 8.8 In July 19XX, Fashion Jewellery recorded a total of $14,500 in the purchases journal. Purchases returns and allowances for the same period were $275; purchases discounts were $260; and freight charges were $570. Calculate the cost of purchases.

EXERCISE 8.9 Following is the accounts payable subsidiary ledger for Kid's Klothes. Calculate the balance after each transaction and prepare a schedule of accounts payable on August 31, 19XX. In the posting reference column, *CP* indicates a payment on account recorded in the cash payments journal. The balance in the accounts payable control account on August 31, 19XX is $2,895.

ACCOUNTS PAYABLE SUBSIDIARY LEDGER

ACCOUNT: ALL-WEATHER COATS

Date		Explanation	Post. Ref.	Debit	Credit	Balance
19XX Aug.	1		P8		500—	
	3		GJ10	150—		
	5		P9		700—	
	11		CP14	350—		

ACCOUNT: CANVAS CLOTHES

Date		Explanation	Post. Ref.	Debit	Credit	Balance
19XX Aug.	4		P8		250—	
	9		P8		460—	
	10		GJ10	100—		
	14		CP14	150—		
	20		P8		300—	

ACCOUNT: KIDDIE KORNER

Date		Explanation	Post. Ref.	Debit	Credit	Balance
19XX Aug.	7		P8		260—	
	9		P8		410—	
	10		P8		520—	
	17		CP14	260—		

ACCOUNT: LITTLE MEN

Date		Explanation	Post. Ref.	Debit	Credit	Balance
19XX Aug.	15		P8		305—	
	16		GJ10	305—		
	17		P8		420—	
	27		CP14	420—		
	31		P8		505—	

EXERCISE 8.10   Give the account classification for each of the following accounts. Classifications are asset, contra asset, liability, owner's equity, revenue, contra revenue, cost of goods sold, contra purchases, and expense. Also indicate whether the account has a normal debit or credit balance, and on which financial statement (income statement or balance sheet) the account appears. The first one has been completed as an example.

	Account Title	Classification	Normal Debit or Credit Balance	Which Financial Statement?
Example	Accumulated Depreciation	contra asset	credit	balance sheet
a.	Mortgage Payable			
b.	Sales			
c.	Unearned Revenue			
d.	Supplies Expense			
e.	GST Charged			
f.	Purchases Discounts			
g.	Freight In			
h.	Depreciation Expense			
i.	Purchases Returns and Allowances			
j.	GST Paid			
k.	Prepaid Advertising			
l.	Supplies			
m.	Provincial Sales Tax Payable			
n.	Merchandise Inventory			
o.	Accounts Receivable			
p.	Drawing			
q.	Sales Returns and Allowances			
r.	Prepaid Insurance			
s.	Sales Discounts			

Problems

PROBLEM 8.1   Carol Ruckle owns a small jewellery store called "Rings 'n Things." Seven percent GST is paid on all purchases. Following are the transactions relating to credit purchases for the month of May 19XX:

May 1   purchased 14K gold chains from M & M Jewellery on invoice 17-420 dated May 1; list price was $3,000 minus a 5 percent trade discount

May 3   purchased 18K rings from Ring Warehouse on invoice 48260 dated May 2; list price was $2,500 minus a trade discount of 10 percent

May 4   issued a $300 debit memo 620-A to Ring Warehouse relating to the May 3 purchase

May 9   purchased pendants from Gold Products Co. on invoice 12411 dated May 7; list price was $1,100 minus a trade discount of 5 percent

May 15   issued a cheque to M & M Jewellery in full payment of the outstanding May 1 balance plus the amount owed on the May 1 invoice 17-420

May 18   purchased earrings from Silver Supplies on invoice 9072-8 dated May 16; list price is $450; no trade discount granted

May 20   issued a $50 debit memo 621-A to Silver Supplies relating to May 18 purchase

May 24   issued a cheque to Ring Warehouse in full payment of the May 3 purchase less the May 4 return

May 26   purchased rings and bracelets from Silver Supplies on invoice 9159-A dated May 25; list price is $570; no trade discount granted

May 28   purchased ankle bracelets from Rich's Supplies on invoice 1049 dated May 27; list price is $400 minus a 10 percent trade discount

INSTRUCTIONS

1. Enter the following account titles, numbers, and May 1 balances into the general ledger and the accounts payable subsidiary ledger.

	General Ledger		Accounts Payable Subsidiary Ledger	
101	Cash	$8,700	Gold Products Co.	0
210	Accounts Payable	7,600	M & M Jewellery	$2,000
220	GST Paid	500	Rich's Supplies	4,500
511	Purchases	0	Ring Warehouse	0
515	Purchases Returns and Allowances	0	Silver Supplies	1,100

2. Use page 5 for the purchases journal and page 21 for the general journal.
3. Assuming that the purchase terms are net 30, record purchases on account in the purchases journal, purchases returns and allowances in the general journal, and cash payments in the general journal. (Later on, you will record all payments of cash in the cash payments journal.)
4. Post to the accounts payable ledger immediately after each transaction is journalized.
5. Post to the general ledger first from the purchases journal and then from the general journal.
6. Prepare a schedule of accounts payable and compare the total with the balance in the accounts payable control account on May 31.

PROBLEM 8.2   Curt Nodd owns a western clothing store called "Curt's Country Clothes." Curt pays 7 percent GST on all purchases. Following are the transactions relating to credit purchases for the month of February 19XX.

February 1   purchased jeans from Cowhand Supplies on invoice 7612 dated February 1; list price was $500; terms 2/10, n/30

February 4   purchased leather vests from Leather Products on invoice 1039 dated February 3; list price was $1,200; terms 1/15, n/30

February 8   issued debit memorandum 16-123 to Leather Products in the amount of $300 relating to their invoice 1039

February 9	purchased shirts from Cowhand Supplies on invoice 7690 dated February 7; list price was $490; terms 2/10, n/30
February 11	wrote a cheque to Cowhand Supplies in full payment of February 1 invoice 7612
February 12	purchased coats from Double R Supplies on invoice 6401 dated February 12; list price was $2,500; terms 2/10, EOM
February 13	issued debit memorandum 16-124 to Double R Supplies in the amount of $150 relating to their invoice 6401 dated February 12
February 14	wrote a cheque to Leather Products in full payment of the February 3 invoice 1039, minus the February 8 return
February 24	wrote a cheque to Cowhand Supplies in full payment of invoice 7690 dated February 7
February 26	purchased boots from Ringo Western Wear on invoice 5622 dated February 25; list price was $1,000; terms 1/15, n/60
February 28	wrote a cheque to Double R Supplies in full payment of February 12 invoice 6401, minus the February 13 return

INSTRUCTIONS

1. Enter the following account titles, numbers, and February 1 balances into the general ledger and the accounts payable subsidiary ledger.

	General Ledger		Accounts Payable Subsidiary Ledger	
101	Cash	$7,230	Cowhand Supplies	$3,000
211	Accounts Payable	6,430	Double R Supplies	2,000
220	GST Paid	420	Leather Products	1,430
511	Purchases	0	Ringo Western Wear	0
515	Purchases Returns and Allowances	0		
520	Purchases Discounts	0		

2. Use page 2 for the purchases journal and page 5 for the general journal.
3. Record purchases on account in the purchases journal, purchases returns and allowances in the general journal, and cash payments (including purchases discounts) in the general journal. (Later on, you will record all payments of cash in the cash payments journal.)
4. Post to the accounts payable ledger immediately after each transaction is journalized.
5. Post to the general ledger first from the purchases journal and then from the general journal.
6. Prepare a schedule of accounts payable and compare the total with the balance in the accounts payable control account on February 28.

PROBLEM 8.3

Following are the transactions relating to credit purchases for Household Supplies for the month of January 19XX. Seven percent GST is paid on all purchases.

January 2	purchased merchandise from A-1 Products on invoice 76403 dated January 2; list price was $5,000 minus a 10 percent trade discount; terms 1/15, n/30
January 2	wrote a cheque to Intra-Province Delivery Co. for $75 plus 7 percent GST relating to A-1 Products' purchase invoice 76403 dated January 2
January 3	purchased merchandise from Zumwalt's on invoice 1240 dated January 3; list price was $4,000; no trade discount allowed; terms 2/10, n/30
January 4	issued debit memo 643-B in the amount of $500 to Zumwalt's relating to its January 3 invoice 1240; merchandise was damaged
January 8	purchased merchandise from Best Products on invoice 6243 dated January 8; list price was $3,500 less trade discount of 10 percent; terms 2/10, EOM
January 8	wrote a cheque to Overnight Delivery Co. for $50 plus 7 percent GST relating to Best Products' invoice 6243
January 12	issued a cheque to Zumwalt's in full payment of its January 3 invoice 1240 less the January 4 return
January 15	purchased merchandise from Klean Homes on invoice 1649 dated January 15; list price was $8,000 less a 5 percent trade discount; terms 1/10, EOM
January 17	issued a cheque to A-1 Products in full payment of its January 2 invoice 76403
January 18	purchased merchandise from Klean Homes on invoice 1701 dated January 18; list price was $2,600 less a 5 percent trade discount; terms 1/10, EOM
January 19	issued debit memo 644-B in the amount of $400 to Klean Homes relating to its January 18 invoice 1701
January 22	purchased merchandise from Zumwalt's on invoice 1322 dated January 22; list price was $3,700; no trade discount allowed; terms 2/10, n/30
January 24	purchased merchandise from Bargain Basement on invoice 16404 dated January 24; list price was $1,500 less a trade discount of 5 percent; terms n/30
January 28	purchased merchandise from A-1 Products on invoice 77106 dated January 28; list price was $4,700 minus a 10 percent trade discount; terms 1/15, n/30
January 28	wrote a cheque to Intra-Province Delivery Co. for $75 plus 7 percent GST relating to A-1 Products' January 28 purchase invoice 77106

INSTRUCTIONS

1. Enter the following account titles, numbers, and January 1 balances into the general ledger and the accounts payable subsidiary ledger:

	General Ledger		Accounts Payable Subsidiary Ledger	
101	Cash	$16,100	A-1 Products	$3,000
211	Accounts Payable	8,900	Bargain Basement	2,500
230	GST Paid	580	Best Products	0
501	Purchases	0	Klean Homes	2,000
510	Purchases Returns and Allowances	0	Zumwalt's	1,400
520	Purchases Discounts	0		
525	Freight In	0		

2. Use page 31 for the purchases journal and page 49 for the general journal.
3. Record purchases on account in the purchases journal, purchases returns and allowances in the general journal, and cash payments in the general journal. Remember, trade discounts are not recorded on the books of the buyer or the seller.
4. Post to the accounts payable ledger immediately after each transaction is journalized.
5. Post to the general ledger first from the purchases journal and then from the general journal.
6. Prepare a schedule of accounts payable and compare the total with the balance in the accounts payable control account on January 31.

PROBLEM 8.4

Following are the transactions relating to credit sales and credit purchases for Ray's Sewing Centre for the month of October 19XX. Seven percent GST is charged on all sales and paid on all purchases.

October 1   purchased merchandise from Kathy's Sewright Machines on invoice 60213 dated October 1; list price was $5,720; terms n/30

October 1   issued a cheque for $70 plus 7 percent GST to Speedee Delivery Co. for delivering the purchase from Kathy's Sewright Machines

October 5   sold merchandise to B.L. Botham; invoice 8037; list price is $60 plus 8 percent provincial sales tax; terms n/30

October 9   purchased merchandise from G & B Fabrics on invoice 9160 dated October 9; list price was $4,200; terms n/30

October 10   issued debit memorandum 581 in the amount of $1,000 plus 7 percent GST to G & B Fabrics relating to invoice 9160; merchandise was returned

October 14   issued a cheque to Kathy's Sewright Machines in full payment of their October 1 invoice 60213

October 17   sold merchandise to The Sewing Corner; invoice 8038 dated October 17; list price is $980 plus 8 percent provincial sales tax, terms are net 30

October 19   issued credit memorandum 603 for $345 to The Sewing Corner relating to invoice 8038 dated October 17; $300 of the amount relates to the list price of the merchandise, $24 relates to the provincial sales tax, and $21 relates to GST

October 22   received a cheque from B.L. Botham in full payment of invoice 8037 dated October 5

October 25   issued a cheque to G & B Fabrics in full payment of invoice 9160 dated October 9, less the return on October 10

October 27   sold merchandise to The Sewing Corner; invoice 8039; list price is $850 plus 8 percent provincial sales tax; terms n/30

October 28   received a cheque from The Sewing Corner in full payment of invoice 8038 dated October 17, less the return on October 19

October 29   purchased merchandise from Kwik-Sew on invoice 1641 dated October 29; list price was $880; terms n/30

October 29   issued a cheque for $50 plus 7 percent GST to Fast Freight for delivering the purchase from Kwik-Sew on October 29

October 30   issued debit memorandum 582 for $106 plus 7 percent GST to Kwik-Sew on October 29

October 31   received a cheque from The Sewing Corner in full payment of invoice 8039 dated October 27

October 31   issued a cheque to Kwik-Sew in full payment of invoice 1641 dated October 29, less the return on October 30

INSTRUCTIONS

1. Listed below is a partial chart of accounts for Ray's Sewing Centre. In this problem, you are not required to post to the general ledger, but you will use the account titles when journalizing.

Partial Chart of Accounts
101   Cash
110   Accounts Receivable
210   Accounts Payable
220   Provincial Sales Tax Payable
230   GST Charged
240   GST Paid
405   Sales
410   Sales Returns and Allowances
505   Purchases
520   Purchases Returns and Allowances
525   Freight In

2. Enter the following names into the accounts receivable and accounts payable ledgers.

Accounts Receivable Subsidiary Ledger	Accounts Payable Subsidiary Ledger
B.L. Botham	G & B Fabrics
The Sewing Corner	Kathy's Sewright Machines
	Kwik-Sew

3. Record all sales on account in a sales journal designed to account for sales tax; use page 18. Record all purchases on account in a purchases journal; use page 10. Record all other transactions in a general journal; begin numbering with page 28.
   a. Post to the accounts receivable and accounts payable subsidiary ledgers immediately after each transaction.
   b. Total, check that the debit column totals equal the credit column totals, and rule the sales and purchases journals.

PROBLEM 8.5   Following are the transactions relating to credit sales and credit purchases for Wing's Mercantile for the month of June 19XX. On all credit sales, Wing's grants charge customers credit terms of 2/10, n/30. Wing's is not required to collect provincial sales tax, but it must charge 7 percent GST on all sales and pay 7 percent GST on all purchases.

June 1   purchased merchandise from Wilson Supplies on invoice 1643 dated June 1; list price was $500; terms n/30

June 2   sold merchandise to A.G. Rogers, invoice 7029; list price was $120; terms 2/10, n/30

June 3   issued debit memo 603 to Wilson Supplies in the amount of $25 plus 7 percent GST; relates to purchase invoice 1643 of June 1

June 5   sold merchandise on account to B.B. Ulrich, invoice 7030; list price was $250; terms 2/10, n/30

June 6   issued credit memo 804 to B.B. Ulrich in the amount of $50 plus 7 percent GST; relates to sales invoice 7030 of June 5

June 8   purchased merchandise from Moreno's Appliances on invoice 32961 dated June 8; list price was $3,000 less a 5 percent trade discount; terms n/30

June 8   issued a cheque to Van's Delivery for $100 plus 7 percent GST relating to the June 8 purchase invoice 32961 from Moreno's Appliances

June 10   purchased merchandise from Van Riper Wholesale House on invoice 20396 dated June 10; list price was $1,650; terms n/30

June 12   received a cheque from A.G. Rogers in full payment of the June 2 invoice 7029

June 14   sold merchandise on account to P.S. Tolstoy, invoice 7031; list price was $370; terms 2/10, n/30

June 15   received a cheque from B.B. Ulrich in full payment of June 5 invoice 7030, minus the return on June 6

June 18   purchased merchandise from Wilson Supplies on invoice 1699 dated June 18; list price was $800; terms n/30

June 20   issued debit memo 604 to Wilson Supplies in the amount of $100 plus 7 percent GST; relates to purchase invoice 1699 of June 18

June 23   sold merchandise to A.G. Rogers, invoice 7032; list price was $325; terms 2/10, n/30

June 24   issued a cheque to Moreno's Appliances in full payment of June 8 purchase, invoice 32961

June 27   purchased merchandise from Moreno's Appliances on invoice 32998 dated June 27; list price was $1,800 less a 5 percent trade discount; terms n/30

June 27   issued a cheque to Van's Delivery for $75 plus 7 percent GST relating to June 27 purchase from Moreno's Appliances

June 29   received a cheque from P.S. Tolstoy in full payment of June 14 invoice 7031

June 30   paid amount owed to Wilson Supplies for purchases on June 1 invoice 1643 and June 18 invoice 1699 minus the returns on June 3 and June 20

INSTRUCTIONS

1. Below is a partial chart of accounts for Wing's Mercantile. In this problem, you are not required to post to the general ledger, but you may use the account titles when journalizing.

Partial Chart of Accounts
101 Cash
110 Accounts Receivable
210 Accounts Payable
220 GST Charged
230 GST Paid
405 Sales
410 Sales Discounts
415 Sales Returns and Allowances
545 Purchases
560 Purchases Returns and Allowances
570 Freight In

2. Enter the following names into the accounts receivable and accounts payable ledgers.

Accounts Receivable Subsidiary Ledger	Accounts Payable Subsidiary Ledger
A.G. Rogers	Moreno's Appliances
P.S. Tolstoy	Van Riper Wholesale House
B.B. Ulrich	Wilson Supplies

3. Record sales on account in the sales journal; use page 32. Record purchases on account in the purchases journal; use page 19. Record sales returns and allowances, sales discounts, purchases returns and allowances, and cash transactions in the general journal; begin numbering with page 68.
4. Total and rule the sales and purchases journals.
5. Post to the accounts receivable ledger and the accounts payable ledger immediately after each transaction.

The Cash Receipts, Cash Payments, and Combined Cash Journals

Learning Objectives

When you have completed this chapter, you should
1. have a better understanding of accounting terminology.
2. have a basic understanding of internal control.
3. have a basic understanding of cash management.
4. be able to account for credit card sales.
5. be able to record entries directly into the cash receipts, cash payments, and combined cash journals.
6. be able to post from the cash receipts, cash payments, and combined cash journals directly into the general ledger and subsidiary ledgers.
7. be able to calculate and account for interest received and interest paid.

Vocabulary

collateral   property that is acceptable as security for a loan

combined journal   a journal that combines all special journals into one journal; also called a synoptic journal

crossfoot   proving that the debit column totals equal the credit column totals of a multicolumn journal

expenditure   the amount expended or spent

foreclose   a legal proceeding whereby the lender deprives the borrower of the right to retain ownership of the property pledged as collateral; foreclosure follows when the borrower is behind in payments

fraud   a dishonest act in which someone is cheated

interest   the charge made for a loan, usually expressed as a percentage of the amount borrowed

interest formula   the simple interest formula for loans:
Interest = Principal × Rate × Time or $I = P \times R \times T$

justify   to show or prove to be just, right, or fair

maker   the person who borrows money and who signs a promissory note

negotiable   capable of being legally transferred from one person to another

payee   the person who lends the money; the person to whom payments of principal and interest will be made

principal   the amount of money borrowed

promissory note   a legal document signed by the borrower (the maker) that specifies the amount borrowed, the interest rate, the time, and the due date of the loan

reimburse   to repay

repossess   to take back possession of

sundry   miscellaneous

valid   sufficiently supported by facts; legally sound

Introduction

The purchases and sales journals and the cash receipts and cash payments journals are designed to meet the needs of the particular company using them and to save the bookkeeper a great deal of time in the journalizing and posting processes. In Chapters Seven and Eight, we learned how Frank Phelps, owner of Sports Haven, handled sales and purchases, returns and allowances, GST charged, sales tax, freight charges, and discounts. In this chapter, we will see how receipts and payments of cash are handled and how special precautions are taken to safeguard against the theft of cash.

Internal Control

Many management decisions are based in part on data obtained from the accounting records. For this reason, accounting information must be accurate. A strong system of internal control will help ensure that this is the case.

Internal control refers to the steps taken by a company to: (1) protect its resources from theft, waste, and inefficiency; (2) ensure that accounting data are accurate; and (3) evaluate employees and departments to determine the level of their performance and whether they are complying with company policy.

One important principle of internal control is that, whenever possible, no one employee should be responsible for handling all phases of a transaction from beginning to end. This is especially true with cash transactions, since cash is particularly susceptible to theft.

Cash Management

Proper management of cash will minimize losses from theft or **fraud** and provide for the accurate accounting of cash. It will ensure that enough cash is on hand for the business to remain solvent and will allow a reserve for emergencies. Proper cash management will also provide for any extra cash to be invested.

For strong internal control of cash, the following guidelines should be observed:

1. Cash receipts should be deposited daily.
2. Cash payments should be made by cheque (not from the cash register or cash on hand unless a petty cash fund has been established).
3. The functions of receiving cash, making cash payments, and accounting for cash should be kept separate.
4. One employee should be designated to verify the amount of every cash payment and to determine whether the payment is **valid**; another employee should be designated to write the cheques. The same person should not be designated to verify the validity and amount of an **expenditure** *and* to write the cheques.
5. Routines for handling cash should be established and carefully followed.

The reasons for these procedures are fairly obvious. When cash is deposited daily, it is not lying around as a temptation. Payments should not be made directly from the cash register, because it may be difficult or too time-consuming to verify amounts and to **justify** payment; thus, unwarranted cash payments may be made. If more than one person is involved in receiving money at the cash register, the chance of error is greater and the chance of finding the person responsible for the error less likely. The functions of receiving cash should be kept separate from the paying of and the accounting for cash to help prevent employee theft. Such theft is made much more difficult when two or more persons have to be involved. When a specific routine has been established for handling cash, management can more easily check to see that the procedures are being followed.

Sources of Cash Receipts

Cash received is primarily from two sources: (1) cash sales and (2) money received on account. Cash sales are normally recorded on a cash register and should be plainly visible to the customer. If the employee fraudulently records an amount different from that charged the customer, management hopes that the customer will complain and thus provide an outside check on the employees.

The use of prenumbered sales tickets also helps to strengthen internal control. One copy of the sales ticket is given to the customer and one copy is retained at the cash register. All tickets must be accounted for at the end of the day. The total of all the tickets must equal the total cash received that day, as verified by the manager or some employee other than the one who received the cash.

Cash Short and Over

Some small errors may be expected in the handling of cash. However, large cash discrepancies, errors made consistently by one employee, or errors that cannot be explained call for immediate attention by management.

Assume that the total amount from the prenumbered sales tickets shows that cash sales on January 11 are $1,240. However, the actual cash in the cash register is only $1,230. (Perhaps the cashier accidentally gave a customer an extra $10 in change.) The general journal entry to record the day's cash sales would be as follows:

GENERAL JOURNAL					PAGE 1
Date	Description	Post. Ref.	Debit	Credit	
19XX Jan. 11	Cash		1230—		
	Cash Short and Over		10—		
	Sales			1240—	
	To Record Cash Sales				

However, if the total of the sales tickets showed sales on January 11 to be $1,240 but the actual cash on hand proved to be $1,250, the general journal entry would appear as follows:

GENERAL JOURNAL					PAGE 1
Date	Description	Post. Ref.	Debit	Credit	
19XX Jan. 11	Cash		1250—		
	Cash Short and Over			10—	
	Sales			1240—	
	To Record Cash Sales				

The Cash Short and Over account is debited when cash is short and credited when cash is over. If the Cash Short and Over account has a credit balance at the end of the accounting period, it is shown on the income statement in a special category called "Other Income," which follows the net income from operations section. If Cash Short and Over has a debit balance, it will appear in the category called "Other Expenses."

Credit Card Sales

Credit cards such as MasterCard and Visa are quite common. After credit approval, the customer is issued the card, which may then be used for purchases in many stores. When making a purchase, the customer signs a credit card draft. The customer then owes the money to the company that issued the credit card, *not* to the store making the sale. The credit card company will **reimburse** the store owner when she or he deposits the credit card draft in the store's bank account. Eventually, the customer reimburses the credit card company. Some credit card drafts cannot be directly deposited; in these cases, the credit card companies require the store making the sale to mail the sales drafts to them and in return they mail a cheque to the store. When this occurs, the store making the sale debits an account receivable from the credit card company at the time of the sale.

The advantages to the merchant of offering credit card sales are many:
1. Cash from credit sales is received quickly.
2. Costly credit checks are not required, because the customer owes money to the credit card company, not to the store making the sale.
3. No uncollectible accounts expense is incurred with credit card sales.

Bank credit card drafts (such as MasterCard or Visa) may be deposited directly into the merchant's bank account, similar to a deposit of a customer's cheque. At the end of the month, the fee for using the credit card company services is deducted directly from the merchant's chequing account, or it may be deducted when the deposit is made. This fee is debited to an account called Credit Card Discount Expense, which shows on the income statement along with the other expenses.

Assume that Audrey Billings purchases merchandise on March 1 from Sports Haven totalling $1,000; she presents an Ultra Charge card for payment. The Ultra Charge Company allows the merchant to deposit the sales drafts minus the 4 percent discount directly to the store's bank account. The entry in the general journal to record the sale would be:

GENERAL JOURNAL				PAGE 17	
Date	Description	Post. Ref.	Debit	Credit
19XX Mar. 1	Cash		1 1 1 0 —	
	Credit Card Discount Expense		4 0 —	
	Sales			1 0 0 0 —
	Provincial Sales Tax Payable			8 0 —
	GST Charged			7 0 —
	To Record Receipt of Cash for Ultra Charge			
	Sales Less a 4% Discount			

The Cash Receipts Journal

The cash receipts journal is, like the other special journals, designed to meet the needs of the particular company using it. All cash received by the company is entered in the cash receipts journal, and every entry in it will be a debit to Cash. Thus, the first column (or the last, as the accountant prefers) will be a cash debit column. If the merchant allows nonbank credit card sales, a special debit column for credit card discount expense may be included. A special debit column may also be included to record sales discounts as customers take advantage of credit terms by paying their invoices early. Credit columns may include accounts receivable, sales, GST charged, and provincial sales tax payable. Other columns may be added if the need arises.

To determine which special columns to use in the cash receipts journal, the accountant must analyze the kinds of transactions that normally occur. For many businesses, the most common examples will be cash received from sales and cash received from customers who are paying on account. These transactions are illustrated in general journal form.

GENERAL JOURNAL				PAGE 1	
Date	Description	Post. Ref.	Debit	Credit
19XX Jan. 4	Cash		2 3 0 —	
	Sales			2 0 0 —
	GST Charged			1 4 —
	Provincial Sales Tax Payable			1 6 —
	To Record Cash Sales			
5	Cash		5 0 —	
	Accounts Receivable—Joe Scott			5 0 —
	To Record Receipt of Money on Account			

Less-frequent transactions might include a cash investment by the owner, a cash sale of assets, or a receipt of money on an outstanding note.

Date		Description	Post. Ref.	Debit	Credit
19XX Jan.	6	Cash		3000—	
		B.J. King, Capital			3000—
		To Record Additional Investment			
	9	Cash		535—	
		GST Charged			35—
		Office Equipment			500—
		To Record Sale of Equipment at Cost			
	11	Cash		750—	
		Notes Receivable			750—
		To Record Cash Received as Payment on Note			
		from P. Santos			

GENERAL JOURNAL   **PAGE 1**

As you are aware, each transaction has been recorded separately and must be posted separately, thus occupying a great deal of the bookkeeper's time. Let's look now at how these transactions, and some others as well, would appear in a multicolumn cash receipts journal.

CASH RECEIPTS JOURNAL

Date		Received From	Account Credited	Post. Ref.
19XX Jan.	4	Cash Sales		
	5	Jo Scott		✓
	6	B.J. King	B.J. King, Capital	310
	9	Cash Sale	Office Equipment	130
	11	P. Santos	Notes Receivable	120
	15	Cash Sales		
	17	Cash Sales		
	19	Pat Kinghorn		✓
	21	Cash Sales		
	24	Phil Valentine		✓
	27	Cash Sales		
	30	Cash Sales		
	31	Cash Sales		
		Totals		

Analysis of Individual Transactions

January 4   This transaction is to record cash sales plus 7 percent GST and 8 percent provincial sales tax. Since there are special columns for each of these accounts, only the words *Cash Sales* and the amounts need to be entered. Similar transactions appear on January 17, 21, 27, and 30.

January 5   A $50 cheque was received from Jo Scott to apply on her outstanding account. The $50 is entered in the accounts receivable credit column and the cash debit column. Her name is written in the received from column so that the $50 may be posted to the accounts receivable subsidiary ledger. The January 19 and 24 transactions are similar. If the company offers cash discounts for prompt payment, an additional column entitled sales discounts would be added.

January 6   B.J. King invested an additional $3,000 cash into the business. This entry requires a debit to Cash and a credit to Capital. Because there is no special column for the Capital account, the amount is entered in the **sundry** credit column and in the cash debit column. For all entries in the sundry column, the account title must be written in the account credited column so that the amount can be posted to the correct general ledger account.

								PAGE 1
Sundry Accounts Credit	Accounts Receivable Credit	Sales Credit	GST Charged Credit	PST Payable Credit	Credit Card Discount Debit	Cash Debit
		200—	14—	16—		230—
	50—					50—
3000—						3000—
500—			35—			535—
750—						750—
		970—	67 90	77 60	44 62	1070 88
		550—	38 50	44—		632 50
	80—					80—
		100—	7—	8—		115—
	75—					75—
		40—	2 80	3 20		46—
		90—	6 30	7 20		103 50
		1940—	135 80	155 20	89 24	2141 76
4250—	205—	3890—	307 30	311 20	133 86	8829 64
(X)	(110)	(401)	(210)	(215)	(630)	(101)

January 9   Surplus office equipment was sold at cost plus 7 percent GST. Again, because there is no special column for office equipment, $500 is entered in the sundry credit column, $35 in the GST charged column, and the total of $535 in the cash debit column. The account title, Office Equipment, must be written in the account credited column so that the amount can be posted to the correct general ledger account.

January 11   Paul Santos paid $750 on a non-interest-bearing note. The amount is entered in the sundry credit and the cash debit columns and *Notes Receivable* is written in the account credited column.

January 15 $1,115.50 (minus a 4 percent credit card discount fee) is received resulting from credit card drafts. Seven percent GST and 8 percent provincial sales tax were deposited in the bank. The total cash received, $1,070.88, is entered in the cash debit column. The amount of the sale, $970, is entered in the sales credit column, the GST charged of $67.90 is entered in the GST charged credit column, and the sales tax of $77.60 is entered in the sales tax payable credit column. There is a similar entry on January 31.

Crossfooting the Cash Receipts Journal

When all the entries for the period have been journalized, total each individual column and enter the totals. Before ruling the journal, **crossfooting** must take place; this is the process whereby the bookkeeper checks to make sure that the debit column totals equal the credit column totals. This proof of balance must occur before summary posting is performed. Crossfooting is performed as follows:

Column	Debit Total	Credit Total
Sundry		$4,250.00
Accounts Receivable		205.00
Sales		3,890.00
GST Charged		307.30
Provincial Sales Tax Payable		311.20
Credit Card Discount	$ 133.86	
Cash	8,829.64	
Totals	$8,963.50	$8,963.50

Ruling and Posting the Cash Receipts Journal

When crossfooting has been completed, a single line is drawn that extends across all account columns beneath the last entry. Beneath the totals, a double line is drawn across all columns except the account titles column.

Posting the Cash Receipts Journal

At the end of the accounting period, summary posting is performed in three steps:

1. All column totals, except the sundry column total, are posted. As each amount is posted, the account number is written beneath the total in parentheses.
2. Daily postings must be made to the general ledger for the amounts that appear in the sundry column. The account numbers are entered in the posting reference column of the journal after each amount is posted, and CR and the page number are entered in the posting reference column of the general ledger accounts. An X is placed beneath the sundry column total at the end of the period to indicate that the column total is not posted.
3. Daily, each amount entered in the accounts receivable credit column is posted separately to the accounts receivable ledger. A check mark is placed in the posting reference column of the journal after posting has been completed.

The completed journal, the T accounts for the general ledger, and the T accounts for the accounts receivable ledger look like this:

Partial General Ledger

Cash   101

1/1	Balance	4,500.00
1/31	CR1	8,829.64

Accounts Receivable   110

1/1	Balance	6,000.00	1/31	CR1	205.00

Notes Receivable   120

1/1	Balance	2,000.00	1/11	CR1	750.00

Office Equipment   130

1/1	Balance	5,000.00	1/9	CR1	500.00

GST Charged   210

			1/1	Balance	28.00
			1/31	CR1	307.30

Provincial Sales Tax Payable   215

			1/1	Balance	30.00
			1/31	CR1	311.20

B.J. King, Capital   310

			1/1	Balance	6,000.00
			1/6	CR1	3,000.00

Sales   401

			1/31	CR1	3,890.00

Credit Card Discount Expense   630

1/31	CR1	133.86

Partial Accounts Receivable Subsidiary Ledger

Pat Kinghorn

1/1	Balance	300.00	1/19	CR1	80.00

Jo Scott

1/1	Balance	120.00	1/5	CR1	50.00

Phil Valentine

1/1	Balance	75.00	1/24	CR1	75.00

Recording Sales Discounts in the Cash Receipts Journal

If it is company policy to allow credit terms, the cash receipts journal should be designed with a special debit column for sales discounts. Assume that on January 10 a sale of $500 plus 7 percent GST is made to Joseph Lee and that credit terms are 2/10, n/30. On January 19, when Joseph Lee sends a cheque in full payment of the purchase, the transaction as entered in the cash receipts journal looks like that shown on page 230.

The Cash Payments Journal

Good internal control of cash requires bills to be paid by cheque, and the cash payments journal is the special journal in which all cheques written are recorded. It may be designed to meet the particular needs of any company; special columns may be added to the journal for those transactions that occur frequently.

In a typical business, cash must be spent in a large number of places, but incoming cash comes from only a few sources. For example, typical transactions where cash is paid out might include payments on account and payments for rent, wages, utilities, advertising, delivery, and phone, while sources of money coming into a business are often limited primarily to cash sales or money received on account.

Some common transactions involving the payment of cash look like this in general journal form:

GENERAL JOURNAL				PAGE 7	
Date		Description	Post. Ref.	Debit	Credit
19XX July	1	Rent Expense		750—	
		Cash			750—
		To Record Payment of Rent			
	3	Purchases		800—	
		GST Paid		56—	
		Cash			856—
		To Record Purchase of Merchandise			
	5	Roberta Smith, Drawing		500—	
		Cash			500—
		To Record Owner's Withdrawal			
	7	Provincial Sales Tax Payable		180—	
		Cash			180—
		To Record Payment of Sales Tax			
	8	Salaries Expense		340—	
		Cash			340—
		To Record Payment of Weekly Salaries			
	10	Accounts Payable—Unity Products		1200—	
		Cash			1176—
		Purchases Discounts			24—
		To Record Payment in Full of Invoice #76432			

If a general journal rather than a cash payments journal is used to record cash transactions, a large number of postings are required. The use of the cash payments journal saves a great deal of time. The general journal entries for cash, along with some other entries, look like those in a typical cash payments journal shown on page 230.

In the cash payments journal, the cheque number is included with every transaction. Strong internal control requires that every cheque be accounted for; even when a cheque is voided, it is recorded so that missing cheque numbers can be easily noticed. For every transaction:
1. The date and cheque number are written.
2. The name of the payee is written in the paid to column and, when there is no special column, the account title to be debited is entered in the account debited column.
3. The amount to be credited to Cash is entered in the cash credit column.
4. The amount to be debited is entered in the sundry column, the accounts payable column, or the GST paid column, as appropriate.
5. If a purchase discount is being recorded, it will appear in the column for purchases discounts. Always make sure before you record such a transaction that the two credits (cash and purchases discounts) equal the debit to accounts payable.

Totalling, Crossfooting, and Ruling the Cash Payments Journal

Once all the entries for the period have been completed, each column is totalled and crossfooting is performed. Once the equality of debits and credits has been proved, a single line is drawn across all the amount columns and a double line is drawn across all columns except the account titles column.

Posting the Cash Payments Journal

The procedure used when posting the cash payments journal is as follows:
1. All debits to Accounts Payable must be posted immediately to the accounts payable ledger. A check mark is placed in the posting reference column of the journal to indicate that posting to the accounts payable ledger has taken place, and CP and the page number are entered in the posting reference column of the ledger.
2. Each entry that is recorded in the sundry column as a debit is posted immediately to the appropriate general ledger account. The ledger account number is written in the posting reference column of the journal, and CP and the page number are written in the posting reference column of the general ledger accounts.
3. The totals of the special columns are posted to the general ledger. The account number in parentheses is placed beneath the column total after posting has taken place, and CP and the page number are written in the posting reference column of the general ledger account. An X must be placed in parentheses beneath the sundry column total to indicate that amounts in that column are posted individually.

CASH RECEIPTS JOURNAL

PAGE 1

Date	Received From	Post. Ref.	Sundry Accounts Credit	Accounts Receivable Credit	Sales Credit	GST Charged Credit	PST Payable Credit	Sales Discount Debit	Cash Debit
19XX									
Jan. 19	Joseph Lee			535 —				10 —	525 —

CASH PAYMENTS JOURNAL

PAGE 7

Date	Cheque No.	Paid To	Account Debited	Post. Ref.	Sundry Accounts Debit	Accounts Payable Debit	GST Paid Debit	Purchases Discount Credit	Cash Credit
19XX July									
1	1071	Star Realty	Rent Expense	610	750 —				750 —
3	1072	Bonland Ltd.	Purchases	501	800 —		56 —		856 —
5	1073	Roberta Smith	R. Smith, Drawing	310	500 —				500 —
7	1074	Treasurer of Ontario	PST Payable	210	180 —				180 —
8	1075	J. Miller	Salaries Expense	615	340 —				340 —
11	1076	Unity Products		✓		1200 —		24 —	1176 —
15	1077	Harold's Cartage	Delivery Expense	630	30 —		2 10		32 10
18	1078	Joy Moroni Company		✓		1000 —		10 —	990 —
20	1079	Roberta Smith	R. Smith, Drawing	310	500 —				500 —
24	1080	C.P. Express	Freight In	540	75 —		5 25		80 25
27	1081	Kozak Lumber	Purchases	501	1400 —		98 —		1498 —
31	1082	Unity Products		✓		1600 —		32 —	1568 —
31	1083	Void							
		Totals			4575 —	3800 —	161 35	66 —	8470 35
					(X)	(201)	(211)	(511)	(101)

Refer now to the completed cash payments journal on page 230. Pay special attention to the posting reference notations. T accounts for the general ledger and the accounts payable ledger look like this:

Partial General Ledger

Cash			101		**Purchases Discount**			511
7/1	Balance	12,500.00	7/31 CP7	8,470.35			7/31 CP7	66.00

Accounts Payable			201		**Freight In**		540
7/31 CP7	3,800.00	7/1	Balance	8,500.00	7/24 CP7	75.00	

GST Paid		211		**Rent Expense**		610
7/31 CP7	161.35		7/1 CP7	750.00	

Provincial Sales Tax Payable			210		**Salaries Expense**		615
7/7 CP7	180.00	7/1 Balance	180.00	7/8 CP7	340.00	

Roberta Smith, Drawing		310		**Delivery Expense**		630
7/5 CP7	500.00		7/15 CP7	30.00	
7/20 CP7	500.00				

Purchases		501
7/3 CP7	800.00	
7/27 CP7	1400.00	

Partial Accounts Payable Subsidiary Ledger

Joy Moroni Company					**Unity Products**			
7/18 CP7	1,000	7/1 Balance	1,000		7/11 CP7	1,200	7/1 Balance	2,800
					7/31 CP7	1,600		

The Combined Cash Journal

Specialized journals like the ones described make it possible for several people to work on the accounting records at the same time and are used by firms that have a relatively large number of repetitive transactions. However, in a small business where all transactions are recorded by one person, a combined journal may be used. The **combined journal** combines all of the special journals into one journal and is sometimes referred to as a synoptic journal.

A combined journal is usually designed to meet the needs of the company using it. The one illustrated in this text has 12 amount columns, but additional columns can be added if there are a sufficient number of each kind of transaction to warrant posting the amounts as a column total.

COMBINED CASH JOURNAL

Cash Debit	Cash Credit	GST Paid Debit	GST Charged Credit	Date		Cheque Number	Account Titles and Explanations
			14—	July	1		Davey Wilkes
		3 50			3		Sales Ret. & Allow., D. Wilkes
		49—			4		Marlwood Fash., Inv. 4206, 2/10, n/30
			14—		6		Pur. Ret. & Allow., Marlwood
	285—				8	147	Utilities Expense
160 50					12		Davey Wilkes
	525—				14	148	Marlwood Fash., Pur. Discounts
856—			56—		15		Cash Sales
			35—		17		Davey Wilkes
		42—			18		Marlwood Fash,. Inv. 5309, 2/10, n/30
1016 50	810—	94 50	119—				
(101)	(101)	(220)	(215)				

Analysis of Individual Transactions

Following is an explanation of the entries included in the combined cash journal.

July 1   Sold $200 in merchandise plus 7 percent GST on account to Davey Wilkes on sales invoice 307. The sale is recorded by entering the customer's name in the account titles and explanations column and the invoice number in the invoice number column. The amount of the sale, $200, is recorded in the sales credit column, and the GST of $14 ($200 × .07) is recorded in the GST charged column. The full amount owing by the customer is recorded in the accounts receivable debit column ($200 + $14 = $214). The entry on July 17 is similar.

July 3   Issued credit memorandum 02-75 to Davey Wilkes for $50 plus 7 percent GST for merchandise returned. This sales return will be recorded by entering the account title Sales Returns and Allowances and the customer's name in the account titles and explanations column. The amount of the sales return, $50, is entered in the sundry debit column, and the 7 percent GST is entered in the GST paid column. The total amount of the return plus GST is entered in the accounts receivable credit column.

July 4   Purchased merchandise for resale from Marlwood Fashions for $700 plus 7 percent GST on invoice 4206; terms 2/10, n/30. This purchase of merchandise is recorded by entering the supplier's name, invoice number, and terms in the account titles and explanations column. The amount of the purchase is recorded in the purchases column, and the 7 percent GST is recorded in the GST paid column. The total amount owing is entered in the accounts payable credit column. The entry on July 18 is similar.

July 6   Issued debit memorandum 123-45 to Marlwood Fashions for $200 plus 7 percent GST for merchandise returned. This purchase return is recorded by entering the account title Purchases Returns and

					Accounts Receivable		Accounts Payable				
Post Ref.	Sundry Debit		Sundry Credit		Debit	Credit	Debit	Credit	Purchases Debit	Sales Credit	Invoice Number
✓					2 1 4 —					2 0 0 —	307
410	5 0 —					5 3 50					
✓								7 4 9 —	7 0 0 —		
510			2 0 0 —				2 1 4 —				
630	2 8 5 —										
✓ /520			1 0 —			1 6 0 50	5 3 5 —				
✓					5 3 5 —					8 0 0 —	
✓								6 4 2 —	6 0 0 —	5 0 0 —	308
	3 3 5 —		2 1 0 —		7 4 9 —	2 1 4 —	7 4 9 —	1 3 9 1 —	1 3 0 0 —	1 5 0 0 —	
	(X)		(X)		(1 1 0)	(1 1 0)	(2 1 0)	(2 1 0)	(5 0 0)	(4 0 1)	

PAGE 17

Allowances and the supplier's name in the account titles and explanations column. The amount of the purchase return of $200 is entered in the sundry credit column, the 7 percent GST is entered in the GST charged column, and the full amount of the return plus GST is entered in the accounts payable debit column.

July 8   Issued cheque 147 for $285 to Bell Canada in payment of the telephone bill. This transaction is recorded by entering the cheque number in the cheque number column, and then the account title Utilities Expense in the account titles and explanations column. The $285 is recorded in the sundry debit column and in the cash credit column.

July 12   Received a cheque from Davey Wilkes in full payment of his July 1 invoice less the sales return of July 3. The receipt of the cheque will be recorded first by entering the customer's name in the account titles and explanations column and then by entering the amount of the payment, $160.50, in the cash debit column and the accounts receivable credit column.

July 14   Issued cheque 148 for $525 to Marlwood Fashions in full payment of its July 4 invoice less the purchase return of July 6. This transaction is recorded by entering the supplier's name and the account title Purchases Discounts in the account titles and explanations column. The full amount outstanding $535 ($700 − $200 = $500 + $35 GST) will be entered in the accounts payable debit column; the purchase discount of $10 ($500 × .02) will be entered in the sundry credit column; and the amount of the cheque, $525, will be entered in the cash credit column.

July 15   Recorded cash sales for the first half of the month totalling $800 plus 7 percent GST. Cash sales are entered by writing the words "Cash Sales" in the account titles and explanations column. The full amount of cash, $856, is entered in the cash debit column; the amount of the cash sales in entered in the sales column; the 7 percent GST ($800 × .07 = $56) is entered in the GST charged column.

July 17   Sold merchandise on account to Davey Wilkes on sales invoice 308; $500 plus 7 percent GST.

July 18   Purchased merchandise for resale from Marlwood Fashions for $600 plus 7 percent GST on invoice 5309; terms 2/10, n/30.

Rules for Recording Transactions in the Combined Journal

Note the following rules for recording transactions in and posting from a combined journal:

1. The date is always entered first for every transaction.
2. If an amount is to be entered in the sundry columns, the accounts receivable columns, or the accounts payable columns, the account title or the person's name must be named in the account titles and explanations column.
3. Any amounts entered in the sundry columns are posted as individual amounts to the accounts named and the column totals are not posted.
4. Any amounts entered in the accounts receivable and accounts payable columns are posted as individual amounts to the subsidiary ledger accounts, and the column totals are posted to the control accounts.
5. All other amounts entered in the journal are posted as column totals.

Crossfooting, Ruling, and Posting the Combined Cash Journal

Once crossfooting is complete, a single line is drawn beneath all amount columns and a double line is drawn beneath all column totals.

Posting to the accounts receivable and accounts payable ledgers is done immediately after each transaction is journalized. A check mark is placed in the journal after posting to the subsidiary ledger, and CJ and the page number are placed in the posting reference column of the subsidiary ledger account. In a similar fashion, posting is performed immediately for all amounts entered in the sundry columns, and the account number is entered in the posting reference column of the journal after posting has been completed. CJ and the page number are entered in the posting reference column of the general ledger accounts, and an X is placed beneath the sundry column totals to indicate that items have been posted individually.

Summary posting is performed at the end of the month; account numbers are placed in parentheses beneath the individual column totals, and CJ and the page number are entered in the posting reference column of the general ledger accounts.

The T accounts relating to the combined journal after posting has been completed appear as follows:

Partial General Ledger

Cash			101
7/31 CJ17	1,016.50	7/31 CJ17	810.00

Purchases			500
7/31 CJ17	1,300.00		

Accounts Receivable			110
7/31 CJ17	749.00	7/31 CJ17	214.00

Purchases Returns and Allowances			510
		7/6 CJ17	200.00

Accounts Payable			210
7/31 CJ17	749.00	7/31 CJ17	1,391.00

GST Charged			215
		7/31 CJ17	119.00

GST Paid			220
7/31 CJ17	94.50		

Sales			401
		7/31 CJ17	1,500.00

Sales Returns and Allowances			410
7/3 CJ17	50.00		

Purchases Discounts			520
		7/14 CJ17	10.00

Utilities Expense			630
7/8 CJ17	285.00		

Partial Accounts Receivable Subsidiary Ledger

Davey Wilkes

7/1 CJ17	214.00	7/3 CJ17	53.50
7/17 CJ17	535.00	7/12 CJ17	160.50

Partial Accounts Payable Subsidiary Ledger

Marlwood Fashions

7/6 CJ17	214.00	7/4 CJ17	749.00
7/14 CJ17	535.00	7/18 CJ17	642.00

Recording Interest Paid

Major purchases of equipment, inventory, vehicles, or other assets are often paid for partially through the issuance of a note. A note is, like a cheque, a **negotiable** instrument; that is, it can be bought and sold. Usually, when a note is issued by the seller, the item sold is held as **collateral** for the note; in other words, title does not fully pass to the buyer until the note is paid in full. The seller normally retains the option to **repossess** the merchandise sold (or to **foreclose** on property) if the terms of the note are not met.

Assume, for example, that Valley Restaurant Supply sold booths and tables to Tony's Pizza on July 1, 19XX at a total cost of $24,000 plus 7 percent GST. Tony paid $14,000 cash as a down payment and signed a note for the other $11,680. The interest rate agreed on was 12 percent per year. Tony agreed to pay the full amount of the note and the interest at the end of one year's time. Tony signed the following **promissory note**.

$11,680.00   Bedford, N.S.   July 1, 19XX

One year   after date   I   promise to pay

to the order of   Valley Restaurant Supply

Eleven Thousand Six Hundred and Eighty --- 00/100 dollars

at   Bank of Nova Scotia, Bedford, N.S.

Value received. Interest at   12%

No. 502   Due   July 1, 19XX

Tony Agostini

Tony's Pizza

Tony Agostini is the borrower, or the **maker**, of the note; he signs the note and is required to pay back the **principal** plus the interest. Valley Restaurant Supply is referred to as the **payee** of the note and is the firm to which payment will be made. The stated interest rate is always to be regarded as an annual rate unless otherwise specified.

A purchase such as Tony's, with a cash down payment and the signing of a note, could be recorded in the general journal as follows:

Date		Description	Post. Ref.	Debit	Credit
GENERAL JOURNAL					**PAGE 18**
19XX July	1	Furniture		24000 —	
		GST Paid		1680 —	
		Cash			14000 —
		Notes Payable			11680 —
		To Record Purchase of Booths and Tables from Valley			
		Restaurant Supply; Signed a One-Year, 12% Note			

Because all payments of cash should be recorded in the cash payments journal, the entry would best be recorded as shown below.

The debit to Furniture for $24,000 is entered as usual in the sundry column; the GST Paid of $1,680 is entered in the GST Paid debit column; and the $14,000 credit to Cash is entered in the cash credit column. Since there is no special credit column for Notes Payable or a sundry credit column, the $11,680

CASH PAYMENTS JOURNAL

Date		Cheque No.	Paid To	Account Debited	Post. Ref.
19XX July	1	1768	Valley Restaurant Supply	Furniture	
				Notes Payable	

CASH PAYMENTS JOURNAL

Date		Cheque No.	Paid To	Account Debited	Post. Ref.
19XX July	1	2691	Valley Restaurant Supply	Notes Payable	
				Interest Expense	

credit to Notes Payable is entered in brackets in the sundry debit column. The brackets indicate that the $11,680 is to be posted with a balance opposite the one indicated in the column head, or, in this case, that the $11,680 is a *credit* rather than a *debit*.

Calculation of Interest

At the end of the year, when Tony pays the $11,680 plus interest to Valley Restaurant Supply, the entry will be recorded in the cash payments journal. The ordinary simple **interest** on the note is calculated as follows:

Interest Formula

$$\text{Interest} = \text{Principal} \times \text{Rate} \times \text{Time}$$
$$I = P \times R \times T$$

where principal = amount borrowed
rate = interest rate
time = length of time for which money is kept

Interest Calculation

1. Change the interest rate into a decimal by moving the decimal point two places to the left:

$$12\% = .12. = .12$$

Sundry Accounts Debit	Accounts Payable Debit	GST Paid Debit	Purchases Discount Credit	Cash Credit
				PAGE 7
2 4 0 0 0 —		1 6 8 0 —		1 4 0 0 0 —
(1 1 6 8 0 —)				

Sundry Accounts Debit	Accounts Payable Debit	GST Paid Debit	Purchases Discount Credit	Cash Credit
				PAGE 19
1 1 6 8 0 —				1 3 0 8 1 60
1 4 0 1 60				

2. Multiply:

$$I = P \times R \times T$$
$$I = \$11,680 \times .12 \times 1 \text{ (1 year)}$$
$$I = \$1,401.60$$

Note: 12 percent means 12 hundredths and may be expressed in decimal form as .12 or in fraction form as 12/100.

The cash payments journal entry to record the payment of the note plus the interest would look like that shown on page 236.

Two or more lines may be used when recording an entry in the cash payments journal. Interest Expense is treated like any other expense account, except that it is shown at the bottom of the income statement in a category called Other Expenses. ("Other" refers to expenses not normally classified as regular operating expenses.)

Recording Interest Received

The transaction between Tony Agostini and Valley Restaurant Supply may be used to illustrate the receipt of interest as well as the payment of interest. The following shows how the transaction would be handled on the books of Valley Restaurant Supply. The original sale of the booths and tables to Tony Agostini could be recorded in the general journal as follows:

Date		Description	Post. Ref.	Debit	Credit
19XX July	1	Notes Receivable		1 1 6 8 0 —	
		Cash		1 4 0 0 0 —	
		Sales			2 4 0 0 0 —
		GST Charged			1 6 8 0 —
		To Record Sale of Booths and Tables to Tony's			
		Pizza; Issued a One-Year, 12% Note			

GENERAL JOURNAL — PAGE 9

However, the transaction should be recorded in a cash receipts journal. Note that there is no special column for provincial sales tax payable because Valley Restaurant Supply is a wholesaler and is not required to pay PST.

CASH RECEIPTS JOURNAL — PAGE 7

Date		Received From	Account Credited	Post. Ref.	Sundry Accounts Credit	Accounts Receivable Credit	Sales Credit	GST Charged Credit	Cash Debit
19XX July	1	Tony Agostini	Notes Receivable		(11 6 8 0 —)		24 0 0 0 —	1 6 8 0 —	14 0 0 0 —

Since there is no sundry debit column in the cash receipts journal, the $11,680 debit to Notes Receivable is entered in brackets in the sundry credit column to indicate that the amount is to be posted as a debit. When, one year later, Valley Restaurant Supply receives the cheque from Tony's Pizza, it will be recorded in the cash receipts journal as follows:

					CASH RECEIPTS JOURNAL						PAGE 7	
Date	Received From	Account Credited	Post. Ref.	Sundry Accounts Credit	Accounts Receivable Credit	Sales Credit	GST Charged Credit	Cash Debit
19XX July 1	Tony Agostini	Notes Receivable		1 1 6 8 0 —				1 3 0 8 1 60
		Interest Income		1 4 0 1 60				

Again, two or more lines may be used for the entry. Interest Income is a miscellaneous income item and is shown at the bottom of the income statement under Other Income.

Other Expenses and Other Income on the Income Statement

The net income figure with which you are already familiar refers to income from operations and is that regular operating income that results from the company's selling its product or service. The net operating income figure is compared and analyzed from period to period, and net income must be compared from the same source. Therefore, income items that are irregular are listed at the bottom of the income statement as an addition after net income from operations has been calculated. Other income might result from interest being received, a credit balance in the Cash Short and Over account, rent income (resulting when the business rents out an unused portion of the premises), or a gain incurred on the sale or disposition of an asset.

Other expense items are those expenses not normally incurred in regular operations and may include interest expense or a debit balance in the Cash Short and Over account. A portion of an income statement, with sections for other income and other expenses, is shown here.

Toy Warehouse Income Statement For Month Ended July 31, 19XX			
Revenue			
Sales		$75,000 —	
Less: Sales Returns and Allowances	$ 4,000 —		
Sales Discounts	1,300 —	5,300 —	
Net Sales			$69,700 —
Net Income from Operations			$ 7,000 —
Other Income			
Interest Income		$ 800 —	
Miscellaneous Income		200 —	
Total Other Income		1,000 —	
Other Expenses			
Interest Expense		350 —	650 —
Net Income			7,650 —

Miscellaneous Ordinary Interest Calculations

When money is borrowed for a period of time other than one year, the time portion of the interest formula will not be 1 (for one year). If, for example, money is borrowed for two years, the ordinary simple interest will be twice as much as if borrowed for one year.

Example $10,000 is borrowed at 9 percent for two years.

Formula: $I = P \times R \times T$
$I = \$10,000 \times 9\% \times 2$
$I = \$10,000 \times .09 \times 2$
$I = \$1,800$

If money is borrowed for half a year, the ordinary simple interest will be one-half of what it would be for a whole year. When the time is expressed in months, a fraction is used in the formula to express it. The numerator is the number of months for which the money is borrowed and the denominator is 12 (for one year).

Example $10,000 is borrowed at 12 percent for six months.

Formula: $I = P \times R \times T$
$I = \$10,000 \times .12 \times 6/12$
$I = \$600$

or, on a calculator,

$I = P \times R \times T$
$I = \$10,000 \times .12 \times .5$
(.5 is one-half or 6/12 of a year)
$I = \$600$

When money is borrowed for a specific number of days, a fraction is also used in the formula to express the time. The numerator will be the number of days for which the money is borrowed and the denominator will be 365.

Example $10,000 is borrowed at 12 percent for 60 days.

Formula: $I = P \times R \times T$
$I = 10,000 \times .12 \times 60/365$
$I = \$197.26$

Summary

A strong system of internal control will help a business protect its resources from theft, waste, and inefficiency; ensure that accounting data are accurate; and evaluate employees and departments to determine their level of performance. A strong system of internal control also provides a basis for regularly evaluating employees and departments and establishes a routine for the handling and management of cash.

Cash is received primarily from cash sales and from customers who are paying on account. Many stores, in addition, allow credit card sales; the store receives from the bank an amount equal to the total credit card sales minus a fee for the service. The amount of the fee is debited to an account called credit card discount expense.

All cash received is recorded in the cash receipts journal, and all cheques written are recorded in the cash payments journal. Every entry in the cash receipts journal is a debit to Cash, and every entry in the cash payments journal is a credit to Cash. Special columns are included in the journals as required. Immediate postings are required to the accounts receivable and accounts payable subsidiary ledgers, and daily postings are required from the sundry columns of the cash receipts and cash payments journals. At the end of the accounting period, the journals are crossfooted and ruled before summary posting is performed.

The combined cash journal is used primarily by professionals or small business owners. The process for journalizing and posting from the combined cash journal is the same as for the cash receipts and cash payments journals.

Sometimes merchandise or services are sold by accepting a promissory note for a portion or all that is owed. The maker of the note normally agrees to pay back the principal and interest within a certain time. The formula for calculating interest is: Interest = Principal $\times$ Rate $\times$ Time ($I = P \times R \times T$). Interest rates are normally expressed in terms of a year. Interest paid is recorded in the cash payments journal, and interest received is recorded in the cash receipts journal.

Vocabulary Review

Following is a list of the words and terms for this chapter:

collateral	maker
combined journal	negotiable
crossfoot	payee
expenditure	principal
foreclose	promissory note
fraud	reimburse
interest	repossess
interest formula	sundry
justify	valid

Fill in the blank with the correct word or term from the list.

1. A legal document that shows the amount borrowed, the interest rate, and the due date of the money borrowed and that is signed by the maker is called a/an _____.
2. A person who borrows money and who signs a note is called the _____ of the note.
3. The lender is called the _____ of the note.
4. The amount of money borrowed is called the _____.
5. An amount spent is a/an _____.
6. Security that is given for a loan is called _____.
7. A dishonest act in which someone is cheated is called _____.
8. The _____ is $I = P \times R \times T$.
9. To show or prove that something is right is to _____.
10. To take back possession of is to _____.
11. Another word for miscellaneous is _____.

12. When a borrower is behind in payments, the lender may choose to _____ on the property, thus depriving the borrower of ownership rights.
13. A charge made for the use of money is called _____.
14. A document that may be transferred from one party to another is said to be _____.
15. To repay is to _____.
16. Having facts to support something makes it _____.
17. To prove that the debit column totals equal the credit column totals of multicolumn journals is to _____.
18. A/An _____ is a journal that combines all special journals into one journal; sometimes called a synoptic journal.

Match the words and terms on the left with the definitions on the right.

19. collateral	a. to take back possession of
20. combined journal	b. the lender
21. crossfoot	c. $I = P \times R \times T$
22. expenditure	d. a dishonest act to deceive someone
23. foreclose	e. the amount borrowed
24. fraud	f. miscellaneous
25. interest	g. to repay
26. interest formula	h. transferable from one person or party to another
27. justify	i. the borrower
28. maker	j. an expense or amount spent
29. negotiable	k. security for a loan
30. payee	l. an amount charged for borrowing money
31. principal	m. legally sound because of facts or evidence
32. promissory note	n. to prove the equality of debit and credit column totals in a multicolumn journal
33. reimburse	o. a legal document indicating an amount of money borrowed, the interest rate, and the time; it is signed by the maker
34. repossess	p. a journal that combines all special journals
35. sundry	q. to prove to be right or fair
36. valid	r. to deprive a borrower of her or his ownership rights

Exercises

EXERCISE 9.1

Record the following in general journal form for Handy Hardware for the month of October 19XX. Handy Hardware is required to collect 8 percent provincial sales tax (PST) and 7 percent GST. Account titles required are Cash, Accounts Receivable, Provincial Sales Tax Payable, GST Charged, Sales, and Credit Card Discount Expense. Use journal page 14.

October 1   sold merchandise for cash to Rick Trevino, $90 plus 7 percent GST and 8 percent provincial sales tax (PST); invoice 143-L

October 4   sold merchandise for cash to Sandra Butler for $120 plus 7 percent GST and 8 percent PST; invoice 172-L

October 9 $658.95 is deposited into the bank for sales to customers who used their credit cards; the $658.95 represents charge sales for the first week of October totalling $600 plus 7 percent GST and 8 percent PST, minus a 4^1/$_2$ percent fee ($31.05).

EXERCISE 9.2   Record the following in general journal form for Noah's Boat Supplies for the month of May 19XX. Noah is not required to collect provincial sales tax, but he must collect and pay 7 percent GST. Account titles required are Cash, Accounts Receivable, Accounts Payable, GST Charged, GST Paid, Sales, Sales Returns and Allowances, Sales Discounts, Purchases, Purchases Returns and Allowances, and Purchases Discounts. Use journal page 6.

May 1   sold $500 plus 7 percent GST in merchandise to Flip Olsen; terms 1/10, n/30; invoice 4269-A.

May 2   issued credit memorandum 643 to Flip Olsen in the amount of $50 plus 7 percent GST; relates to invoice 4269-A dated May 1

May 4   purchased $850 plus 7 percent GST of merchandise from Water World; terms 2/10, n/60; invoice 72643

May 5   issued debit memo 916 to Water World in the amount of $100 plus 7 percent GST; relates to invoice 72643 dated May 4

May 11   received a cheque from Flip Olsen in full payment of invoice 4269-A, minus the May 2 return

May 14   sent cheque 1688 to Water World in full payment of its invoice 72643, minus the May 5 return

EXERCISE 9.3   Calculate the ordinary simple interest for the following. Round your answers to the nearest penny if necessary.

	Interest	=	Principal	×	Rate	×	Time
a.	_____	=	$ 5,000	×	14%	×	1 year
b.	_____	=	3,000	×	8	×	3 months
c.	_____	=	8,500	×	10	×	6 months
d.	_____	=	12,000	×	9	×	3 months
e.	_____	=	1,000	×	7	×	60 days
f.	_____	=	2,400	×	11	×	30 days
g.	_____	=	10,000	×	6	×	1 month
h.	_____	=	25,000	×	12	×	5 months
i.	_____	=	50,000	×	10	×	15 days
j.	_____	=	14,000	×	9	×	6 months

EXERCISE 9.4   Following are some of the account balances for Roger's Antiques on June 30, 19XX. Determine (a) the amount of net sales and (b) the cost of purchases.

Sales	$12,000
Purchases	7,500
Purchases Discounts	75
Sales Discounts	180
Freight In	500
Sales Returns and Allowances	370
Purchases Returns and Allowances	180
Delivery Expense	275

EXERCISE 9.5   Prepare the following entries in general journal form for Atlantic Marina. Account titles required are Cash, Notes Payable, and Interest Expense. Use journal page 2.

February 1   borrowed $5,000 from Commonwealth Bank, signed a six-month, 11 percent note payable; record the receipt of the cash

August 1   wrote a cheque to Commonwealth Bank in full payment of the February 1 note plus the 11 percent interest

EXERCISE 9.6   Prepare the following entries in general journal form for Wanda's Wholesale Jewellery. Account titles required are Cash, Notes Receivable, GST Charged, Sales, and Interest Income. Use journal page 2.

September 1   sold $7,000 plus 7 percent GST in merchandise to Gold House; accepted a three-month, 15 percent note in payment

December 1   received a cheque from Gold House in full payment of the September 1 note plus interest

EXERCISE 9.7   At the end of the day on March 18, Geri's Jeans had total cash sales of $590 plus 7 percent GST and 8 percent PST as evidenced by the cash register total. However, the actual cash on hand was only $673.50. In general journal form, prepare the entry to record the cash sales on March 18. Account titles required are Cash, PST Payable, GST Charged, Sales, and Cash Short and Over. Use journal page 9.

EXERCISE 9.8   1. Record the following cash sales in a general journal (page 10) for Geri's Jeans for the first week in March. (You may omit explanations.)
2. Determine whether the Cash Short and Over account has a debit or a credit balance and the amount of the balance.

Date	Sales	Actual Cash on Hand	Cash Short and (Over)
March 1	$2,754	$2,774	($20)
March 2	2,329	2,334	($5)
March 3	1,645	1,635	$10
March 4	1,520	1,519	$1
March 5	2,116	2,166	($50)
March 6	2,904	2,886	$18
March 7	1,592	1,590	$2

EXERCISE 9.9   After looking over the following different kinds of transactions, determine into which journal each should be recorded. Identify the journals by their posting reference notations: sales journal, S; purchases journal, P; cash receipts journal, CR; cash payments journal, CP; and general journal, GJ.

Type of Transaction	Which Journal?
a. paid monthly telephone bill	_____
b. purchase of merchandise for resale on account	_____
c. receipt of cash from a customer who is paying on account	_____
d. purchase of furniture on account	_____
e. sale of merchandise on account	_____
f. owner withdrew cash for personal use	_____
g. made payment to a creditor	_____
h. sold extra item of office equipment; will receive payment within 90 days	_____
i. owner invested additional cash into the business	_____
j. adjusting entries	_____
k. purchase of office equipment for cash	_____
l. borrowed money from a bank	_____
m. issued credit memorandum to a customer to whom merchandise was originally sold on account	_____
n. made payment on a loan, plus interest	_____
o. cash purchase of merchandise for resale	_____
p. recorded cash sales plus 6 percent sales tax	_____
q. received payment less a 2 percent discount from a customer to whom merchandise was sold earlier	_____
r. owner invested personal property into the business	_____
s. closing entries	_____
t. issued a debit memorandum to creditor from whom merchandise was purchased on account	_____

Problems

PROBLEM 9.1   Suzie Niessen owns a retail gift shop. Suzie makes sales for cash, sales on account, and credit card sales through the Horizon Credit Card Company. Seven percent GST is collected on all sales. Following are a partial chart of accounts and the transactions relating to cash received for the month of October 19XX.

Partial Chart of Accounts

101	Cash
110	Accounts Receivable
120	Notes Receivable
130	Office Equipment
220	GST Charged
301	Suzie Niessen, Capital
401	Sales
410	Interest Income
610	Credit Card Discount Expense

TRANSACTIONS

October 1   cash sales, $175 plus 7 percent GST

October 4   received a cheque for $189 from Ron King to apply on his account

October 8   deposited some credit card sales drafts in the bank; the sales totalled $1,500 plus 7 percent GST; the credit card discount charged is $71

October 12   cash sales, $290 plus 7 percent GST

October 15   Suzie Niessen invested an additional $6,000 in the business

October 17   Suzie decided to sell to Al Torino an extra item of office equipment for $5,500 cash, plus 7 percent GST; this was her original cost for the equipment

October 20   received a cheque for $52.50 from Barbara Goode to apply on her account

October 24   deposited some credit card sales drafts in the bank; the sales totalled $2,500 plus 7 percent GST; the credit card discount charged is $118

October 27   cash sales, $700 plus 7 percent GST

October 31   received a cheque from Andrew Pate for $1,200; this represents full payment of his $1,000 outstanding note of a year ago, plus interest

INSTRUCTIONS

1. Journalize the transactions in a cash receipts journal. Use page 10.
2. Total, crossfoot, and rule the journal.
3. Indicate, by check marks and account numbers, how the journal would look if posting were complete.

PROBLEM 9.2

Wayne Werner owns a retail store called Artists' Supply Shop. Wayne takes advantage of all purchases discounts offered. Following are a partial chart of accounts and the transactions relating to cash payments for the month of April 19XX.

Partial Chart of Accounts	
101	Cash
220	Accounts Payable
230	Notes Payable
235	GST Paid
240	Payroll Taxes Payable
320	Wayne Werner, Drawing
501	Purchases
510	Purchases Discount
520	Freight In
605	Rent Expense
610	Utilities Expense
620	Insurance Expense
630	Interest Expense

TRANSACTIONS   April 1   wrote cheque 5203 to Star Realty for $650 for April rent

April 3   wrote cheque 5204 for $125 plus 7 percent GST to Kwik Delivery when it delivered an out-of-town purchase

April 6   Wayne Werner withdrew $500 for personal use; cheque 5205

April 8   wrote cheque 5206 for $175 to Revenue Canada for payroll taxes due

April 11   wrote cheque 5207 for $1,890 to Sandberg's Paints in payment of its invoice 1643-2 for $1,800 plus 7 percent GST, less a 2 percent discount

April 15   wrote cheque 5208 for $140 to Ontario Hydro for electricity bill

April 19   wrote cheque 5209 for $1,272 to Art Corner in payment of its invoice 469-20 for $1,200 plus 7 percent GST, less a 1 percent discount

April 22   wrote cheque 5210 to Bell Canada for $92 in payment of telephone bill

April 25   wrote cheque 5211 to Royal Bank for $525 in full payment of a $500 note plus interest

April 28   Wayne Werner withdrew $500 for personal use; cheque 5212

April 30   wrote cheque 5213 for $525 to Sandberg's Paints in payment of its invoice 1740-2 for $500 plus 7 percent GST, less a 2 percent discount

April 30   wrote cheque 5214 to Creative Concepts for $642 plus 7 percent GST for purchase of art supplies for resale (note: this is a cash purchase of merchandise for resale)

INSTRUCTIONS
1. Journalize the transactions in a cash payments journal. Use page 4.
2. Total, crossfoot, and rule the journal.
3. Indicate, by check marks and account numbers, how the journal would look if posting were complete.

PROBLEM 9.3   Grace O'Brien owns a retail store called The Book Depot. Grace sells merchandise for cash and on account and also accepts credit card sales through the Wonder Charge Company. Grace takes advantage of all purchases discounts by paying within the discount period. Seven percent GST is charged on each sale and is paid on each purchase. Following are a partial chart of accounts with balances for selected accounts as of December 1, partial schedules of accounts receivable and accounts payable as of December 1, and the cash transactions for December.

Partial Chart of Accounts		
101 Cash	$3,800	
110 Accounts Receivable	5,000	
120 Notes Receivable	400	
201 Accounts Payable		$3,000
210 Notes Payable		2,500
220 GST Charged		600
230 GST Paid	280	
301 Grace O'Brien, Capital		7,500
310 Grace O'Brien, Drawing		
401 Sales		
410 Interest Income		
501 Purchases		
510 Purchases Discounts		
601 Credit Card Discount Expense		
610 Salaries Expense		
620 Utilities Expense		
630 Rent Expense		
640 Interest Expense		

Partial Schedule of Accounts Receivable		Partial Schedule of Accounts Payable	
Ellen Brown	$ 150.00	Book Wholesalers	$802.50
Kenneth Kong	150.00	Paperbacks, Inc.	963.00
Wonder Charge Company	3,531.00		

TRANSACTIONS

December 1 — cash sales, $320 plus 7 percent GST

December 2 — wrote cheque 9013 to East Coast Realty for December rent; $1,500

December 5 — received a $70 cheque from Ellen Brown to apply on her account

December 6 — wrote cheque 9014 to Book Wholesalers for $787.50 in full payment of its invoice 1620-A for $750 plus 7 percent GST, less a 2 percent discount

December 9 — received payment from Wonder Charge Company for sales that totalled $1,100 plus 7 percent GST; the credit card discount charged was $52

December 10 — wrote cheque 9015 to Cheryl Stinson for her part-time salary, $220

December 11 — wrote cheque 9016 to Bell Canada in payment of telephone bill, $82

December 12 — Grace O'Brien invested an additional $4,500 into the business

December 15 — cash sales, $570 plus 7 percent GST

December 16   Grace O'Brien withdrew $800 for personal use; cheque 9017

December 17   wrote cheque 9018 to Paperbacks, Inc. for $954, which represents payment in full of its invoice 16204 for $900 plus 7 percent GST, less a 1 percent discount

December 18   received a $50 cheque from Kenneth Kong to apply on his account

December 24   received a cheque from Thomas Payne for $440, which represents full payment of his outstanding note for $400 plus interest

December 26   wrote cheque 9019 to Ontario Hydro in payment of electricity bill, $230

December 26   wrote cheque 9020 to Books Unlimited for $520 plus 7 percent GST for purchase of books for resale

December 28   cash sales, $900 plus 7 percent GST

December 29   wrote cheque 9021 for $2,750 to Eastern Savings Company in full payment of outstanding note of $2,500 plus interest

December 30   received cheque from Ellen Brown for $80 to apply on her account

December 31   received payment from Wonder Charge Company for sales that totalled $2,200 plus 7 percent GST; the credit card discount charged is $104

INSTRUCTIONS

1. Transfer the account balances to the general ledger accounts and to the subsidiary ledger accounts.
2. Journalize December's transactions into a cash receipts journal, page 16, and a cash payments journal, page 20.
3. As an entry is journalized to accounts receivable or accounts payable, post immediately to the appropriate account in either the accounts receivable or the accounts payable ledger.
4. When journalizing is complete, total, crossfoot, and rule the journals.
5. Perform the required posting from the cash receipts journal and the cash payments journal. Remember, amounts appearing in the sundry columns must be posted individually.

PROBLEM 9.4

Willie Davis owns a retail store called Family Cycles. He sells bicycles and parts, both for cash and on account. Willie uses a cash receipts journal, a cash payments journal, sales and purchases journals, and a general journal. Willie is required to collect 7 percent GST on all sales and pay 7 percent GST on all purchases; terms of credit sales are n/30. Following are the partial chart of accounts and the transactions for Family Cycles for the month of May 19XX.

Partial Chart of Accounts

---

101 Cash
110 Accounts Receivable
130 Office Equipment
210 Accounts Payable
220 GST Charged
230 GST Paid
301 Willie Davis, Capital
310 Willie Davis, Drawing
401 Sales
410 Sales Returns and Allowances
501 Purchases
510 Purchases Returns and Allowances
601 Rent Expense
620 Utilities Expense
630 Credit Card Discount Expense

TRANSACTIONS

May 1   purchased unassembled bicycles from Bike World on account; $1,750 plus 7 percent GST; invoice 72403 dated May 1; terms n/30

May 2   wrote cheque 4039 to Olympic Realty for $800 for the May rent

May 3   sold a bicycle to Hortense Wiggins on account; $250 plus 7 percent GST; invoice 2031-14.

May 4   wrote cheque 4040 to B.C. Hydro for $180 for electricity bill

May 5   received in the mail a $400 cheque from Bob Dole in partial payment of his account

May 10   purchased bicycle parts on account from The Cyclery; $800 plus 7 percent GST; invoice 6043-A dated May 10; terms n/30

May 11   sold a bicycle to Doc Smoley for $275 cash plus 7 percent GST; invoice 2031-15

May 12   Willie Davis wrote cheque 4041 for $600 for personal use

May 15   sold bicycle parts on account to Wayne Dyke; $50 plus 7 percent GST; invoice 2031-16

May 15   deposited credit card sales drafts in the bank; the sales totalled $2,450 plus 7 percent GST; the credit card discount charged is $98

May 16   wrote cheque 4042 to Bike World in full payment of Family Cycles' May 1 purchase; invoice 72403

May 18   sold five bicycles to Riders Anonymous for $1,250 cash plus 7 percent GST; invoice 2031-17

May 19   purchased bicycle parts on account from Cycle World; $570 plus 7 percent GST; invoice 42137 dated May 19; terms n/30

May 20   Family Cycles issued debit memorandum 231-B for $60 plus 7 percent GST to Cycle World relating to its invoice 42137 of May 19; Family Cycles is returning some parts to Cycle World

May 21   wrote cheque 4043 to The Cyclery in full payment of Family Cycles' May 10 purchase, invoice 6043-A

May 21   wrote cheque 4044 to Atlas Cycles for $922 plus 7 percent GST for purchase of bicycle parts for resale

May 23   sold three bicycles to Rose Santiago on account; $950 plus 7 percent GST; invoice 2031-18

May 24   received a $100 cheque in the mail from Hortense Wiggins to apply on her account

May 25   wrote cheque 4045 to World Sports for $800 plus 7 percent GST for the purchase of bicycles for resale

May 26   purchased a small computer on account for office use from Computer World; $4,000 plus 7 percent GST; invoice 9034-21 dated May 26; terms n/30

May 27   wrote cheque 4046 to Bell Canada in payment of phone bill, $90

May 28   sold bicycle parts on account to Joe Yamaha; $160 plus 7 percent GST; invoice 2031-19

May 29   Family Cycles issued credit memorandum 603-C for $10 plus 7 percent GST to Joe Yamaha relating to May 28 invoice 2031-19; he returned a portion of the parts he had purchased

May 31   purchased bicycle parts on account from Bikes 'N Cycles; $350 plus 7 percent GST; invoice 30116 dated May 31; terms n/30

May 31   deposited credit card sales drafts in the bank; the sales totalled $3,190 plus 7 percent GST; the credit card discount charged is $127.60

INSTRUCTIONS   1. Journalize sales of merchandise on account in the sales journal, page 5; purchases of merchandise on account in the purchases journal, page 6; cash receipts in the cash receipts journal, page 7; cash payments in the cash payments journal, page 8; and the miscellaneous entries in the general journal, page 15.
2. Total, crossfoot (where required), and rule each journal.
3. Indicate, by using check marks and account numbers, how the journals would look if posting were complete.

PROBLEM 9.5   Butler Products sells kitchen cabinets to wholesale outlets. It does not have to collect provincial sales tax, but it must charge and pay 7 percent GST on all sales and purchases. All sales and purchases on account have credit terms of n/30. Following is a partial chart of accounts, the names in the accounts receivable and accounts payable ledgers, and the transactions for the month of March 19XX.

Partial Chart of Accounts

101	Cash
110	Accounts Receivable
210	Accounts Payable
215	Bank Loan Payable
220	GST Charged
230	GST Paid
310	Jack Daniels, Capital
320	Jack Daniels, Drawing
401	Sales
410	Sales Returns and Allowances
510	Purchases
520	Purchases Returns and Allowances
610	Salaries Expense
620	Advertising Expense
630	Rent Expense

Accounts Receivable Subsidiary Ledger

Creative Cookery
Dawson Designs
Krafty Kitchens

Accounts Payable Subsidiary Ledger

Allistar Supplies
International Importers
Kitchen Kupboards

March 1   paid rent of $650, cheque 1101

March 3   paid for advertising in *The Tribune*, $330 plus 7 percent GST, cheque 1102

March 3   purchased unassembled cabinets from International Importers on account, $1,450 plus 7 percent GST, invoice 506

March 5   sold cabinets to Dawson Designs on account, $750 plus 7 percent GST, invoice 107

March 7   purchased products from Kitchen Kupboards on account, $1,240 plus 7 percent GST, invoice 5092

March 9   issued a debit memorandum to Kitchen Kupboards in the amount of $280 plus 7 percent GST for damaged merchandise received on the May 7 invoice 5092 (note: the $19.60 credit to GST paid will be recorded in parentheses in the GST paid *debit* column)

March 12   sold cabinets to Krafty Kitchens on account, $2,200 plus 7 percent GST, invoice 108

March 15   Paid semimonthly salaries in the amount of $1,080, cheque 1103

March 18   purchased materials from Allistar Supplies on account, $490 plus 7 percent GST, invoice 6042

March 19   sold cabinets to Dawson Designs on account, $1,480 plus 7 percent GST, invoice 109

March 21   borrowed $2,000 from the Toronto Dominion Bank on a 12-month loan with interest at 8 percent

March 22   sold cabinets to Creative Cookery on account, $1,750 plus 7 percent GST, invoice 110

March 23   issued credit memorandum to Creative Cookery in the amount of $400 plus 7 percent GST as an allowance for defective merchandise received by it on invoice 110 dated March 22 (note: the $28 debit to GST charged will be recorded in parentheses in the GST charged *credit* column)

March 24   received a cheque from Dawson Designs in full payment of March 5 invoice 107

March 25   issued cheque 1104 to International Importers in full payment of its March 3 invoice 506

March 27   Jack Daniels invested an additional $2,000 in the business

March 28   sold cabinets to Creative Cookery on account, $1,290 plus 7 percent GST, invoice 111

March 29   received a cheque from Krafty Kitchens in full payment of the March 12 invoice 108

March 31   paid semimonthly salaries in the amount of $1,080, cheque 1105

March 31   received a cheque from Creative Cookery in full payment of the March 22 invoice 110, less the March 23 allowance

March 31   issued cheque 1106 to Allistar Supplies in full payment of its March 18 invoice 6042

March 31   Jack Daniels withdrew $300 for personal use, cheque 1107

INSTRUCTIONS
1. Record all the transactions in a combined journal, page 9.
2. Post all amounts to the general ledger as required. Remember, the amounts appearing in the sundry columns must be posted individually.
3. Post all amounts to accounts receivable and accounts payable to the subsidiary ledgers immediately after journalizing.
4. Total, crossfoot, and rule the journal.

PROBLEM 9.6   The Surfside Company does not have to collect provincial sales tax, but it must charge and pay 7 percent GST on all sales and purchases. Terms of sale are 2/10, n/30. Following are a partial chart of accounts, the names in the accounts receivable and accounts payable ledgers, and the transactions completed during February of the current year.

Partial Chart of Accounts

101	Cash
110	Accounts Receivable
120	Office Equipment
210	Accounts Payable
220	GST Charged
230	GST Paid
401	Sales
410	Sales Returns and Allowances
420	Sales Discounts
501	Purchases
510	Purchases Returns and Allowances
520	Purchases Discounts
620	Rent Expense
630	Advertising Expense

Accounts Receivable Subsidiary Ledger

Terry Long
Geri Nash

Accounts Payable Subsidiary Ledger

Bestco Company
Goode Company
Western Company

February 1   purchased merchandise on an invoice dated January 30 from Goode Company; terms 2/10, n/60, $1,385 plus 7 percent GST

February 2   issued cheque 567 to *The Star* for advertising, $115 plus 7 percent GST

February 4   sold merchandise on account to Terry Long, invoice 862, $750 plus 7 percent GST, terms 2/10, n/30

February 5   returned for credit defective merchandise purchased from Goode Company on February 1, $135 plus 7 percent GST (note: the credit to GST Paid will be recorded by placing $9.45 in parentheses in the GST paid *debit* column)

February 7   cash sales for the week ended February 7, $1,045 plus 7 percent GST

February 8   issued cheque 568 to Goode Company in payment of its invoice of January 30 less the return of February 5 and the discount

February 9   sold merchandise on account to Geri Nash, invoice 863, $570 plus 7 percent GST, terms 2/10, n/30

February 10   purchased office equipment on account from Western Company, terms n/10, EOM, $345 plus 7 percent GST

February 11   issued a credit memorandum to Geri Nash for defective merchandise sold to her on February 9 and returned by her, $70 plus 7 percent GST (note: the debit to GST charged will be recorded by placing $4.90 in parentheses in the GST charged *credit* column)

February 13   received a cheque from Terry Long in full payment of the February 4 invoice 862 less the discount

February 14   cash sales for the week ended February 14, $990 plus 7 percent GST

February 15   issued cheque 569 to Lakeland Realty for one month's rent, $850

February 16   issued a debit memorandum in the amount of $75 plus 7 percent GST to Western Company for defective office equipment purchased on February 10 (note: the credit to GST paid will be recorded by placing $5.25 in parentheses in the GST paid *debit* column)

February 17   purchased merchandise from Bestco Company on an invoice dated February 15; terms 2/10, n/60; $1,000 plus 7 percent GST

February 19   received a cheque from Geri Nash in full payment of the February 9 invoice 863 less the return of February 11 and the discount

February 21   cash sales for the week ended February 21, $1,120 plus 7 percent GST

February 23   purchased merchandise from Goode Company on an invoice dated February 21; terms 1/10, n/60; $785 plus 7 percent GST

February 24   sold merchandise on account to Geri Nash; invoice 864; $635 plus 7 percent GST; terms 2/10, n/30

February 25   issued cheque 570 to Bestco Company in payment of its invoice of February 15 less the discount

February 28   cash sales for the week ended February 28, $1,015 plus 7 percent GST

INSTRUCTIONS
1. Record all the transactions in a combined journal, page 4.
2. Post all amounts to the general ledger. Remember, the amounts appearing in the sundry columns must be posted individually.
2. Post all amounts to accounts receivable and accounts payable immediately to the subsidiary ledgers after journalizing.
4. Total, crossfoot, and rule the journal.

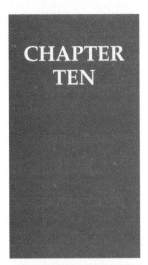

The Bank Account and Cash Funds

Learning Objectives

When you have completed this chapter, you should
1. have an increased understanding of accounting terminology.
2. have a basic understanding of bank accounts.
3. be able to reconcile a bank statement.
4. be able to prepare the journal entries necessary to bring the books up to date after bank statement reconciliation is complete.
5. be able to prepare the journal entries to establish and replenish a petty cash fund.
6. be able to prepare the journal entries required to establish a change fund.

Vocabulary

accessible   easily obtained

automated   automatically controlled or operated

cancelled cheque   a cheque that has been paid by the bank and that is marked paid

change fund   a certain amount of cash that is kept on hand for use in the company's cash register

denomination   a unit in a system of money (for example, a $10 bill, a $1 coin, a nickel, a dime)

deposit in transit   a deposit that has been made but that does not appear on the bank statement until later

endorsement   a signature or a company stamp on the back of a cheque; required before cashing or depositing the cheque.

non-sufficient funds/NSF cheque   a cheque previously deposited but debited back to the payee's account because there were not sufficient funds in the maker's account to cover it

outstanding cheque   a cheque that has been written but that has not yet been presented to the bank for payment

petty cash   a cash fund that is kept on hand from which small cash payments may be made

reconcile   to bring into agreement

restrictive endorsement   an endorsement that prohibits further circulation of a cheque

serial   arranged in a series; for example, 1001, 1002, 1003, 1004 . . .

Introduction

Most businesses pay their bills by cheque. The cheque and its accompanying stub provide information for the accountant. Entries are made in the cash payments journal from the stubs. Paying bills by serially numbered cheques provides an important element of internal control over cash; only certain persons will be authorized to write the cheques and the cheques that are written are returned as cancelled to the business. It is then easy to check to see whether any are missing and whether the information recorded in the cash payments journal agrees with the cheque information on the cheque itself.

Opening a Bank Account

Before a bank account may be opened, personal information (social insurance number, name, address, and so on) must be provided to the bank. A signature card is filled out and signed by each person who is authorized to sign cheques on the account. If there is any doubt about the validity of a signature on an incoming cheque, the bank employee will use the signature card to verify that the signature on the cheque is an authorized one.

   Serially numbered cheques are obtained from the bank with the depositor's name, address, and phone number printed on each. The numbered cheques allow the business owner to easily discover any missing cheques and thus help maintain the system of internal control over cash. In addition to the serial numbers at the top of each cheque, each depositor is assigned an account number that is printed on the cheque in magnetic ink so that cheques may be processed by computer.

Deposits

It is recommended business practice to make daily deposits of all cash received. Deposit slips contain a space to list currency, coins, and cheques. The following illustrates a deposit slip for Robert's Pastries:

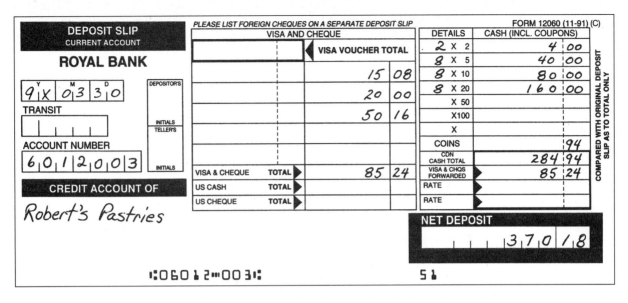

Most banks also provide deposit slips in book form with space to record the name of the person or the company paying by cheque. The carbon copy duplicate of the deposit slip is retained on file by the depositor and used as the source document for entering in the cash receipts journal.

Restrictive Endorsements

Deposits may be made by mail or in person. In either case, an **endorsement** in the form of a signature or company stamp is required. Cash deposits should not be sent through the mail because of the possibility of theft. Cheques, however, may be protected from theft by a **restrictive endorsement**, which stops any further circulation. The restrictive endorsement shown should be stamped or handwritten on the backs of the cheques as soon as they are received.

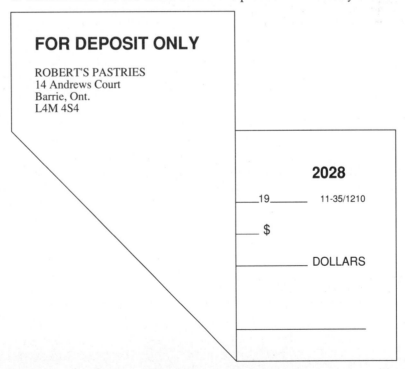

Automated Banking Machines

Deposits may be made at an **automated** banking machine (if one is available), which makes the bank **accessible** for deposits and withdrawals 24 hours a day. The automated tellers, as they are sometimes called, are convenient and easy to use. A plastic card, similar to an ordinary credit card, and a code number (known only to the depositor) are all that are required for their use. The automatic teller "talks" to the depositor on a television-like screen, processes the deposit or withdrawal, and gives the depositor a record of the transaction.

It is good business practice to have the services of an automated banking machine available. Because they may be used at any hour of the day or night, cash may conveniently be deposited after banking hours. When an automated banking machine is not available, the business owner may wish to use a night depository so that large sums of cash are not lying around. The bank will provide deposit bags and a key to the night depository if the depositor wishes to take advantage of this service.

Cheque Stubs

Before a cheque is written, the accompanying cheque stub should be carefully filled in. The cheque stub should show the date the cheque was written, to whom, for what amount, and for what reason. In addition, it will show the balance in the cash account before and after the cheque is written.

The cheque stubs are used as the source documents for entries in the cash payments journal.

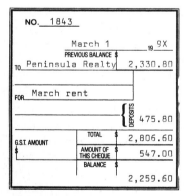
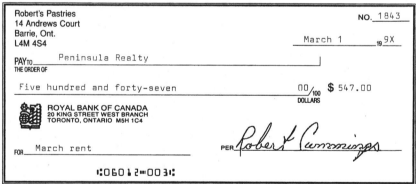

Stop Payment Orders

Once a cheque has been written and presented to someone as payment, it is the issuer's order to the bank to make payment. If the issuer changes her or his mind, a stop payment order may be issued that instructs the bank not to make the payment. The bank will charge the issuer a fee for the stop payment order, which is most effective if issued soon after the cheque is written. Of course, the bank cannot stop payment if the cheque has already been paid.

The Bank Statement

Once a month the bank sends a statement to the depositor showing all the transactions that occurred in that account. Each cheque presented to the bank for payment is listed on the statement; each deposit made is listed; and each miscellaneous transaction is shown (sometimes by a code letter or a prepared list). Miscellaneous transactions are referred to as debits or credits to the account. Debit entries are deductions from the account (such as cheques) and credit entries are additions to the account (such as deposits). On the accounting records of the bank, each depositor's account is handled like an account payable. A **cancelled cheque** is a cheque that has been paid by the bank and that is in some way marked paid or cancelled.

Bank Statement Reconciliation

When the bank statement is received, it will show the cash balance at the beginning and at the end of the period. In most cases, the ending cash balance will not agree with the depositor's general ledger balance. There are many reasons for this difference. The depositor must **reconcile** the bank statement balance, or bring it and the general ledger balance into agreement. Once reconciliation is complete, the depositor knows the correct cash balance. If reconciliation is completed at the end of the month, the cash balance determined by reconciliation will appear on the balance sheet as well as in the general ledger.

Some causes for the discrepancy between the ending bank balance and the general ledger balance follow:

1. **Outstanding cheques** have not yet been presented to the bank for payment. They must be subtracted from the bank statement balance when reconciling.
2. **Deposits in transit** have been made but do not yet appear on the bank statement. All such deposits must be added to the bank balance when reconciling.
3. Service charges are made by the bank for handling the account. The service charge is usually based on the amount of the average daily balance in the account and the number of transactions that occur each month. A service charge will show on the bank statement as a debit entry (reducing the depositor's balance) and must be subtracted from the balance in the general ledger when reconciling.
4. Special collections are made by the bank for the depositor and will appear on the bank statement as miscellaneous credits (increasing the depositor's balance). Often, a depositor will designate the bank as payee on an outstanding note receivable. When the note becomes due, the maker will pay the face amount of the note plus the interest to the lender's bank, which will in turn deposit the money into the lender's account. Special collections will be added to the general ledger balance when reconciling.
5. Miscellaneous charges are made by the bank and will appear on the bank statement as miscellaneous debits reducing the depositor's balance. Such charges might include: (a) safe deposit box rental fee; (b) cheque printing charge; (c) fee for a stop payment order; and (d) charges for **NSF cheques** (non-sufficient funds in the bank to cover the amount of the cheque). In addition to bank charges, the depositor might authorize another firm to deduct money from the account on a regular basis. Such deductions might be for a loan payment, an insurance premium, or a savings account. They will appear on the bank statement as debits (or deductions) from the depositor's balance. Miscellaneous charges are subtracted from the chequebook balance when reconciling, and will be journalized and posted.
6. Errors may be made either by the bank or by the depositor and will, of course, cause a discrepancy when reconciling. When a bank error is discovered, the depositor should notify the bank immediately. Errors on the depositor's books should be corrected when reconciling.

Steps in Preparing a Bank Statement Reconciliation

Before reconciliation can take place, the depositor needs the bank statement, the cancelled cheques, and the cash payment and cash receipts journals. Most bank statements provide a reconciliation form on the back of the statement. Although each one is a little different, they are generally similar. Basically, the depositor must do the following:

1. Check to make sure that all deposits recorded in the cash receipts journal are entered on the bank statement. Deposits that do not appear on the bank statement are called deposits in transit and are added to the bank balance. It is possible, too, that a deposit that appears on the bank statement does not appear in the cash receipts journal. This indicates that the depositor forgot to record the deposit when it was made. If this is the case, the depositor must add the deposit to the general ledger when reconciling.
2. If cancelled cheques are included with the bank statement, place them in numerical order. Compare the amounts on the cheques with the amounts written in the cash payments journal to make sure that they are the same.
3. Check the miscellaneous debits and credits (subtractions and additions) on the bank statement. The debit entries will be subtracted from the general ledger balance, and the credit entries will be added to the general ledger balance when reconciling (if this has not been done already).

Illustration of a Bank Statement Reconciliation

When Robert Cummings received the bank statement for Robert's Pastries, it showed a balance on March 31 of $5,571.39. The general ledger balance on this date was $5,957.88.

Robert took the following steps to reconcile the bank statement:
1. He compared the deposits in the cash receipts journal with those on the bank statement. There was one deposit in transit on March 31 for $371.50.
2. He put the cancelled cheques in numerical order and compared the amounts on the cheques with the amounts entered in the cash payments journal. Robert noticed that cheque number 1872 written for $60 in payment of the electricity bill was recorded incorrectly in the cash payments journal as $90.
3. He compared the cancelled cheques with the cash payments journal and found that there were five outstanding cheques:

1885	$ 20.00	1894	$10.00
1888	$ 32.14	1896	$48.50
1893	$150.16		

4. Robert noted the debit entries listed on the bank statement.
   a. March 10 — an NSF cheque from Customer M for $150 and a debit memo from the bank for $10 representing the bank's charge for the NSF cheque.
   b. March 12 — Robert's cheque to Provincial Life Insurance for $137.79 cleared the bank. This is a pre-authorized cheque that comes directly from the insurance company to the bank and is automatically deducted from Robert's account for an insurance policy on the manager's life. Robert entered into the agreement and signed the necessary papers some time ago.
   c. Bank service charge—$8.

None of these debit entries were recorded on Robert's books before reconciliation.

Account Statement

	Account No.
	6012003

Robert's Pastries
14 Andrews Court
Barrie, ON
L4M 4S4

Period	
From	**To**
02/28	03/31/9X

Enclosures	Page
34	1

Date	Transaction Description	Cheques & Debits	Deposits & Credits	Balance
02 28				2651 80
03 01		321 00	475 80	
		547 00		2259 60
03 02		92 17	340 18	2507 61
03 03		50 00	353 06	
		113 06		2697 61
03 04		40 00	321 17	
		91 34		2887 44
03 05		20 00	350 60	3218 04
03 08		150 00	482 10	3550 14
03 09		51 00	330 18	
		57 26		
		30 00		3742 06
03 10	NSF Cheque	150 00		
	NSF Charge	10 00		
		59 68	340 79	3863 17
03 11		150 00	320 18	
		52 59		3980 76
03 12	Provincial Life	137 79	356 01	4198 98
03 15		124 82	403 50	
		60 00		4417 66
03 16		20 00	351 07	4748 73
03 17		86 96	348 32	5010 09
03 18		30 16	360 24	5340 17
03 19		120 00	366 80	
		54 84		5532 13
03 22		113 77	490 14	5908 50
03 23		330 00	340 06	5918 56
03 24		19 95	350 64	
		547 00		5702 25
03 25		503 57	353 90	5552 58
03 26		324 15	360 08	5588 51
03 29		50 00	365 20	5903 71
03 30		549 00	370 18	
		145 50		5579 39
03 31	Service Charge	8 00		5571 39

To reconcile the bank statement, Robert must do the following:

Step 1.	Write in the ending bank balance	$5,571.39
Step 2.	Add deposit in transit, March 31	+ 371.50
	Subtotal	$5,942.89
Step 3.	Subtract outstanding cheques:	
	1885	$ 20.00
	1888	32.14
	1893	150.16
	1894	10.00
	1896	48.50
	Total	− 260.80

Step 4.	Determine adjusted bank balance	$5,682.09
Step 5.	Write in the ending general ledger balance	$5,957.88
Step 6.	*Add* the amount of the error in recording cheque number 1872	
	$90.00 − $60.00 = $30.00	+ 30.00
	Subtotal	$5,987.88
Step 7.	Subtract the bank statement debits:	

a. NSF cheque (Customer M) plus Service charge (debit memo)	$ 160.00
b. Insurance premium	137.79
c. Bank service charge	8.00
Total deductions	− 305.79

Step 8.	Determine adjusted general ledger balance	$5,682.09

Required Journal Entries

When reconciliation is complete and the correct cash account balance has been determined, certain journal entries must be made to bring the books up to date. Normally, a journal entry will be required for every correction made on the general ledger portion of the reconciliation. For Robert's Pastries, the general journal entries are:

GENERAL JOURNAL						PAGE 8
Date		**Description**	**Post. Ref.**	**Debit**		**Credit**
19XX Mar.	31	Cash		30 —		
		Utilities Expense				30 —
		To Correct Incorrect Amount Recorded for Cheque Number				
		1872 (Bank Reconciliation, March 31, 19XX)				
	31	Accounts Receivable, Customer "M"		160 —		
		Insurance Expense		137 79		
		Bank Charges Expense		8 —		
		Cash				305 79
		To Record Amounts Necessary after Bank Statement				
		Reconciliation, March 31, 19XX				

The first entry debiting Cash and crediting Utilities Expense was made because $30 *too much* was subtracted from the cash account in the cash payments journal (a $60 cheque was recorded as $90). Therefore, $30 has to be added back to the cheque stubs and to the cash account, and the Utilities Expense account must, too, be corrected.

The entry debiting Accounts Receivable for $160 places Customer M back on the books, because there were insufficient funds in M's account to cover the cheque given to Robert's Pastries. Notice that the $10 service charge is also debited to M's account in the hope that both the amount of the cheque and the service charge will be recovered from the customer.

The other entries record the debits to Insurance Expense and Bank Charges Expense and the corresponding credits to Cash.

After these entries have been posted, the books will be up to date. The ledger account for Cash will be equal to the corrected bank statement balance. The corrections must also be recorded in the cheque stubs so that they will agree with the ledger account for Cash.

T Account Bank Statement Reconciliation

A simple form may be used when reconciling the bank statement if a printed form is not available. The form simply lists the ending bank balance and any additions and subtractions on the left-hand side of the page and the ending general ledger balance and any additions or subtractions on the right-hand side of the page.

For Robert's Pastries, a T account reconciliation looks like this:

Robert's Pastries
Bank Reconciliation
March 31, 19XX

Bank balance, 3/31		$5,571.39	General ledger balance, 3/31		$5,957.88
Add: Deposit in transit, 3/31		+ 371.50	Add: Error in recording cheque 1872		+ 30.00
		$5,942.89			$5,987.88
Deduct:			Deduct:		
Outstanding cheques			a. NSF cheque (M) plus service		
#1885—	$ 20.00		charge (DM)	$160.00	
#1888—	32.14		b. Insurance premium		
#1893—	150.16		(manager's life)	137.79	
#1894—	10.00		c. Service charge	8.00	
#1896—	48.50	− 260.80			305.79
Adjusted bank balance		$5,682.09	Adjusted general ledger balance		$5,682.09

The Petty Cash Fund

While business owners are advised to pay most bills by cheque, there are some payments that may be made in cash because it is so much more convenient. For example, payments to the mail carrier for postage due, payments for packages delivered, or small payments for supplies would best be made with cash. For such expenditures, a special cash fund called **petty cash** is established.

The amount of money put into the petty cash fund depends on the needs of the business. If there is danger of theft, the petty cash fund should be kept small and should be reimbursed often. If there is little danger of theft, the owner may choose to establish a fund that will last through the month.

Establishing the Fund

To establish the petty cash fund, a cheque is written in favour of the petty cashier. It is cashed and the money is put into a strong box or some other safe place. The entry will be recorded in the cash payments journal.

The entry simply takes money from one cash account and puts it into another. The petty cash account is an asset and will be listed on the balance sheet along with the cash account.

After the original entry to establish the fund, the account for petty cash will not be debited again unless it is decided to increase or decrease the amount of money kept in the fund.

CASH PAYMENTS JOURNAL						Sundry Accounts Debit	Accounts Payable Debit	Purchases Discount Credit	Cash Credit	PAGE 10
Date		Cheque No.	Paid To	Account Debited	Post. Ref.	Sundry Accounts Debit	Accounts Payable Debit	Purchases Discount Credit	Cash Credit	
19XX Oct.	1	1075	Petty Cashier	Petty Cash		75—			75—	

Making Petty Cash Payments

Vouchers are kept with the petty cash so that a record of all payments made out of the fund will be shown there. If, for example, $6 is paid out of petty cash for the monthly charge for a local newspaper, a voucher would be filled out as follows:

PETTY CASH VOUCHER

No. _1_   Date _Oct 3, 19XX_

PAID TO _Bay Area Press_

AMOUNT PAID _$6.00_

ACCOUNT DEBITED _Miscellaneous Expense_

APPROVED BY   PAYMENT RECEIVED BY

_R.C._   _Sandy Odette_

Usually one or two persons will be given access to the petty cash fund and will make cash payments from it. The person(s) so designated should initial each voucher and have the one who is receiving the cash sign the voucher. Making one or two persons responsible for the fund and having the payee sign each voucher gives some internal control over the cash.

The Petty Cash Disbursements Register

While some companies prefer simply to put the vouchers into their various categories and find totals for each category, many firms require that petty cash disbursements be recorded in a register similar to the cash payments journal. On the facing page is a petty cash disbursements register for the month of March.

Note that the amount of the fund, $75, is entered on the first line of the register. Each expenditure is recorded in the payments column and also is recorded under its appropriate column heading. When petty cash is replenished at the end of the month or sooner, each column is totalled. Crossfooting ensures that no errors have been made before the journal entry is prepared.

PETTY CASH DISBURSEMENTS REGISTER FOR MONTH OF MARCH　　　**PAGE 1**

Date	Voucher No.	Explanation	Receipts	Payments	Supplies 140	Delivery Exp. 640	Misc. Exp. 690	Sundry Debits Acct. No.	Amount
March 1		To Establish Fund	$75.00						
3	1	Bay Area Press		6.00			6.00		
5	2	Sam Strauss—Cleaning		10.00				615	10.00
6	3	E & L Stationery		4.50	4.50				
9	4	United Delivery		8.40		8.40			
12	5	Sam Strauss—Cleaning		10.00				615	10.00
18	6	Burke's Drug Store		3.15	3.15				
20	7	Bay Area Press		6.00			6.00		
20	8	Postage		5.00			5.00		
25	9	Belmont Delivery		7.25		7.25			
30	10	R. Cummings, Drawing		10.00				360	10.00
		Totals	75.00	70.30	7.65	15.65	17.00		30.00
		Balance, March 31		4.70					
			75.00	75.00					
March 31		Balance	4.70						
		To Replenish, March 31	70.30						
April 1		Balance	75.00						

Distribution of Payments	Amount	Total of Payments Column
Supplies	$ 7.65	
Delivery Expense	15.65	
Miscellaneous Expense	17.00	
Sundry	30.00	
Total	$70.30	= $70.30

Reimbursing the Petty Cash Fund

The petty cash fund may be reimbursed at any time, and is usually done when the funds are low. Even if the fund is not particularly low at the end of the month (or at the end of the accounting period), petty cash should be reimbursed so that the proper expense accounts may be debited before the trial balance is prepared.

The entry to reimburse the petty cash fund will appear in the cash payments journal. The accountant will debit the accounts for which expenditures from the fund have been made and will credit cash for the total. The information for the entry is taken from the petty cash disbursements register where each column total represents cash spent for a particular expense during the period. In addition, the expenses listed in the sundry column will be journalized at this time. Remember, the petty cash disbursements record is not a formal journal. It is similar to a worksheet; it is a place where the accountant summarizes the information about petty cash. Until the entry to reimburse petty cash is made in the cash disbursements journal, no formal record has been made of the petty cash expenditures.

The information for the following entry was taken from the petty cash disbursements register for the month of March.

							CASH PAYMENTS JOURNAL											PAGE 10	
Date		Cheque No.	Paid To	Account Debited		Post. Ref.	Sundry Accounts Debit			Accounts Payable Debit			Purchases Discount Credit			Cash Credit				
19XX																			
Mar.	31	1104	Petty Cashier	Supplies				7	65											
				Delivery Expense			1	5	65											
				Miscellaneous Expense			1	7	—											
				R. Cummings, Drawing			1	0	—											
				Cleaning Expense			2	0	—							7	0	30	

Notice that when the petty cash fund is reimbursed, the Petty Cash account is not debited again. The ledger account for petty cash will contain the same balance that it had originally (in this case $75) unless it is decided to make the fund either larger or smaller.

The credit to cash, $70.30, represents a cheque written and cashed for that amount. The sum of $70.30 will be put back into the petty cash fund for use in the next period.

The Change Fund

Most businesses have on hand a **change fund**, which is cash that is used in the cash registers so that change may be made for customers. The journal entry to establish the change fund is as follows:

							CASH PAYMENTS JOURNAL											PAGE 10	
Date		Cheque No.	Paid To	Account Debited		Post. Ref.	Sundry Accounts Debit			Accounts Payable Debit			Purchases Discount Credit			Cash Credit				
19XX Oct.	1	1076	Cashier	Change Fund			2	0	0	—							2	0	0	—

The $200 will be obtained from the bank and will be in various **denominations** —that is, in nickels, dimes, $1 coins, $20 bills, and so on. The money will be placed in the cash register to be used for making change for customers. Assume that at the end of the day on October 7 the cash register tape shows total sales of $450. The amount of money that should be in the cash register is $717.50 which includes 7 percent GST, 8 percent PST, and the $200 change fund. The actual cash when counted, however, is $712.50; the register is $5 short. In general journal form, the entry to record the day's sales will be:

					GENERAL JOURNAL												PAGE 29		
Date		Description		Post. Ref.		Debit					Credit								
19XX Oct.	7	Cash				5	1	2	50										
		Cash Short and Over						5	—										
		Sales										4	5	0	—				
		Provincial Sales Tax Payable											3	6	—				
		GST Charged											3	1	50				
		To Record Cash Sales and $5.00 Shortage																		

The same entry recorded in the cash receipts journal looks like this:

CASH RECEIPTS JOURNAL															**PAGE 10**		
Date	Received From	Account Credited	Post. Ref.	Sundry Accounts Credit	Accounts Receivable Credit	Sales Credit	GST Charged Credit	PST Payable Credit	Cash Short and Over Dr./(Cr.)	Cash Debit
19XX Oct. 7	Cash Sales					4 5 0 —	3 1 50	3 6 —	5 —	5 1 2 50

Notice that the cash receipts journal has a special column for recording shortages and overages. Remember that the cash short and over account may have either a debit or a credit balance because it is debited for shortages and credited for overages. The column head is titled Cash Short and Over—Dr./(Cr.). Credit entries in the column will be enclosed in parentheses to indicate that they are credits. At the end of the accounting period, when the column is totalled, the accountant will determine whether the account has a debit or a credit balance.

After the day's receipts are accounted for, the $200 change fund is put back into the cash register. The accountant may need to make a trip to the bank to ensure that enough change is on hand for the following day's business.

The T accounts for the three cash accounts appear as follows:

Cash	101		**Change Fund**	110
	10/31 Balance 3,588		10/31 Balance 200	

Petty Cash	105
10/31 Balance 75	

Each of these accounts appears on the balance sheet for Super Cookies on October 31, 19XX as follows:

Super Cookies Balance Sheet October 31, 19XX		
Assets		
Cash	$3,588 —	
Petty Cash	75 —	
Change Fund	200 —	
Accounts Receivable	780 —	
Notes Receivable	4,300 —	
Total Assets		$37,641 —

Summary

It is common business practice to pay bills by cheque. The cheque stubs and the cancelled cheques provide valuable information to the accountant. The stubs are used when preparing the journal entries for cash payments; the journals and cancelled cheques are used when reconciling the bank statement; and the cancelled cheques provide proof of payment.

Once a bank account has been opened, deposits of cash should be made daily. The depositor may wish to use an automated banking machine or a night depository so that she or he will not be restricted to regular banking hours. Daily bank deposits of cash help reduce the possibility of theft.

A restrictive endorsement should be placed on incoming cheques as soon as they are received. Again, this helps to safeguard against theft because the restrictive endorsement prohibits further circulation.

The bank will send the depositor a bank statement once a month. This provides the depositor with the opportunity to reconcile her or his cash records with the bank's records. Once reconciliation is complete, the depositor may be relatively sure that the cash balance obtained is the correct one.

In addition to a bank account, many businesses will establish a cash fund out of which small cash payments may be made. Payments from this fund, called petty cash, are recorded on a voucher and in a petty cash disbursements register.

If sales are made in the store, a change fund is necessary. This fund provides small cash denominations so that change may be given to customers.

Cash, petty cash, and the change fund usually appear on the balance sheet as three separate accounts.

Vocabulary Review

Following is a list of the words and terms for this chapter:

accessible	non-sufficient funds/NSF
automated	outstanding cheque
cancelled cheque	petty cash
change fund	reconcile
denominations	restrictive endorsement
deposit in transit	serial
endorsement	

Fill in the blank with the correct word or term from the list.

1. A signature is sometimes referred to as a/an _____.
2. A fund that is kept on hand for making small cash payments is called _____.
3. An endorsement that prohibits further circulation of a cheque is a/an _____.
4. A word that means easily obtained is _____.
5. A cheque that has been paid by the bank is called a/an _____.
6. An automatically controlled banking machine is called a/an _____ teller.
7. Units in a system of money, such as a dime or a quarter, are referred to as _____ of money.
8. A cheque that has not yet been presented to the bank for payment is called a/an _____.

9. To bring into agreement is to _____.

10. Numbers arranged in a series (1, 2, 3, 4, 5, . . .) are _____ numbers.

11. A deposit that has been made but that does not appear on the bank statement is referred to as a/an _____.

12. Cash that is kept on hand for use in the cash register is the _____.

13. A customer's cheque previously deposited but debited back to her or his account because of a lack of funds is a/an _____ cheque.

Match the words and terms on the left with the definitions on the right.

14. accessible	a. a signature
15. automated	b. a cheque paid by the bank
16. cancelled cheque	c. a cheque not yet presented to the bank for payment
17. change fund	d. easily obtained
18. denominations	e. cash kept on hand for use in the cash register
19. deposit in transit	f. automatically controlled
20. endorsement	g. units in a money system
21. non-sufficient funds/ NSF	h. in a series
22. outstanding cheque	i. an endorsement that prohibits further circulation
23. petty cash	j. a deposit that does not yet appear on the bank statement
24. reconcile	k. to bring into agreement
25. restrictive endorsement	l. cash fund out of which small cash payments may be made
26. serial	m. not enough money in a chequing account to cover a cheque

Exercises

EXERCISE 10.1 On May 22, at the end of the business day, the cash register for Mom's Auto Parts showed total sales of $472.18. The actual cash on hand was $682.18, which included a $200 change fund that would be placed back in the cash register. The daily deposit included the following: $2.18 in coins; $150.00 in currency; and three cheques: $96.14, $83.04, and $150.82. In the cash receipts journal, prepare the entry to record the day's sales and prepare a deposit slip for the daily deposit of cash. Use journal page 5.

EXERCISE 10.2 Following is the cash receipts journal for the first week in October showing the total cash sales and the cash short and over for each day. Assuming that cash short and over had a zero balance on October 1, what is the balance of the account on October 7? Is it a debit or a credit balance?

	CASH RECEIPTS JOURNAL						PAGE 10	
Date	Received From	Account Credited	Post. Ref.	Sales Credit	PST Payable Credit	Cash Short and Over Dr./(Cr.)	Cash Debit	
19XX Oct. 1	Cash Sales			300 —	15 —	50	314 50	
2	Cash Sales			320 —	16 —	(10 —)	346 —	
3	Cash Sales			480 —	24 —	4 —	500 —	
4	Cash Sales			518 —	25 90	1 —	542 90	
5	Cash Sales			590 —	29 50	(5 —)	624 50	
6	Cash Sales			502 —	25 10		527 10	
7	Cash Sales			417 20	20 86	20 —	418 06	

EXERCISE 10.3   Marcy Lennon sells accessories for pets in her small specialty store called "Pets 'n' People." In the past, she has had one cash register in the store with a change fund of $150 in it. On July 1, however, Marcy enlarged her store and bought a second cash register. She also wants to put $150 in this register. Answer the following questions:

    a. To establish a change fund for the second cash register, what accounts should be debited and credited, and for how much?

    b. What will be the balance in the Change Fund account after the journal entry in Step a has been made?

    c. On which financial statement will the Change Fund account appear?

EXERCISE 10.4   Prepare general journal entries if necessary to record the following bank statement reconciliation adjustments. Use journal page 7.

    a. Collection of a note by the bank for $6,000 plus interest of $910.

    b. A deposit in transit of $1,215.

    c. Four cheques were found to be outstanding: cheque number 604, $1,204.06; cheque number 609, $475.18; cheque number 614, $22.40; and cheque number 623, $573.20.

    d. A service charge of $8.50 was deducted by the bank.

    e. An NSF cheque in the amount of $372.18 from Jim Butler was returned by the bank. The bank charged a $30 fee.

    f. A debit memo in the amount of $15, which represented the charge for a safe deposit box rental, was included with the bank statement.

EXERCISE 10.5   When the bank statement was received on March 2, it showed a balance of $4,116.80 on February 28 before reconciliation. After reconciliation, the adjusted general ledger balance is $4,120.02. If there was one deposit in transit of $520.50, what was the total amount of the outstanding cheques, assuming that there were no other adjustments to be made to the bank statement?

EXERCISE 10.6   After the bank statement was reconciled, the adjusted bank balance was $2,792.58. The general ledger balance before reconciliation was $2,286.58. The bank collected a note for $500 plus $10 in interest for the depositor. If there were no other adjustments to be made to the general ledger, what was the amount of the bank service charge?

EXERCISE 10.7   When reconciling the bank statement, tell whether the following would be additions to the bank statement, subtractions from the bank statement, additions to the general ledger, or subtractions from the general ledger.

	Add to Bank Statement	Subtract from Bank Statement	Add to General Ledger	Subtract from General Ledger
a. Outstanding cheques	_____	_____	_____	_____
b. Cheque-printing charge	_____	_____	_____	_____
c. A collection made by the bank for the depositor	_____	_____	_____	_____
d. A cheque written for $72.98 was recorded in the cash payments journal as $79.28	_____	_____	_____	_____
e. A deposit in transit	_____	_____	_____	_____
f. Bank service charges	_____	_____	_____	_____
g. A cheque written for $543.56 was recorded in the cash payments journal as $534.56	_____	_____	_____	_____
h. An automatic cheque for an insurance premium is included with the cancelled cheques	_____	_____	_____	_____

EXERCISE 10.8   Heinrich Zimler owns Heinrich's Foreign Auto Sales. On August 1, he decides to establish a petty cash fund of $150. On August 31, after the petty cash vouchers have been categorized and totalled for the month, the expenditures are found to be: $18 for postage; $30.75 for owner's drawing; $10.80 for delivery expense; $16.42 for supplies; $12 for a magazine subscription for customers' use; and $6.00 for a newspaper subscription for the waiting room. The amount of cash on hand on August 31 is $56.03. Prepare the entry in the cash payments journal, page 8, to (a) establish the petty cash fund on August 1 (cheque 1075) and (b) replenish the fund on August 31 (cheque 1146). Account titles are: Cash, 101; Petty Cash, 105; Supplies, 140; Heinrich Zimler, Drawing, 320; Postage Expense, 640; Miscellaneous Expense, 650; and Delivery Expense, 660.

EXERCISE 10.9   The petty cash fund for Betty's Barber Shop had a balance of $25 on September 1, 19XX. On September 9, Betty noticed that the fund was nearly used up. The cash on hand on September 9 was 35 cents. The totals of the petty cash payments register showed the following: Postage Expense, 640, $4.20; Miscellaneous Expense, 650, $5; and Entertainment Expense, 690, $15.45. Betty decided to make the fund $50 larger so that it would not have to be replenished so often. Prepare an entry in the cash payments journal, page 9, on September 9 that will both replenish the petty cash fund and enlarge the fund by $50. Use cheque 1902. The account number for Petty Cash is 135.

Problems

PROBLEM 10.1   Zorba's Delicatessen received a bank statement on November 2, 19XX. The bank balance for October 31 was $4,982.02. The general ledger balance at the time of reconciliation was $4,566.64. When reconciling, the following were found: four outstanding cheques, 1742, $462.81; 1745, $198.40; 1746, $42.69; and 1747, $51.08; two deposits in transit, October 30, $300 and October 31, $119.60; a bank service charge, $12; a cheque-printing charge, $18; a $90 automatic cheque for an insurance premium; and a $200 note receivable left with the bank for collection had been paid in full at the bank.

INSTRUCTIONS   1. Prepare a bank statement reconciliation on October 31 for Zorba's Delicatessen.
2. Prepare the necessary entries in general journal form to bring the books up to date after reconciliation. Use journal page 11. A partial chart of accounts includes the following: Cash, 101; Notes Receivable, 120; Insurance Expense, 650; and Bank Service Charges, 670.

PROBLEM 10.2   Geri Speir owns Fillie's Frocks, a western wear store. On June 2, Geri received the bank statement. It showed a balance on May 31 of $6,420.95. The general ledger balance at the time of reconciliation was $6,446.11. When reconciling, Geri found one deposit in transit of $645.80. There were five outstanding cheques: 2016, $29.40; 2020, $150; 2025, $490; 2026, $10.50; and 2027, $65.04. The bank service charge was $10.50, and there was a cheque-printing charge of $16.50. When comparing the cancelled cheques with the cash payments journal, Geri noticed that cheque 1998, written on May 15 to Western Wear in payment of an account payable, was actually written for $75.87 but was recorded in the cash payments journal as $78.57. Geri also noticed that she forgot to record a $100 cash withdrawal from an automated teller on May 27 (the cash was for personal use).

INSTRUCTIONS   1. Prepare a bank statement reconciliation on May 31 for Fillie's Frocks.
2. Prepare the necessary entries in general journal form to bring the books up to date after reconciliation. Use journal page 27. A partial chart of accounts includes the following: Cash, 101; Accounts Payable, 210; Geri Speir, Drawing, 310; and Bank Service Charges, 640.

PROBLEM 10.3   Marie Bouchard, owner of A–Z Novelties, received her bank statement on February 2. The January 31 bank balance was $3,240.60. The general ledger balance at the time of reconciliation was $3,223.59. During reconciliation, Marie noted that the bank service charge was $15. Also, a note receivable left at the bank for collection had been paid in full, $600 plus $60 interest. There were two deposits in transit: January 30, $649.28 and January 31, $596.81. The bank charge for cheque printing was $18. There were three outstanding cheques: 972, $450; 973, $95.40; and 974, $150. When comparing the cancelled cheques with the cash payments journal, Marie noticed that two errors had been made. Cheque 952, written on January 10 in payment of the electric bill, was actually written for $98.20 but was recorded in the cash payments journal as $89.20. Cheque 965, written on January 19 in payment for a desk for the office, was actually written for $370.32 but was recorded in the cash payments journal as $390.32. An automatic cheque for $70.30 in payment of an insurance premium was included with the cancelled cheques.

INSTRUCTIONS   1. Prepare a bank statement reconciliation on January 31 for A–Z Novelties.
2. Prepare the necessary entries in general journal form to bring the books up to date after reconciliation. Use journal page 33. A partial chart of accounts includes the following: Cash, 101; Notes Receivable, 110; Office Furniture, 170; Interest Income, 420; Utilities Expense 650; Insurance Expense, 660; and Bank Charges Expense, 670.

PROBLEM 10.4   The following information was available to reconcile Holiday Handicrafts' general ledger balance and the bank statement balance as of December 31, 19XX.
  a. The December 31 cash balance according to the accounting records was $7,063.50, and the bank statement balance for that date was $10,362.50.
  b. Cheque 124 for $178 and cheque 129 for $200, both written and entered in the accounting records in December, were not among the cancelled cheques. Two cheques, 117 for $587 and 119 for $95, were outstanding on November 30 when the bank and general ledger balances were reconciled. Cheque 119 was returned with the December cancelled cheques, but cheque 117 was not.
  c. When the December cheques were compared with entries in the accounting records, it was found that cheque 121 in payment for office supplies had been correctly written for $654 but was erroneously entered in the accounting records as $645.
  d. Two debit memoranda and a credit memorandum were included with the bank statement. The credit memorandum indicated that the bank had collected a $5,900 note receivable for Holiday Handicrafts, and had deducted a $25 service charge for the collection. One of the debit memoranda was for $215 for an NSF cheque from J. Warren in the amount of $205. The bank charged a $10 fee for the NSF cheque. The second debit memorandum was for $72 to cover interest on an outstanding bank loan.
  e. The December 31 deposit in the amount of $3,245 had been placed in the bank's night depository after banking hours and did not appear on the bank statement.

INSTRUCTIONS   1. Prepare a T account bank statement reconciliation for Holiday Handicrafts on December 31, 19XX.
2. Prepare the necessary general journal entries (page 24) to bring the books up to date after the bank statement reconciliation. A partial chart of accounts includes the following: Cash, 101; Accounts Receivable, 110; Notes Receivable, 120; Office Supplies, 130; Bank Service Charges, 630; and Interest Expense, 650.

PROBLEM 10.5   Shown below are the cash columns of the cash receipts and cash payments journals for Okanagan Valley Ski Resort for the month of October 19XX.

Cash Receipts Journal		Cash Payments Journal	
October 4	$ 3,174	113	$ 1,930
7	1,407	114	1,472
10	1,559	115	2,413
15	187	116	689
17	2,130	117	230
22	1,404	118	118
23	721	119	307
25	4,208	120	1,326
29	5,105	121	640
Total	$19,895	122	3,016
		123	741
		Total	$12,882

The cash account in the general ledger showed the following:

ACCOUNT: CASH   **ACCT. NO. 101**

Date		Explanation	Post. Ref.	Debit	Credit	Balance
19XX Oct.	1	Balance				13,542—
	31		CR4	19,895—		33,437—
	31		CP8		12,882—	20,555—

Okanagan Valley Ski Resort received the following bank statement:

Okanagan Valley Ski Resort
321 Spring Road
Peace River, B.C.

Date		Explanation	Cheques	Deposits	Balance
Oct.	1				13,542
	3	113	1,930		
		115	2,413		9,199
	4			3,174	12,373
	5	116	689		11,684
	7			1,407	
		118	118		12,973
	9	119	307		12,666
	10			1,559	14,225
	15			187	14,412
	16	CM*		4,225	18,637
	17	120	1,326		
				2,130	19,441
	22			1,404	20,845
	24	122	3,016		
				721	18,550
	26			4,208	22,758
	31	SC**	10		22,748
	31	DM***	285		22,463
	31	123	714		21,749

*CM = Credit Memo   **SC = Service Charge   ***DM = Debit Memo

The credit memorandum from the bank indicated that the bank had collected a note receivable in the amount of $4,000 plus interest for Okanagan Valley Ski Resort. The debit memorandum indicated that a cheque in the amount of $260 from R. Walters had been returned because of non-sufficient funds. The bank assessed a service charge of $25 for the NSF cheque. Cheque 123 had been written in payment of the utilities bill.

INSTRUCTIONS

1. Prepare a T account bank statement reconciliation for Okanagan Valley Ski Resort as of January 31, 19XX.
2. Prepare the necessary general journal entries (page 19) to bring the books up to date after bank statement reconciliation. A partial chart of accounts includes the following: Cash, 101; Accounts Receivable, 110; Notes Receivable, 120; Interest Revenue, 420; Utilities Expense, 640; and Bank Service Charges, 670.

PROBLEM 10.6

The following petty cash transactions occurred in October for the Jackson House of Guitars:

October 1 established a petty cash fund of $100; cheque 1716

October 3 paid $5 for delivery charges; voucher 1

October 4 Herb Jackson took $20 cash for his personal use; voucher 2

October 7 paid $7.50 for newspaper subscription for customers' use; voucher 3

October 10 paid $15 to have windows washed; voucher 4

October 12 paid $5 for postage stamps; voucher 5

October 15 paid $9.50 for express mail charges; voucher 6

October 18 Herb Jackson took a customer to lunch, $17.80; voucher 7

October 21 paid $3.60 for office supplies, voucher 8

October 25 mailed a package to a customer, $3.70; voucher 9

October 27 paid $8 for an ad in a shoppers' newspaper; voucher 10

INSTRUCTIONS

1. Record the entry in the cash payments journal to establish the petty cash fund on October 1. Use page 18 for the journal.
2. Record in a petty cash register (page 10) the initial $100 deposit into the fund and the disbursements for the month. Column headings in the register should include postage expense, delivery expense, and entertainment expense. A partial chart of accounts includes: Cash, 101; Petty Cash, 110; Office Supplies, 120; Herb Jackson, Drawing, 310; Advertising Expense, 610; Delivery Expense, 620; Cleaning Expense, 630; Postage Expense, 640; Entertainment Expense, 650; and Subscription Expense, 660.
3. Total and rule the petty cash register.
4. Prepare the October 31 entry in the cash disbursements journal, cheque 1762, to replenish the petty cash fund.
5. Complete the petty cash register by indicating the October 31 balance, the deposit into the fund, and the balance on November 1.

PROBLEM 10.7   The following petty cash transactions occurred in January for Cowhide Products:

January 1   established a petty cash fund of $50; cheque 2640

January 2   paid $4.60 for office supplies; voucher 100

January 5   paid $12 for a magazine subscription for customers' use; voucher 101

January 6   owner Marge Wade took a customer to lunch, $15.20; voucher 102

January 7   paid $3.20 for office supplies; voucher 103

January 9   bought postage stamps, $6; voucher 104

January 14   Marge Wade withdrew $5 for personal use; voucher 105

January 15   bookkeeper replenished the petty cash fund and made it $50 larger; cheque 2682

January 17   Marge Wade took a client to lunch, $16.40; voucher 106

January 19   paid $15 postage to have parcels sent to a customer; voucher 107

January 20   bought $6.40 in office supplies; voucher 108

January 24   Marge Wade withdrew $10 for personal use; voucher 109

January 25   took packages to the post office for mailing; cost, $8.70; voucher 110

January 26   bought a fern for the store, $17.50 (debit Miscellaneous Expense); voucher 111

January 27   bought plant food for the fern, $3.90 (debit Miscellaneous Expense); voucher 112

January 31   sent flowers to a customer in the hospital, $19.70 (debit Miscellaneous Expense); voucher 113

INSTRUCTIONS   1. Record the entry in the cash payments journal (page 13) to establish the petty cash fund on January 1.
2. Record in a petty cash register (page 12) the initial $50 deposit into the fund and the disbursements from January 1 to January 14. Column headings for the register should include Office Supplies, Postage Expense, and Miscellaneous Expense. A partial chart of accounts includes: Cash, 101; Petty Cash, 110; Office Supplies, 120; Marge Wade, Drawing, 310; Advertising Expense, 610; Postage Expense, 640; Entertainment Expense, 650; Subscription Expense, 660; and Miscellaneous Expense, 670.
3. Total and rule the petty cash register.
4. Prepare the January 15 entry in the cash disbursements journal to replenish the petty cash fund and to make the fund $50 larger. Use page 14 for the journal and cheque 2682.

5. Complete the petty cash register for the January 1–14 time period by writing in the amounts required to replenish the fund and to make the fund $50 larger. The new balance on January 15 will be $100.
6. Continuing on with the month's transactions in a new petty cash register (page 13), record the disbursements from January 15 to January 31. Total and rule the register again.
7. Prepare the entry in the cash disbursements journal on January 31 (cheque 2731), to replenish the petty cash fund and restore it to a $100 balance.
8. Record in the petty cash register, page 13, the balance on January 31, the deposit into the fund, and the balance on February 1.

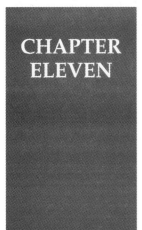

Worksheets, Financial Statements, and Closing Entries for a Merchandising Business

Learning Objectives

When you have completed this chapter, you should
1. have a better understanding of accounting terminology.
2. be able to prepare a ten-column worksheet for a merchandising business.
3. have a basic understanding of cost of goods sold.
4. be able to prepare an income statement for a merchandising business.
5. be able to prepare a classified balance sheet.
6. be able to calculate current ratio and working capital.
7. be able to journalize and post the adjusting and closing entries for a merchandising business.

Vocabulary

classified   separated into categories

current ratio   one of the indicators of short-term debt-paying ability; obtained by dividing current assets by current liabilities

gross profit   net sales minus cost of goods sold

liquid asset   an asset that is cash or easily converted into cash

working capital   one of the indicators of short-term debt-paying ability; obtained by subtracting current liabilities from current assets

Introduction

The material presented in this chapter completes the accounting cycle for a merchandising business. The accounting cycle, remember, refers to the sequence of accounting procedures that are performed during an accounting period. The cycle begins when a transaction occurs and is journalized and ends with the closing of the books. The steps in the accounting cycle, from beginning to end, are as follows:

1. Journalize transactions.
2. Post transactions.
3. Prepare a worksheet that includes:
    a. a trial balance,
    b. adjustments,
    c. an adjusted trial balance,
    d. income statement calculations, and
    e. balance sheet calculations.
4. Prepare an income statement.

Ron's Appliances — Worksheet — For Month Ended June 30, 19XX

Acct. No.	Account Titles	Trial Balance Debit	Trial Balance Credit	Adjustments Debit	Adjustments Credit
101	Cash	11600—			
110	Accounts Receivable	13600—			
120	Notes Receivable	7200—			
130	Merchandise Inventory	46000—			
140	Supplies	1960—			a. 640—
150	Prepaid Insurance	3100—			b. 100—
160	Office Equipment	28000—			
161	Accumulated Depreciation: OE		5500—		c. 500—
170	Delivery Equipment	57000—			
171	Accumulated Depreciation: DE		11250—		c. 750—
180	Building	130000—			
181	Accumulated Depreciation: Building		7500—		c. 500—
210	Accounts Payable		5150—		
220	Notes Payable		25000—		
240	Unearned Revenue		3500—	d. 900—	
250	Mortgage Payable		90000—		
310	Ron Renner, Capital		124390—		
320	Ron Renner, Drawing	6000—			
410	Sales		104100—		d. 900—
420	Sales Returns and Allowances	2100—			
430	Sales Discounts	2900—			
501	Purchases	58000—			
520	Purchases Returns and Allowances		620—		
530	Purchases Discounts		2400—		
540	Freight In	2000—			
610	Rent Expense	3500—			
620	Utilities Expense	750—			
630	Wages Expense	5700—		e. 200—	
	Totals	379410—	379410—		
650	Supplies Expense			a. 640—	
660	Insurance Expense			b. 100—	
670	Depreciation Expense			c. 1750—	
230	Wages Payable				e. 200—
				3590—	3590—
	Net Income				

5. Prepare a balance sheet.
6. Prepare schedules of accounts receivable and accounts payable.
7. Journalize and post the adjusting entries.
8. Journalize and post the closing entries.
9. Prepare a post-closing trial balance.

This chapter will concentrate on preparing the worksheet and financial statements and journalizing and posting the closing entries for a merchandising business. The worksheet for Ron's Appliances for the month ended June 30, 19XX is below. The trial balance is prepared directly from the ledger on June 30. Once it is complete and in balance, it should be double ruled. Look over the worksheet and then read the discussion material about merchandise inventory and the adjustments.

Adjusted Trial Balance		Income Statement		Balance Sheet	
Debit	Credit	Debit	Credit	Debit	Credit
11600—				11600—	
13600—				13600—	
7200—				7200—	
46000—		46000—	45100—	45100—	
1320—				1320—	
3000—				3000—	
28000—				28000—	
	6000—				6000—
57000—				57000—	
	12000—				12000—
130000—				130000—	
	8000—				8000—
	5150—				5150—
	25000—				25000—
	2600—				2600—
	90000—				90000—
	124390—				124390—
6000—				6000—	
	105000—		105000—		
2100—		2100—			
2900—		2900—			
58000—		58000—			
	620—		620—		
	2400—		2400—		
2000—		2000—			
3500—		3500—			
750—		750—			
5900—		5900—			
640—		640—			
100—		100—			
1750—		1750—			
	200—				200—
381360—	381360—	123640—	153120—	302820—	273340—
		29480—			29480—
		153120—	153120—	302820—	302820—

The Merchandise Inventory Account on the Worksheet

The merchandise inventory figure that appears on the trial balance represents the balance in the account on June 1 and is referred to as the beginning inventory. The beginning inventory appears on the worksheet as a debit in three places: on the original trial balance, on the adjusted trial balance, and on the income statement, where it will be used in calculating the cost of goods sold.

At the end of the period, June 30 in this case, the periodic inventory was taken, and the value of the actual merchandise on hand was $45,100. This is referred to as the ending inventory and is the current value of the asset. It appears on the worksheet in two places: as a credit on the income statement, where it will be used in the cost of goods sold calculation, and as a debit on the balance sheet, where it represents the actual value of merchandise on hand.

The merchandise inventory appears five times on the worksheet: four times as a debit and once as a credit.

Beginning Inventory Appears	Ending Inventory Appears
As a **debit** on the trial balance	As a **debit** on the balance sheet
As a **debit** on the adjusted trial balance	As a **credit** on the income statement
As a **debit** on the income statement	

Adjustments on the Worksheet

Adjustments are made at the end of the accounting period to bring certain accounts up to date. Each adjustment involves both an income statement account and a balance sheet account. Following is a brief explanation of the adjustments on the worksheet for Ron's Appliances.

a. This adjustment records the amount of supplies used during June by debiting Supplies Expense and crediting Supplies for $640. The value of the ending inventory of supplies is the figure that should appear on the adjusted trial balance and on the balance sheet.

b. This adjustment records the insurance expense for June by debiting Insurance Expense and crediting Prepaid Insurance for $100.

c. This adjustment records depreciation expense for June on all the depreciable assets (office equipment, delivery equipment, and the building). The debit in each case is to Depreciation Expense and the credit is to the contra-asset account, Accumulated Depreciation. The three debits to Depreciation Expense may be added together and shown as one figure—$1,750—on the worksheet, but the credits must be made individually to the Accumulated Depreciation accounts ($500, $750, and $500).

d. At some point in the past, Ron received cash in advance of actually delivering the merchandise. This transaction was recorded at the time as a debit to Cash and as a credit to the liability account, Unearned Revenue. This adjusting entry is to transfer a portion ($900) of the balance in Unearned Revenue to Sales, an earned revenue account.

e. This adjustment records wages expense that have accrued at the end of the accounting period by debiting Wages Expense and crediting Wages Payable for $200.

Once all the adjustments are entered on the worksheet, the adjustments column should be totalled and ruled.

Completing the Worksheet

The next step involves combining the original trial balance with the adjustments for the adjusted trial balance. (If necessary, you may wish to review Chapter Five for details on preparing the worksheet.) Once the adjusted trial balance is complete and in balance, extensions may be made to the balance sheet and income statement columns of the worksheet. Extensions include entering the beginning merchandise inventory as a debit on the income statement and entering the ending inventory as a credit on the income statement and a debit on the balance sheet.

When extensions are complete, the income statement columns are totalled and the net income (or net loss) is determined. A net income figure is entered as a debit on the income statement and as a credit on the balance sheet. Finally, the remaining parts of the worksheet are totalled and ruled.

Cost of Goods Sold

After the worksheet is complete, the accountant may wish to prepare the financial statements. Before discussing the income statement for a merchandising business, however, a discussion about the cost of goods sold is in order. When an item is sold by a retail store, several things have to be taken into consideration before a net income or loss figure can be determined. In addition to determining the related expenses, the *cost of the merchandise sold* must be calculated.

For example, assume that you buy a used car from a friend for $1,200. You pay $800 to have it painted, $150 to have it tuned, and $350 for new tires. Then you place a $50 ad in the newspaper offering to sell the car for $3,500. After a week's time, you sell the car for $3,400. To calculate your net income, you would do the following:

Revenue from Sale of Car		$3,400
Minus Cost of Purchase of Car		1,200
Gross Profit		$2,200
Minus Expenses		
Painting	$800	
Tune-up	150	
Tires	350	
Ad in Paper	50	
Total Expenses		1,350
Net Income from Sale		$ 850

The **gross profit** is profit *before* expenses have been deducted; it is simply the revenue minus the cost of the item sold. When a large item such as an automobile is sold, the direct cost of the merchandise sold is relatively easy to figure. When a store sells smaller items that are difficult to identify individually, a different procedure is used to calculate the cost of goods sold.

Calculation for Cost of Goods Sold

Before the cost of goods sold can be calculated, three things must be known: (1) the cost of the beginning inventory, (2) the cost of purchases, and (3) the cost of the ending inventory.

Cost of Goods Sold		
Beginning Inventory	$21,500	What the merchant had to start with
Add: Cost of Purchases	46,200	Add what was purchased during the period
Total Goods Available for Sale	$67,700	Everything that was available for sale during the period
Minus: Ending Inventory	19,600	Minus what was left at the end of the period
Cost of Goods Sold	$48,100	Equals the cost of what was sold

Goods Available for Sale

When the cost of purchases for the period is added to beginning inventory, the result is the total goods available for sale. The total goods available for sale does not equal the cost of goods sold, however, because not every item that was available for sale was sold. Some items remain in the store at the end of the accounting period; these items represent ending inventory, or the remaining goods. When the ending inventory is subtracted from all the goods available for sale, the result is the goods sold, or the cost of goods sold. The goods available for sale represents both the goods sold and the goods not sold, because it represents *everything that was available for sale in the store during the entire accounting period.*

The Merchandising Income Statement

The income statement for a merchandising business contains three main sections: (1) the revenue section, (2) the cost of goods sold section, and (3) the expense section. The three sections appear in this order:

1. Sales
2. −Cost of Goods Sold
   Gross Profit
3. −Expenses
   Net Income (or Net Loss)

The gross profit, remember, is profit before related expenses are deducted; it is the net sales minus cost of goods sold. The income statement is prepared directly from the worksheet, where many of the calculations have already been made. A partial worksheet showing the income statement columns for Ron's Appliances appears on page 285.

The net income has already been calculated. The accountant can now prepare the formal income statement for Ron's Appliances directly from the worksheet.

Ron's Appliances
Worksheet (Partial)
For Month Ended June 30, 19XX

Acct. No.	Account Titles	Adjusted Trial Balance Debit	Adjusted Trial Balance Credit	Income Statement Debit	Income Statement Credit
101	Cash	11600 —			
110	Accounts Receivable	13600 —			
120	Notes Receivable	7200 —			
130	Merchandise Inventory	46000 —		46000 —	45100 —
140	Supplies	1320 —			
150	Prepaid Insurance	3000 —			
160	Office Equipment	28000 —			
161	Accumulated Depreciation: OE		6000 —		
170	Delivery Equipment	57000 —			
171	Accumulated Depreciation: DE		12000 —		
180	Building	130000 —			
181	Accumulated Depreciation: Bldg.		8000 —		
210	Accounts Payable		5150 —		
220	Notes Payable		25000 —		
240	Unearned Revenue		2600 —		
250	Mortgage Payable		90000 —		
310	Ron Renner, Capital		124390 —		
320	Ron Renner, Drawing	6000 —			
410	Sales		105000 —		105000 —
420	Sales Returns and Allowances	2100 —		2100 —	
430	Sales Discounts	2900 —		2900 —	
501	Purchases	58000 —		58000 —	
520	Purchases Returns and Allowances		620 —		620 —
530	Purchases Discounts		2400 —		2400 —
540	Freight In	2000 —		2000 —	
610	Rent Expense	3500 —		3500 —	
620	Utilities Expense	750 —		750 —	
630	Wages Expense	5900 —		5900 —	
	Totals				
650	Supplies Expense	640 —		640 —	
660	Insurance Expense	100 —		100 —	
670	Depreciation Expense	1750 —		1750 —	
230	Wages Payable		200 —		
		381360 —	381360 —	123640 —	153120 —
	Net Income			29480 —	
				153120 —	153120 —

The following income statement for Ron's Appliances contains the three main elements: (1) revenue, (2) cost of goods sold, and (3) expenses.

Ron's Appliances
Income Statement
For Month Ended June 30, 19XX

Revenue from Sales			
Sales		$105,000	
Less: Sales Returns and Allowances	$ 2,100		
Sales Discounts	2,900	5,000	
Net Sales			$100,000
Cost of Goods Sold			
Merchandise Inventory, June 1, 19XX		46,000	
Purchases	58,000		
Less: Purchases Returns and Allowances	$ 620		
Purchases Discounts	2,400	3,020	
Net Purchases		54,980	
Add: Freight In		2,000	
Cost of Purchases		56,980	
Cost of Merchandise Available for Sale		102,980	
Less: Merchandise Inventory, June 30, 19XX		45,100	
Cost of Goods Sold			57,880
Gross Profit			42,120
Expenses			
Rent Expense		3,500	
Utilities Expense		750	
Wages Expense		5,900	
Supplies Expense		640	
Insurance Expense		100	
Depreciation Expense		1,750	
Total Expenses			12,640
Net Income			$ 29,480

The cost of goods sold section contains the calculation for cost of purchases, which makes the income statement appear to be more complicated than it really is. The following shows the three main elements of the cost of goods sold section: (1) beginning inventory, (2) cost of purchases, and (3) ending inventory.

Cost of Goods Sold			
1. **Merchandise Inventory, June 1, 19XX**			**$ 46,000**
Purchases		$58,000	
Less: Purchases Returns and			
Allowances	$ 620		
Purchases Discounts	2,400	3,020	
Net Purchases		54,980	
Add: Freight In		2,000	
2. **Cost of Purchases**			**56,980**
Total Cost of Merchandise Available			
for Sale			102,980
3. **Less: Merchandise Inventory, June 30, 19XX**			**45,100**
Cost of Goods Sold			$57,880

The Classified Balance Sheet

The balance sheet, too, is prepared directly from the worksheet. The accounts have already been adjusted, and the net income (or net loss) has already been calculated. The balance sheet portion of the worksheet for Ron's Appliances follows on page 288.

Assets and liabilities are **classified** on the balance sheet. That is, assets and liabilities are separated into categories: for assets, the categories are (1) current assets and (2) plant and equipment; for liabilities, the categories are (1) current liabilities and (2) long-term liabilities.

Current Assets

Current assets are listed on the balance sheet in their order of liquidity. A **liquid asset** is cash or an asset that can easily be converted into cash. Therefore Cash is always listed first, followed by Accounts Receivable, Notes Receivable, and Merchandise Inventory. The other current assets may be listed in any order.

Plant and Equipment

Items of plant and equipment are assets held for use in producing other assets. Those items of plant and equipment that are depreciable are shown with their Accumulated Depreciation accounts as illustrated on page 289.

Ron's Appliances
Worksheet (Partial)
For Month Ended June 30, 19XX

Acct. No.	Account Titles	Adjusted Trial Balance Debit	Adjusted Trial Balance Credit	Balance Sheet Debit	Balance Sheet Credit
101	Cash	11600—		11600—	
110	Accounts Receivable	13600—		13600—	
120	Notes Receivable	7200—		7200—	
130	Merchandise Inventory	46000—		45100—	
140	Supplies	1320—		1320—	
150	Prepaid Insurance	3000—		3000—	
160	Office Equipment	28000—		28000—	
161	Accumulated Depreciation: OE		6000—		6000—
170	Delivery Equipment	57000—		57000—	
171	Accumulated Depreciation: DE		12000—		12000—
180	Building	130000—		130000—	
181	Accumulated Depreciation: Bldg.		8000—		8000—
210	Accounts Payable		5150—		5150—
220	Notes Payable		25000—		25000—
240	Unearned Revenue		2600—		2600—
250	Mortgage Payable		90000—		90000—
310	Ron Renner, Capital		124390—		124390—
320	Ron Renner, Drawing	6000—		6000—	
410	Sales		105000—		
420	Sales Returns and Allowances	2100—			
430	Sales Discounts	2900—			
501	Purchases	58000—			
520	Purchases Returns and Allowances		620—		
530	Purchases Discounts		2400—		
540	Freight In	2000—			
610	Rent Expense	3500—			
620	Utilities Expense	750—			
630	Wages Expense	5900—			
	Totals				
650	Supplies Expense	640—			
660	Insurance Expense	100—			
670	Depreciation Expense	1750—			
230	Wages Payable		200—		200—
		381360—	381360—	302820—	273340—
	Net Income				29480—
				302820—	302820—

Plant and Equipment

Office Equipment	$ 28,000	
Less: Accumulated Depreciation:	6,000	$ 22,000
Office Equipment		
Delivery Equipment	57,000	
Less: Accumulated Depreciation:	12,000	45,000
Delivery Equipment		
Building	130,000	
Less: Accumulated Depreciation: Building	8,000	122,000
Total Plant and Equipment		$189,000

Plant and equipment items are recorded originally at their historic cost. The balance sheet shows the historic cost, the accumulated depreciation, and the book value. If a firm owns land, it will show on the balance sheet beneath the last depreciable item listed.

Current and Long-Term Liabilities

Current liabilities are those that are due within a relatively short period of time, usually one year. Current liabilities are paid out of current assets. On the balance sheet, Accounts Payable is listed first, followed by Notes Payable (that portion that is due within one year). The other current liabilities are listed in no particular order. A portion of the Mortgage Payable is usually listed as a current liability, but only the amount that is due and payable within one year.

Long-term liabilities are those that are due after one year's time. Mortgage Payable and Notes Payable (those portions due after one year's time) usually fall into this category.

Owner's Equity

There are no changes in presentation of owner's equity on the balance sheet. However, many business owners prepare a separate statement of owner's equity and show only the ending capital on the balance sheet. The balance sheet for Ron's Appliances follows.

Ron's Appliances
Balance Sheet
June 30, 19XX

Assets

Current Assets

Cash	$ 11,600	
Accounts Receivable	13,600	
Notes Receivable	7,200	
Merchandise Inventory	45,100	
Supplies	1,320	
Prepaid Insurance	3,000	
Total Current Assets		$ 81,820

Plant and Equipment

Office Equipment	$ 28,000		
Less: Accumulated Depreciation: Office Equipment	6,000	22,000	
Delivery Equipment	57,000		
Less: Accumulated Depreciation: Delivery Equipment	12,000	45,000	
Building	130,000		
Less: Accumulated Depreciation: Building	8,000	122,000	
Total Plant and Equipment			189,000
Total Assets			$270,820

Liabilities

Current Liabilities

Accounts Payable	$ 5,150	
Notes Payable	25,000	
Wages Payable	200	
Unearned Revenue	2,600	
Mortgage Payable (current portion)	12,000	
Total Current Liabilities		44,950

Long-Term Liabilities

Mortgage Payable		78,000
Total Liabilities		$122,950

Owner's Equity

Ron Renner, Capital, June 1, 19XX	$124,390	
Add: Net Income	29,480	
Subtotal	153,870	
Less: Ron Renner, Drawing	6,000	
Ron Renner, Capital, June 30, 19XX		147,870
Total Liabilities and Owner's Equity		$270,820

Current Ratio

The **current ratio** is a good indicator of a firm's ability to pay its debts when they are due; it is determined by dividing total current assets by total current liabilities. For Ron's Appliances, the current ratio is:

$$\frac{\text{Current Assets}}{\text{Current Liabilities}} = \frac{\$81,820}{\$44,950} = 1.82{:}1.$$

The 1.82:1 figure (rounded to the nearest hundredth) indicates that current assets are 1.82 times as much as current liabilities. Most lenders and other readers of financial statements are concerned with the current ratio and would like to see it be at least 2:1 (twice as many current assets as current liabilities), because the current liabilities must be paid out of the current assets. Although a 2:1 ratio may be desirable, in reality the average in Canadian industry is around 1.7:1 or 1.8:1. A current ratio of 3:1 would be a strong current position, while a ratio of 1:1 would be weak. A 1:1 ratio indicates that every dollar of current assets is targeted for payment of short-term debt and nothing would be left over for emergencies or working capital.

Working Capital

The excess of current assets over current liabilities is **working capital**. For Ron's Appliances, it is:

$$
\begin{array}{ccccc}
\text{Current Assets} & - & \text{Current Liabilities} & = & \text{Working Capital} \\
\$81,820 & - & \$44,950 & = & \$36,870
\end{array}
$$

The working capital figure is, like the current ratio, an indication of a firm's short-term financial strength. It represents an amount of cash that a firm may put into, for example, volume buying, inventories, advertising, or favourable credit terms to customers.

Closing Entries

The previous discussion of closing entries showed that there are four entries to be made for a service business. They are entries to (1) close all revenue accounts, (2) close all expense accounts, (3) transfer profit or loss to the capital account, and (4) transfer the balance of drawing to the capital account.

The first two closing entries are a little different for a merchandising business, because all of the cost of goods sold accounts must be closed in addition to the revenue and expense accounts. However, there are still four general journal entries required to close the books of a merchandising business, and they are made directly from the worksheet as before:

1. Close each account that appears in the credit column of the income statement.
2. Close each account that appears in the debit column of the income statement.
3. Transfer the profit or loss to the capital account.
4. Transfer the balance of the drawing account to the capital account.

Only the first two entries are different from those of a service business; the last two are exactly the same. The following shows the income statement columns of the worksheet for Ron's Appliances.

Ron's Appliances
Worksheet (Partial)
For Month Ended June 30, 19XX

Acct. No.	Account Titles	Adjusted Trial Balance Debit	Adjusted Trial Balance Credit	Income Statement Debit	Income Statement Credit
101	Cash	11 600 —			
110	Accounts Receivable	13 600 —			
120	Notes Receivable	7 200 —			
130	Merchandise Inventory	46 000 —		46 000 —	45 100 — ✓
140	Supplies	1 320 —			
150	Prepaid Insurance	3 000 —			
160	Office Equipment	28 000 —			
161	Accumulated Depreciation: OE		6 000 —		
170	Delivery Equipment	57 000 —			
171	Accumulated Depreciation: DE		12 000 —		
180	Building	130 000 —			
181	Accumulated Depreciation: Bldg.		8 000 —		
210	Accounts Payable		5 150 —		
220	Notes Payable		25 000 —		
240	Unearned Revenue		2 600 —		
250	Mortgage Payable		90 000 —		
310	Ron Renner, Capital		124 390 —		
320	Ron Renner, Drawing	6 000 —			
410	Sales		105 000 —		105 000 — ✓
420	Sales Returns and Allowances	2 100 —		2 100 —	
430	Sales Discounts	2 900 —		2 900 —	
501	Purchases	58 000 —		58 000 —	
520	Purchases Returns and Allowances		620 —		620 — ✓
530	Purchases Discounts		2 400 —		2 400 — ✓
540	Freight In	2 000 —		2 000 —	
610	Rent Expense	3 500 —		3 500 —	
620	Utilities Expense	750 —		750 —	
630	Wages Expense	5 900 —		5 900 —	
	Totals				
650	Supplies Expense	640 —		640 —	
660	Insurance Expense	100 —		100 —	
670	Depreciation Expense	1 750 —		1 750 —	
230	Wages Payable		200 —		
		381 360 —	381 360 —	123 640 —	153 120 — ✓
	Net Income			29 480 —	
				153 120 —	153 120 —

The First Closing Entry

The first closing entry debits each account that appears in the credit column of the income statement; the total is credited to Income Summary. Add check marks to the worksheet next to the amounts as they are journalized.

Date		Description	Post. Ref.	Debit	Credit
		GENERAL JOURNAL			**PAGE 6**
19XX		Closing Entries			
June	30	Merchandise Inventory	130	45 100 —	
		Sales	410	105 000 —	
		Purchases Returns and Allowances	520	620 —	
		Purchases Discounts	530	2 400 —	
		Income Summary	360		153 120 —
		To Close Income Statement Accounts with			
		Credit Balances and to Enter the Ending			
		Inventory on the Books			

After this first closing entry has been posted, the Merchandise Inventory account will look like this:

Merchandise Inventory		130
6/1 Balance	46,000	
6/30 Closing GJ6	45,100	

The effect of the first closing entry on the Merchandise Inventory account is to transfer the value of the ending inventory to the account. The beginning inventory figure is removed from the account in the second closing entry.

The Second Closing Entry

The second closing entry credits every account that appears on the debit side of the income statement and debits Income Summary. The following shows the income statement columns of the worksheet. Check marks have been placed opposite the accounts in the worksheet debit and credit columns for which closing entries have been made.

		Ron's Appliances Worksheet (Partial) For Month Ended June 30, 19XX					
		Adjusted Trial Balance		Income Statement			
Acct. No.	Account Titles	Debit	Credit	Debit		Credit	
101	Cash	11600—					
110	Accounts Receivable	13600—					
120	Notes Receivable	7200—					
130	Merchandise Inventory	46000—		46000 ✓		45100 ✓	
140	Supplies	1320—					
150	Prepaid Insurance	3000—					
160	Office Equipment	28000—					
161	Accumulated Depreciation: OE		6000—				
170	Delivery Equipment	57000—					
171	Accumulated Depreciation: DE		12000—				
180	Building	130000—					
181	Accumulated Depreciation: Bldg.		8000—				
210	Accounts Payable		5150—				
220	Notes Payable		25000—				
240	Unearned Revenue		2600—				
250	Mortgage Payable		90000—				
310	Ron Renner, Capital		124390—				
320	Ron Renner, Drawing	6000—					
410	Sales		105000—			105000 ✓	
420	Sales Returns and Allowances	2100—		2100 ✓			
430	Sales Discounts	2900—		2900 ✓			
501	Purchases	58000—		58000 ✓			
520	Purchases Returns and Allowances		620—			620 ✓	
530	Purchases Discounts		2400—			2400 ✓	
540	Freight In	2000—		2000 ✓			
610	Rent Expense	3500—		3500 ✓			
620	Utilities Expense	750—		750 ✓			
630	Wages Expense	5900—		5900 ✓			
	Totals						
650	Supplies Expense	640—		640 ✓			
660	Insurance Expense	100—		100 ✓			
670	Depreciation Expense	1750—		1750 ✓			
230	Wages Payable		200—				
		381360—	381360—	123640 ✓		153120 ✓	
	Net Income			29480			
				153120—		153120—	

GENERAL JOURNAL							PAGE 6	
Date		Description	Post. Ref.	Debit			Credit	
19XX		Closing Entries						
	30	Income Summary	360		1 2 3 6 4 0 —			
		Merchandising Inventory	130				4 6 0 0 0 —	
		Sales Returns and Allowances	420				2 1 0 0 —	
		Sales Discounts	430				2 9 0 0 —	
		Purchases	501				5 8 0 0 0 —	
		Freight In	540				2 0 0 0 —	
		Rent Expense	610				3 5 0 0 —	
		Utilities Expense	620				7 5 0 —	
		Wages Expense	630				5 9 0 0 —	
		Supplies Expense	650				6 4 0 —	
		Insurance Expense	660				1 0 0 —	
		Depreciation Expense	670				1 7 5 0 —	
		To Close Income Statement Accounts with						
		Debit Balances and to Close Out Beginning						
		Merchandise Inventory						

After the second closing entry has been posted, the Merchandise Inventory account appears as follows.

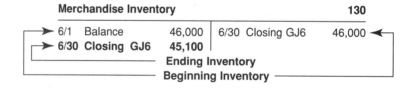

Merchandise Inventory   **130**

| 6/1 | Balance | 46,000 | 6/30 Closing GJ6 | 46,000 |
| 6/30 | Closing GJ6 | 45,100 | | |

Ending Inventory
Beginning Inventory

The account now reflects the value of the ending inventory. The ending inventory for this period becomes the beginning inventory of the next period.

The Third and Fourth Closing Entries

The third closing entry transfers the profit (or loss) to the owner's capital account, and the fourth transfers the balance of the drawing account to the owner's capital account.

GENERAL JOURNAL							PAGE 6	
Date		Description	Post. Ref.	Debit			Credit	
19XX		Closing Entries						
	30	Income Summary	360		2 9 4 8 0 —			
		Ron Renner, Capital	310				2 9 4 8 0 —	
		To Transfer Net Income to Capital						
	30	Ron Renner, Capital	310		6 0 0 0 —			
		Ron Renner, Drawing	320				6 0 0 0 —	
		To Transfer Balance of Drawing to Capital						

After the third closing entry is posted, the Income Summary account is closed as follows:

Income Summary   **360**

6/30 Closing GJ6 123,640	6/30 Closing GJ6 153,120
6/30 Closing GJ6 29,480	

The General Ledger after the Adjusting and Closing Entries Are Posted

The adjusting and closing entries are shown now, followed by T accounts representing the general ledger after they have been posted.

GENERAL JOURNAL				PAGE 5	
Date	Description	Post. Ref.	Debit	Credit	
19XX	Adjusting Entries				
June 30	Supplies Expense	650	640 —		
	Supplies	140		640 —	
	To Record Supplies Used for June				
30	Insurance Expense	660	100 —		
	Prepaid Insurance	150		100 —	
	To Record Insurance Expense for June				
30	Depreciation Expense	670	1750 —		
	Accumulated Depreciation: OE	161		500 —	
	Accumulated Depreciation: DE	171		750 —	
	Accumulated Depreciation: Building	181		500 —	
	To Record Depreciation Expense				
30	Unearned Revenue	240	900 —		
	Sales	410		900 —	
	To Transfer a Portion of Unearned Revenue				
	to Sales				
30	Wages Expense	630	200 —		
	Wages Payable	230		200 —	
	To Record Accrued Wages				

GENERAL JOURNAL   PAGE 6

Date	Description	Post. Ref.	Debit	Credit
19XX	Closing Entries			
June 30	Merchandise Inventory	130	45100—	
	Sales	410	105000—	
	Purchases Returns and Allowances	520	620—	
	Purchases Discounts	530	2400—	
	Income Summary	360		153120—
	To Close Income Statement Accounts with			
	Credit Balances and to Enter the Ending			
	Inventory on the Books			
30	Income Summary	360	123640—	
	Merchandise Inventory	130		46000—
	Sales Returns and Allowances	420		2100—
	Sales Discounts	430		2900—
	Purchases	501		58000—
	Freight In	540		2000—
	Rent Expense	610		3500—
	Utilities Expense	620		750—
	Wages Expense	630		5900—
	Supplies Expense	650		640—
	Insurance Expense	660		100—
	Depreciation Expense	670		1750—
	To Close Income Statement Accounts with			
	Debit Balances and to Close Out			
	Beginning Merchandise Inventory			
30	Income Summary	360	29480—	
	Ron Renner, Capital	310		29480—
	To Transfer Net Income to Capital			
30	Ron Renner, Capital	310	6000—	
	Ron Renner, Drawing	320		6000—
	To Transfer Balance of Drawing to Capital			

Cash   101

6/30 Balance	11,600	

Accounts Receivable   110

6/30 Balance	13,600	

Notes Receivable   120

6/30 Balance	7,200	

Merchandise Inventory   130

6/1 Balance	46,000	6/30 Closing GJ6	46,000
6/30 Closing GJ6	45,100		

Supplies   140

6/1 Balance	1,960	6/30 Adjusting GJ5	640
	1,320		

Prepaid Insurance   150

6/1	Balance	3,100	6/30	Adjusting GJ5	100
		3,000			

Office Equipment   160

6/30	Balance	28,000	

Accumulated Depreciation: Office Equipment   161

		6/1	Balance	5,500
		6/30	Adjusting GJ5	500
				6,000

Delivery Equipment   170

6/30	Balance	57,000	

Accumulated Depreciation: Delivery Equipment   171

		6/1	Balance	11,250
		6/30	Adjusting GJ5	750
				12,000

Building   180

6/30	Balance	130,000	

Accumulated Depreciation: Building   181

		6/1	Balance	7,500
		6/30	Adjusting GJ5	500
				8,000

Accounts Payable   210

		6/30	Balance	5,150

Notes Payable   220

		6/30	Balance	25,000

Wages Payable   230

		6/30	Adjusting GJ5	200

Unearned Revenue   240

6/30	Adjusting GJ5	900	6/1	Balance	3,500
					2,600

Mortgage Payable   250

		6/30	Balance	90,000

Ron Renner, Capital 310

6/30 Closing GJ6	6,000	6/1 Balance	124,390
		6/30 Closing GJ6	29,480
			153,870
			147,870

Ron Renner, Drawing 320

| 6/30 Balance | 6,000 | 6/30 Closing GJ6 | 6,000 |

Income Summary 360

| 6/30 Closing GJ6 | 123,640 | 6/30 Closing GJ6 | 153,120 |
| 6/30 Closing GJ6 | 29,480 | | |

Sales 410

| 6/30 Closing GJ6 | 105,000 | 6/30 Balance | 104,100 |
| | | 6/30 Adjusting GJ5 | 900 |

Sales Returns and Allowances 420

| 6/30 Balance | 2,100 | 6/30 Closing GJ6 | 2,100 |

Sales Discounts 430

| 6/30 Balance | 2,900 | 6/30 Closing GJ6 | 2,900 |

Purchases 501

| 6/30 Balance | 58,000 | 6/30 Closing GJ6 | 58,000 |

Purchases Returns and Allowances 520

| 6/30 Closing GJ6 | 620 | 6/30 Balance | 620 |

Purchases Discounts 530

| 6/30 Closing GJ6 | 2,400 | 6/30 Balance | 2,400 |

Freight In 540

| 6/30 Balance | 2,000 | 6/30 Closing GJ6 | 2,000 |

Rent Expense 610

| 6/30 Balance | 3,500 | 6/30 Closing GJ6 | 3,500 |

Utilities Expense 620

| 6/30 Balance | 750 | 6/30 Closing GJ6 | 750 |

Wages Expense   630

| 6/30 Balance | 5,700 | 6/30 Closing GJ6 | 5,900 |
| 6/30 Adjusting GJ5 | 200 | | |

Supplies Expense   650

| 6/30 Adjusting GJ5 | 640 | 6/30 Closing GJ6 | 640 |

Insurance Expense   660

| 6/30 Adjusting GJ5 | 100 | 6/30 Closing GJ6 | 100 |

Depreciation Expense   670

| 6/30 Adjusting GJ5 | 1,750 | 6/30 Closing GJ6 | 1,750 |

The Post-Closing Trial Balance

All the revenue, cost of goods sold, and expense accounts have zero balances after the closing entries are posted. In addition, the capital account has been brought up to date (by adding the net income and subtracting the drawing), and the drawing account has been closed. The only accounts that remain open are the assets, liabilities, and owner's capital accounts.

The post-closing trial balance is prepared to ensure that debits equal credits in the accounts that remain open — the balance sheet accounts — before work is started for the next accounting period. It should be prepared directly from the ledger after the closing entries are posted. Following is the post-closing trial balance for Ron's Appliances.

Ron's Appliances Post-Closing Trial Balance June 30, 19XX	Debit	Credit
Cash	$ 11,600	
Accounts Receivable	13,600	
Notes Receivable	7,200	
Merchandise Inventory	45,100	
Supplies	1,320	
Prepaid Insurance	3,000	
Office Equipment	28,000	
Accumulated Depreciation: OE		$ 6,000
Delivery Equipment	57,000	
Accumulated Depreciation: DE		12,000
Building	130,000	
Accumulated Depreciation: Building		8,000
Accounts Payable		5,150
Notes Payable		25,000
Wages Payable		200
Unearned Revenue		2,600
Mortgage Payable		90,000
Ron Renner, Capital		147,870
Totals	$296,820	$296,820

Summary

The complete accounting cycle includes (1) journalizing, (2) posting, (3) preparing a worksheet with adjustments, (4) preparing an income statement, (5) preparing a balance sheet, (6) preparing schedules of accounts receivable and accounts payable, (7) journalizing and posting adjusting entries, (8) journalizing and posting closing entries, and (9) preparing a post-closing trial balance.

The worksheet for a merchandising business contains both the beginning and ending merchandise inventories. The beginning inventory figure is obtained from the general ledger and appears on the worksheet as a debit on the trial balance, the adjusted trial balance, and the income statement. The ending inventory figure, obtained by a physical count or an estimate, appears on the worksheet in two places: as a credit on the income statement and as a debit on the balance sheet. The inventory figures are used when calculating cost of goods sold on the income statement.

The income statement for a merchandising business contains three major sections: (1) revenue, (2) cost of goods sold, and (3) expenses. Revenue minus cost of goods sold produces the gross profit figure, and expenses subtracted from gross profit produces the net profit figure. The cost of goods sold is calculated as follows:

Beginning Inventory
+ Cost of Purchases
Cost of Merchandise Available for Sale
− Ending Inventory
Cost of Goods Sold

The income statement is prepared directly from the income statement columns of the worksheet, and the balance sheet is prepared from the balance sheet columns. The asset section of the balance sheet is classified into current assets and plant and equipment. Current assets are cash, items that can easily be converted into cash, or items that will be used up within one year's time. Plant and equipment includes assets that are used in the production of other assets; such items might be furniture, office equipment, delivery vehicles, or land. Items of plant and equipment, when depreciable, are shown on the balance sheet at their historic cost. Accumulated depreciation is subtracted from cost, and the book value is calculated on the balance sheet.

Liabilities are also classified into two categories: current and long-term. Current liabilities must be paid within one year's time, and long-term liabilities will be due after one year.

The current ratio is an indicator of a firm's short-term debt-paying ability and is calculated by dividing current assets by current liabilities. A ratio of 2:1 is considered to be adequate; a ratio of 3:1 is considered to be strong. Another indicator of short-term debt-paying ability is the working capital figure, which is obtained by subtracting current liabilities from current assets. Working capital represents the portion of current assets that is not targeted for paying current liabilities.

The closing entries, prepared directly from the income statement columns of the worksheet, accomplish the following:
1. All the revenue and contra-revenue accounts are closed.
2. All the cost of goods sold accounts (including purchases and contra-purchases accounts) are closed.
3. All the expense accounts are closed.

4. The merchandise inventory account is brought up to date by closing out the beginning inventory and entering the ending inventory figure on the books.
5. The drawing account is closed.
6. The capital account is brought up to date by adding the net income, or deducting the net loss, and by deducting drawing.

Once the closing entries are posted, the only remaining step in the accounting cycle is to prepare a post-closing trial balance. It ensures the equality of debits and credits in the ledger accounts that remain open—all of the balance sheet accounts except drawing.

Vocabulary Review

Following is a list of the words and terms for this chapter:

classified	liquid asset
current ratio	working capital
gross profit	

Fill in the blank with the correct word or term from the list.

1. The _____ is obtained by dividing current assets by current liabilities and is an indicator of short-term debt-paying ability.
2. Net sales minus cost of goods sold equals _____.
3. Current assets minus current liabilities is called the _____ and is an indicator of a firm's short-term debt-paying ability.
4. When items are separated into categories, they are said to be _____.
5. A/an _____ is cash or is easily converted to cash.

Match the words and terms on the left with the definitions on the right.

6. classified
7. current ratio
8. gross profit
9. liquid asset
10. working capital

a. separated into categories
b. net sales minus cost of goods sold
c. cash or easily converted into cash
d. current assets minus current liabilities
e. current assets divided by current liabilities

Exercises

EXERCISE 11.1   Record the adjusting entries in a general journal (page 6) for the month of September 19XX for Ma and Pa Grocery. Use the following account titles: Supplies, Prepaid Insurance, Prepaid Advertising, Accumulated Depreciation: Computer, Unearned Revenue, Wages Payable, Grocery Revenue, Depreciation Expense, Insurance Expense, Advertising Expense, Supplies Expense, and Wages Expense.

a. The computer, purchased on January 2 of this year for $8,000, is expected to be useful for four years and will have a salvage value of $2,000.
b. On September 1 of this year, Ma and Pa Grocery received a cheque for $2,000 from a local orphanage. The money was for supplies and groceries

to be delivered after September 1 and was credited to Unearned Revenue. During September, $800 worth of groceries were delivered to the orphanage.

c. On January 2 of this year, $1,800 was paid for a two-year insurance policy.

d. On September 1 of this year, $900 was paid for three months of advertising.

e. Three days' wages of $210 per day had accrued at the end of September.

f. The balance in the Supplies account on September 1 was $440. Additional supplies were purchased on September 18 for $120 and on September 24 for $70. The value of the supplies on hand on September 30 was $310.

EXERCISE 11.2   Tell on which section of the balance sheet each of the following accounts appears. The sections should be identified as current assets (CA), plant and equipment (PE), current liabilities (CL), long-term liabilities (LTL), or owner's equity (OE). Also tell what the normal account balance is for each account listed.

	Account Titles	Which Section of the Balance Sheet?	Normal Account Balance?
a.	Prepaid Insurance	_____	_____
b.	Owner's Drawing	_____	_____
c.	Accounts Payable	_____	_____
d.	Building	_____	_____
e.	Cash	_____	_____
f.	Unearned Revenue	_____	_____
g.	Accumulated Depreciation	_____	_____
h.	Office Furniture	_____	_____
i.	Mortgage Payable (all due in 10 years)	_____	_____
j.	Merchandise Inventory	_____	_____

Now tell on which section of the income statement each of the following accounts appears. Sections should be identified as revenue (R), cost of goods sold (CGS), or expense (E). Also tell the normal account balance for each.

	Account Titles	Which Section of the Income Statement?	Normal Account Balance?
k.	Sales Discounts	_____	_____
l.	Purchases Discounts	_____	_____
m.	Wages Expense	_____	_____
n.	Sales Returns and Allowances	_____	_____
o.	Merchandise Inventory	_____	_____
p.	Sales	_____	_____
q.	Supplies Expense	_____	_____
r.	Freight In	_____	_____
s.	Purchases	_____	_____
t.	Purchases Returns and Allowances	_____	_____

EXERCISE 11.3   The Merchandise Inventory account for Sam's Glass Shop shows a debit balance on February 1 of $17,640. Answer the following questions about this account:

a. What is the account classification for merchandise inventory?

b. How is the dollar value of the ending merchandise inventory determined?

c. The beginning merchandise inventory figure appears on the ten-column worksheet in three different places. What are those three places?

d. Assuming that the value of Sam's merchandise inventory on February 28 is $16,500, on which two worksheet columns will this ending inventory figure appear?

e. Where will the merchandise inventory figure appear on the financial statements?

EXERCISE 11.4   Following are the steps in the accounting cycle. Rearrange them in correct order, numbering each. As an example, the first is "(1) Journalize period's regular transactions."

Prepare trial balance, calculate adjustments, and complete worksheet.
Prepare a balance sheet.
Prepare a post-closing trial balance.
Journalize period's regular transactions.
Journalize and post closing entries.
Post regular transactions to ledger.
Prepare an income statement.
Journalize and post adjusting entries.
Prepare schedules of accounts receivable and payable.

EXERCISE 11.5   Given the following account balances, calculate (1) net sales and (2) cost of purchases.

Cash	$10,550
Sales Discounts	1,470
Purchases Discounts	3,880
Sales	94,000
Freight In	3,190
Merchandise Inventory	31,000
Purchases	49,600
Sales Returns and Allowances	2,630
Purchases Returns and Allowances	4,020

EXERCISE 11.6   From the following account balances, prepare the cost of goods sold section of an income statement for the month of August 19XX.

Purchases	$29,400
Merchandise Inventory, August 31	12,300
Purchases Returns and Allowances	410
Freight In	1,100
Purchases Discounts	290
Merchandise Inventory, August 1	11,400

EXERCISE 11.7   Following are the asset and liability accounts and their balances as of May 31, 19XX for Carlo's Italian Restaurant after the adjusting entries have been posted. Determine (1) the dollar amount of current assets, (2) the dollar amount of current liabilities, (3) the current ratio, (4) the working capital, and (5) the total dollar value of plant and equipment as it would appear on the balance sheet.

Cash	$ 9,120
Accounts Payable	2,500
Merchandise Inventory	9,235
Equipment	15,000
Accumulated Depreciation: Equipment	2,300
Payroll Taxes Payable	320
Supplies	940
Accounts Receivable	3,630
Wages Payable	550
Prepaid Insurance	500
Furniture	7,500
Accumulated Depreciation: Furniture	1,800
Mortgage Payable ($6,000 due within 12 months)	50,000
Land	75,000

EXERCISE 11.8   Following are the income statement columns of the May 19XX worksheet for Goodlife Vitamins, owned by Nancy Swanson. The balance of the owner's drawing account on May 31, 19XX was $3,600. Prepare the closing entries to: (1) close all accounts with credit balances and enter the ending merchandise inventory on the books, (2) close all accounts with debit balances and remove the beginning inventory from the books, (3) transfer the net income to the owner's capital account, and (4) transfer the balance of drawing to capital. Use general journal page 31.

	Income Statement	
	Debit	**Credit**
Merchandise Inventory	13,700	14,100
Sales		47,000
Sales Returns and Allowances	410	
Sales Discounts	520	
Purchases	29,000	
Purchases Returns and Allowances		330
Purchases Discounts		260
Freight In	1,100	
Rent Expense	1,800	
Advertising Expense	2,010	
Salary Expense	2,740	
Supplies Expense	390	
Depreciation Expense	1,740	
Utilities Expense	330	
Totals	53,740	61,690
Net Income	7,950	
	61,690	61,690

EXERCISE 11.9   Following are the income statement columns of the March 19XX worksheet for Puffy Pastries, owned by Sam Yee. The balance of the owner's drawing account on March 31 was $1,500. Prepare the closing entries to: (1) close all accounts with credit balances and enter the ending inventory figure on the books, (2) close all accounts with debit balances and remove the beginning inventory figure from the books, (3) transfer the net loss to the owner's capital account, and (4) transfer the balance of drawing to capital. Use general journal page 56.

	Income Statement	
	Debit	Credit
Merchandise Inventory	3,000	2,100

Sales		14,300
Sales Returns and Allowances	390	
Purchases	8,000	
Purchases Discounts		740
Rent Expense	1,100	
Utilities Expense	310	
Salary Expense	1,200	
Supplies Expense	140	
Depreciation Expense	3,500	
	17,640	17,140
Net Loss		500
	17,640	17,640

Problems

PROBLEM 11.1   Following are the closing entries and the related T accounts for Higgins' Grocery on January 31, 19XX.

GENERAL JOURNAL				PAGE 13	
Date	Description	Post. Ref.	Debit	Credit	
19XX	Closing Entries				
Jan. 31	Merchandise Inventory		1 2 1 0 0 —		
	Sales		2 5 0 0 0 —		
	Purchases Returns and Allowances		4 8 0 —		
	Purchases Discounts		1 6 5 —		
	Income Summary			3 7 7 4 5 —	
	To Close Income Statement Accounts with Credit				
	Balances and to Enter the Ending Inventory on				
	the Books				
31	Income Summary		3 4 2 1 0 —		
	Merchandise Inventory			1 3 4 0 0 —	
	Sales Returns and Allowances			1 4 0 0 —	
	Sales Discounts			9 0 0 —	
	Purchases			1 6 5 0 0 —	
	Rent Expense			9 0 0 —	
	Utilities Expense			3 8 0 —	
	Advertising Expense			5 2 0 —	
	Insurance Expense			2 1 0 —	
	To Close Income Statement Accounts with Debit				
	Balances and to Close Out the Beginning				
	Merchandise Inventory				
31	Income Summary		3 5 3 5 —		
	Henry Higgins, Capital			3 5 3 5 —	
	To Transfer Net Income to Capital				
31	Henry Higgins, Capital		2 2 0 0 —		
	Henry Higgins, Drawing			2 2 0 0 —	
	To Transfer the Balance of Drawing to Capital				

Merchandise Inventory		130
1/31 Balance	13,400	

Purchases		510
1/31 Balance	16,500	

Henry Higgins, Capital		310
	1/31 Balance	15,200

Purchases Returns and Allowances		520
	1/31 Balance	480

Henry Higgins, Drawing		320
1/31 Balance	2,200	

Purchases Discounts		530
	1/31 Balance	165

Income Summary		330

Rent Expense		610
1/31 Balance	900	

Sales		410
	1/31 Balance	25,000

Utilities Expense		620
1/31 Balance	380	

Sales Returns and Allowances		420
1/31 Balance	1,400	

Advertising Expense		630
1/31 Balance	520	

Sales Discounts		430
1/31 Balance	900	

Insurance Expense		640
1/31 Balance	210	

INSTRUCTIONS

1. Post the closing entries to the T accounts provided. As posting is completed, be sure to place account numbers in the journal and the journal page number (GJ13) in the T accounts.
2. After posting has been completed, answer the following questions:
   a. What is the balance of the Income Summary account after posting has been completed?
   b. What is the balance of the Merchandise Inventory account after posting has been completed?
   c. Which income statement accounts remain open after posting has been completed?
   d. What is the balance of the drawing account after posting has been completed?
   e. What is the balance of the capital account on January 31, 19XX?
   f. What is the dollar amount of the net income for January?

PROBLEM 11.2

Following are the income statement columns of the worksheet for Koffee Kitchen, owned by Raymond White, for the month of February 19XX.

		Income Statement	
		Debit	**Credit**
130	Merchandise Inventory	11,400	10,600
410	Sales		27,400
420	Sales Returns and Allowances	600	
430	Sales Discounts	730	
501	Purchases	14,200	

520	Purchases Returns and Allowances		190
530	Purchases Discounts		510
540	Freight In	540	
610	Rent Expense	850	
620	Utilities Expense	240	
630	Wages Expense	1,500	
640	Advertising Expense	1,000	
650	Supplies Expense	190	
660	Insurance Expense	70	
670	Depreciation Expense	850	
		32,170	38,700
	Net Income	6,530	
		38,700	38,700

INSTRUCTIONS

1. Journalize the four required closing entries. Use general journal page 6. The balance of the owner's drawing account on February 28 is $3,400.
2. Prepare an income statement for the month.

PROBLEM 11.3

Following are the balance sheet columns of the worksheet for Special Effects, a retail store owned by Betsy Rawlings, on September 30, 19XX.

		Balance Sheet	
		Debit	**Credit**
101	Cash	9,350	
110	Accounts Receivable	5,120	
120	Notes Receivable	5,700	
130	Merchandise Inventory	24,600	
140	Supplies	730	
150	Prepaid Insurance	1,500	
160	Office Equipment	14,000	
161	Accumulated Depreciation: OE		5,000
170	Store Equipment	21,000	
171	Accumulated Depreciation: SE		6,000
180	Building	55,000	
181	Accumulated Depreciation: Bldg.		16,400
210	Accounts Payable		6,200
220	Notes Payable		14,600
230	Wages Payable		470
240	Unearned Revenue		1,370
250	Mortgage Payable		42,000
310	Betsy Rawlings, Capital		43,980
320	Betsy Rawlings, Drawing	3,650	
		140,650	136,020
	Net Income		4,630
		140,650	140,650

INSTRUCTIONS

1. Prepare a classified balance sheet as of September 30, 19XX. The balance in Notes Payable is due in 6 months and $12,000 of the balance in Mortgage Payable is due within the next 12 months. Include a complete statement of owner's equity on the balance sheet.
2. Determine the current ratio. (Round to the nearest tenth of a percent.) Does it indicate a strong or a weak current position?
3. Determine the dollar amount of working capital.

PROBLEM 11.4   Following are the trial balance columns of the worksheet for the month of April 19XX for Gail Greenwood, owner of Woman Source, a bookstore.

		Trial Balance Debit	Trial Balance Credit
101	Cash	10,400	
110	Accounts Receivable	3,300	
120	Notes Receivable	9,600	
130	Merchandise Inventory	31,000	
140	Supplies	760	
150	Prepaid Insurance	2,300	
160	Office Equipment	27,000	
161	Accumulated Depreciation: OE		6,750
170	Delivery Equipment	40,000	
171	Accumulated Depreciation: DE		9,375
180	Building	35,000	
181	Accumulated Depreciation: Bldg.		1,500
210	Accounts Payable		5,100
220	Notes Payable		40,000
240	Unearned Revenue		1,800
250	Mortgage Payable		30,000
310	Gail Greenwood, Capital		67,265
320	Gail Greenwood, Drawing	4,400	
410	Sales		60,000
420	Sales Returns and Allowances	690	
430	Sales Discounts	1,600	
501	Purchases	49,000	
520	Purchases Returns and Allowances		1,110
530	Purchases Discounts		980
540	Freight In	2,500	
610	Rent Expense	1,400	
620	Utilities Expense	370	
630	Wages Expense	3,160	
640	Advertising Expense	1,400	
		223,880	223,880

INSTRUCTIONS

1. Enter the account names, numbers, and balances into T accounts representing a general ledger and onto the trial balance columns of a worksheet. In addition to the accounts listed on the trial balance, add the following: Supplies Expense, 650; Insurance Expense, 660; Depreciation Expense, 670; Wages Payable, 260; and Income Summary, 330.
2. Calculate the adjustments for April and enter the amounts in the adjustments columns of the worksheet. The necessary information is:
   a. The supplies inventory on April 30 is $310.
   b. A two-year insurance policy was purchased on March 1 of this year for $2,400.
   c. Office equipment was purchased on January 2 of last year; cost, $27,000; life, five years; salvage value, 0.
   d. Delivery equipment was purchased on January 4 of last year; cost, $40,000; life, four years; salvage value, $10,000.
   e. A building was purchased on January 2 of last year; cost, $35,000; life, 20 years; salvage value, $11,000.
   f. Wages payable on April 30 are $760.
   g. $800 of the unearned revenue has been earned during April.
3. The value of the merchandise inventory on April 30 is $34,000. Enter the inventory figures in their appropriate places on the worksheet.
4. Complete the worksheet.

5. Prepare an income statement for Woman Source for the month of April 19XX.

6. Prepare a statement of owner's equity for Woman Source for the month of April 19XX.

7. Prepare a classified balance sheet for Woman Source as of April 30, 19XX. Include only the ending capital figure in the owner's equity section. $12,000 of the balance in Notes Payable is due within 12 months, and the mortgage is all due and payable in 10 years.

8. Journalize and post the adjusting entries. Use general journal page 48.

9. Journalize and post the closing entries. Use general journal page 49.

10. Prepare a post-closing trial balance.

PROBLEM 11.5   Following are the income statement and balance sheet columns of the worksheet for Pete Stavros, owner of Stavros Imports, for the month of August 19XX.

	Income Statement		Balance Sheet	
	Debit	Credit	Debit	Credit
Cash			15,340	
Accounts Receivable			6,050	
Notes Receivable			14,290	
Merchandise Inventory	12,290	15,450	15,450	
Supplies			1,020	
Prepaid Insurance			1,900	
Office Equipment			24,000	
Accumulated Depreciation: OE				7,400
Store Equipment			34,000	
Accumulated Depreciation: SE				17,500
Building			42,000	
Accumulated Depreciation: Bldg.				20,600
Accounts Payable				3,030
Notes Payable				36,200
Wages Payable				1,420
Unearned Revenue				1,140
Mortgage Payable				25,700
Pete Stavros, Capital				44,420
Pete Stavros, Drawing			2,490	
Sales		49,740		
Sales Returns and Allowances	600			
Sales Discounts	500			
Purchases	35,000			
Purchases Returns and Allowances		1,610		
Purchases Discounts		700		
Freight In	1,960			
Rent Expense	1,500			
Utilities Expense	590			
Wages Expense	5,640			
Depreciation Expense	4,470			
Advertising Expense	1,940			
Insurance Expense	160			
Repairs Expense	3,120			
Supplies Expense	600			
Totals	68,370	67,500	156,540	157,410
Net Loss		870	870	
	68,370	68,370	157,410	157,410

INSTRUCTIONS

1. Prepare an income statement for Stavros Imports for the month of August 19XX.
2. Prepare a classified balance sheet for Stavros Imports on August 31, 19XX, assuming that $12,000 of the balance in Notes Payable is due within a year's time and that $6,000 of the balance in Mortgage Payable is due within a year's time.
3. Journalize the closing entries on August 31. Use general journal page 29.
4. Determine the current ratio. (Round to the nearest tenth of a percent.)
5. Determine the dollar amount of working capital.

Comprehensive Problem 2 for Review of Chapters Seven–Eleven

Holly Harris owns a business called "Hobby House." It is a novelty store that sells model kits for cars, planes, and railroad equipment, accessories for model kits, miniature furniture and houses, unusual games and puzzles, and other novelty items. The chart of accounts and account balances for Hobby House on January 1, 19XX follow. The schedules of accounts receivable and payable showing the balance owed on January 1 appear below. The bank statement that Hobby House received from the Bank of Nova Scotia follows the transactions. Read all of the instructions (which follow the bank statement) before you begin work on the problem.

Hobby House
Schedule of Accounts Receivable
January 1, 19XX

Dave Culver	$275.15
Jill Goode	291.05
Lynda Morrison	143.50
Peter Vermont	214.60
Total	$924.30

Hobby House
Schedule of Accounts Payable
January 1, 19XX

Adult Toys	$ 900.94
Model Supplies	714.76
The Toy Place	462.24
Total	$2,077.94

Chart of Accounts

101	Cash	$15,399.63
105	Petty Cash	—0—
110	Change Fund	300.00
120	Accounts Receivable	924.30
130	Prepaid Insurance	—0—
140	Office Supplies	642.50
145	Merchandise Inventory	17,895.00

311

150	Office Equipment	12,400.00	
151	Accumulated Depreciation: Office Equipment		$ 4,800.00
160	Store Equipment	18,600.00	
161	Accumulated Depreciation: Store Equipment		4,500.00
170	Office Furniture	2,790.00	
171	Accumulated Depreciation: Office Furniture		1,395.00
180	Van	21,800.00	
181	Accumulated Depreciation: Van		7,200.00
210	Accounts Payable		2,077.94
220	Notes Payable		30,620.00
230	Provincial Sales Tax Payable		605.40
240	GST Charged		529.73
242	GST Paid	306.25	
244	GST Owing (Refund)		—0—
301	Holly Harris, Capital		39,329.61
310	Holly Harris, Drawing		
320	Income Summary		
410	Revenue from Sales		
420	Sales Returns and Allowances		
510	Purchases		
520	Purchases Returns and Allowances		
530	Purchases Discounts		
540	Freight In		
610	Rent Expense		
620	Utilities Expense		
625	Office Supplies Expense		
630	Interest Expense		
635	Insurance Expense		
640	Wages Expense		
650	Advertising Expense		
655	Depreciation Expense		
660	Delivery Expense		
670	Subscription Expense		
680	Postage Expense		
690	Entertainment Expense		
695	Bank Service Charges		

TRANSACTIONS

January 1   issued cheque 405 for $360 to Business Insurance Company in payment for a two-year fire insurance policy

January 1   sold merchandise on account to Lynda Morrison on sales invoice 320; $52 plus PST and GST

January 1   received a cheque from Jill Goode for $291.05 in full payment of her account

January 1   issued cheque 406 for $100 to establish a petty cash fund (enter the receipt of the $100 into the petty cash register after the cheque is recorded)

January 2   purchased merchandise for resale from Adult Toys for $408 plus GST on invoice 2982 dated January 2; terms 2/10, n/30

January 2   issued cheque 407 for $50 plus GST to Mercury's Trucking Company for delivering the purchase from Adult Toys

January 3   issued cheque 408 to Olympic Realty for $1,400 for January rent

January 4   issued cheque 409 to Model Supplies for $701.40 in full payment of December 29 purchase of $668 plus GST, less a 2 percent discount

January 5   issued cheque 410 to Adult Toys for $884.10 in full payment of December 30 purchase of $842 plus GST, less a 2 percent discount

January 5   sold merchandise on account to Dave Culver on sales invoice 321, $76 plus PST and GST

January 6   record petty cash voucher 1 for $6.45 plus GST, payment for monthly subscription for the local newspaper

January 7   cash sales for the week are $3,642 plus PST and GST

January 8   issued cheque 411 for $275.60 to Ontario Hydro for electricity for the month

January 9   received a cheque from Peter Vermont for $100 in partial payment of his account

January 9   issued cheque 412 for $30.90 plus GST to Grand & Toy for office supplies

January 9   issued cheque 413 to The Toy Place for $462.24 in full payment of January 1 balance (no discount granted)

January 10   sold merchandise on account to Jill Goode on sales invoice 322; $125 plus PST and GST

January 10   record petty cash voucher 2 for $8.30 plus GST spent for postage

January 11   issued credit memorandum 60-A to Jill Goode for $20 plus PST and GST relating to invoice 322 dated January 10

January 11   received a cheque from Dave Culver for $150 in partial payment of his account

January 12   issued cheque 414 for $428.40 to Adult Toys in full payment of invoice 2982 dated January 2

January 12   purchased merchandise for resale from Model Supplies for $1,540 plus GST on invoice 333 dated January 12; terms 2/10, n/30

January 13   received a cheque from Lynda Morrison for $143.50 in partial payment of her account

January 14   issued debit memorandum 321-13 to Model Supplies for $120 plus GST for merchandise returned to them

January 14   record petty cash voucher 3 for $18.90 plus GST; Holly took a customer to lunch

January 15   cash sales for the week are $4,016 plus PST and GST

January 15   issued cheque 415 for $970 to Royal Trust for monthly payment on the outstanding note; $459 is for interest expense and the rest is for principal

January 16   issued cheque 416 to Grant Tudor for $700 in payment of semi-monthly wages

January 17   issued cheque 417 to Treasurer of Ontario for $605.40 in payment of balance owed for sales tax payable on January 1

January 17   issued cheque 418 to Holly Harris for $1,600 for personal use

January 18   sold merchandise on account to Peter Vermont on sales invoice 323; $70 plus PST and GST

January 19   purchased merchandise for resale from The Toy Place for $622 plus GST on invoice 78-32 dated January 19; terms n/30

January 21   cash sales for the week are $4,906 plus PST and GST

January 21   record petty cash voucher 4 for $17.30 plus GST; Holly took a customer to lunch

January 22   issued credit memorandum 61-A to Peter Vermont for $10 plus PST and GST relating to invoice 323 dated January 18

January 22   issued cheque 419 to Model Supplies for $1,491 in full payment of invoice 333-A dated January 12, less the return on January 14

January 22   Holly purchased a word processor and computer from Computerland for use in the office at a total cost of $10,700 plus GST; she paid no cash down, but signed a three-year, 9 percent note for the purchase

January 23   issued cheque 420 to *The Toronto Star* for $150 plus GST for advertising in January

January 24   record petty cash voucher 5 for $8.45 plus GST for delivery expense

January 24   purchased merchandise for resale from Adult Toys for $750 plus GST on invoice 3053 dated January 24; terms 2/10, n/30

January 24   issued cheque 421 to Mercury's Trucking Company for $50 plus GST for delivering the purchase from Adult Toys

January 26   sold merchandise on account to Lynda Morrison on sales invoice 324; $190 plus PST and GST

January 27   received a cheque from Lynda Morrison for $59.80 in full payment of invoice 320 dated January 1

January 28   record petty cash voucher 6 for $30 plus GST for a magazine subscription

January 28   issued cheque 422 to Grant Tudor for $775 in payment of semi-monthly wages

January 28   cash sales for the week are $3,760 plus PST and GST

January 29   received a cheque from Peter Vermont for $100 in partial payment of his account

January 30   purchased merchandise for resale from Model Supplies for $1,250 plus GST on invoice 461 dated January 30; terms 2/10 n/30

January 31   received a cheque from Dave Culver for $50 in partial payment of his account

January 31   issued cheque 423 for $95.65 to replenish the petty cash fund. Stop now and total and rule the petty cash register. (See instruction 9.)

January 31   issued cheque 424 to the Receiver General of Canada in full payment of the GST owing. (Before recording the cheque in the cash payments journal, prepare the general journal entry to close the GST Charged and GST Paid accounts to GST Owing (Refund) to calculate the amount owing. This entry will require a debit to GST Charged and credits to GST Paid and GST Owing (Refund).)

Bank of Nova Scotia
327 South Street
Hamilton, Ontario

Date		Explanation	Cheques	Deposits	Balance
Jan.	1	Balance			15,399.63
	1			291.05	15,690.68
	1	406	100.00		15,590.68
	3	405	280.00		15,310.68
	3	407	53.50		15,257.18
	5	408	1,400.00		13,857.18
	5	409	701.40		13,155.78
	7	410	884.10		12,271.68
	7			4,188.30	16,459.98
	9			100.00	16,559.98
	10	411	275.60		16,284.38
	10	413	462.24		15,822.14
	11	412	33.06		15,789.08
	11			150.00	15,939.08
	13			143.50	16,082.58
	14	414	428.40		15,654.18
	15			4,618.40	20,272.58
	15	415	970.00		19,302.58
	15	Cheque Printing	32.50		19,270.08
	17	416	700.00		18,570.08
	17	418	1,600.00		16,970.08
	19	417	605.40		16,364.68
	21			5,641.90	22,006.58
	24	419	1,491.00		20,515.58
	27	420	160.50		20,355.08
	27	421	53.50		20,301.58
	27			59.80	20,361.38
	28			4,324.00	24,685.38
	29	422	775.00		23,910.38
	29			100.00	24,010.38
	31	Service Charge	18.50		23,991.88

INSTRUCTIONS

1. Copy the account names, numbers, and balances into the general ledger.
2. Copy the names and balances into the accounts receivable and accounts payable subsidiary ledgers. Post to the subsidiary ledgers immediately after each transaction.
3. Record sales on account in a sales journal, page 11, with the following column headings: sales credit, PST payable credit, GST charged credit, and accounts receivable debit. Hobby House is required to collect 8 percent provincial sales tax and 7 percent GST on all sales. Terms of sale are n/30.
4. Record credit purchases of merchandise for resale in a purchases journal, page 10, with the following column headings: purchases debit, GST paid

debit, and accounts payable credit. Holly always pays within the discount period when terms are offered.

5. Record all cash receipts in a cash receipts journal, page 12, with the following column headings: sundry credits, accounts receivable credit, sales credit, PST payable credit, GST charged credit, and cash debit.

6. Record all cash payments in a cash payments journal, page 13, with the following column headings: sundry debits, accounts payable debit, purchases discounts credit, and cash credit.

7. Record all transactions that do not belong in a special journal in a general journal, page 24.

8. Record all payments out of petty cash in the petty cash register, page 14. Use the following column headings: receipts, payments, subscription expense, postage expense, entertainment expense, GST paid, and sundry debits.

9. On January 31, total and rule the petty cash register, and then record cheque 423 for $95.65 to replenish the fund.

10. Total, crossfoot, and rule the sales, purchases, cash receipts, and cash payments journals.

11. Perform all the required summary and individual posting from the special journals.

12. Prepare a bank statement reconciliation as of January 31. All incoming cash and cheques are deposited daily.

13. Prepare all necessary entries in the general journal to bring the books up to date after reconciliation.

14. Perform all the required posting from the general journal.

15. Prepare a trial balance of the general ledger on January 31 in the trial balance columns of the worksheet.

16. Prepare a schedule of accounts receivable on January 31. Compare the total with the balance in the accounts receivable control account in the general ledger.

17. Prepare a schedule of accounts payable on January 31. Compare the total with the balance in the accounts payable control account in the general ledger.

18. Calculate the adjustments for January and enter the amounts in the adjustments columns of the worksheet. The necessary information is:

   a. The supplies inventory on January 31 is $453.50.

   b. A two-year insurance policy was purchased on January 1 of this year for $360.

   c. Office equipment was purchased two years ago; cost, $12,400; life, 5 years; salvage value, $400.

   d. Store equipment was purchased one year ago; cost, $18,600; life, 4 years; salvage value, $600.

   e. Office furniture was purchased one year ago; cost, $2,790; life, 2 years; salvage value, zero.

   f. The van was purchased two years ago; cost, $21,800; life, 5 years; salvage value, $3,800.

19. The value of the merchandise inventory on January 31 is $16,695. Enter the inventory figures in their appropriate places on the worksheet.

20. Complete the worksheet.

21. Prepare an income statement for Hobby House for the month of January 19XX.

22. Prepare a statement of owner's equity for Hobby House for the month of January 19XX.

23. Prepare a classified balance sheet for Hobby House as of January 31, 19XX. $6,132 of the note payable is due within the next 12 months.

24. Journalize and post the adjusting entries. Use general journal page 26.

25. Journalize and post the closing entries. Use general journal page 27.

26. Prepare a post-closing trial balance as of January 31, 19XX.

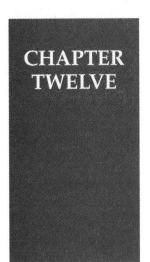

Payroll—Employee Deductions

Learning Objectives

When you have completed this chapter, you should
1. have an increased understanding of accounting terminology.
2. have a basic understanding of the employer–employee relationship.
3. be able to calculate regular, overtime, and total earnings.
4. be able to determine Canada Pension Plan (CPP) and unemployment insurance (UI) premiums.
5. be able to determine income tax deductions.
6. be able to complete a payroll register.
7. be able to prepare the journal entry to record the payroll.

Vocabulary

employee   one who performs services for an employer and whose work may be directed by the employer

employer   an organization or a person who receives the services of an employee; the employer may provide the working place of, direct the activities of, and hire or fire the employee

exempt   to free from a duty or an obligation required of others; to excuse

gross wages   total earnings before any deductions

independent contractor   one whose services may be hired for a fee, but whose work is not directed by the person or organization doing the hiring; the independent contractor is not considered to be an employee and therefore no payroll taxes are withheld

net wages   gross pay minus deductions

overtime   in this text, refers to hours worked over a weekly total of 40 hours

317

overtime earnings   in this text, wages earned for hours worked over a weekly total of 40 hours; paid at time and a half or double the rate of regular earnings

regular earnings   in this text, earnings for hours worked up to a weekly total of 40

Revenue Canada   the federal agency that is responsible for collecting income taxes

salary   in this text, refers to earnings stated in yearly, monthly, or weekly terms

TD1, personal tax credit return   government form completed by an employee indicating various personal exemptions that exempt a portion of gross earnings from federal income tax

wages   in this text, refers to earnings stated in hourly terms

withhold   to refrain, or hold back, from giving

Introduction

Nearly every adult has received a paycheque at one time or another. The stub that accompanies the cheque shows the total amount earned, all the deductions, and the take-home pay. The amount that an employee takes home is usually much less than the amount earned.

A great deal of work goes into the preparation of a payroll. Employees should be aware of the tax laws so that they can protect their own interests. Employers, too, must be knowledgeable about the tax laws as they relate to the employer–employee relationship and to the payment of wages and the withholding of taxes. Revenue Canada requires, for example, that employers **withhold** certain taxes each payroll period, remit those taxes at certain times, and file regular reports relating to the payroll and amounts withheld. Employers who are not totally familiar with Revenue Canada requirements sometimes remit taxes withheld after the deadline; if that is the case, a 10 percent penalty will be assessed for the first late remittance in a calendar year. If, during the same calendar year, there are subsequent late remittances, the penalty may increase to 20 percent.

Payroll Deductions Tables

Revenue Canada, a federal government department, provides employers with all the necessary information for the withholding of taxes. It publishes a booklet, *Payroll Deductions Tables*, each year, for each province, that is provided to each registered employer and to anyone who requests it. The tables are regularly updated as tax laws and rates of tax change. The booklet provides basic information that an employer needs to know. Among others, topics include "What's new," "Some information about deducting," "Need help?" and many others.

Tables also show the amounts of *combined* provincial and federal income taxes that are required to be deducted.

Amounts required to be deducted for Canada Pension Plan (CPP) and unemployment insurance (UI) premiums are shown together with their regulations in the same booklet. Every employer must be familiar with all of the regulations in this booklet.

The Employer–Employee Relationship

An **employer** is a person or an organization that receives the services of an employee. The employer usually provides the place to work and the required tools. An employer may discharge an employee and has the right to tell the employee when, where, and how a job is to be done.

An **employee** performs services for an employer and his or her work may be controlled by the employer.

An **independent contractor**, in contrast, is someone who is hired to do a specific job but may decide how the job is to be completed. Plumbers, doctors, tutors, and repair persons, for example, fall into this category.

It is important to make the distinction between employees and independent contractors because employers are required by law to withhold certain taxes from wages paid to employees, while payroll taxes are not withheld on fees paid to independent contractors.

Payroll Tax Laws

Both the federal and the provincial governments have legal requirements that pertain, among other things, to the withholding of payroll taxes, to the payment of a certain minimum wage, and to the payment of workers' compensation insurance.

Labour Standards

Except for certain industries, hours of work, minimum wages, and **overtime** provisions as well as general labour standards are regulated by provincial governments and differ somewhat from province to province. Often, working conditions are established by a union contract at a level above those legislated.

Income Taxes Withheld (ITD)

In 1917, legislation was passed allowing the federal government to tax the incomes of its people. However, this applied to only a few individuals having high earnings. It was not until World War II that the government began taxing the income of virtually all employees. Since the federal government recognized the difficulty of employees saving to pay a lump sum once a year, it introduced a system in which taxes are withheld each payday at their source. In this system, the employer is required to act as the collection agent.

Canada Pension Plan Contributions (CPP)

The CPP applies to all employees between the ages of 18 and 70, with few exceptions. One should consult Revenue Canada's publication *Payroll Deductions Tables* for employment that may not be subject to these contributions.

The contributions to be deducted are based on maximum pensionable earnings of $34,400 for 1994, with a basic exemption of $3,400. The rate for 1994 is 2.6 percent of pensionable earnings, for a maximum contribution of $806 per year. The rates are subject to change each year.

Unemployment Insurance Premiums

In 1940, the Unemployment Insurance Act created a federal agency, the Unemployment Insurance Commission, to administer a plan that would alleviate the hardships caused by unemployment. In 1971, this plan was revised and under the new Act, unemployment insurance coverage is compulsory for all Canadian workers under the age of 65 who are not self-employed. There are exceptions to this compulsory coverage, and one should consult Revenue Canada's publication *Payroll Deductions Tables* for verification.

Effective January 1, 1994, the employer is required to deduct an amount equal to 3.07 percent of the insurable earnings. The maximum 1994 insurable earnings are $780 per week or $40,560 per year, resulting in a maximum employee premium payable of $23.95 per week, or $1,245.40 ($23.95 × 52) on a 52-week basis. The rates are subject to change each year.

Salaries and Hourly Wages

Although the terms salary and wages are often used interchangeably, **salary** normally refers to earnings that are stated in weekly, monthly, or yearly terms. Usually management, teachers, engineers, and supervisory personnel are paid salaries. **Wages** normally refer to earnings stated on an hourly basis.

Calculating the Gross Payroll

Gross payroll is the total amount earned by all employees before any deductions are taken. It involves calculating the **gross wages** for employees who earn salaries and for those who earn hourly wages.

Assume that Wright's Accounting Service has six employees; two are management and are paid yearly salaries, and four are accounting clerks who are paid hourly wages, with time and a half for all hours worked over 40 in a week. The gross payroll calculations for the last week in March follow:

Management Personnel	
Susan Harris	$36,400 per year
	$36,400/52 = $700 per week
Anthony LaMarca	$31,200 per year
	$31,200/52 = $600 per week

As you can see, the yearly salary is divided by the number of weeks in a year. Once the weekly salary has been calculated, it need not be recalculated for each new pay period.

Wage Earners

The four hourly employees for Wright's Accounting Service and their wages per hour are as follows:

Non-Management Personnel

Richard McIntosh	$12.00 per hour, worked 50 hours
Carolyn Seaver	$10.50 per hour, worked 35 hours
Thomas Wyman	$11.00 per hour, worked 60 hours
Virginia Colter	$11.00 per hour, worked 45 hours

Each hourly employee is paid time and a half for hours worked over 40 in a week. To calculate each employee's weekly gross wage, determine: (1) the regular wage, which is the hourly rate times 40 hours (or less, if the employee worked fewer than 40 hours during the week); (2) the overtime premium, which is the hourly overtime rate times the number of hours worked overtime; and (3) the total of the regular wage and the overtime wage.

McIntosh
1. Determine regular wage.
   $12.00 × 40 hours = $480.00
2. Determine overtime wage.
   $12.00 × 1.5 = $18.00
   $18.00 × 10 hours =   180.00
3. Determine gross wage.
   Add the results of Steps 1 and 2. $660.00

Seaver
1. Determine regular wage.
   $10.50 × 35 hours = $367.50

Wyman
1. Determine regular wage.
   $11.00 × 40 hours = $440.00
2. Determine overtime wage.
   $11.00 × 1.5 = $16.50
   $16.50 × 20 hours =   330.00
3. Determine gross wage.
   Add the results of Steps 1 and 2. $770.00

Colter
1. Determine regular wage.
   $11.00 × 40 hours = $440.00
2. Determine overtime wage.
   $11.00 × 1.5 = $16.50
   $16.50 × 5 hours =   82.50
3. Determine gross wage.
   Add the results of Steps 1 and 2. $522.50

The total gross payroll for Wright's Accounting Service for the last week in March is as follows:

Employee	Gross Wages
Susan Harris	$ 700.00
Anthony LaMarca	600.00
Richard McIntosh	660.00
Carolyn Seaver	367.50
Thomas Wyman	770.00
Virginia Colter	522.50
Total	$3,620.00

Calculating the gross payroll is just the first step in the process. Once the gross wages have been calculated, the bookkeeper must calculate each employee's deductions.

Deductions for CPP and UI

The CPP and UI deductions may be determined by referring to the appropriate columns in the *Payroll Deductions Tables*, or by simply calculating the amount. Remember, the maximum taxable CPP earnings are $34,400 a year and the basic yearly exemption is $3,400. This $3,400 figure may be converted to smaller amounts that may be deducted for weekly, biweekly, or monthly pay periods as shown. Amounts are generally rounded; however, when the $3,400 basic exemption is prorated for the appropriate deduction, it is not rounded, according to Revenue Canada guidelines.

The appropriate deduction for weekly pay periods is:

$$\frac{\$3,400}{52} = \$65.38 \text{ per pay period.}$$

The appropriate deduction for biweekly pay periods is:

$$\frac{\$3,400}{26} = \$130.76 \text{ per pay period.}$$

The appropriate deduction for semimonthly pay periods is:

$$\frac{\$3,400}{24} = \$141.66$$

Since Wright's Accounting Service has weekly pay periods, $65.38 is deducted from each person's gross salary and the remaining amount is multiplied by 2.6 percent (.026).

Employee	Gross Earnings	Basic Exemption	Pensionable Earnings	CPP Deducted
Harris	$ 700.00	$ 65.38	$ 634.62 × .026	$16.50
LaMarca	600.00	65.38	534.62 × .026	13.90
McIntosh	660.00	65.38	594.62 × .026	15.46
Seaver	367.50	65.38	302.12 × .026	7.86*
Wyman	770.00	65.38	704.62 × .026	18.32
Colter	522.50	65.38	457.12 × .026	11.89*
Totals	$3,620.00	$392.28	$3,227.72	$83.93

* Rounded to the nearest penny.

Note: If you are using the tables provided by Revenue Canada, you will find discrepancies between the figures you have calculated and the amounts listed in the tables if the gross pay is $662 or more. The reason for this is that Revenue Canada uses $10 increments for calculating the CPP when the gross pay figure reaches $661.73.

When multiplying to find the amount of CPP and UI, round your answers to the nearest penny. When rounding to the nearest penny, look at the digit immediately to the right of the hundredths position. If that number is 0, 1, 2, 3, or 4, simply drop all the unnecessary digits. If the number is 5, 6, 7, 8, or 9, round up one penny. For example:

Number	Digit to the Right of the Hundredths Position	Number Rounded to the Nearest Penny
$31.3775	$31.37**75**	$31.38
29.324	29.3**2**4	29.32
4.6987	4.69**87**	4.70
.793	.79**3**	.79

To calculate the UI premiums, multiply the gross earnings by 3.07 percent, keeping in mind that the maximum taxable earnings for a year are $40,560 and the maximum yearly deduction is $1,245.40. When payroll periods are weekly, the maximum taxable amount is $780 and the maximum deduction is $23.95.

Employee	Gross Earnings	UI Premiums
Harris	$ 700.00 × .0307	$ 21.49
LaMarca	600.00 × .0307	18.42
McIntosh	660.00 × .0307	20.26
Seaver	367.50 × .0307	11.28
Wyman	770.00 × .0307	23.64
Colter	522.50 × .0307	16.04
Totals	$3,620.00	$111.13

Income Tax Deductions

Before the income tax to be withheld for each employee can be determined, the gross wage, the marital status, and the tax credits claimed by the employee must be known. A tax credit allows an employee to **exempt** a certain amount of her or his wages from income tax. As of January 1, 1994, each individual is entitled to a $6,456 basic personal credit. Also, an employee may be entitled to additional tax credits, such as credits for a dependent spouse, child, or other relative.

When an employee begins work, he or she will fill out and sign a **TD1**, **personal tax credit return**. The TD1 will show the employee's name, address, and social insurance number. In addition, it will show the total tax credits claimed by the individual.

In recent years, the most common credits are:
1. Basic personal $6,456
2. Married or equivalent   5,380

Once the total credits have been calculated, the net claim code must be determined according to the following table:

CLAIM CODES	
Total Claim Amount	**Claim Code**
No claim amount	0
$0 – $ 6,456	1
6,456.01 – 8,037	2
8,037.01 – 9,619	3
9,619.01 – 11,202	4
11,202.01 – 12,783	5
12,783.01 – 14,364	6
14,364.01 – 15,946	7
15,946.01 – 17,527	8
17,527.01 – 19,109	9
19,109.01 – 20,693	10
20,693.01 and over *Manual calculation required by employer or payer*	X
No tax withholding required	E

If the employee does not complete and sign a TD1 form, the employer is required to withhold income tax for that employee as if she or he were single with no tax credits.

The actual amount of the income tax to be withheld may be determined by referring to the wage bracket tables in Revenue Canada's *Payroll Deductions Tables* publication. The tables are separated into varying pay periods. Two pages of these tables for a weekly payroll period are reproduced on pages 325 and 326.

Let's now determine the amount of income tax withholding for the employees of Wright's Accounting Service.

Susan Harris is entitled to the basic personal credit of $6,456. According to the table above, her net claim code would be 1.

In the income tax table, find the amount of Susan's earnings in the left-hand column. The appropriate bracket is $697–$705. With your finger, follow across the column until you reach the amount listed under net claim code 1. The amount of income tax to be withheld for Susan Harris is $166.85.

Continue this process to determine the income tax to be withheld from each employee.

Employee	Net Claim Code	Earnings	Income Tax Payable
Harris	1	$ 700.00	$166.85
LaMarca	0	600.00	158.65
McIntosh	2	660.00	146.30
Seaver	3	367.50	48.75
Wyman	1	770.00	196.40
Colter	6	522.50	64.55
Totals		$3,620.00	$781.50

D-2

Ontario
Tax Deductions
Weekly (52 pay periods a year)

Ontario
Retenues d'impôt
Hebdomadaire (52 périodes de paie par année)

Pay Rémunération			If the employee's claim code from form TD1 is Si le code de demande de l'employé selon la formule TD1 est										
		0	1	2	3	4	5	6	7	8	9	10
From De	Less than Moins que		Deduct from each pay Retenez sur chaque paie									
237.-	241.	62.15	28.20	24.05	15.20	4.70						
241.-	245.	63.20	29.20	25.05	16.75	5.40	.05					
245.-	249.	64.25	30.25	26.10	17.75	6.05	.70					
249.-	253.	65.25	31.30	27.15	18.80	6.70	1.35					
253.-	257.	66.30	32.30	28.15	19.85	7.95	2.05					
257.-	261.	67.35	33.35	29.20	20.85	9.75	2.70					
261.-	265.	68.35	34.40	30.25	21.90	11.50	3.35					
265.-	269.	69.40	35.40	31.25	22.95	13.30	4.00					
269.-	273.	70.45	36.45	32.30	23.95	15.10	4.70					
273.-	277.	71.45	37.50	33.30	25.00	16.65	5.35					
277.-	281.	72.50	38.50	34.35	26.05	17.70	6.00	.65				
281.-	285.	73.55	39.55	35.40	27.05	18.75	6.65	1.35				
285.-	289.	74.55	40.60	36.40	28.10	19.75	7.85	2.00				
289.-	293.	75.60	41.60	37.45	29.15	20.80	9.65	2.65				
293.-	297.	76.65	42.65	38.50	30.15	21.85	11.40	3.30				
297.-	301.	77.65	43.70	39.50	31.20	22.85	13.20	4.00				
301.-	305.	78.70	44.70	40.55	32.25	23.90	14.95	4.65				
305.-	309.	79.75	45.75	41.60	33.25	24.95	16.60	5.30				
309.-	313.	80.75	46.80	42.60	34.30	25.95	17.65	5.95	.65			
313.-	317.	81.80	47.80	43.65	35.35	27.00	18.65	6.60	1.30			
317.-	321.	82.85	48.85	44.70	36.35	28.05	19.70	7.75	1.95			
321.-	325.	83.85	49.90	45.70	37.40	29.05	20.75	9.55	2.60			
325.-	329.	84.90	50.90	46.75	38.40	30.10	21.75	11.30	3.30			
329.-	333.	85.90	51.95	47.80	39.45	31.15	22.80	13.10	3.95			
333.-	337.	86.95	53.00	48.80	40.50	32.15	23.85	14.85	4.60			
337.-	341.	88.00	54.00	49.85	41.50	33.20	24.85	16.55	5.25			
341.-	345.	89.00	55.05	50.90	42.55	34.25	25.90	17.60	5.90	.60		
345.-	349.	90.05	56.05	51.90	43.60	35.25	26.95	18.60	6.60	1.25		
349.-	353.	91.10	57.10	52.95	44.60	36.30	27.95	19.65	7.65	1.90		
353.-	357.	92.10	58.15	54.00	45.65	37.30	29.00	20.70	9.40	2.60		
357.-	361.	93.15	59.15	55.00	46.70	38.35	30.05	21.70	11.20	3.25		
361.-	365.	94.20	60.20	56.05	47.70	39.40	31.05	22.75	13.00	3.90		
365.-	369.	95.20	61.25	57.10	48.75	40.40	32.10	23.75	14.75	4.55		
369.-	373.	96.25	62.25	58.10	49.80	41.45	33.15	24.80	16.50	5.20		
373.-	377.	97.30	63.30	59.15	50.80	42.50	34.15	25.85	17.50	5.90	.55	
377.-	381.	98.30	64.35	60.15	51.85	43.50	35.20	26.85	18.55	6.55	1.20	
381.-	385.	99.35	65.35	61.20	52.90	44.55	36.25	27.90	19.60	7.55	1.90	
385.-	389.	100.40	66.40	62.25	53.90	45.60	37.25	28.95	20.60	9.30	2.55	
389.-	393.	101.40	67.45	63.25	54.95	46.60	38.30	29.95	21.65	11.10	3.20	
393.-	397.	102.45	68.45	64.30	56.00	47.65	39.30	31.00	22.70	12.85	3.85	
397.-	401.	103.50	69.50	65.35	57.00	48.70	40.35	32.05	23.70	14.65	4.50	
401.-	405.	104.50	70.55	66.35	58.05	49.70	41.40	33.05	24.75	16.40	5.20	
405.-	409.	105.55	71.55	67.40	59.10	50.75	42.40	34.10	25.80	17.45	5.85	.50
409.-	413.	106.60	72.60	68.45	60.10	51.80	43.45	35.15	26.80	18.50	6.50	1.15
413.-	417.	107.60	73.65	69.45	61.15	52.80	44.50	36.15	27.85	19.50	7.45	1.85
417.-	421.	108.65	74.65	70.50	62.20	53.85	45.50	37.20	28.90	20.55	9.20	2.50
421.-	425.	109.70	75.70	71.55	63.20	54.90	46.55	38.25	29.90	21.60	11.00	3.15
425.-	429.	110.70	76.75	72.55	64.25	55.90	47.60	39.25	30.95	22.60	12.75	3.80
429.-	433.	111.75	77.75	73.60	65.30	56.95	48.60	40.30	31.95	23.65	14.55	4.45
433.-	437.	112.75	78.80	74.65	66.30	58.00	49.65	41.35	33.00	24.70	16.30	5.15
437.-	441.	113.80	79.85	75.65	67.35	59.00	50.70	42.35	34.05	25.70	17.40	5.80
441.-	445.	114.85	80.85	76.70	68.35	60.05	51.70	43.40	35.05	26.75	18.40	6.45
445.-	449.	115.85	81.90	77.75	69.40	61.10	52.75	44.45	36.10	27.80	19.45	7.30
449.-	453.	116.90	82.90	78.75	70.45	62.10	53.80	45.45	37.15	28.80	20.50	9.10
453.-	457.	117.95	83.95	79.80	71.45	63.15	54.80	46.50	38.15	29.85	21.50	10.85

Ontario
Tax Deductions
Weekly (52 pay periods a year)

Ontario
Retenues d'impôt
Hebdomadaire (52 périodes de paie par année)

D-3

Pay Rémunération From De	Less than Moins que	0	1	2	3	4	5	6	7	8	9	10
457.-	465.	119.50	85.50	81.35	73.00	64.70	56.35	48.05	39.70	31.40	23.05	13.55
465.-	473.	121.55	87.55	83.40	75.10	66.75	58.45	50.10	41.80	33.45	25.15	16.80
473.-	481.	123.60	89.65	85.50	77.15	68.80	60.50	52.15	43.85	35.55	27.20	18.85
481.-	489.	125.70	91.70	87.55	79.20	70.90	62.55	54.25	45.90	37.60	29.25	20.95
489.-	497.	127.75	93.75	89.60	81.30	72.95	64.65	56.30	48.00	39.65	31.35	23.00
497.-	505.	129.80	95.85	91.65	83.35	75.00	66.70	58.35	50.05	41.70	33.40	25.05
505.-	513.	131.90	97.90	93.75	85.40	77.10	68.75	60.45	52.10	43.80	35.45	27.15
513.-	521.	133.95	99.95	95.80	87.50	79.15	70.80	62.50	54.20	45.85	37.55	29.20
521.-	529.	136.00	102.05	97.85	89.55	81.20	72.90	64.55	56.25	47.90	39.60	31.25
529.-	537.	138.10	104.10	99.95	91.60	83.30	74.95	66.65	58.30	50.00	41.65	33.35
537.-	545.	140.15	106.15	102.00	93.70	85.35	77.00	68.70	60.35	52.05	43.75	35.40
545.-	553.	142.20	108.25	104.05	95.75	87.40	79.10	70.75	62.45	54.10	45.80	37.45
553.-	561.	144.25	110.30	106.15	97.80	89.50	81.15	72.85	64.50	56.20	47.85	39.50
561.-	569.	146.35	112.35	108.20	99.85	91.55	83.20	74.90	66.55	58.25	49.90	41.60
569.-	577.	149.00	115.00	110.85	102.50	94.20	85.85	77.55	69.20	60.90	52.55	44.25
577.-	585.	152.20	118.20	114.05	105.75	97.40	89.10	80.75	72.45	64.10	55.80	47.45
585.-	593.	155.45	121.45	117.30	108.95	100.65	92.30	84.00	75.65	67.35	59.00	50.70
593.-	601.	158.65	124.65	120.50	112.20	103.85	95.55	87.20	78.90	70.55	62.25	53.90
601.-	609.	161.90	127.90	123.75	115.40	107.10	98.75	90.45	82.10	73.80	65.45	57.15
609.-	617.	165.10	131.10	126.95	118.65	110.30	102.00	93.65	85.35	77.00	68.70	60.35
617.-	625.	168.35	134.35	130.20	121.85	113.55	105.20	96.90	88.55	80.25	71.90	63.60
625.-	633.	171.55	137.55	133.40	125.10	116.75	108.45	100.10	91.80	83.45	75.15	66.80
633.-	641.	174.80	140.80	136.65	128.30	120.00	111.65	103.35	95.00	86.70	78.35	70.05
641.-	649.	178.00	144.00	139.85	131.55	123.20	114.90	106.55	98.25	89.90	81.60	73.25
649.-	657.	181.25	147.25	143.10	134.75	126.45	118.10	109.80	101.45	93.15	84.80	76.50
657.-	665.	184.45	150.45	146.30	138.00	129.65	121.35	113.00	104.70	96.35	88.05	79.70
665.-	673.	187.75	153.75	149.60	141.25	132.95	124.60	116.30	107.95	99.65	91.30	83.00
673.-	681.	191.00	157.05	152.85	144.55	136.20	127.90	119.55	111.25	102.90	94.60	86.25
681.-	689.	194.30	160.30	156.15	147.85	139.50	131.15	122.85	114.50	106.20	97.90	89.55
689.-	697.	197.55	163.60	159.45	151.10	142.80	134.45	126.15	117.80	109.50	101.15	92.85
697.-	705.	200.85	166.85	162.70	154.40	146.05	137.75	129.40	121.10	112.75	104.45	96.10
705.-	713.	204.15	170.15	166.00	157.65	149.35	141.00	132.70	124.35	116.05	107.70	99.40
713.-	721.	207.40	173.45	169.30	160.95	152.60	144.30	135.95	127.65	119.35	111.00	102.65
721.-	729.	210.70	176.70	172.55	164.25	155.90	147.60	139.25	130.95	122.60	114.30	105.95
729.-	737.	214.00	180.00	175.85	167.50	159.20	150.85	142.55	134.20	125.90	117.55	109.25
737.-	745.	217.25	183.30	179.10	170.80	162.45	154.15	145.80	137.50	129.15	120.85	112.50
745.-	753.	220.55	186.55	182.40	174.10	165.75	157.40	149.10	140.80	132.45	124.15	115.80
753.-	761.	223.85	189.85	185.70	177.35	169.05	160.70	152.40	144.05	135.75	127.40	119.10
761.-	769.	227.10	193.15	188.95	180.65	172.30	164.00	155.65	147.35	139.00	130.70	122.35
769.-	777.	230.40	196.40	192.25	183.90	175.60	167.25	158.95	150.60	142.30	133.95	125.65
777.-	785.	233.70	199.70	195.55	187.20	178.90	170.55	162.25	153.90	145.60	137.25	128.95
785.-	793.	237.05	203.05	198.90	190.55	182.25	173.90	165.60	157.25	148.95	140.60	132.30
793.-	801.	240.40	206.40	202.25	193.90	185.60	177.25	168.95	160.60	152.30	143.95	135.65
801.-	809.	243.70	209.75	205.60	197.25	188.95	180.60	172.30	163.95	155.65	147.30	139.00
809.-	817.	247.05	213.10	208.95	200.60	192.30	183.95	175.65	167.30	159.00	150.65	142.35
817.-	825.	250.40	216.45	212.30	203.95	195.65	187.30	179.00	170.65	162.35	154.00	145.65
825.-	833.	253.75	219.80	215.65	207.30	199.00	190.65	182.35	174.00	165.70	157.35	149.00
833.-	841.	257.10	223.15	219.00	210.65	202.30	194.00	185.70	177.35	169.05	160.70	152.35
841.-	849.	260.45	226.50	222.35	214.00	205.65	197.35	189.05	180.70	172.40	164.05	155.70
849.-	857.	263.80	229.85	225.70	217.35	209.00	200.70	192.35	184.05	175.75	167.40	159.05
857.-	865.	267.15	233.20	229.00	220.70	212.35	204.05	195.70	187.40	179.05	170.75	162.40
865.-	873.	270.50	236.55	232.35	224.05	215.70	207.40	199.05	190.75	182.40	174.10	165.75
873.-	881.	273.85	239.90	235.70	227.40	219.05	210.75	202.40	194.10	185.75	177.45	169.10
881.-	889.	277.20	243.25	239.05	230.75	222.40	214.10	205.75	197.45	189.10	180.80	172.45
889.-	897.	280.55	246.60	242.40	234.10	225.75	217.45	209.10	200.80	192.45	184.15	175.80

Miscellaneous Payroll Deductions

In addition to deductions for CPP, UI, and income tax, there are many other deductions that might be taken. Among the many possibilities, an employee may have money deducted for

1. registered pension plans
2. Canada Savings Bonds
3. health insurance
4. union or professional dues
5. insurance premiums
6. contributions to a charity
7. loan payments.

It should be noted that deductions in categories numbered 1 and 4 on this list are deductible for the purposes of calculating taxable income and therefore should be deducted from gross pay when determining the amount of income taxes to be withheld from an employee.

The Payroll Register

The bookkeeper uses the payroll register much as a worksheet, summarizing in it all the information necessary for the calculation of the net wages and the recording of wages expense, the payroll tax liabilities, and wages payable. The payroll register for the last week in March for Wright's Accounting Service follows:

Employee	Total Hours	Hourly Rate	Regular Earnings	Overtime Earnings	Total Earnings	Net Claim Code	CPP Contri-butions	UI Prem-iums	Income Tax	Health Insurance	Deduc-tions	Net Pay
Harris	Mgmt	—	700.00	—	700.00	1	16.50	21.49	166.85	—	204.84	495.16
LaMarca	Mgmt	—	600.00	—	600.00	0	13.90	18.42	158.65	—	190.97	409.03
McIntosh	50	12.00	480.00	180.00	660.00	2	15.46	20.26	146.30	6.50	188.52	471.48
Seaver	35	10.50	367.50	—	367.50	3	7.86	11.28	48.75	6.50	74.39	293.11
Wyman	60	11.00	440.00	330.00	770.00	1	18.32	23.64	196.40	6.50	244.86	525.14
Colter	45	11.00	440.00	82.50	522.50	6	11.89	16.04	64.55	6.50	98.98	423.52
Totals			3027.50	592.50	3620.00		83.93	111.13	781.50	26.00	1002.56	2617.44

Steps in Completing the Payroll Register

Complete the payroll register in this order:

1. Calculate each employee's regular, overtime, and total wages. Total each of these columns before determining payroll deductions.
2. Prove the accuracy of your work so far by adding the total **regular earnings** to the total **overtime earnings**. Your answer must be the total earnings. For Wright's Accounting Service, the calculations are as follows:

Total regular earnings	$3,027.50
Total overtime earnings	592.50
Total earnings	$3,620.00

3. Determine the payroll deductions for each individual employee and total each individual deductions column.
4. Calculate the total deductions for each employee and determine the column total.
5. Before continuing, add the totals of the individual deductions columns. The sum must equal the total of the total deductions column or else an error has been made and must be found before continuing. For Wright's Accounting Service, this calculation is:

Total CPP	$ 83.93
Total UI	111.13
Total income tax	781.50
Total health insurance	26.00
Total deductions	$1,002.56

6. Calculate the **net wages** for each employee by subtracting her or his total deductions from total earnings, then find the column total.
7. Prove that the column total is accurate by subtracting the total of the total deductions column from the total of the total earnings column.

Total earnings	$3,620.00
Total deductions	1,002.56
Net wages	$2,617.44

It is important that the bookkeeper check the accuracy of the work at each appropriate step in the preparation of the payroll. If the work is proved at intervals along the way, and if a mistake is made, it is much easier to find than if the proofs were delayed until after the net wages have been calculated.

The Journal Entry to Record the Payroll

Once the payroll register has been completed, the bookkeeper has all the necessary information for the journal entry. The total gross earnings represents the employer's total wages expense for the week. The amounts withheld by the employer represent liabilities, because each amount must be submitted by the employer to a government agency, an insurance company, an employee union, and so on.

The entry to record the week's payroll for Wright's Accounting Service is as follows:

GENERAL JOURNAL				PAGE 9	
Date	Description	Post. Ref.	Debit	Credit	
19XX Mar. 31	Wages Expense		3620 —		
	Canada Pension Plan Payable			83 93	
	Unemployment Insurance Payable			111 13	
	Income Tax Deductions Payable			781 50	
	Health Insurance Payable			26 —	
	Wages Payable			2617 44	
	To Record the Week's Wages Expense and Related				
	Payroll Liabilities				

The Payroll Bank Account

Many firms have a separate payroll bank account. After the entries to record the gross wages, the deductions, and net wages have been recorded, the following entry will be made:

Date		Description	Post. Ref.	Debit	Credit
Mar.	31	Wages Payable		2 6 1 7 44	
		Cash			2 6 1 7 44
		To Record Payment of Wages			

GENERAL JOURNAL — PAGE 1

A cheque must now be written for the net amount of the payroll, $2,617.44, and it must be deposited in the payroll bank account. Individual cheques will then be written for the employees; after they have cashed their cheques, the payroll bank account will have a zero balance.

Summary

Employers must be familiar with the laws as they relate to payroll. They are required, for example, to withhold from the wages of most employees CPP and UI premiums and income taxes, and they must remit those taxes to the proper government agency within a certain amount of time. For the employer to deduct the correct amounts, each employee must file with the employer a TD1 that shows the employee's marital status and number of withholding allowances claimed. If the employer does not have a TD1 form on hand for an employee, deductions must be taken as though the employee were single with no dependants.

Much of the information that an employer needs concerning payroll and payroll deductions is found in the Revenue Canada booklet *Payroll Deductions Tables*, which may be obtained free of charge from Revenue Canada.

The entire payroll may be calculated on a payroll register, after which time the cheques are written and the journal entry to record the payroll is made. The entire gross payroll is debited to wages expense, and amounts withheld from employees' earnings are credited to liability accounts.

Vocabulary Review

Following is a list of the words and terms for this chapter:

employee
employer
exempt
gross wage
independent contractor
net wage
overtime

overtime earnings
regular earnings
Revenue Canada
salary
TD1, personal tax credit return
wages
withhold

Fill in the blank with the correct word or term from the list.

1. A word that means to refrain or hold back from giving is _____.
2. Earnings for the first 40 hours in a week are referred to as _____.
3. Earnings for hours worked over a weekly total of 40 hours are referred to as _____.
4. The federal government department responsible for collecting CPP, UI, and income taxes withheld by the employer is _____.
5. A/An _____ may have her or his work directed by the employer.
6. A word that means to free from an obligation is _____.
7. _____ refer to earnings before any deductions are taken.
8. _____ refer to gross earnings minus all deductions for the period.
9. Hours worked over a weekly total of 40 hours are referred to as _____.
10. A/An _____ may direct the activities of an employee and may hire and fire the employee.
11. Earnings stated in terms of a month or a year are referred to as _____.
12. Earnings stated in terms of an hourly payment are referred to as _____.
13. An employer may hire a/an _____ to perform services for a fee, but the employer will probably not direct the activities of this person, nor will the employer withhold payroll taxes upon payment.
14. A government form completed by an employee indicating various personal exemptions from federal income tax is the _____.

Match the words and terms on the left with the definitions on the right.

15. employee
16. employer
17. exempt
18. gross wage
19. independent contractor
20. net wage
21. overtime
22. overtime earnings
23. regular earnings
24. Revenue Canada
25. salary
26. TD1, personal tax credit return
27. wages
28. withhold

a. gross pay minus deductions
b. earnings for the first 40 hours worked in a week
c. one who may direct the activities of an employee
d. hours worked over a weekly total of 40 paid at time and a half or double time
e. to free from an obligation
f. one who performs services for an employer but who is not an employee
g. earnings stated in yearly or monthly terms
h. total earnings before any deductions are taken
i. to hold back from giving
j. federal government department
k. one who performs services for and is under the direction of an employer
l. earnings stated on an hourly basis
m. earnings for hours worked over a weekly total of 40
n. a government form completed by an employee indicating various personal exemptions from federal income tax

Exercises

EXERCISE 12.1

For each employee listed, determine the regular earnings, overtime earnings, and gross earnings and find the total for each column. Assume that overtime is paid at time and a half for all hours worked over a weekly total of 40. Round your answers to the nearest penny.

Employee	Hours Worked	Hourly Wage	Regular Earnings	Overtime Earnings	Gross Earnings
Wickham	48	$6.50	_____	_____	_____
McDonald	50	7.10	_____	_____	_____
Murray	42	9.60	_____	_____	_____
Kauffman	46	8.80	_____	_____	_____
Totals			_____	_____	_____

EXERCISE 12.2

For the first weekly payroll period of the year, determine the CPP contribution and UI premiums to be deducted for each employee; also determine the column totals. Round your answers to the nearest penny.

Employee	Gross Pay	CPP Contribution	UI Premium
Douglas	$312.00	_____	_____
Warner	500.00	_____	_____
Olsen	335.00	_____	_____
Jenkins	562.00	_____	_____
Wade	196.00	_____	_____
Bartz	326.00	_____	_____
Totals		_____	_____

EXERCISE 12.3

Determine the net claim codes for each of the following Grason employees:

Employee	Total Exemptions	Net Claim Code
Mandrake	$6,900	_____
Graham	6,456	_____
Williams	7,120	_____
Culver	8,490	_____
Cropier	9,815	_____

EXERCISE 12.4

Glenda Thomson earns $9.64 an hour and is paid time and a half for hours worked over a weekly total of 40. Calculate Glenda's net pay for a week in which she works 47 hours. In addition to the compulsory deductions, Glenda has $4.50 per week withheld for health insurance. She has total tax credits of $6,456 for income tax purposes. Round your answers to the nearest penny.

EXERCISE 12.5

Auburn Company has a four-day work week. Time and a half is paid for all hours worked over a daily total of 10. Calculate the regular earnings, overtime earnings, and gross earnings for each of the following, as well as the column totals.

	Hours Worked				Hourly	Regular	Overtime	Gross
	M	Tu	W	Th	Wage	Earnings	Earnings	Earnings
Habib	10	10	12	8	$7.20			
Wiggins	10	10	14	10	6.50			
Jackson	12	12	12	12	8.40			
Drummer	14	12	10	10	9.20			
Totals								

EXERCISE 12.6

Calculate the income tax deduction and the total income tax deductions for each of Debrondan Industries' employees for the first week in May.

Employee	Net Claim Code	Earnings	Income Tax Deduction
Graham	1	$485.00	
Thomson	3	315.00	
Culver	2	390.00	
Davidson	4	410.00	
Schmidt	6	764.00	
Total			

EXERCISE 12.7

Following are some figures from the payroll register of Alpha Company. Determine the amounts of the missing figures.

Regular earnings		$1,269.38
Overtime earnings	a.	
Total gross earnings		1,737.70
CPP contributions		31.74
UI premiums	b.	
Income tax deductions		352.14
Health insurance premium withheld		89.00
Union dues withheld		18.00
Total deductions	c.	
Net pay		$1,204.55

EXERCISE 12.8

Prepare the journal entry to record the wages payable on March 28 from the following information taken from the payroll register of East Coast Real Estate:

Total regular earnings	$2,368.50
Total overtime earnings	512.48
Total earnings	2,880.98
CPP contributions	49.38
UI premiums	54.19
Income taxes deducted	201.67
Union dues withheld	64.00
Total deductions	369.24
Net pay	2,511.74

The following payroll accounts are used: Wages Expense, CPP Payable, UI Payable, Income Taxes Payable, Union Dues Payable, and Wages Payable. Use journal page 6.

Problems

PROBLEM 12.1 Atlantic Consultants has five employees; two are management and are not paid overtime, and three are office personnel who are paid double time for hours worked over a weekly total of 40. Following are the employees' names and the amounts they are paid:

Ann Suter, Management	$36,400 per year
Wayne Heintz, Management	$33,800 per year
Doris Barstow, Office Personnel	$8.50 per hour
Robert Bracken, Office Personnel	$9.20 per hour
Richard Chicos, Office Personnel	$7.75 per hour

[handwritten: 36400 ÷ 52 = 700 (weekly); 33,800 ÷ 52 = 650 (weekly)]

INSTRUCTIONS Calculate (a) the total regular earnings, (b) the total overtime earnings, and (c) the total gross earnings for the employees of Atlantic Consultants during the week of August 9–15, 19XX. Also calculate the column totals for regular earnings, overtime earnings, and total gross earnings. The employees worked the following number of hours:

Suter	50 hours
Heintz	48 hours
Barstow	46 hours
Bracken	50 hours
Chicos	60 hours

[handwritten: 700; 650; 6×2×8.5 =; 10×2×9.2 =; 20×2×7.75 =]

PROBLEM 12.2 The following information is available for ABC Products for the week of October 10–16, 19XX:

Employee	Net Claim Code	Hours Worked	Hourly Wage
Gilbert	4	36	$12.08
Harris	1	44	7.50
Johnstone	3	48	8.10
Kelly	5	31	10.20
Laurin	2	51	12.50

[handwritten: 434.88]

INSTRUCTIONS
1. Complete a payroll register for ABC Products for the week of October 10–16, 19XX. Each employee is paid time and a half for hours worked over a weekly total of 40. Round your calculations to the nearest penny if necessary.
   a. Calculate regular earnings, overtime earnings, and total earnings.
   b. Calculate the CPP contributions. No employee has earned over $34,400.
   c. Calculate the UI premiums. No employee has earned over $40,560.
   d. Determine the income tax deductions.
   e. Include in the deductions $18 for health insurance for each employee.
   f. Calculate total deductions.
   g. Calculate net pay.
2. Prepare the general journal entry to record the wages payable. Use journal page 33.

PROBLEM 12.3 The following payroll information is available on December 10 for Timeshare, a firm employing six people:

Employee	Total Exemptions	Hours Worked	Hourly Wage	Health Insurance
Campbell	$ 6,500	45	$13.80	$12.50
Cressie	7,180	46	14.20	12.50
Drendel	6,456	50	12.90	8.00
Nelson	8,940	36	9.40	8.00
Trickle	7,460	44	15.06	12.50
Weaver	10,420	40	8.32	8.00

INSTRUCTIONS

1. Complete a payroll register for Timeshare for the week of December 4–10, 19XX. Each employee is paid time and a half for hours worked over a weekly total of 40. Round calculations to the nearest penny if necessary.
   a. Calculate regular earnings, overtime earnings, and total earnings.
   b. Calculate the CPP contributions. No employee has earned over $34,400.
   c. Calculate the UI premiums. No employee has earned over $40,560.
   d. Determine the net claim code for each employee, using the table on page 324.
   e. Determine the amount of income taxes to be withheld.
   f. Include in your calculations for total deductions the amount withheld for health insurance.
   g. Calculate total deductions.
   h. Calculate net pay.
2. Prepare the general journal entry to record the wages payable. Use journal page 19.

PROBLEM 12.4

The following payroll information is available for The Shirt House on August 31, 19XX:

Employee	Total Exemptions	Hours Worked	Hourly Wage	Canada Savings Bonds
McIntosh	$6,456	Mgmt	—	$40.00
Boling	7,500	49	$14.10	—
Strauss	6,456	55	11.30	20.00
Williams	6,750	54	8.00	20.00
Jones	9,030	40	9.30	—

INSTRUCTIONS

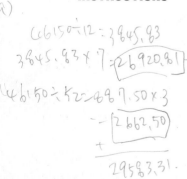

1. Complete a payroll register for The Shirt House for the week ended August 31, 19XX. Employees, except management, are paid double time for hours worked over a weekly total of 40. Round your calculations to the nearest penny if necessary.
   a. Calculate regular earnings, overtime earnings, and total earnings. The manager, McIntosh, earns $46,150 a year.
   b. Calculate the CPP contributions.
   c. Calculate the UI premiums. Remember, the maximum UI deduction is $23.95 per week.
   d. Determine the net claim code for each employee, using the table on page 324.
   e. Determine the amount of income taxes to be withheld.
   f. Include in your calculations for total deductions the amount withheld for Canada Savings Bonds.
   g. Calculate total deductions.
   h. Calculate net pay.
2. Prepare the general journal entry to record the wages payable. Use journal page 17.

CHAPTER THIRTEEN

Payroll—Employer Taxes and Other Obligations

Learning Objectives

When you have completed this chapter, you should
1. have an increased understanding of accounting terminology.
2. have a basic understanding of the employer's obligation for payroll taxes.
3. be able to calculate the employer's tax liability for Canada Pension Plan and for federal unemployment insurance.
4. be able to prepare the journal entry to record the employer's payroll tax expense.
5. be able to calculate the monthly remittance to Revenue Canada for employees' income tax, Canada Pension Plan, and unemployment insurance.
6. be able to complete a T4 statement and a T4 summary.
7. be able to calculate workers' compensation insurance expense.
8. be able to calculate the employers' health tax expense.

Vocabulary

compensation   payment for

cumulative   acquired by or resulting from accumulation

employers' health tax (EHT)   a tax imposed on employers by the provincial government to provide health-care coverage for all citizens of the province

form PD7AR   a form provided by Revenue Canada that is to be used by employers making monthly remittances of employee income taxes, Canada Pension Plan, and unemployment insurance

T4 statement   a form provided by Revenue Canada that the employer must complete and give to each employee on or before the last day of February each year showing the employee's total earnings from the employer for the year just ended (January 1–December 31), taxable benefits received from the employer, income taxes withheld, and deductions for Canada Pension Plan, unemployment insurance, and registered pension plans; a copy of each T4 statement must also be remitted to Revenue Canada

T4 summary   a form that must be forwarded to Revenue Canada on or before the last day of February each year summarizing the information shown on each employee's T4 statement

workers' compensation insurance   a provincial government insurance program that is paid for by the employer and that will provide payments to employees who miss work because of job-related injuries

Introduction

Employers, as well as employees, are liable for the payment of certain payroll taxes. While amounts withheld from employees' earnings are liabilities of the employer, amounts of tax levied on the employer are expenses and will appear on the income statement as a reduction in net income.

The employer is responsible for keeping accurate payroll records and for filing forms with Revenue Canada at regular intervals. For late payments of payroll taxes, the employer may be charged a fine and will have to pay interest on amounts owed.

Information relating to required employment taxes, tax rates and bases, required forms and their due dates, and so on is available by telephoning Revenue Canada's nearest District Taxation Office (the toll-free number may be found in the federal government section of the blue pages of the telephone directory).

Employer's Payroll Taxes

The employer's payroll taxes are based on the earnings of employees. The two main categories of employer taxes are: (1) Canada Pension Plan, and (2) federal unemployment insurance.

Canada Pension Plan

The employer must contribute each month for Canada Pension Plan (CPP) an amount equal to the amount deducted from the employees' wages for this purpose, as shown by the payroll records for the previous month.

Federal Unemployment Insurance

The employer must contribute each month for federal unemployment insurance (UI) an amount equal to 1.4 times the amount deducted from the employees' wages for this purpose, as shown by the payroll records for the previous month.

Employee's Individual Earnings Record

For each employee, an individual earnings record must be kept. It contains gross and net earnings and all the deductions for each payroll period, and it shows annual totals for each item.

Periodic totals are also useful because they contain important information for the bookkeeper. Once an employee has exceeded the maximum earnings for CPP purposes, the employer is no longer required to deduct for the plan for that employee for the remainder of that year. By referring to the **cumulative** earnings for each employee, shown on the individual earnings record, the bookkeeper will know how much to deduct. For example, suppose that by the beginning of November Herb Gardener has already earned $32,000 for the year and that $760 has already been deducted from his earnings for Canada Pension Plan. If $806 is the maximum contribution required of any employee for that year, then in November Herb's deduction for Canada Pension Plan will be only $46 ($806 − $760) and not some higher figure called for by the deduction tables for his monthly salary of $3,200. Then, in December, no deduction at all is required for Canada Pension Plan for Herb.

Employee's Individual Earnings Record

Name Gardener, Herb   **Employee No.** 6432-8   **Date Employed** Feb. 28, 1985

Address 17 West St., Brandon, Man.   **Social Insurance No.** 987-654-231

Female ____ **Male** ✓   **Net Claim Code**   3

Married ____ **Single** ✓   **Pay Rate** $3,200 **Per** Month

Phone No. 643-1728   **Date of Birth** 8-14-45

Period Ending	Gross Earnings	CPP	UI Premiums	Income Tax	Union Dues	Canada Savings Bonds	Total Deduc- tions	Net Pay	Cheque No.
Cumulative to Sept. 30	$28,800	$684	$ 884	$4,896	$270	$ 900	$7,634	$21,166	
October 31	3,200	76	98	544	30	100	848	2,352	2134
Cumulative to Oct. 31	32,000	760	982	5,440	300	1,000	8,482	23,518	
November 30	3,200	46	98	544	30	100	818	2,382	2417
Cumulative to Nov. 30	35,200	806	1,080	5,984	330	1,100	9,300	25,900	

The Calculation of Employer's Payroll Taxes

When the payroll register has been completed and the accumulated earnings for each employee have been determined, the calculations are made to determine the amount of the employer's payroll taxes.

Assume the following information from the payroll register for Adam 'N' Eve's Natural Foods on November 26, 19XX:

Payroll Register
Week of November 20–26, 19XX

Employee	Gross Wages	Canada Pension Plan	Unemploy- ment Insurance	Income Tax	Total Deduc- tions	Net Wages
Wiseman	$ 750	$ 0	$ 23	$183	$206	$ 544
O'Connor	725	0	22	177	199	526
Wong	600	14	18	112	144	456
Merino	650	15	20	143	178	472
Adolfi	570	13	17	94	124	446
Totals	$3,295	$42	$100	$709	$851	$2,444

The amounts in the deductions columns were determined separately for each employee. For Canada Pension Plan, the employer must pay an amount equal to the employee's deductions; for unemployment insurance, the employer must pay 1.4 times the employee deductions.

The payroll tax expense for Adam 'N' Eve's Natural Foods for the week ending November 26, 19XX is calculated as follows (refer to the payroll register, week of November 20–26):

For Canada Pension Plan	1	× $ 42 =	$ 42.00
For unemployment insurance	1.4	× $100 =	140.00
Total payroll tax expense for the week		=	$182.00

The employer will record this payroll tax expense at the time the wages are paid. However, the CPP premiums and the UI premiums will not actually be paid at the same time the wages are paid. The payroll taxes will be recorded and carried on the books as liabilities until they are paid in the following month.

The journal entry to record the employer's payroll tax expense is as follows:

		GENERAL JOURNAL				PAGE 30	
Date		**Description**	**Post. Ref.**	**Debit**		**Credit**	
19XX Nov.	26	Payroll Tax Expense		182—			
		Canada Pension Plan Payable				42—	
		Unemployment Insurance Payable				140—	
		To Record Payroll Tax Expense and Related Liabilities					

The total amount debited to Payroll Tax Expense will appear on the income statement along with the other expenses and will be subtracted from revenue to determine net income or net loss. The credits are liabilities and will appear on the balance sheet along with the other liabilities until they are paid.

The Journal Entry to Record Wages Expense

In addition to the recording of the payroll tax expense, a journal entry is made to record the wages expense and the amounts withheld from employees' wages. That entry is as follows:

		GENERAL JOURNAL				PAGE 30	
Date		**Description**	**Post. Ref.**	**Debit**		**Credit**	
19XX Nov.	26	Wages Expense		3295—			
		Canada Pension Plan Payable				42—	
		Unemployment Insurance Payable				100—	
		Income Tax Deductions Payable				709—	
		Wages Payable				2444—	
		To Record Payroll Register Totals for the Week					

The Canada Pension Plan Payable, Unemployment Insurance Payable, and Income Tax Deductions Payable in this entry represent liabilities of the employer. This is logical because the employer is responsible for withholding the money from the employees' wages and for remitting the money to the proper taxing authorities.

The General Ledger Accounts Relating to Payroll

The T accounts, after the entries to record the Payroll Tax Expense and the Wages Expense have been journalized and posted, are shown below.

Wages Payable   215

	Nov. 26 GJ30	2,444	Employees' net wages owing

Canada Pension Plan Payable   220

	Nov. 26 GJ30	42	Withheld from employee's wages
	Nov. 26 GJ30	42	Employer's portion of CPP liability
	Nov. 30 Balance	84	

Unemployment Insurance Payable   225

	Nov. 26 GJ30	100	Withheld from employees' wages
	Nov. 26 GJ30	140	Employer's portion of UI liability
	Nov. 30 Balance	240	

Income Tax Deductions Payable   230

	Nov. 26 GJ30	709	Withheld from employees' wages

Wages Expense   610

Nov. 26 GJ30	3,295		Employees' total gross wages

Payroll Tax Expense   620

Nov. 26 GJ30	182		Employer's portion of CPP and UI

Remitting Income Tax Deductions, Canada Pension Plan Contributions, and Unemployment Insurance Premiums

An employer who has not previously remitted income tax deductions, CPP contributions, and UI premiums should contact her or his District Taxation Office by telephoning a toll-free number found in the Government of Canada section of the blue pages of the telephone directory (look under Revenue Canada—Taxation). The employer will then be provided with an account number and other relevant information. A cheque or money order payable to the receiver general for Canada for the combined amount due under these three pieces of legislation must be sent in to the Taxation Centre at the indicated address (along with an explanatory letter and the account number) by the fifteenth day of the month following the month for which the employees are being paid. This will result in a **form PD7AR** being sent to the employer each month thereafter, and this form will then always be used when the employer makes monthly remittances.

For most employers, these remittances must be made to Revenue Canada by the fifteenth day of the following month. However, larger employers whose average monthly deductions are $15,000 or more are required to remit twice a month, and they use form PD7A-RB.

The Journal Entries to Record Remittances to the Receiver General

The remittance to the receiver general must be mailed in time to reach Revenue Canada by the fifteenth day of the month following the payroll. The journal entry required when CPP, UI, and income tax deduction obligations are paid is:

Date		Description	Post. Ref.	Debit	Credit
19XX Dec.	14	Canada Pension Plan Payable		84—	
		Unemployment Insurance Payable		240—	
		Income Tax Deductions Payable		709—	
		Cash			1033—
		To Record Monthly Remittance to the Receiver General for			
		Payroll Deductions and Payroll Taxes for November			

GENERAL JOURNAL — PAGE 35

The figures for this journal entry are found in the T accounts for Adam 'N' Eve's Natural Foods for the month of November as found on the previous page. (For simplicity, assume that the business was open only the one week in November.)

Form T4—Statement of Remuneration Paid

Employers give a **T4 statement** annually to each employee to whom remuneration was paid. The T4 will show, among other things, total wages paid, any tips or benefits reported, and amounts deducted for income tax, Canada Pension Plan, unemployment insurance, and registered pension plan.

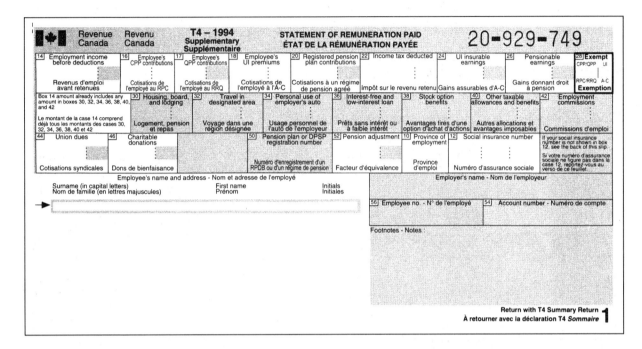

The information for the preparation of the T4 is obtained from the employee's individual earnings record. The T4 shows wages for the calendar year. A copy must be given to each employee and to Revenue Canada by the last day of February of the year following the payment of wages. Revenue Canada must also be given a summary of total amounts reported on all T4 slips issued for the year on a form known as the **T4 summary**. It is unlawful for an employer to willfully fail to supply an employee with a T4 Statement. It is also unlawful to willfully supply false information on the form.

Revenue Canada / Revenu Canada

T4 SUMMARY / SOMMAIRE

0505   44111

Complete this return using the instructions in the
Employers' Guide to Payroll Deductions - Basic Information.

1994

Vous devez remplir cette déclaration selon les instructions du
Guide de l'employeur – Retenues sur la paie : Renseignements de base.

SUMMARY OF REMUNERATION PAID
(For the year ending December 31, 1994)

SOMMAIRE DE LA RÉMUNÉRATION PAYÉE
(Pour l'année se terminant le 31 décembre 1994)

Copy
Copie **1**

If you file your T4 return on tape or diskette, you no longer need to complete this form. See the guide called *Computer Specifications for Data filed on Magnetic Media* for more information.

Si vous produisez votre déclaration T4 sur disquette ou sur bande, vous n'avez plus à remplir ce formulaire. Consultez le guide *Spécifications informatiques pour données produites sur support magnétique* pour obtenir plus d'informations.

Important
Employer's name and number must be the same as those shown on your PD7A remittance form. The T4 Summary must be filed on or before February 28, 1995.

Le nom et le numéro de l'employeur doivent être les mêmes que ceux qui figurent sur le formulaire de versement PD7A. La T4 *Sommaire* doit être produite au plus tard le 28 février 1995.

Account number
Numéro de compte

Name and address of employer
Nom et adresse de l'employeur

Taxation centre / Centre fiscal

DO code / Code du BD

T4 Supplementary slips totals

For returns with over 300 T4 slips, please see instructions in the *Employers' Guide to Payroll Deductions - Basic Information* about the breakdown of large returns.

Totaux des feuillets T4 *Supplémentaire*

Pour les déclarations renfermant plus de 300 feuillets T4, consultez le *Guide de l'employeur – Retenues sur la paie : Renseignements de base* pour la répartition des déclarations volumineuses.

		Box	
Total number of T4 slips filed / Nombre total de feuillets T4 produits		88	
Employment income before deductions	Revenus d'emploi avant retenues	14	
Registered pension plan contributions	Cotisations à un régime de pension agréé	20	
Pension adjustment	Facteur d'équivalence	52	
Unemployment Insurance insurable earnings	Gains assurables d'assurance-chômage	24	
Employee's Canada Pension Plan contributions	Cotisations de l'employé au Régime de pensions du Canada	16	
Employer's Canada Pension Plan contributions	Cotisations de l'employeur au Régime de pensions du Canada	27	
Employee's Unemployment Insurance premiums	Cotisations de l'employé à l'assurance-chômage	18	
Employer's Unemployment Insurance premiums	Cotisations de l'employeur à l'assurance-chômage	19	
Income tax deducted	Impôt sur le revenu retenu	22	

Of the total number at left, indicate how many T4 slips are for employees whose addresses are in the U.S.A.

Indiquez le nombre de feuillets T4 total émis pour des employés dont l'adresse est au É.-U.

Departmental use only

		Box	
Total deductions reported (16 + 27 + 18 + 19 + 22) / Total des retenues déclarées (16 + 27 + 18 + 19 + 22)		80	
Minus: remittances – Moins : versements		82	
Difference – Différence			

We do not charge or refund a difference of less than $2.00.
Une différence inférieure à 2 $ ne sera ni exigée ni remboursée par le Ministère.

Overpayment / Montant du trop-payé   84

* Balance due / Solde à payer   86

* If you have not paid the total deductions reported, include the balance with this completed return. You may have to pay a penalty for late payment if you have any balance owing.

Si vous n'avez pas payé le montant total des retenues déclarées, veuillez joindre le solde à payer, à la présente déclaration. Tout solde à payer est assujetti à une pénalité pour paiement tardif.

Amount enclosed / Somme jointe

Revenue Canada issued - registration number(s) for RPP or DPSP – Numéro(s) d'enregistrement émis par Revenu Canada pour le RPA ou le RPDB

71   72   73

Canadian-controlled private corporations or unincorporated employers: list the social insurance number of the main shareholder(s) or proprietor(s).
Sociétés privées dont le contrôle est canadien ou employeurs non constitués: inscrivez le numéro d'assurance sociale de l'(des) actionnaire(s) ou du(des) propriétaire(s).

Réservé au Ministère

74   75

Person to contact about this return – Personne avec qui communiquer au sujet de cette déclaration

76   First name – Prénom   Surname – Nom de famille

78   Telephone number – Numéro de téléphone   Area code – Indicatif régional

Certification – Attestation

I certify that the information given in this T4 return (T4 Summary and related T4 Supplementary slips) is, to the best of my knowledge, correct and complete.
J'atteste que les renseignements fournis dans cette déclaration T4 (la T4 *Sommaire* et les feuillets T4 *Supplémentaire* connexes) sont, à ma connaissance, exacts et complets.

Date	Name and surname (in capital letters) – Nom et prénom (en lettres majuscules)	Signature of authorized person – Signature de la personne autorisée	Position or office – Titre ou poste

For departmental use only: please do not write in this area – Réservé au Ministère : Ne rien écrire ici

90			91			93			
	1	Last to current / Précédente à courante		1	No / Non			Date	Memo – Note
Transfer / Transfert	2	No action / Aucune mesure	Pro Forma	2	Yes / Oui	94		A	
	3	Other / Autre						B	

Late-filing penalty / Pénalité pour production tardive

Prepared by – Établi par   Date

		Code 2	Correspond.	Inc.	TPC – CCT	Dressed – MAP	Rev. – Rév.	No Accounts – Aucun n°
Initials – Initiales								
Date								

* Keep this without copy of the T4 *Summary* for your records.
Send copies 1 and 2 of the *Summary* and copy 1 of the related T4 *Supplementary* to the appropriate taxation centre address shown on the back of this form.

* Conservez la troisième du formulaire T4 *Sommaire* pour vos dossiers.
Envoyez les copies 1 et 2 du formulaire T4 *Sommaire* ainsi que la copie 1 du T4 *Supplémentaire* connexe au centre fiscal approprié, dont l'adresse figure à la case A, au verso de ce formulaire.

Canadian Human Rights Act Federal Information Bank Number: 15615.

Loi canadienne sur les droits de la personne : Numéro de la banque fédérale de données : 15615.

The employer will prepare at least four copies of each T4. They are distributed as follows:

1. Employer remits one copy to Revenue Canada.
2. Employer gives one copy to employee to be filed with the employee's income tax return.
3. Employer gives one copy to employee for his or her records.
4. Employer retains one copy.

Workers' Compensation Insurance

Most employers are required to pay **workers' compensation insurance**, which provides certain payments to employees who are injured on the job or who become sick as a result of something that is job-related. The workers' compensation insurance rates are based on the degree of risk involved in various job categories. For example, restaurant kitchen workers (because of the possibility of cuts, falling, burns, etc.) have a higher risk of becoming injured on the job than an usher in a theatre; thus, the restaurant owner would pay a higher workers' compensation insurance rate per kitchen worker than the theatre owner would pay per usher.

The premium is normally paid a year in advance and based on the year's estimated gross payroll.

Assume that the estimated payroll for the year for Adam 'N' Eve's Natural Food Store is $170,000 and that the workers' compensation rate is .2 percent (or 20 cents on every $100). The premium for the year would be determined as follows:

a. Move decimal point two places to the left
   before multiplying $.2 = .002$
b. Multiply rate by estimated payroll $.002 \times \$170,000 = \$340$

The entry at the beginning of the year to record the insurance premium would be:

GENERAL JOURNAL				PAGE 40	
Date		Description	Post. Ref.	Debit	Credit
19XX Jan.	10	Workers' Compensation Insurance Expense		3 4 0 —	
		Cash			3 4 0 —
		To Record Payment of Yearly Premium for Workers'			
		Compensation Insurance			

At the end of the year, the accounting records show wages for Adam 'N' Eve's Natural Foods to be $173,940. An additional premium is required because the original premium was based on $170,000. The additional premium payment is calculated as follows:

a. Figure extra amount on which premium is to be calculated		$173,940
		−170,000
		$ 3,940
b. After moving the decimal point two places to the left, multiply the extra amount by .2 percent		3,940
		× .002
		$ 7.88

The additional premium is $7.88. The journal entry to record the payment for workers' compensation for the additional premium is:

GENERAL JOURNAL				PAGE 40
Date	**Description**	**Post. Ref.**	**Debit**	**Credit**
19XX Jan. 4	Workers' Compensation Insurance Expense		7 88	
	Cash			7 88
	To Record Additional Premium for Last Year's Workers'			
	Compensation Insurance			

Of course, if the actual payroll is less than the amount estimated, the company would be entitled to a refund.

Employers' Health Tax

In most provinces, there is now a legislated **employers' health tax (EHT)**, which is intended to provide health-care coverage to all of the citizens of that province.

In the province of Ontario, the rate of EHT that must be paid by employers is based on the total gross payroll for the calendar year. The current rates are shown in the following table:

Total Annual Ontario Remuneration	Rate (%)
Up to $200,000.00	0.98
$200,000.01 to $230,000.00	1.101
$230,000.01 to $260,000.00	1.223
$260,000.01 to $290,000.00	1.344
$290,000.01 to $320,000.00	1.465
$320,000.01 to $350,000.00	1.586
$350,000.01 to $380,000.00	1.708
$380,000.01 to $400,000.00	1.829
Over $400,000.00	1.95

All employers are required to submit an annual return, stating their total gross payroll for the calendar year just ended, to the Ministry of Finance by March 15 of the following calendar year.

If the total gross payroll is up to and including $200,000, the EHT payment is due by March 15 of the following calendar year. If the total gross payroll is over $200,000 and up to and including $400,000, the employer is required to remit quarterly installments. Employers with a total annual gross payroll in excess of $400,000 must make monthly EHT installment payments.

If the gross annual payroll for Adam 'N' Eve's Natural Food Store were actually $173,940 as stated previously, the required remittance for EHT would be calculated as follows:

$$\$173,940 \times .0098 = \$1,704.61.$$

Since the total gross payroll is less than $200,000, the required payment will be due by March 15 of the following calendar year.

The general journal entry to record this payment is as follows:

		GENERAL JOURNAL				PAGE 58
Date		Description	Post. Ref.	Debit		Credit
19XX Mar.	10	Employers' Health Tax Expense		1 7 0 4 61		
		Cash				1 7 0 4 61
		To Record Payment of EHT for the				
		Previous Calendar Year				

Summary

Because employers must pay various payroll taxes based on the earnings of their employees, they need to be familiar with the tax laws relating to payroll.

Employers are required to pay, for example, an amount equal to the amounts paid by their employees for Canada Pension Plan. Also, employers must contribute an amount equal to 1.4 times the UI premiums deducted from their employees.

Amounts actually paid by the employer, as opposed to amounts withheld from employees' wages, are expenses and are deducted from revenue when determining net income.

Employers are usually required to pay, in addition to payroll taxes, a workers' compensation insurance premium. The insurance is designed to make certain payments to employees who are injured on the job or who become sick because of something that is job-related. The workers' compensation premium is based on the total gross payroll and the degree of hazard present.

In most provinces, employers must also pay an employers' health tax, which is designed to pay for the health-care coverage of all residents of that province. The employer's rate is based on the total annual gross payroll.

Employers must supply employees with information relating to total wages paid and amounts withheld for Canada Pension Plan, unemployment insurance, and income taxes. This information is provided on a T4 statement and is given to each employee by the last day of February. By the end of the same month (February) the employer also remits copies of all T4s to Revenue Canada along with the T4 summary.

Vocabulary Review

Following is a list of the words and terms for this chapter:

compensation   T4 statement
cumulative   T4 summary
employers' health tax (EHT)   workers' compensation insurance
form PD7AR

Fill in the blank with the correct word or term from the list.

1. _____ is a form provided by Revenue Canada that is used by employers making monthly remittances of income taxes, CPP, and UI.
2. The form that summarizes the information shown on a T4 statement is called a _____ .
3. A word that means to accumulate is _____.
4. _____ is a form provided by Revenue Canada that the employer must complete to show the employee's total earnings and deductions for the year.
5. _____ provides insurance for employees who incur job-related injuries.
6. Something given or received as a satisfactory equivalent for a loss or an injury is called _____.
7. _____ is a tax imposed on employers so that health-care coverage might be provided to all the citizens of a province.

Match the words and terms on the left with the definitions on the right.

8. compensation
9. employers' health tax
10. cumulative
11. form PD7AR
12. T4 statement
13. T4 summary
14. workers' compensation insurance

a. acquired by or resulting from accumulation
b. a provincial government insurance program paid for by the employer
c. payment for
d. the form that must be completed and given to each employee on or before the last day of February
e. the form that must be forwarded to Revenue Canada on or before the last day of February
f. the form that employers use to remit monthly employee deductions
g. a tax imposed on employers by the provincial government to provide health-care coverage

Exercises

EXERCISE 13.1   Dorothy London, owner of London's Tax Service, employs six people. The gross wages for the year are:

Employee	Gross Wages
1	$39,000
2	32,600
3	27,400
4	22,600
5	18,400
6	15,200

The employees' premium rates for CPP contributions and UI are as described in Chapter Twelve.

    a. Calculate the employees' total CPP contributions for the year. Remember, the maximum taxable amount for each employee for a year under CPP is $34,400 and the basic yearly exemption is $3,400. The CPP rate is 2.6 percent of the earnings subject to taxation ($34,400 − $3,400).

    b. Calculate the total UI premiums for the year if the rate is 3.07 percent of each employee's gross wages.

    c. Calculate the employer's total wages expense for the year.

    d. Calculate the employer's total payroll tax expense for the year. The employer's UI premium is 1.4 times the amount paid by employees for their UI premium.

Round your answers to the nearest penny.

EXERCISE 13.2

Wanda Nelson earns $16 an hour as an electrician. She receives double time for working more than 40 hours in a week. For the week ended January 30, 19XX, Wanda worked 50 hours. Her payroll deductions for the week are: Canada Pension Plan, $23.26; unemployment insurance, $23.95; income tax, $163.20; union dues, $9.00; and health insurance, $4.60.

    a. Prepare the general journal entry (page 25) to record Wanda's gross earnings, her deductions from gross earnings, and the wages payable. The CPP contribution rate is 2.6 percent of pensionable earnings and the UI premium rate is 3.07 percent of the gross wage.

    b. Prepare the general journal entry to record the employer's payroll tax expense. The employer's UI premium is 1.4 times the amount withheld from the employee's wages. Continue on journal page 25.

EXERCISE 13.3

On April 30, the general ledger for Rayco had the following balances: Canada Pension Plan Payable, $98; Unemployment Insurance Payable, $105; and Employees' Income Taxes Payable, $890. These amounts represent the employees' deductions only.

    a. Prepare a general journal entry on May 10 to record the remittance that the employer must send to Revenue Canada before May 15. Remember, the employer pays 1.4 times the UI premium withheld from the employees. Use cheque number 2516 and journal page 34.

    b. Determine what portion of this payment represents an expense to the employer.

EXERCISE 13.4

Payroll data for Mack's Home Cleaning include the following for the first week in February:

	Employee Deductions		
Gross Wages	Canada Pension Plan	Unemployment Insurance	Income Tax
$4,200.00	$100.70	$128.94	$714.00

a. Prepare a general journal entry dated February 7 to record the gross wages, the employee deductions, and the wages payable. Use journal page 44.

b. Prepare a general journal entry on February 7 to record the employer's payroll tax expense. Continue on journal page 44.

EXERCISE 13.5 On January 3, Year 1, the bookkeeper for Sunrise Repairs estimated that the annual payroll would be $98,620 and, on the basis of this estimate, paid a workers' compensation premium of .3 percent of the gross payroll. On January 4, Year 2, the bookkeeper figured the actual payroll for Year 1 to have been $104,700.

a. Prepare a general journal entry on January 3, Year 1 to pay the estimated premium for Year 1. Use journal page 39.

b. Prepare a general journal entry on January 4, Year 2 to pay the additional amount due in Year 2. Use journal page 84.

EXERCISE 13.6 The total annual gross payroll for Huronia Artifacts for the last calendar year was $397,450. Using the EHT rates given in the text

a. Calculate the amount of the employers' health tax the employer will be required to pay.

b. Determine how often the employer will have to make remittances to the Ministry of Finance.

EXERCISE 13.7 Carlos Pietro owns a business called Pietro's Travel Agency. The business address is 496 West Main Street, Hinsdale, N.S. He employs Nathaniel Joseph Emerson, whose address is 420 North Oak, Hinsdale N.S. L4Y 2G4. The employee's individual earnings record shows Emerson's social insurance number to be 321-324-321. He earned $41,800 for the year and had income tax of $3,046.19 withheld. He also had $1,245.40 (the maximum for the year) deducted for unemployment insurance. If the maximum pensionable earnings for the year for the purposes of Canada Pension Plan are $34,400, if the first $3,400 of that is exempt, and if the CPP contribution rate for employees is 2.6 percent, complete Emerson's T4 slip.

Problems

PROBLEM 13.1 Perry Hobson is single and has no dependants. His address is 97 Sylvan Avenue, Englewood, Ontario; his telephone number is 321-0685; his birthdate is 03/24/65; and his social insurance number is 987-654-321. Perry works for M & M Storage Company. His semimonthly wages are $1,250. His net claim code is 1 and in each pay period his income tax is $253.40. His CPP contributions are 2.6 percent of his pensionable earnings, his UI premiums are 3.07 percent of earnings, and union dues are $7.50. Assume that his gross pay, deductions, and net pay have been the same in each pay period of the year.

INSTRUCTIONS Prepare an individual earnings record for Perry for the first four pay periods of the year. Assume that wages are paid on the fifteenth and the last day of each month. At the end of the fourth pay period, calculate and enter year-to-date totals. Use cheque numbers 109, 328, 407, and 515.

PROBLEM 13.2   Cowboy Buck's employs eight people. The T accounts that relate to payroll and their June 1 balances are:

Cash	110
June 1 Balance 11,600	

Wages Expense	610

Canada Pension Plan Payable	210
	June 1 Balance 340.20

Payroll Tax Expense	620

Unemployment Insurance Payable	215
	June 1 Balance 543.80

Income Tax Deductions Payable	220
	June 1 Balance 1,230.15

Wages Payable	225

The following transactions relating to payroll occurred in June and July:

June 15   issued a cheque for monthly payment of amounts owed for Canada Pension Plan, unemployment insurance, and employees' income taxes (use the June 1 balances in the ledger)

June 15   recorded semimonthly wages expense and amounts withheld for employees' wages

Gross wages	$4,280.00
CPP contributions	81.82
UI premiums	131.40
Income tax deductions	727.60

June 15   recorded the employer's payroll tax expense

June 15   issued a cheque for the net pay, made payable to the payroll bank account (debit Wages Payable, credit Cash)

June 30   recorded semimonthly wages expense and amounts withheld from employees' wages

Gross wages	$4,460.00
CPP contributions	86.50
UI premiums	136.92
Income tax deductions	758.20

June 30   recorded the employer's payroll tax expense

June 30   issued a cheque for the net pay, made payable to the payroll bank
           account

July 15   issued a cheque for the amount due to Revenue Canada for June

INSTRUCTIONS

1. Enter the account names and June 1 balances into the general ledger.
2. Journalize each transaction in a general journal. Begin numbering with
   page 86. Post to the general ledger immediately after each transaction so
   that the amounts owed can be determined.
3. Answer the following questions about the accounts after all the entries
   have been journalized and posted:
   a. What was the total wages expense for June?
   b. What was the total payroll tax expense for June?

PROBLEM 13.3

The payroll records of Sasha Records for the month of May 19XX show the
following totals, which represent the amounts withheld from employees'
wages during May:

CPP contributions	$ 920.40
UI premiums	1,204.80
Income tax deductions	4,281.50

INSTRUCTIONS

Calculate the amounts that will be shown on form PD7AR and that will be
remitted to Revenue Canada by the fifteenth of June.

PROBLEM 13.4

On January 4, Year 1, the bookkeeper of Arco Metals estimated that the total
annual gross payroll would be $143,270. On the basis of this estimate, he paid
a workers' compensation premium of .42 percent (.0042) of the gross payroll.
On January 3, Year 2, the bookkeeper calculated the actual payroll for Year 1
to have been $198,490.

INSTRUCTIONS

1. Prepare a general journal entry on January 4, Year 1 to pay the estimated
   workers' compensation premium. Use journal page 2.
2. Prepare a general journal entry on January 3, Year 2 to pay the additional
   workers' compensation premium owed for Year 1. Use journal page 49.
3. Prepare a general journal entry on March 10 to pay the EHT owing for
   Year 1. Use journal page 64.

PROBLEM 13.5

Thompson, Inc. is located at 543 High Street, Peterborough, Ontario L4S 1K0.
Its employer account number is 12345 and its telephone number is (613) 287-
1589. Thompson, Inc. has a total of six employees and the following information is available from the end-of-year payroll records. Thompson, Inc. has
weekly payroll periods.

Employee	Gross Salary	Income Tax Deducted
Graham	$48,640	$12,646.40
Crozier	42,190	10,969.40
Culver	39,780	9,640.20
Mandrake	32,100	7,560.80
Reynolds	29,640	6,928.70
Weir	27,560	5,281.30

The CPP contributions deducted for each employee were 2.6 percent of pensionable earnings, and the UI premiums withheld were 3.07 percent of insurable earnings.

The employees' addresses and social insurance numbers are as follows:

Name	Address	Social Insurance Number
Crozier, James	294 First Street Peterborough, Ontario L4S 1K0	321-654-832
Culver, David	74 Summerhill Avenue Peterborough, Ontario L4S 2K0	204-368-215
Graham, Daniel	104 Forest Lane Peterborough, Ontario L4S 2K0	123-456-789
Mandrake, Rodger	68 Queens Quay Peterborough, Ontario L4S 2N0	237-822-069
Reynolds, Carl	2703 Burton Road Peterborough, Ontario L4S 2R0	174-281-326
Weir, Terry	79 Cuthbert Drive Peterborough, Ontario L4S 1R0	437-289-163

INSTRUCTIONS

1. Complete T4 statements for each employee.
2. Complete a T4 summary for the year. Assume that the total remittance to Revenue Canada for the year was $77,464.54.

Comprehensive Problem 3 for Review of Chapters Twelve–Thirteen

On Monday, December 4, 19X4, Jan Howard began a new position as the payroll clerk for Hillcrest Industries, which is located at 307 Main Street, Owen Sound, Ontario L4R 3X2. The employer account number is 54321. Before Jan joined the firm, the owner, Malcolm Rhodes, had kept all of the payroll records.

During Jan's discussion with Malcolm, she was told that Hillcrest Industries is a sole proprietorship that has five employees including Jan. The plant is open every week from Monday through Friday and never opens on weekends. A normal working day is 8 hours per day and all hourly employees are paid time and a half for all hours in excess of 40 hours per week. Employees paid an annual salary do not receive overtime pay, but when they work more than 40 hours a week, they are given an equal number of hours off at a mutually agreed upon time.

December 25, Christmas Day, and December 26 are paid holidays for all employees, regardless of the length of time they have been employed. December 30 and 31 fall on a Saturday and Sunday; thus, the books are closed for the year as of December 29.

All employees paid an hourly wage are paid $14 per hour and have $4 deducted from their second and fourth cheques each month for union dues.

After three months of continuous service, 6 percent of the regular earnings are deducted each pay period from *all employees* for registered pension plans (RPPs).

Malcolm insists that the union dues deducted from the employees' wages be paid to their union on the same date that they are deducted. RPP contributions are paid to Great West Life Assurance Company on the fifteenth day of the month following the deduction.

All payroll journal entries to date have been correctly prepared and all amounts have been correctly posted to the general ledger. All general ledger balances as of Friday, December 1 are correct.

Furthermore, when Malcolm estimated the total amount of the gross payroll for the year, he estimated that it would be $137,400; on the basis of this amount, he paid .39 percent (.0039) of the gross payroll for workers' compensation insurance.

Malcolm then gave Jan the payroll register and the employees' individual earnings records, which have been correctly completed to December 1. Malcolm had already prepared an individual earning record for Jan.

The remittances already made to Revenue Canada for the year are:

CPP employee deductions	$ 2,715.62
CPP employer contributions	2,715.62
UI employee deductions	3,649.17
UI employer contributions	5,108.84
Income tax deductions	27,541.09

The payroll register used, employees' individual earnings records, and the general ledger follow.

Payroll Register

Employee	Total Hours	Hour Rate	Regular Earnings	Overtime Earnings	Gross Earnings	Net Claim Code	Deductions — CPP Contributions	Deductions — UI Premiums	Deductions — Income Tax	Deductions — Union Dues	Deductions — RPP Contributions	Total Deductions	Net Pay

---

Employee's Individual Earnings Record

Name Mathers, Doug   **Employee No.** 1   **Date Employed** Nov. 3, 19X1

Address 1702 Wellington St.   **Social Insurance No.** 304-628-917

Owen Sound, Ont. L4R 3X9

Female ___ **Male** ✓   **Net Claim Code** 2

Married ✓ **Single** ___   **Pay Rate** $42,640 **Per** Year

Phone No. 123-4556   **Date of Birth** 09/06/53

Period Ending	Gross Earnings	Deductions — CPP Contributions	Deductions — UI Premiums	Deductions — Income Tax	Deductions — Union Dues	Deductions — RPP Contributions	Total Deductions	Net Pay
Cumulative to Dec. 1	$39,360	$806.00	$1,149.60	$10,190.40		$2,361.60	$14,507.60	$24,852.40

Employee's Individual Earnings Record

Name Livingston, Brenda   **Employee No.** 2   **Date Employed** Jan. 5, 19X2

Address 42 Summerside Dr.   **Social Insurance No.** 406-281-755

Owen Sound, Ont. L4R 3X9

Female ✓ **Male** ___   **Net Claim Code** 1

Married ✓ **Single** ___   **Pay Rate** $14 **Per** Hour

Phone No. 123-7852   **Date of Birth** 10/06/69

Period Ending	Gross Earnings	Deductions — CPP Contributions	Deductions — UI Premiums	Deductions — Income Tax	Deductions — Union Dues	Deductions — RPP Contributions	Total Deductions	Net Pay
Cumulative to Dec. 1	$33,402	$786.86	$1,025.44	$7,852.80	$96.00	$1,612.80	$11,373.90	$22,028.10

Employee's Individual Earnings Record

Name Tomlin, Scott   **Employee No.** 3   **Date Employed** Feb. 7, 19X3

Address 324 Queen St. E.   **Social Insurance No.** 409-672-815

Owen Sound, Ont. L4R 3X7

Female _____ **Male** ✓   **Net Claim Code** 3

Married _____ **Single** ✓   **Pay Rate** $14 **Per** Hour

Phone No. 123-9003   **Date of Birth** 07/28/74

| Period Ending | Gross Earnings | Deductions | | | | | Total Deductions | Net Pay |
		CPP Contributions	UI Premiums	Income Tax	Union Dues	RPP Contributions		
Cumulative to Dec. 1	$28,992	$672.20	$890.05	$5,539.20	$96.00	$1,500.00	$8,697.45	$20,294.55

Employee's Individual Earnings Record

Name Tremblay, Jill   **Employee No.** 4   **Date Employed** May 4, 19X3

Address 275 Dunedin Rd.   **Social Insurance No.** 503-287-152

Meaford, Ont. L0L 1S4

Female ✓ **Male** _____   **Net Claim Code** 2

Married ✓ **Single** _____   **Pay Rate** $14 **Per** Hour

Phone No. 532-0129   **Date of Birth** 04/23/72

| Period Ending | Gross Earnings | Deductions | | | | | Total Deductions | Net Pay |
		CPP Contributions	UI Premiums	Income Tax	Union Dues	RPP Contributions		
Cumulative to Dec. 1	$30,912	$722.12	$949.00	$6,712.80	$96.00	$1,730.40	$10,210.32	$20,701.68

Employee's Individual Earnings Record

Name Howard, Jan   **Employee No.** 5   **Date Employed** Dec. 4, 19X4

Address 193 Highview Drive   **Social Insurance No.** 208-113-564

Thornbury, Ont. L0L 2V0

Female ✓ **Male** _____   **Net Claim Code** 1

Married _____ **Single** ✓   **Pay Rate** $20,800 **Per** Year

Phone No. 428-1702   **Date of Birth** 09/26/70

| Period Ending | Gross Earnings | Deductions | | | | | Total Deductions | Net Pay |
		CPP Contributions	UI Premiums	Income Tax	Union Dues	RPP Contributions		
Cumulative to Dec. 1	0	0	0	0	0	0	0	0

GENERAL LEDGER

ACCOUNT: CASH   **ACCT. NO. 101**

Date		Explanation	Post. Ref.	Debit	Credit	Balance
19XX Dec.	1	Balance				1 9 0 4 4 35

ACCOUNT: WAGES PAYABLE   **ACCT. NO. 205**

Date		Explanation	Post. Ref.	Debit	Credit	Balance
19XX Dec.	1	Balance				

ACCOUNT: CANADA PENSION PLAN PAYABLE   **ACCT. NO. 210**

Date		Explanation	Post. Ref.	Debit	Credit	Balance
19XX Dec.	1	Balance				5 4 3 12

ACCOUNT: UNEMPLOYMENT INSURANCE PAYABLE   **ACCT. NO. 215**

Date		Explanation	Post. Ref.	Debit	Credit	Balance
19XX Dec.	1	Balance				8 7 5 81

ACCOUNT: INCOME TAX DEDUCTIONS PAYABLE   **ACCT. NO. 220**

Date		Explanation	Post. Ref.	Debit	Credit	Balance
19XX Dec.	1	Balance				2 7 5 4 11

ACCOUNT: UNION DUES PAYABLE   **ACCT. NO. 225**

Date		Explanation	Post. Ref.	Debit	Credit	Balance
19XX Dec.	1	Balance				

ACCOUNT: REGISTERED PENSION PLAN PAYABLE   **ACCT. NO. 230**

Date		Explanation	Post. Ref.	Debit	Credit	Balance
19XX Dec.	1	Balance				6 5 4 98

ACCOUNT: EMPLOYERS' HEALTH TAX PAYABLE   **ACCT. NO. 240**

Date		Explanation	Post. Ref.	Debit	Credit	Balance
19XX Dec.	1	Balance				

ACCOUNT: MALCOLM RHODES, CAPITAL   ACCT. NO. 301

Date		Explanation	Post. Ref.	Debit	Credit	Balance
19XX Dec.	1	Balance				1 5 6 0 2 5 10

ACCOUNT: INCOME SUMMARY   ACCT. NO. 315

Date		Explanation	Post. Ref.	Debit	Credit	Balance
19XX Dec.	1	Balance				

ACCOUNT: WAGES EXPENSE   ACCT. NO. 610

Date		Explanation	Post. Ref.	Debit	Credit	Balance
19XX Dec.	1	Balance				1 3 2 6 6 6 00

ACCOUNT: PAYROLL TAX EXPENSE   ACCT. NO. 615

Date		Explanation	Post. Ref.	Debit	Credit	Balance
19XX Dec.	1	Balance				8 6 0 6 91

ACCOUNT: WORKERS' COMPENSATION INSURANCE EXPENSE   ACCT. NO. 620

Date		Explanation	Post. Ref.	Debit	Credit	Balance
19XX Dec.	1	Balance				5 3 5 86

ACCOUNT: EMPLOYERS' HEALTH TAX EXPENSE   ACCT. NO. 630

Date		Explanation	Post. Ref.	Debit	Credit	Balance
19XX Dec.	1	Balance				

PAYROLL TRANSACTIONS   (Post immediately after each transaction.)

December 8   complete the payroll register for the week using the following information (refer to the individual earnings records for rates of pay; remember, employees paid an annual salary are not paid overtime):

Doug Mathers	44 hours
Brenda Livingston	42 hours
Scott Tomlin	48 hours
Jill Tremblay	36 hours
Jan Howard	40 hours

December 8   record the employee earnings in their individual employee earnings records

December 8   calculate cumulative-to-date totals in the employees' individual earnings records

December 8   prepare the journal entry to record the wages payable for the week

December 8   prepare the journal entry to record employer's payroll tax expense

December 8   issue a cheque for the net pay, made payable to the payroll bank account (debit Wages Payable and credit Cash)

December 12   prepare the journal entry to record the amount due to Revenue Canada for payroll taxes for November (the CPP payable consists of $271.56 deducted from employees' wages and $271.56 as the employer's contribution; the UI payable consists of $364.92 in employee deductions and $510.89 for the employer's contribution)

December 15   complete the payroll register for the week using the following information (be sure to check each employee's individual earnings record for cumulative earnings before calculating CPP deductions; also, remember that union dues are deducted the second and fourth pay periods for hourly workers):

Doug Mathers	50 hours
Brenda Livingston	40 hours
Scott Tomlin	42 hours
Jill Tremblay	44 hours
Jan Howard	45 hours

December 15   record the employee earnings in the individual employee earnings records

December 15   calculate cumulative-to-date totals in the employees' individual earnings records

December 15   prepare the journal entry to record the wages payable for the week

December 15   prepare the journal entry to record the employer's payroll tax expense

December 15   issue a cheque for the net pay made payable to the payroll bank account

December 15   prepare the journal entry to record payment of union dues deducted

December 15   prepare the journal entry to record payment for the RPP contributions deducted from the employees' wages in November

December 22   complete the payroll register for the week using the following information:

Doug Mathers	40 hours
Brenda Livingston	44 hours
Scott Tomlin	40 hours
Jill Tremblay	46 hours
Jan Howard	40 hours

December 22   record the employee earnings in the individual employee earnings records

December 22   calculate cumulative-to-date totals in the employees' individual earnings records

December 22   prepare the journal entry to record the wages payable for the week

December 22   prepare the journal entry to record employer's payroll tax expense

December 22   issue a cheque for the net pay made payable to the payroll bank account

December 29   complete the payroll register for the week using the following information:

Doug Mathers	24 hours
Brenda Livingston	24 hours
Scott Tomlin	24 hours
Jill Tremblay	24 hours
Jan Howard	24 hours

December 29   record the employee earnings in the individual employee earnings records

December 29   calculate cumulative-to-date totals in the employees' individual earnings records

December 29   prepare the journal entry to record the wages payable for the week

December 29   prepare the journal entry to record employer's payroll tax expense

December 29   issue a cheque for the net pay made payable to the payroll bank account

December 29   prepare the journal entry to record payment of union dues deducted

December 29   prepare the journal entry to record the additional premium paid for workers' compensation insurance expense based on actual wages for the year

December 29   record the amount due for employers' health tax based on gross wages in 19X4 (refer to the table on page 344 for the appropriate percentage)

December 29   record closing entries for all expense accounts relating to payroll

December 29   close Income Summary to Owner's Capital account (note: not all closing entries will be prepared at this time)

January 10   prepare the journal entry to record payment for amount due to Revenue Canada for December

January 15   prepare journal entry to record amount due to Great West Life Assurance Company for the RPP contributions deducted from the employees' wages during December

February 20   prepare T4 statements for all employees

February 20   prepare a T4 summary for Revenue Canada

March 1   prepare the journal entry to record payment to the Ministry of Finance for the EHT owing based on the 19X4 annual gross payroll

INSTRUCTIONS

1. Assume that you are Jan Howard, the payroll clerk, and complete the work required for each payroll transaction.
2. When calculating the gross earnings for each employee in the payroll register, use the following:
   a. For income tax, use the tables on pages 325 and 326.
   b. For CPP, the total yearly taxable earnings are $34,400 and the basic yearly exemption is $3,400; the maximum yearly pensionable earnings are $31,000. The weekly exemption is $65.38 and the rate is 2.6 percent.
   c. For UI, the maximum taxable earnings are $780 per week and the maximum weekly deduction is $23.95. For employees, the UI rate is 3.07 percent; for employers, the rate is 1.4 times the amount deducted from employees' wages.
   d. For RPP, after three months of continuous service, 6 percent of *regular earnings* is deducted *each pay period for each employee.*
3. Record all required journal entries in a general journal, beginning with page 9.
4. Post immediately following each transaction.
5. Prepare T4 statements for each employee. The CPP pensionable earnings for Tomlin and Tremblay are calculated by subtracting $3,400 from their gross yearly earnings. For Howard, multiply $65.38 by 4 (the number of pay periods) and subtract the result from her total wages for the year— $1,600.
6. Prepare a T4 summary for Revenue Canada. Take your information from the remittances made to Revenue Canada as of December 4, and from the individual earnings records.

Appendix:
Check Figures
for Problems

Problem Number	Instruction Number	Check Figure
1.1	1	Cash balance, $3,200
1.2	1	Total assets, $16,700
1.3	2	Total assets, $24,000
1.4	1b	Total assets, $20,575
1.5	2	Total assets, $5,870
2.1	1	Cash balance, $3,545
2.2	1	Net loss, $500
2.3	1	Cash balance, $3,765
2.4	1	Net income, $7,560
2.5	1	Total assets, $19,860
2.6		No check figure
3.1	3	Trial balance total, $27,300
3.2	4	Trial balance total, $135,577
3.3	5	Trial balance total, $69,065
3.4	4	Trial balance total, $38,695
3.5	2	Trial balance total, $39,870
3.6	2	Corrected net income, $8,790
4.1	3	Trial balance total, $359,979
4.2	4	Trial balance total, $120,575
4.3	3	Trial balance total, $19,475
4.4	5	Corrected net income, $3,970
5.1	5	Net income, $1,049
5.2	3	Net income, $1,645
5.3	3	Net income, $2,540
5.4	3	Net income, $7,710
5.5	4	Net loss, $85
5.6	2	Corrected net income, $1,985
6.1		No check figure
6.2	2	Capital, September 30, 19XX, $6,185
6.3	3	Capital, December 31, 19XX, $16,466
6.4	3	Net loss, $2,036

6.5	3	Net income, $104
6.6	2	Trial balance total, $37,115
CP#1	4	Trial balance total, $386,782.64
	7	Net income, $2,465.18
7.1	7	Schedule of accounts receivable, $5,852.10
7.2	7	Schedule of accounts receivable, $9,448.60
7.3	7	Schedule of accounts receivable, $1,270.50
7.4	7	Schedule of accounts receivable, $4,012.50
7.5	7	Schedule of accounts receivable, $368
8.1	6	Schedule of accounts payable, $8,141.25
8.2	6	Schedule of accounts payable, $7,500
8.3	6	Schedule of accounts payable, $32,627.25
8.4	3b	Sales journal, total accounts receivable debit column, $2,173.50
8.5	4	Purchases journal, total accounts payable credit column, $8,035.70
9.1	2	Total cash debit, cash receipts journal, $18,664.05
9.2	2	Total cash credit, cash payments journal, $7,089.69
9.3	4	Total cash debit, cash receipts journal, $10,430.30
9.4	2	Total cash debit, cash receipts journal, $7,940.95
9.5	4	Total cash debit, combined journal, $8,601
9.6	4	Total cash debit, combined journal, $5,774.40
10.1	1	Adjusted bank balance, $4,646.64
10.2	1	Adjusted bank balance, $6,321.81
10.3	1	Adjusted bank balance, $3,791.29
10.4	1	Adjusted bank balance, $12,642.50
10.5	1	Adjusted bank balance, $24,512
10.6	3	Total petty cash disbursements, $95.10
10.7	6	Total petty cash disbursements, January 16–31, $97.60
CP#2	14	Balance, Cash account #101, December 31, $23,632.67
	15	Trial balance total, $102,061.47
11.1	2f	Net income, $3,535
11.2	2	Net income, $6,530
11.3	1	Total asset, $109,600
11.4	4	Net income, $3,285
11.5	1	Net loss, $870
12.1	1c	Total gross earnings, $2,964
12.2	1g	Total net pay, $1,654.06
12.3	1h	Total net pay, $2,474.48
12.4	1h	Total net pay, $2,341.71
13.1	1	Year-to-date net pay, February 28, $3,687.60
13.2	2	Balance in Cash account, July 15, $201.88
13.3	1	Total remittances, $6,406.70
13.4	2	Workers' compensation additional premium, $231.92
13.5	2	Total employment income, $219,910
CP#3	4	Balance, Cash account #101, March 1, 19X5, zero

Index

READER REPLY CARD

We are interested in your reaction to *Accounting*, Second Canadian Edition, by Nanci Lee and Elaine Hales. With your comments, we can improve this book in future editions. Please help us by completing this questionnaire.

1. What was your reason for using this book?

   ☐ university course   ☐ college course   ☐ continuing education courses

   ☐ professional development   ☐ personal interest   ☐ other (please specify) _____

   _____

2. If you are a student, please identify your school and course. If you used this text for a program, what was the name of that program?

   _____

3. Approximately how much of the book did you use?

   ☐ all   ☐ 3/4   ☐ 1/2   ☐ 1/4

4. Which chapters or sections were omitted from your course?

   _____

5. What is the best aspect of this book?

   _____

6. Is there anything that should be added?

   _____

7. Was the information in this text presented in an interesting manner?

   _____

8. Was there enough problem material to support the level of difficulty in the text?

   _____

9. Please add any comments or suggestions for the text.

   _____

10. What did you like best/least about the Working Papers? Why?

    _____

11. Please make any suggestions to improve the Working Papers.

    _____

(fold here and tape shut)

0116870399-M8Z4X6-BR01

Heather McWhinney
Publisher, College Division
HARCOURT BRACE & COMPANY, CANADA
55 HORNER AVENUE
TORONTO, ONTARIO
M8Z 9Z9